DICTIONARY OF GERMAN SLANG AND COLLOQUIAL EXPRESSIONS

Henry Strutz
Formerly Associate Professor of Languages
State University of New York
Alfred State College of Technology

All inquiries should be addressed to:
Barron's Educational Series, Inc.
250 Wireless Boulevard
Hauppauge, NY 11788
http://www.barronseduc.com

International Standard Book Number 0-7641-0966-9

Library of Congress Catalog Card Number 99-75493

Printed in Canada
9 8 7 6 5

Contents

PREFACE

The Range of German—Starry Heights and Lower Depths

The German you've studied is Hochdeutsch or "High German," as distinct from the Plattdeutsch or "Low German," still spoken by some in the lowlands of the North. You've probably also concentrated on the high points of the German literary and philosophical tradition, so rich in romantic, rhapsodic abstractions and so devoted to the "true, good, and beautiful." Joseph Campbell, renowned scholar and popularizer of mythology, once contrasted English, "a practical language," with German, "a poetic language, a mystic language." If you haven't had much contact with ordinary German-speaking people, you may have concluded that German is essentially a superbly resonant instrument most suited to the articulation of poetic, scientific, and philosophic abstractions. It is that. But it also has other strings to its bow for expressing the whole range of human experience.

Luther, Goethe, and Mozart were aware of the depth and variety of that experience. All three reveled in ribald humor, and neither was afraid of "strong language." Luther's German was effective because he listened to the way people really talked: "the mother at home, children playing on the streets, the man in the street, people in the marketplace." Scaling poetic and philosophic heights is a necessary and desirable part of language study. After such rarified air however, you may want to come down to earth. Mountains, and titans of creativity too, are earth-based—however high spirits may soar and fancy may fly (see KAISER; KAISERIN). This dictionary should help you to enjoy the earthy journey and familiarize you with how truck drivers, bakers, computer hackers, sports fans, motor bikers, soldiers, and all sorts of ordinary, and not-so-ordinary people (such as professional criminals, convicts, drug addicts, pimps, and prostitutes) talk, especially when they're having a few beers.

Types and Characteristics of Slang

Many languages, including English and German, have a "thieves' cant," i.e. language used to conceal illegal activity (see ROTWELSCH). Underworld language is still an element in slang, but, as lexicographer Eric Partridge points out, slang is "now merely the unconventional speech of all classes." Besides thieves' cant, the *Fachchinesisch* (shop talk, jargon) of people engaged in a specific activity, and the speech of people from a particular culture or subculture can be sources of slang.

The *Oxford English Dictionary* contains many slang entries that are well researched. But both it and the *Oxford Dictionary of English Etymology* have scarcely a good word to say in the entries labeled "slang." In the latter dictionary slang is characterized as "offensive language" (twice), "abusive language," and is called "colloquial speech of an undignified kind." In the *Oxford English Dictionary* we are told that it is "low, vulgar language . . . below the level of standard, educated speech" and "spoken by people of a low, disreputable character." In the excellent *Oxford Dictionary of Modern Slang,* however, slang fares better. Its entries are drawn largely from the *Oxford English Dictionary.* There is no entry for *slang,* but in their introduction, lexicographers John Ayto and John Simpson call slang "colorful, alternative vocabulary . . . English with its sleeves rolled up . . . its shirt-tails dangling, and its shoes covered in mud." Nevertheless, they repeat that it is "below the level of standard, educated speech."

At the opposite end of the spectrum, far from the entries in the two Oxford dictionaries, is Walt Whitman. In his *Slang in America* he defines slang as "an attempt of common humanity to escape from bald literalism, and express itself illimitably." In contrast to the class-conscious, class-bound, deprecatory dicta of the Oxford entries, it is more on the mark to associate slang with the "unconventional speech of all classes" (Partridge) and "common humanity" (Whitman).

To create that "unconventional speech," all the classes,

including the educated and the least educated, often resort to poetic devices such as rhyme, assonance, alliteration, similes, and metaphors. You will find hundreds of such "poetic" instances in both the German and English examples given in this dictionary. "You're a poet and you don't know it" is a hackneyed expression. Yet people (certainly the many "rappers" that now flourish in Germany, too) usually do know it, and deliberately employ elements of poetry to be unconventional or sometimes to make the vulgar or unpleasant humorous and thus easier to deal with. *Dann ist aber die Kacke am Dampfen,* for instance, uses assonance. Its English equivalent, "then the shit will really hit the fan," employs rhyme. *Keine müde Mark* uses alliteration. "Not a red cent" employs assonance.

To give greater impact to what they're saying, slang speakers seek to substitute the unusual, the colorful, the taboo for the standard, the humdrum. That can mean being vulgar—or simply being witty, clever, not at all crude. In the right context, much slang can be used by very dignified, eminently respectable, educated speakers. Slang can be sassy, sexy lingo. It can also be vituperative and vitriolic, aggressive, whimsical, picturesque, and, above all, different. Of course, slang and colloquial expressions that are boldly innovative today may enter the standard language tomorrow. Language is involved in constant processes of change.

Knowing the Tune

Mark Twain's wife was dismayed by his predilection for profanity. Once, hoping to shock and revolt him, she spewed a filthy litany of obscenities at him. "You know the words, my dear, but you don't know the tune," was his reaction. Mozart knew the tune. He was proficient in profanities in several languages, including his native German. Brain researchers report that music and sequential, chanted prayer, as well as strings of profanity, are processed in the same lower right area of the brain. All should strive to integrate the poetic, musical right brain with the rational, scientific left brain. Familiarizing yourself with the whole range of language is part of that process. Yet you must proceed with caution when using slang. Wait until you know the tune better, till you are familiar with the inner music, the rhythms of German. To "know the tune" you have to know the tone of the conversation, the social context, the situation. Wait until you have acquired language habit patterns before slinging slang at speakers of German.

Levels of Language

Familiarity with the full range of a language and its different levels is one thing. Finding the appropriate level for a particular social situation is another. Sensibilities, as well as dialect and class distinctions, are all less rigid than they once were. Nevertheless, there are still some lines one should not cross, unless one deliberately wants to shock or create humor by juxtaposing disparate elements, such as sending sailors to take tea with the bishop and turning church ladies out to carouse in sleazy bars. Normally, church ladies at a tea party would use a level of language different from that of sailors boozing it up in a waterfront tavern. I have made a consistent effort to let the English translations reflect the German. But it should be noted that the English sometimes sounds more vulgar than the German, perhaps because in Europe "strong" language has long been more acceptable over a broader social spectrum than has been the case in puritanical America. For *Scheißkerl,* for instance, the slang translations that suggest themselves are "shitbag/shitface/shithead." Yet they are a bit stronger than the German. "SOB," "bastard," "louse" are closer equivalents.

Contemporary Slang and Youth Slang—
Looking for Alternatives

Nowadays many declare: *wir leben alternativ* (we've adopted an alternative lifestyle). This "otherness" is reflected in dress, behavior codes, religion, ecological concerns, and language. Speakers of slang could well say, *wir spre chen alternativ.* Nevertheless, youth slang is often nowhere near as *alternativ* as its speakers think. For one thing, "youth" doesn't stay young forever. For another, older people have been merrily adopting youth slang terms, probably because they want to show they're "with it" and not really old.

Some Characteristics of Youth Slang

In German, as in English, there is a long tradition of converting originally negative words to a positive sense in order to emphasize or intensify, as in "terribly good" or "awfully nice." Youth slang is much concerned with being intense. Therefore, many entries have a positive slang definition in addition to the original negative one. This use of "bad" for "good," of "wicked" for "wonderful" has accelerated greatly in recent years. Sociologists and moralists have drawn the obvious conclusions about a "loss of absolute values" and "confusion in ethical behavior." When dealing with subjects such as drugs, drug-fueled techno-raves, gang violence, and body art such as piercing and branding, I have attempted not to make value judgments.

More Youthful Intensity

Most people want more out of life, want to explore the possibilities. Youth, and a few elderly Faustian types too, often not only want to go the limit, but go beyond it. As some of the entries indicate, drugs are sometimes an unfortunate concomitant of that endeavor. The motto of the O lympics is Citius, Altius, Fortius (Faster, Higher, Stronger). In seeking to push the language beyond its limits, youth slang makes use of a whole series of intensifiers, such as *elch-, end-, galaktisch, giga-, hyper-, maxi-, mega-, ober-, super-, turbo-, ultra-,* and more. You will find many intensifiers among the entries. Of course, all that intensifying leads to inflated linguistic currency that you may be inclined to take at less than face value. Youth may scorn the establishment, but the culture is full of media hype, and impressionable youth is not immune to it either. Overusing all those intensifiers, all that "mind-blowing, awesome, stupendous, super, tremendous" can make for absurdity. Even if you agree with Anatole France's pronouncement, "I prefer the foolishness of enthusiasm to the cynicism of wisdom," it will be useful and good for you to determine which is which, and to inform enthusiasm with wisdom. Despite Oscar Wilde's quip, "The only opinions worth listening to are those of youth," you might not want to give full weight to much of the hyperbole characteristic of youth slang. Wilde, long identified with elegantly brittle upper-class wit and flowery aestheticism, is paradoxically something of a hero to many British punk rockers. Lady Bracknell, a character in his *The Importance of Being Earnest,* announces her opposition to French and declares, "German is a very moral language." After reading some of the entries in this dictionary, you may well disagree with her.

Youth and Old Age

Youth sees itself as new, unique. It is, of course—but so is every new day that dawns. Much youth slang strives for linguistic newness, uniqueness and expresses contempt for the establishment (parents, teachers, police, politicians, priests, authority figures, the elderly [i.e. those over 30], all "squares"). But neither language nor people are created *ex nihilo,* from nothing. Nor do they exist in a void. Most often, slang meanings grow out of the literal meaning. I list the literal meaning first or put it in parentheses. Pursuing connections with slang meanings should be of interest even to the casual reader.

Youth often aggressively seeks to mock the establishment by dressing, behaving, believing, and speaking in socially provocative ways. There are therefore many contemptuous terms for what youth considers old. (See the entries AB-; ABGEJUBELT; KOMPI/KOMPOSTI; GRUFTI; VOR-GRUFTI, among others.) Fortunately, some of those terms aren't as sinister as they sound, and some young speakers use them ironically, even good-naturedly. Youth's hostility to the establishment is by no means an exclusively contemporary phenomenon. That hostility is almost as much a cliché as the conviction of many older people in every generation that the new generation is hell-bent on destroying good order.

People don't stay young. Nor do words. Slang expressions once oh so hip in the 60s, 70s, and 80s are still heard. But they've grown old with their users. Demographically, Germany is moving toward a society with a majority of seniors.

Don't be discouraged if some entries, especially youth slang entries, seem weirdly difficult to you. Many native Germans have trouble with them too, and dictionaries of Neudeutsch (primarily borrowings from American English) and Jugendsprache (youth slang) have proliferated. Some of the more recent ones are listed in the bibliography. I hope the brief explanations given for a few of the more "far out" words will be helpful to you. Some stretches and distortions of German words, to say nothing of all the foreign, or pseudo-foreign words combined with German, perplex many speakers of German too.

Geographical Designations

Globalization is a planetary phenomenon. Homogenization, including language standardization due to communications and schooling, has occurred in many countries, including German-speaking ones. An additional factor is the post-WWII influx of German-speaking refugees from former parts of Germany into what is present-day Germany, a population upheaval that also helped to blur dialect boundaries. Many dialect distinctions still exist, however. Swiss Germans, Swabians, Bavarians and Austrians, Franconians, Saxons, and others often, but not always, retain a local accent even when speaking standard German. A *Weißwurstgrenze* (veal sausage) or any other *Grenze* (border), or dialect lines (like the *Benrather Linie* dividing High and Low German) don't really exist anymore, or they are very slack. Therefore the designations "N., S., E." (North, South, East) are not absolute. Rather, they usually indicate the area where the word in question is more likely to be used. "West" has not been used because of the many dialect variations that occur in and near the Rhine valley, from Switzerland to the

North Sea. "East" refers to the territory of the former German Democratic Republic. There are many dialects in that area too. Some of the entries designated "East" reflect a Soviet Russian presence of almost half a century.

Foreign Influences

American English is the largest source of foreign words. Business persons with international contacts frequently use English. Young speakers are among the particularly eager borrowers from American English. One is not likely to hear them speak of a *Tanzkapelle* (dance band); instead, it's *die Band.* And youthful speakers will always call the music or sound that band makes *der Sound,* never *der Klang.* Sometimes English is transliterated; sometimes German and English are grotesquely mixed, as Germans in America have been doing for many centuries. Current European speakers of what they call *Neudeutsch* (*neu* and *deutsch* are both really misnomers) are very serious about their use—or often misuse—of English. They perceive it as very smart, chic. They are impressed by how much English they know (or think they know), and want to impress others.

In addition to American English, other languages, such as Spanish and Italian, or more often pseudo-Italian, figure prominently in current slang. Today, *Fantástico!* is popular with young speakers. Their grandmothers and great-grandmothers said *Fantastisch!* (Fantastic!). Some slang is also drawn from Latin or Greek, often via English. (See the entries KANAKE; NULLO PROBLEMO; PALAZZO PROTZO.)

Long Words and Contractions

German is famous for its long words. In slang and colloquial speech many contractions are used, and words are often shortened.

Women are a majority of the electorate, and politicians generally open their speeches with, *Liebe Bürgerinnen, liebe Bürger* (Dear female and male citizens). For generic nouns some feminists advocate using feminine forms exclusively and telling males to feel themselves included, if they so wish. Nevertheless, there is a unisex tendency to dispense with *-in* and *-innen*. A woman who doesn't smoke will usually say: *ich bin Nichtraucher* instead of *Nichtraucherin*.

Many contractions continue to be indicated by an apostrophe, but, according to the new Duden rules, it is now correct to omit it in many instances. Duden also favors writing separately many words formerly written as one word, and also allows for many hyphenated spellings (the opposite of the usual process in English, where words that started out separately are first linked by a hyphen, then, come to be written as one-word compounds).

Prefix Verbs

As you know, German has a whole panoply of prefixes— separable, inseparable, and doubtful. Often, in addition to the basic verb, I also provide entries beginning with a prefix, especially if there is a semantic change. But it would have made the dictionary too long to include all the possible prefix variations on basic verbs. If you don't find a particular slang expression using a prefix verb, try looking up the basic verb, or the basic verb with another prefix.

Having Fun with Language

Learning verb prefixes and other topics in German grammar probably wasn't your idea of fun. Goethe complained to Herder that nasty pedants were out to sour all *Sprachspielerei* (playfulness in language). Many researchers, including Einstein, have said that the urge to play is the source of all creativity. (Einstein also said, "God does not play dice with the universe," but quantum physics disputes that.) Many religious traditions teach that God is, or that the Gods and Goddesses are, at play in the universe and that all creation is an expression of that play. There's plenty of playfulness in slang and colloquial expressions. I hope this dictionary will help you to play the language game better and to have fun while playing it.

BIBLIOGRAPHY

The following books and dictionaries may be useful to you for additional study.

Besserwisser, Gertrude. *Scheisse!* New York: Plume, 1994.

Burke, David. *Street German-1.* Berkeley: Optima Books, 1996.

Duden, vol. 1. Rechtschreibung der deutschen Sprache. Mannheim: Dudenverlag, 1996.

Duden, vol. 11. Redewendungen und sprichwörtliche Redensarten. Mannheim: Dudenverlag, 1992.

Ehmann, Hermann. *Affengeil. Ein Lexikon der Jugendsprache.* Munich: C. H. Beck, 1996.

Ehmann, Hermann. *Oberaffengeil. Neues Lexikon der Jugendsprache.* Munich: C. H. Beck, 1996.

Graves, Paul. *Streetwise German.* Lincolnwood: Passport Books, 1994.

Gruner, Dorothea. *Hesch a Kioschk an der Eigernordwand?* Bern, 1990.

Henscheid, Eckhard. *Dummdeutsch.* Stuttgart: Reclam, 1993.

Hoppe, Ulrich. *Neudeutsch. Von Asche bis Zombie.* Munich, 1989.

Horx, Matthias. *Trendwörter von Acid bis Zippies.* Düsseldorf: Econ Verlag, 1995.

Schlobinski, Peter; Kohl, Gaby; Ludewigt, Irmgard. *Jugendsprache.* Opladen: Westdeutscher Verlag, 1993.

Schönfeld, Eike. *Alles easy. Wörterbuch des Neudeutschen.* Munich: C. H. Beck, 1995.

ABBREVIATIONS

abbr. = abbreviation
adj. = adjective
Aust. = Austrian
Brit. = British
cf. = compare
comb. = combination
dim. = diminutive
E. = East
Eng. = English
esp. = especially
euph. = euphemism
expr. = expression
f. = feminine
Fr. = French
GDR = German Democratic Republic
Ger. = German/Germany
Gk. = Greek
Hebr. = Hebrew
h.s. = herself/himself
hum. = humorous
infl. = influence/influenced
It. = Italian
Japn. = Japanese
jmdm. (Ger.) = *jemandem* (someone)
jmdn. = *jemanden*
jmds. = *jemandes*
Lat. = Latin
lit. = literally

m. = masculine
mil. = military
m.s. = myself
n. = neuter
N. = North
orig. = originally
o.s. = oneself
pej. = pejorative
pl. = plural
Pol. = Polish
pop. = popular
poss. = possible
prev. = previous
pron. = pronounced/pronunciation
prov. = proverb
rel. = related
S. = South
sent. = sentence
sl. = slang
s.o. = someone
s.t. = something
Sp. = Spanish
stand. = standard
tr. = translated/translation
translit. = transliteration
t.s. = themselves
var. = variant/variation
W. = West
y.s. = yourself

AA MACHEN, *children.* To do #2/go on the potty. *Musst du wieder Aa machen?* "Do you have to go on the potty again?"

(SICH) AALEN. To stretch out (from *Aal,* eel). *Du aalst dich in der Sonne und schaust zu, während ich maloche.* "You stretch out in the sun and watch while I work my fingers to the bone."

AB-. Off, away. In youth sl., the past participles of many separable prefix verbs are used to describe s.t. passé, past it, finished, old-fashioned, done for. See ABGEEBT; ABGEFEIERT; ABGEFUCKT; ABGELUTSCHT; ABGEJUBELT; ABGEMACKERT.

AB DIE POST!/AB DURCH DIE MITTE! Off you go!/ Head on out!

ABER RAPIDO!/ABER RASANTO!/ABER SUBITO! Make it fast! See RAPIDO; RASANTO; SUBITO.

AB NACH KASSEL! = **AB DIE POST!**

AB UND AN/AB UND ZU. Now and then. *Ab und an gehen wir ins Kino.* "Once in a while we go to the movies."

ABARTIG, *youth.* Extremely; excruciatingly (lit. deviant, abnormal). *Das Piercing tat abartig weh; alle finden's aber abartig toll.* "The (body) piercing hurt like hell, but everybody thinks it's terrific."

(SICH) ABASTEN. To slave away. ***Sich einen abasten.*** To

1

struggle with s.t. *Da hab ich mir einen abgeastet!* "I really took on a whopper there."

ABBEIßEN. To bite off. *Einen abbeißen. (N).* To have a drink. *Beißen wir schnell noch einen ab!* "Let's have another quick drink."

ABBLITZEN. To scram. *Blitz ab, Depp!* "Beat it, nerd!" *Bei jmdm. abblitzen.* To get nowhere with s.o. *Tim versuchte alles, aber bei ihr hat er abgeblitzt.* "Tim tried everything, but he got nowhere with her." *Jmdn. abblitzen lassen.* To send s.o. packing. *Dir hab ich so viel geschenkt; jetzt lässt du mich abblitzen.* "I gave you so many presents; now you send me packing."

ABBLÖDELN, *youth.* To fool/horse around. *Blödelt euch einen ab, aber hier nicht!* "Go horse around, but not here!"

ABBÜRSTEN, *youth.* See BÜRSTEN **1**; NIEDERBÜRSTEN.

ABDAMPFEN. To scram (lit. to evaporate). *Sie ist nach Hamburg abgedampft.* "She's gone off to Hamburg."

ABDANKEN, *youth.* **1.** To give up (lit. to abdicate, resign). *Hättest nicht gleich abdanken sollen.* "You shouldn't have bowed out right away." **2.** To die. *Er dankte endlich ab.* "He finally gave up the ghost."

ABDACKELN, *youth.* To go off/away. (*Dackel* = dachshund; also infl. of *wackeln,* to shake, wiggle. Cf. DACKELN **1**.) *Ich muss jetzt endlich abdackeln.* "I've really got to shove off now."

ABDRÜCKEN. To fire a gun. In sl. = RAUSRÜCKEN.

ABDÜSEN. To speed off. *Die sind schnell abgedüst.* "They sped off fast."

ABEND, *m.* Evening. *Am Abend besuchen.* To visit in the evening; euph. for *am Arsch lecken,* to lick ass. Cf. ÄRMEL. *Wenn er mich wieder enttäuscht, kann er mich mal am Abend besuchen.* "If he disappoints me again, he can kiss my ass."

ABER SUBITO! See SUBITO.

2

ABFACKELN, *N., youth.* To torch. *Urs war total durchge-knallt und versuchte die Penne abzufackeln.* "Urs was totally freaked out and tried to burn down the school." Cf. VERKOKELN.

ABFAHREN. To go for/turn on to (lit. to depart). *Mein Mann fährt wahnsinnig auf meine sexy Dessous ab.* "My husband really turns on to my sexy lingerie." Cf. ABGE-FAHREN.

ABFINGERN. See ARSCH.

ABFLOTTIEREN, *youth.* To buzz off (cf. FLOTT 1). *Wenn du nicht rapido abflottierst, bügeln wir dir's Fell.* "If you don't make tracks fast, we'll knock your block off."

ABFLUG, *m.* Takeoff (of planes, birds). *Mach 'nen Abflug! (Youth.)* Get the hell away!/Buzz off! *Den großen Abflug machen.* To die. *Der DJ hat den großen Abflug gemacht.* "The DJ's now in that great disco in the sky."

ABFLUPPEN = ABFLOTTIEREN.

ABFRIEREN. To get frostbite. *Sich einen abfrieren.* To be cold through and through. *Im ungeheizten Zug haben wir uns ganz schön einen abgefroren.* "We practically froze to death in the unheated train." *Sich den Arsch abfrieren.* To freeze one's ass off. *Wir schauten den Schiläufern zu und froren uns dabei den Arsch ab.* "We froze our asses off watching the skiers."

ABFÜTTERUNG, *f., youth.* Meal (lit. animal feeding). *Die Abfütterungen im Internat waren nichts für Fein-schmecker.* "The meals at boarding school weren't for gourmets."

ABGANG, *youth.* **1.** Exit from a scene on stage. *Mach 'nen Abgang!* Clear off!/Beat it! Cf. ABFLUG! **2.** Sexual climax. *Einen Abgang kriegen.* To find incredible; experience orgasm. *Wenn du das hörst, kriegst du 'n Abgang!* "When you hear that, you'll cream your jeans!"

ABGEBAGGERT, *youth.* Pooped/burned out (lit. dredged off). *Gestern war ich total abgebaggert.* "I was really bushed yesterday."

ABGEBRANNT, *youth.* Flat broke (lit. burned down). *In Las Vegas war ich völlig abgebrannt, aber da fand ich die große Liebe.* "I was flat broke in Las Vegas, but I found the love of my life there."

ABGEBROCHENER, *E.,* *m.* **1.** School dropout. *Sie sind alle fünf Abgebrochene, abgebrochene Mediziner und Juristen.* "All five of them broke off their studies in med school and law school." **2.** Underaged (used pejoratively by older youth). *Der Macker verkauft falsche Flebben an Abgebrochene.* "That guy sells fake IDs to minors."

ABGEBRÜHT. Hard boiled (lit. blanched by boiling). *Er ist doch kein abgebrühter Schwerverbrecher.* "He's far from being a hardened criminal." Cf. AUSGEKOCHT.

ABGEDREHT = **ABGEFAHREN.**

ABGEEBT, *youth.* Boring (lit. faded away, receded; cf. EBBE). *Alles findet ihr abgeebt, aber ihr seid ja selber die leibhaftige Langeweile.* "You find everything boring, but you y.s. are boredom personified."

ABGEFACKT = **ABGEFUCKT.**

ABGEFAHREN, *youth.* Terrifically good/bad; stylish/out of style (only the context will tell you whether the meaning is laudatory or pej.). *Ihre letzte Rille ist echt abgefahren!* "Her last record's s.t. else!"

ABGEFEIERT = **ABGEJUBELT 1,2.**

ABGEFUCKT, *youth.* Bored; useless; down and out; played out. *Dieser Drogi ist voll abgefuckt.* "That junkie's a total washout." Cf. ABGELUTSCHT.

ABGEFEIERT/ABGEGESSEN/ABGEGURGELT/ ABGEHALFTERT = **ABGEJUBELT.**

ABGEHEN, *youth.* **1.** To leave. **Mit etwas abgehen.** To perform brilliantly (lit. to go off with s.t.). *Uli geht mit dem Tastenkasten echt ab.* "Uli really goes to town on the piano." **2.** To happen; be where it's at. *Im Winter geht hier nichts ab; aber im Sommer, wenn die Berliner kommen,* *da geht aber was ab.* "In the winter there's no action here; but in the summer, when the Berliners come, we're where it's really happening." **3.** To ejaculate. *Beim bloßen Anblick der üppigen Stripperin ging ihm einer ab.* "At the mere sight of the voluptuous stripper, he shot a load." Cf. ABGANG **2.**

ABGEHOBEN. High, exhilarated. *Die Kiffer fanden die Stimmung bei der Fete voll abgehoben.* "The potheads found the party out of this world." Cf. ABHEBEN.

(SICH) ABGEILEN, *youth.* To calm down (slangier than SICH ABREGEN). *Hast 'n Furz gefressen? Geil dich ab, Mann!* "What the hell's gotten into you? Simmer down, man!"

ABGEJUBELT, *youth, pej.* **1.** Old; old hat. (*Jubeln* = to celebrate. *Abgejubelt* is therefore "no longer celebrated/ worth celebrating.") *Ihr findet alles abgejubelt, abgegessen, abgegriffen, abgezopft, weil ihr von ewigen Wahrheiten nichts wissen wollt.* "You find everything stale, passé, because you don't believe in eternal truths." **2.** Uninteresting. *Vor allem wollen wir von dir nichts wissen, abgejubelter Grufti.* "It's really you we don't want to know anything about, decrepit old bore."

ABGEKLUNKERT. Bankrupt. *Jetzt ist er voll abgeklunkert.* "He's flat broke now." Cf. BEKLUNKERT; KLUNKER.

ABGELEIERT = **ABGEDROSCHEN.**

ABGELUTSCHT, *youth.* Old-fashioned; played out (lit. sucked off). *Der Schnuffi ist voll abgelutscht.* "That cokehead's had it." Cf. ABGEFUCKT.

ABGEMACHT! It's a deal!

ABGEMACKERT = **ABGEJUBELT 1.**

ABGEPFIFFEN/ABGESCHLAFFT = **ABGEFACKT/ ABGEFUCKT.**

ABGESOFFEN. Dead drunk (lit. drowned). *Er erinnert sich nicht mehr daran; er war ja voll abgesoffen.* "He doesn't remember it; he was too drunk." See ABSAUFEN.

ABGETAKELT. Washed up (lit. unrigged [nautical]). *Ihr haltet mich für abgetakelt, aber ich werde euch zeigen, was ich noch kann.* "You think I've had it, but I'll show you what's still in me." Cf. AUFGETAKELT.

ABGEWÖHNEN. To break a habit. *Noch einen zum Abgewöhnen trinken/noch eine zum Abgewöhnen rauchen.* (*Hum.*) To have just one more drink/cigarette. *Ja, morgen gehen wir unter die Abstinenzler, aber jetzt trinken wir uns noch einen zum Abgewöhnen.* "Yes, tomorrow we'll go on the wagon, but let's have one for the road now." *Zum Abgewöhnen sein.* To be a big turnoff. *Der Typ ist richtig zum Abgewöhnen!* "That guy's bad news/is no good (and should be avoided)."

ABGEWRACKT. Down and out (lit. scrapped; decrepit). *Was will die abgewrackte alte Wachtel hier?* "What does that broken down old bag want here?"

ABGEZIPFELT/ABGEZOPFT = ABGEJUBELT 1.

ABGREIFEN, *youth.* To shoplift. *Hättest wenigstens einen größeren Brilli abgreifen können.* "You could at least have ripped off a larger diamond ring." Cf. KLAUFEN; STAUCHEN.

ABHABEN. See EINEN ABHABEN.

ABHAUEN. To scram. *Ich muss jetzt abhauen.* "I've got to hit the road now."

ABHEBEFETE/ABHEBEPARTY, *f., youth.* Splendid party; rave. *Von wegen Abhebeparty! 's war voll tote Hose.* "What do you mean, 'big blast'? It was a real dud."

ABHEBEN, *youth.* To feel very high (to take/lift off). *Heb nicht gleich ab! Bleib doch aufm Teppich!* "Don't get carried away; stay grounded!"

(SICH) ABHOTTEN = (SICH) HOTTEN.

ABJACKEN, *youth.* To take off one's jacket. *Keine Zeit abzujacken; 's geht gleich los!* "No time to take off jackets; it's starting right now." See ABMANTELN.

ABKEIMEN, *E., youth.* To scram (*keimen* = to sprout).

Zum Glück konnten wir rasanto abkeimen. "Fortunately, we were able to make tracks fast."

ABKLATSCHEN. 1. To take the ball away. *Der flinke Tim hat mir den Ball abgeklatscht.* "Swifty Tim took the ball away from me." **2.** To cut in (dance). *Darf ich abklatschen?* "May I cut in?" **3.** To beat up. See KLATSCHEN 3.

ABKLAVIEREN. See ARSCH.

ABKNALLEN. To gun down. *Die Räuber knallten alle in der Bank ab.* "The robbers gunned down everyone in the bank." Cf. WEGBALLERN.

ABKNUTSCHEN/(SICH) ABKNUTSCHEN = KNUT-SCHEN.

ABKÖNNEN, *N.* To stand; tolerate. *Schnaps kann er nicht mehr ab.* "He can't handle hard liquor anymore."

ABKRÄBELN, *E.* = **ABKRATZEN.**

ABKRATZEN. To croak (lit. to scratch off). *Die Maschine kam ins Trudeln und ich dachte, jetzt kratz ich ab.* "The plane went into a spin and I thought 'I'm done for now.' "

ABKUPFERN. To copy (etchings are struck [copied] from copper plates [*Kupferstiche*]). *Beim Matheexamen hat er wieder bei mir abgekupfert.* "He copied from me again during the math test."

ABLASSEN = RAUSLASSEN 2.

ABLATSCHEN. To shuffle off (lit. to wear out shoes/slippers). *Latsch nur sachte ab!* "Just move along, now."

ABLAUFEN. 1. To wear down by walking. ***Sich den Arsch ablaufen.*** To run around trying to do/get s.t. (lit. to walk one's ass off). *Ich hab mir den Arsch abgelaufen, das alles für dich zu kriegen, und jetzt lässt du mich ablaufen.* "I busted my buns getting all that for you, and now you're giving me the cold shoulder." **2.** To drain off. *Solch fiese Kritik läuft nur an mir ab.* "I just shrug off nasty criticism like that."

ABLAUFEN LASSEN. To reject disdainfully. *Er ver-*

suchte, sich bei mir lieb Kind zu machen, aber ich ließ ihn ablaufen. "He tried to get into my good graces, but I sent him packing."

ABLINKEN, *N., youth.* **1.** To treat shabbily; usher out; deceive. (Left-handed people complain of the "sinister" meanings of *links* [left] in many langs. Cf. LINKS *liegen lassen;* LINKEN; LINKE TITTE.) *Ich war bereit einzulenken, aber man linkte mich gleich ab.* "I was ready to make concessions, but they shut me out right away." **2.** To deceive. See LINKEN.

ABLUTSCHEN. To suck/lick off. *Jmdm. einen ablutschen.* To perform fellatio. *Täglich muss ich ihm einen ablutschen.* "I have to go give him his daily blow job." Cf. ABGELUTSCHT.

ABMALEN. To paint a picture of s.t./s.o. *Dort verkehrt die Schickeria, aber da möcht ich nicht abgemalt sein.* "That's where the trendy hang out, but I wouldn't be caught dead there."

ABMANTELN, *youth.* To take one's coat off. *Der Exhibitionist mantelt selten ab.* "That flasher rarely takes off his coat."

ABMELDEN. To cancel; disconnect (telephone). *Bei jmdm. abgemeldet sein.* Not to exist for s.o. *Seit er mich betrogen hat, ist er bei mir abgemeldet.* "Ever since he betrayed me, he doesn't exist for me."

ABMISCHEN, *youth.* To beat up. *Den Schiri sollten wir mal abmischen.* "We ought to beat up the umpire!"

ABMÜLLEN. To unload garbage. *Mein Mann müllt bei mir ab und fühlt sich dann erleichtert.* "My huband dumps his stress on me and then feels better." See DIPLOMMÜLLOLOGE **2.**

ABMURKSEN. To bump off. *Wie viele wurden beim Valentinstagsmassaker in Chicago abgemurkst?* "How many got rubbed out in the Chicago St. Valentine's Day massacre?"

ABNIBBELN, *youth.* To die (lit. to stop nibbling). *Beim*

Rodeln ist er fast abgenibbelt. "He almost died when tobogganing." Cf. BESTECK; GABEL; LÖFFEL **1.**

ABNUDELN = RUNTERNUDELN.

ABPFEIFEN, *youth.* To clear out. *Warum bist gleich abgepfiffen?* "Why'd you run off like that?"

ABPROTZEN, *mil.* To defecate (from a term formerly used for detaching part of an artillery cannon). (Military life is often characterized by a jump-to-it, spit-and-polish, parade-discipline atmosphere. Showing off while defecating is difficult; thus some pomposity and pretention are temporarily shed, "excreted," when defecating.) *Abmarschieren mussten wir sofort—nicht mal Zeit zum Abprotzen!* "We had to march off right away—no time to take a crap."

(SICH) ABREGEN. To calm down. *Reg dich ab!* "Simmer down!/Cool it!" Cf. (SICH) ABGEILEN.

ABREIBEN = ABSCHMIRGELN.

ABREIBUNG, *f.* Beating (lit. rubdown). *Er droht mir mit 'ner saftigen Abreibung, wenn ich abtreibe.* "He threatens to beat me up good if I get an abortion."

ABSAHNEN. To siphon off money (lit. to skim off the cream). *Der Senator hat da tüchtig abgesahnt.* "The senator got his hefty cut out of it."

ABSAUFEN. To drown; sink. *Die Kiste ist abgesoffen.* "The old tub sank." *Sich einen absaufen.* To get drunk. *Saufen wir uns einen ab!* "Let's tie one on!" Cf. ABGESOFFEN.

ABSCHLEPPEN, *youth.* To pick up (lit. to drag off). *Die Tussi hab ich mir im Park abgeschleppt.* "I picked up that broad in the park."

ABSCHMETTERN. To reject brusquely. *Der Präsident schlug eine Steuererhöhung vor und wurde abgeschmettert.* "The president suggested a tax increase and was told to get lost."

ABSCHMIEREN. 1. To copy (lit. to grease). *Du versuchst immer bei mir abzuschmieren.* "You always try to copy from me." **2.** To lose altitude by side-slipping (aviation); to decline (finance). *Diese Aktien werden weiter abschmieren.* "These stocks will continue to go down." **3.** To clear out. *Schmier ab, aber rapido!* "Beat it, fast!" **4.** To die. *Beim Tauchen ist er abgeschmiert.* "He croaked while diving."

ABSCHMINKEN. To put out of one's mind (lit. to remove makeup). *Den neuen Flitzer kannst du dir abschminken; wir sind pleite.* "You can forget about that new car; we're broke."

ABSCHMIRGELN, *youth.* To beat up (lit. to sand down). *Die Skins haben ihn in der U-Bahn grell abgeschmirgelt.* "The skinheads beat him to a pulp in the subway."

ABSCHNACKEN, *N.* To coax; talk s.o. into s.t. *Versuch nicht, mir's abzuschnacken.* "Don't try to wheedle it out of me."

ABSCHNALLEN. To be floored (lit. to unbuckle). *Nicht abschnallen, cool bleiben!* "Don't be flabbergastered; stay cool!"

ABSCHRAMMEN. 1. To graze (skin). *Beim Rollschuhlaufen hat sie sich das Knie abgeschrammt.* "She scraped her knee while skating." **2.** (*Youth.*) To go away. *Wir müssen jetzt abschrammen.* "We've got to shove/push off now." **3.** To die. *Er zog seinen Revolver, und ich dachte, jetzt schramm ich ab.* "He drew his revolver, and I thought 'I'm done for now.'"

ABSCHUSS, *m.* Shooting down. **Auf der Abschussliste stehen.** To be on s.o.'s hit/black list. *Der Postbeamte glaubte auf der Abschussliste zu stehen.* "The postal employee thought he was going to get the axe (be fired)."

ABSCHWATZEN = **ABSCHNACKEN.**

ABSCHWEBEN = **ABSCHWIRREN.**

ABSCHWIRREN, *youth.* To buzz off. *Schwirr ab, Stecher, aber rapido!* "Buzz off fast, fucko!"

(SICH) ABSEILEN, *youth.* **1.** To buzz off; back off (lit. to lower o.s. by a rope). *Sie sprach von ewiger Liebe und ich* *wusste, es war Zeit, mich abzuseilen.* "She started talking about everlasting love, and I knew it was time for me to hit the road." **2.** To disappear; commit suicide. *Der Depri hat sich abgeseilt.* "That Gloomy Gus checked out permanently."

ABSITZARSCH, *m.* Phlegmatic old fogey. *Diese Absitzärsche tun doch nichts für dich.* "Those foggy-bottoms won't do anything for you."

ABSOCKEN, *youth.* To get going. See SOCKEN.

ABSPRITZEN = ABHEBEN.

ABSTAUBEN. 1. To mooch (lit. to dust). *Bei mir will er immer Hugos abstauben.* "He's always trying to bum joints off me." **2.** To take away from. *Bette staubte ihrer Schwester die Macker ab.* "Bette used to make off with her sister's boyfriends." **3.** To score high in school; score an easy football goal. *Den Kurs hat sie abgestaubt.* "She aced the course."

ABSTOTTERN. To pay in installments. *Jeden Monat müssen wir 900 DM abstottern.* "We've got to meet payments of 900 marks every month."

ABSTURZ, *m.* Plane crash. ***Einen Programmabsturz/ Systemabsturz haben.*** (*Youth.*) To be in a fog/feel fuzzy (lit. to have a [computer] program/[computer] system breakdown). *Beim Matheexam hatte ich 'n totalen Systemabsturz.* "I drew a total blank during the math exam."

ABTANZEN, *youth.* To die (lit. to dance off). *Wann ist er abgetanzt?* "When'd he kick the bucket?"

ABTÖRNEN, *youth.* To turn off (from Eng.) *Ihre Scheißmucke törnte uns total ab.* "Their lousy music really turned us off."

ABTURNEN = ABTÖRNEN.

ABWICHSEN. To masturbate. ***Sich/jmdm. einen abwichsen.*** To jerk o.s./s.o. off. *Könntest mir wenigstens einen abwichsen.* "You could at least give me a hand job."

ABWIMMELN. To get rid of. *Der Türsteher der Disko hat*

die Skins abgewimmelt. "The disco's doorman turned away the skinheads."

ABWISCHEN. To wipe off. *Sich mit etwas den Arsch/Hinten abwischen können.* (Lit. to wipe one's ass/behind with s.t.) *Mit deinem Liebesbrief kannst du dir den Arsch abwischen.* "You can go wipe your ass with your love letter."

ABZIEHEN. 1. To leave. *Zieh ab, Fiesling.* "Beat it, creep!" **2.** To stage. *Eine Nummer/Schau abziehen.* To put on an act/show. *Heiligabend zieht Opa seine Weihnachtsmannschau ab.* "On Christmas Eve, grandpa puts on his Santa Claus act."

ABZISCHEN. To buzz off. *Zisch ab, Knallkopf!* "Beat it, dweeb!"

(SICH EINEN) ABZITTERN. 1. To be afraid. *Ich hab ganz schön einen abgezittert, aber sie haben mich nicht erwischt.* "I was really scared, but they didn't catch me." **2.** To be cold. *Wie lange müssen wir hier noch einen abzittern, bevor geheizt wird?* "How long are we gonna have to freeze here till you turn the heat on?" **3.** To go away. *Zitter nur jetzt ab!* "Just be on your way."

ABZOCKEN. To swindle. *Der Witwe hat er den letzten Pfennig abgezockt.* "He swindled the widow out of her last cent."

ABZOCKER, *m.* Con man. *Warum ist sie diesem Abzocker aufn Leim gegangen?* "Why'd she fall for that con man's scam?"

ABZOCKEREI, *f.* Scam. *Wir trauten dem Braten nicht und wussten es war nur Abzockerei.* "We were suspicious and knew it was a con."

ABZWITSCHERN. To drive/go off (lit. to chirp off). *Wir müssen jetzt abzwitschern.* "We've got to buzz off now."

ACHOKARACHO. Intensifies KARACHO.

ACKER, *m.* Field. *Sich vom Acker machen.* To scram. *Mach dich vom Acker!* "Get out of here."

ACKERGAUL, *m., pej.* Prostitute (lit. farm horse; old nag). *Ich muss viele Nummern schieben; bin halt nur 'n alter Ackergaul.* "I've got to turn lots of tricks; I'm just an old workhorse hooker." Cf. PFERDCHEN (less pej.).

ACKERN. To slave away at s.t. (lit. to till the soil). *Ich musste die ganze Nacht ackern, sonst hätt ich's nicht geschafft.* "I had to plug away all night, or I wouldn't have made it."

ÄCKTSCH(E)N, *f., youth.* Dynamism; action (translit. of Eng. "action"). *Keine Szene-Konnäcktschens zu machen in dem Kaff; voll tote Hose, nullo Äcktschn.* "No (drug) scene connections in that hick burg; really deadbeat, no action."

AFFE, *m.* **1.** Monkey. *Einen Affen sitzen haben.* To be drunk/drugged. *Er hat wieder 'n Affen sitzen.* "He's got a load on again." *Sich einen Affen kaufen/antrinken.* To get drunk. *Trink dir wieder keinen Affen an!* "Don't get soused again." *Wie vom wilden Affen gebissen sein.* To be crazy. *Der war wie vom wilden Affen gebissen.* "He was like s.o. out of his senses." *Auf (dem) Affe* = AUF TURKEY. See ANGEBEN; FRESSEN; LAUSEN; LORE. **2.** Jerk. *Du alter, eingebildeter Affe!* "You conceited old jackass!" See BRÜLLAFFE (a noisy jerk). **3.** Homosexual. See AFFENSUSE.

AFFENARSCH. Intensifies AFFE **2.**

AFFENGEIL, *youth.* Really terrific (lit. monkey horny). *Mannomann ist Hanuman aber ein affengeiler Gott!* "Man oh man, Hanuman is one totally fantastic God!"

AFFENGESCHWINDIGKEIT. See AFFENZAHN.

AFFENHART. Var. of **AFFENGEIL.**

AFFENKÄFIG, *m., youth.* School gymnasium. *Schwitz du im Affenkäfig; ich hau ab.* "You go sweat in the gym; I'm going to make tracks."

AFFENKASTEN, *m., youth.* School. *Den Affenkasten hab ich geschmissen.* "I quit school."

AFFENKOPF = **AFFE 2.**

AFFENSPITZ/AFFENSTARK, *youth.* Var. of **AF-FENGEIL.**

AFFENSUSE, *f., pej.* Male homosexual. *Im Knast hatte ich kein süßes Törtchen, dafür aber eine scharfe Affensuse.* "In the slammer I had no sweet pussy pie but, instead, a nifty piece of faggot fruit."

AFFENTEMPO. See AFFENZAHN.

AFFENZAHN, *m.* Monkey's tooth. ***Mit einem Affenzahn.*** Extremely fast. *Mit seinem Flitzer fährt er immer mit einem Affenzahn.* "He always drives at breakneck speed in his new sports car."

AFTERSAUSEN, *f.* Fear (lit. anal rumbling). ***Aftersausen haben/kriegen.*** To be/get scared. *Ich mach's lieber ohne dich; du kriegst immer gleich Aftersausen.* "I'd rather do it without you; you always get scared shitless right away." Cf. FRACKSAUSEN; MUFFENSAUSEN.

ÄITSCH, *m.* Heroin (translit. of Eng. drug sl. "H" or "Big H"). *Er ist Äitschabhängig.* "He's hooked on the Big H."

AKTIENMUFFEL, *m.* S.o. wary of the stock market. *Einst waren die Deutschen Aktienmuffel, aber jetzt nicht mehr!* "Once the Germans were leery of stocks, but no longer!"

ALK, *m.* **1.** Alcohol (for stand. *Alkohol*). *Hast schon genug Alk getankt.* "You've already guzzled enough booze." Cf. RIESENALK. **2.** Alcoholic. Cf. ALKER.

ALKEN. To booze it up. *Gehen wir alken.* "Let's tie one on."

ALKER/ALKI, *m.* Alcoholic (for stand. *Alkoholiker*). *Alle in der Familie sind Alker.* "They're all heavy drinkers in that family."

ALKOHOLSELIG. High on alcohol. *Bei der alkoholseligen Verbrüderung schwuren sie sich ewige Freundschaft.* "They buddied up, high on alcohol, and pledged eternal friendship."

ALKOLENKER, *m.* Drunk driver (play on *Alkohol* and *Autolenker*). *Alkolenkern wird der Führerschein entzogen.* "Drunk drivers get their licenses taken away."

ALLE. All. *Alle sein/alle machen.* To be/make all gone, finish off. *Der Schnaps ist alle.* "We've killed off all the booze." *Nicht mehr alle haben.* To be crazy (cf. *nicht alle TASSEN im Schrank haben*). *Haste (hast du) nicht mehr alle?* "Are you off your rocker?"

ALLES PALETTI! Everything's fine/OK! *Alles paletti in Cincinnati.* "Everything's fine in Cincinnati."

ALLTAGSTROTT, *m.* Daily routine. *Ich hab wenig Chance dem Alltagstrott zu entfliehen.* "I have little chance of getting away from the daily grind."

ALPENDOLLAR, *m., hum.* Austrian schilling (lit. Alpine dollar). *Wenn der Euro kommt, ist's auch mit dem Alpendollar aus.* "When the euro comes, it'll be all over for the Austrian schilling too."

ALT. See OLL.

ALTBACKEN. Stale; old-fashioned. *Ihre Mucke klingt altbacken.* "Their music's old stuff."

ALTE KLAMOTTE/ALTE KLAMOTTEN. Old-fashioned (lit. old clothes). *Dass man solche Stücke noch aufführt! Alles alte Klamotten.* "It's incredible that they're still putting on plays like that. It's old hat."

ALTE MESSE. See MESSE.

ALTENTEIL, *n.* Rights retained by a farmer after deeding most property to a successor. *Jmdn. aufs Altenteil setzen/abschieben.* To squeeze s.o. out; force s.o. to retire. *Meine Kinder wollen mich aufs Altenteil setzen, aber ich denk nicht daran, den König Lear zu spielen.* "My children want to move me out (of a business, etc.), but I have no intention of playing King Lear."

ALTER KNACKER, *m.* Old crock/fogey. *Mein Mann hält sich noch für einen tollen Hecht aber aus ihm ist nur 'n alter Knacker geworden.* "My husband still thinks he's hot stuff, but he's just an old fart."

ALTER SCHWEDE, *m.* Chum (lit. old Swede). *Zischen wir noch einen, alter Schwede.* "Let's have another beer, old buddy."

ALTES REGISTER, *n., dated.* Old person. *Du denkst, ich bin nur ein altes Register, aber ich könnte dich mal angenehm überraschen, süßes Törtchen.* "You think I'm just an old fart, but I might give you a pleasant surprise, my little sweetie."

AMI, *m., often pej.* American; Yank; GI. When many Europeans resentfully perceived Americans as rich, rude, and stupid. U.S. soldiers stationed in Britain, 1942–1945, were often described by the natives as "overpaid, overfed, oversexed, and over here." *In Amerika gibt's keine Amis, behauptete einer.* "S.o. said there are no 'ugly Americans' in America."

AMINUTTE, *f.* Prostitute whose clientele consists principally of American soldiers. *Diese Aminutte spricht Englisch mit dem Akzent des Südens.* "That Yank tramp speaks English with a Southern accent."

AMISCHLITTEN, *m.* Big American car (such as a Cadillac or Lincoln). *Die Aminutte hat viele Kunden, aber keiner hat ihr bisjetzt einen Amischlitten geschenkt.* "That girl who hustles for Yanks has many customers, but none of them's given her a Cadillac yet." See SCHLITTEN.

AMIZONE (play on *Amazone* [Amazon] and American Zone of Occupation). See AMINUTTE; ZONI.

ANARCHO, *m., youth.* Anarchist. *Manch Harmloser schimpft sich heutzutage Anarcho.* "Many mild-mannered sorts style t.s. anarchists today."

ANBAGGERN, *youth.* To come on to; try to pick up. *Als Rockstar werd ich oft angebaggert. Klaro!* "I'm a rock star and many try to make it with me. Natch!" Cf. ANGRABEN.

ANBEAMEN, *youth.* To turn on (from Eng. "beam"). *Ihr Sound beamte uns schrill an.* "Their sound really turned us on."

ANBLASEN = **ANBLÖKEN.**

ANBLÖKEN, *youth.* To feed a load of baloney to s.o. (*blöken* = to bleat). *Der Kragen will mich immer mit* *seinen Müllsprüchen anblöken.* "That stuffed shirt's always trying to lay a load of crap on me."

ANDIPPELN = ANFLASCHEN.

ANDUDELN. *Sich einen andudeln.* To get tipsy. *Sie hatten sich einen angedudelt und begannen zu singen.* "They'd gotten a little high and began to sing."

ANFLASCHELN, *Aust.* To drink alcohol. *Seit dem Tod seiner Frau, flaschelt er sich an.* "Since his wife's death he's taken to the bottle."

ANFLUNKERN. To put one over on. *Du hast versucht, uns anzuflunkern.* "You tried to sell us the Brooklyn Bridge."

ANGEFEGT KOMMEN. To arrive at the last moment (*fegen* = to sweep). *Endlich ist er angefegt gekommen.* "He finally swept in at the last moment."

ANGEILEN. To arouse. *Er versuchte mich anzugeilen, aber ich wollte nicht mit ihm poofen.* "He tried to get me hot, but I didn't want to sleep with him."

ANGELATSCHT KOMMEN. To come ambling in. *Er hat sich kein Bein ausgerissen, kam aber doch angelatscht.* "He didn't break a leg getting here, but just ambled in." Cf. LATSCHEN.

ANGESCHISSEN. Screwed up (lit. shat on). *Angeschissen kommen.* To show up with one's tail between one's legs. *Komm mir nicht wieder angeschissen! Bleib mir vom Leibe!* "Don't show your shit-ass face around me again. Stay away from me." See ANSCHEIßEN.

ANGRABEN. To come on to. *Einige Macker kriegen Angst, wenn ich sie angrabe.* "Some guys get scared when I come on to them." Cf. ANBAGGERN.

ANHAUEN, *youth.* **1.** To scrounge. *Versuch nicht, mich wieder um Kohle anzuhauen.* "Don't try to hit me up for any more money." **2.** To lay down the law to. *Der Lernfuzzi wollte mich anhauen.* "The teach tried to preach to me."

ANHIMMELN. To adore. *Ja, er himmelt mich an, liebt mich abgöttisch; aber er beginnt mich anzuöden.* "Yes, he worships the ground I walk on, idolizes me; but he's beginning to bore me."

ANKER, *m.* Anchor. *Den Anker werfen.* To get married (lit. to cast anchor). *Er hat endlich den Anker geworfen.* "He finally got hitched."

ANKERN = **Den ANKER werfen.**

ANKLOPFEN. To knock. *Bei jmdm. um etwas anklopfen.* To try to get s.t. from s.o. *Er wollte bei mir um noch mehr Kies anklopfen.* "He wanted to hit me up for even more money." Cf. ANHAUEN 1. *Bei Petrus anklopfen.* To die (lit. to knock on Peter's door). *Opa hat schon längst bei Petrus angeklopft; in meinen Träumen spricht er aber noch zu mir.* "Grandpa appeared at the pearly gates long ago, but he still speaks to me in dreams."

ANKOTZEN. To throw up on; disgust. *Dein Benehmen kotzt mich an.* "Your behavior makes me want to throw up." Cf. KOTZEN.

ANKRATZ FINDEN/HABEN. To find social contacts. *Mit 'nem solchen Vorbau fand sie natürlich sofort Ankratz auf der Party.* "Of course she made a hit at the party, stacked the way she is."

ANLACHEN. To smile at. *Sich jmdn. anlachen.* To pick s.o. up (by giving them a sexy little smile). *Wo hast du dir diesen Typ angelacht?* "Where'd you pick up that guy?"

ANMACHE, *f.* Coming on; making sexual advances. *Der Macke ist ein Meister der Anmache.* "That guy's a master at handing a line."

ANMACHEN. 1. To turn on (lit. and fig.). *Die Band hat das Publikum wirklich angemacht.* "The band really turned the audience on." **2.** To sweet talk, come on to. *Er versucht noch, mich anzumachen, aber ich kann ihn nicht riechen.* "He still tries to hand me a line, but I can't stand him." **3.** To harass. *Mach mich nicht an!* "Quit bugging me."

ANMEIERN = ANBLÖKEN.

ANNO DAZUMAL/ANNO TOBAK/ANNO X. In days gone by; former times. *Oft wird die Mode von anno (Anno) dazumal wieder populär.* "Out-of-date fashion often becomes popular again."

ANNO DUNNEMALS. Hum. var. of ANNO DAZUMAL.

ANÖDEN. To bore stiff. *Er wird uns mit denselben Geschichten wieder anöden.* "He's going to bore us to death again with the same stories." Cf. ÖDIG.

ANPESEN, *youth.* **1.** To show/drive up fast. *Sie kam mit Achokaracho angepest.* "She showed up in no time flat." Cf. PESEN. **2.** To bawl out. *Meine Fossilien haben mich tierisch angepest.* "My parents gave me one hell of a chewing out."

ANPFLAUMEN. To poke fun at. *Den Armen hättest du nicht so anpflaumen sollen.* "You shouldn't have made fun like that of the poor guy."

ANPINKELN/ANPISSEN, *youth.* To urinate on. *Jmdn. anpinkeln.* To cheat s.o.; to bug s.o.; put s.o. down. *Versuch nur nicht, mich anzupinkeln!* "Just don't try to piss me off!"

(SICH) ANPISSEN, *youth.* To get all worked up. *Mann, piss dich nicht gleich an! Geil dich doch ab!* "Man, hold your water! Simmer down!" Cf. SICH NASS MACHEN.

ANPOWERN, *youth.* To turn on intensely. *Der blöde Macho glaubt, nur er wisse, Tussis voll anzupowern.* "That macho dork thinks he's the only one who knows how to turn on chicks."

ANRANZEN. To bawl out. *Mutti hat mich vielleicht angeranzt.* "Mom really chewed me out."

ANSABBELN. See SABBELN.

ANSÄUSELN. *Sich einen ansäuseln.* To have a little drink/get a buzz. *Wenn er sagt, er wolle sich einen ansäuseln, weiß ich wie das endet.* "When he says he wants to have a wee drop, I know how that will end up." Cf. SAUSE.

ANSCHAFFE, *f.* Procurement. *Auf (die) Anschaffe gehen.* To engage in prostitution. *Mein Mann weiß, dass ich manchmal noch auf Anschaffe gehe.* "My husband knows I still hustle a little sometimes."

ANSCHAFFEN, *youth.* **1.** To steal (lit. to acquire; buy). *Diesen Brilli hab ich mir gestern angeschafft.* "I swiped this diamond ring yesterday." Cf. KLAUFEN. **2.** To engage in prostitution. *Für mich selber geh ich anschaffen; ich brauch keinen Kuppelmacker.* "I'm in business for m.; I don't need a pimp."

ANSCHAFFER. See NAHRUNGSBESCHAFFER.

ANSCHEIßEN. 1. To deceive (lit. to shit on). *Der Schwindler hat sie alle angeschissen.* "The swindler conned them all." Cf. ANPISSEN. **2.** To bawl out. *Sie wird mich richtig anscheißen.* "She'll give me a real chewing out."

ANSCHISS, *m.s.* Bawling out (lit. shitting on). *Er kam besoffen nach Hause und kriegte einen Anschiss von seiner Alten.* "He came home drunk and got a chewing out from his old lady (wife)."

ANSCHLEIFEN. Drag/bring along. *Brauchst nicht immer Wein anzuschleifen, wenn wir dich einladen.* "You don't always have to bring us wine when we invite you."

ANSCHMEIßEN, *youth.* To use one's head (with words meaning "head; brains"). *Schmeiß doch mal deine Nuss an!* "Use your noodle, will ya!"

ANSCHMIEREN. To con (lit. to grease). *Dich hat man ganz schön angeschmiert.* "You really got taken for a ride." Cf. EINSEIFEN.

ANSCHWALLEN. See SCHWALLEN.

ANSINGEN = OPERN.

ANSPITZEN. 1. To induce; prod (lit. to sharpen). *Vielleicht kann ich den Alten anspitzen, mir den Wagen zu lassen.* "Maybe I can get the old man to let me have the car." **2.** To talk s.o.'s head off. *Wie lange willst du mich noch anspitzen? Den Wagen bekommst du nicht!*

"How much longer are you going to keep harassing me? You're not getting the car!" **3.** To put s.o. on. See ZUSPITZEN.

ANSTANDSWAUWAU, *hum., youth.* Chaperon; parent. (*Anstand* = decency. *Wauwau* is children's lang. for dog [bow-wow]; thus a watchdog for propriety). *Meine Anstandswauwaus gehen mir echt tierisch auf den Keks.* "My parents really bug the hell out of me."

ANSTINKEN. *Gegen jmdn./etwas nichts anstinken können.* Not to be able to do shit about s.o./s.t. *Der Chef hat mich beschissen aber ich kann nichts dagegen anstinken.* "The boss cheated me, but I can't do shit about it."

ANSÜLZEN, *youth.* To babble. *Mann, der Kragen hat uns voll angesülzt!* "Man, that square sure fed us a crock o' crap."

ANTANZEN, *youth.* To show up fast; drive up. *Verzupft euch, da kommen die Tangobrüder angetanzt!* "Beat it, the cops are coming!"

ANTENNE, *f.* **1.** Antenna. *Eine Antenne für etwas haben.* To have a feeling for s.t. *Du hast keine Antenne dafür.* "You have no feeling for that." **2.** Brains. *Streng doch mal deine Antenne an!* "Put your thinking cap on!" **3.** Penis. *Ich brauch kein Kabelfernsehen; seine Antenne sorgt voll und ganz für meine Unterhaltung.* "I don't need cable TV; his dick takes care of all my entertainment needs."

ANTÖRNEN/ANTURNEN. To turn on. *Sich einen anturnen.* To get stoned. *Turnen wir uns einen voll an!* "Let's get really stoned!" *Sich angeturnt haben.* To be turned on. *Beim Rave hatten wir uns alle angeturnt.* "We were all turned on during the rave." See ANMACHEN **1.** Cf. ABTURNEN; OBERANTÖRNER.

ANZUG, *m.* Suit. *Aus dem Anzug gehen/springen.* To fly off the handle. *Spring doch nicht gleich aus dem Anzug; ich geh nur auf ein Bier mit den Kumpels.* "Keep your shirt on, I'm just going for a beer with the boys."

APFEL, *m.* Apple. ***Für einen Apfel/Appel und 'n Ei.*** For practically nothing. *Ja, ich tu's, aber nicht für einen Apfel und 'n Ei.* "Yes, I'll do it, but not for peanuts."

APOSTEL. See GESUNDHEITSAPOSTEL; MORALAPOSTEL.

ÄRGERN. To annoy. ***Sich die Krätze/die Schwindsucht an den Hals ärgern*** (lit. to get a throat full of scabies/consumption). To be infuriated. *Mit dir ärgere ich mir die Schwindsucht an den Hals und du lachst mich nur aus.* "You're driving me into my grave, yet you laugh at me." See PLATZE.

ARIE, *f.* Same old story (lit. aria). *Deine Arien kenn ich alle schon; leg doch 'ne andere Rille auf!* "I've heard that tune before; put another record on!"

ARM, *m.* **1.** Arm. ***Jmdn. auf den Arm nehmen.*** To make fun of s.o. *Ich glaube, du nimmst mich wieder auf den Arm.* "I think you're putting me on again." ***Jmdn. in den Arm fallen.*** To obstruct s.o. *Die Baubehörde fällt uns in den Arm.* "The housing authority is giving us a hard time." ***Jmdm. in die Arme laufen.*** To meet s.o. by chance. *Hoffentlich laufen wir keinem Bekannten meines Mannes in die Arme.* "I hope we don't run into any of my husband's acquaintances." **2.** Poor. ***Arm dran sein.*** To be in a bad way. ***Lieber/besser arm dran als Arm ab.*** "It's better to have a hard time than to be without an arm."

ARMLEUCHTER, *m.* Dimwit (lit. chandelier). *Dieser Armleuchter wird's nie peilen.* "That dimwit'll never get it."

ARSCH, *m.* **1.** Ass. ***Ein ganzer Arsch voll.*** A great many. *Du hast schon 'nen ganzen Arsch voll solcher religiösen Bücher, die du nicht gelesen hast.* "You've already got a whole shit pile of similar religious books you haven't read." ***Einen kalten Arsch haben.*** To be dead. *Die Feuerwehr kam zu spät; er hatte schon einen kalten Arsch.* "The firefighters came too late; he'd already kicked the bucket." ***Einen kalten Arsch kriegen/Sich einen kalten Arsch holen*** (lit. to get a cold ass). To croak. *Hier halt* *ich's nicht länger aus, wenn ich nicht abhaue, hol ich mir 'n kalten Arsch.* "I can't take it here anymore; if I don't clear out, I'll be done for." ***In den Arsch gehen.*** To go down the drain; be ruined. *Der Computer ist total in den Arsch gegangen.* "The computer's all fucked up." ***Im Arsch sein.*** To be ruined. *Was, der Computer wieder im Arsch?* "What, the computer's in the toilet again?" ***Jmdm. den Arsch aufreißen.*** To beat the shit out of s.o. (lit. to rip open s.o.'s ass). *Ich reiß euch allen den Arsch auf, ihr Scheißkerle!* "I'll beat the shit out of all of you, you bastards!" ***Jmdn. beim Arsch haben.*** To have s.t. on s.o. *Ich glaubte, es vertuscht zu haben; aber die Chefin hat's erfahren und sie hat mich jetzt beim Arsch.* "I thought I'd hushed it up; but the boss found out and now she's got me by the short hairs." ***Sich etwas am Arsch abfingern/abklavieren können.*** To figure out/ imagine. *Was mit dir jetzt geschieht, kannste (kannst du) dir jetzt am Arsch abklavieren.* "Even you can figure out what's going to happen to you now." ***Am Arsch vorbeigehen.*** To leave indifferent. *Ja, schimpft nur ruhig weiter! 'S geht mir nur am Arsch vorbei.* "Yeah, keep on complaining. It's no skin off my ass." **2.** Stupid bastard. *Du Arsch, lass mich in Ruhe.* "Leave me alone, you asshole!" See ABSITZARSCH; AFFENARSCH; PARAGRAPHENARSCH. **3.** Insignificant person. *Wir sind die Ärsche hier.* "We're the nobodies here." See SCHÜTZE ARSCH.

ARSCH MIT OHREN, *m.* Repulsive person. *Hau ab, du Arsch mit Ohren!* "Beat it, shithead!"

ARSCHFICKER, *m.* SOB (lit. butt fucker). *Zieh Leine, aber rasanto, Arschficker!* "Get lost fast, asshole!"

ARSCHGEIGE, *f.* = **ARSCH 2.**

ARSCHIG. Asinine. *Ist der aber arschig.* "What an asshole he is."

ARSCHKRIECHER, *m.* Ass kisser (lit. ass crawler/licker). *Der Chef will nur Arschkriecher um sich.* "The boss just wants ass kissers around him."

ARSCHLECKER = ARSCHKRIECHER.

ARSCH-UND-TITTEN-PRESSE, *f.* Trashy print media (lit. ass-and-tits-press). *Omi liest gern die Regenbogenpresse; Opa hingegen, liebt die Arsch-und-Titten-Presse.* "Granny likes romantic tabloids; but grandpa likes raunchy scandal sheets."

ASCHE, *f.* Money (lit. ashes). *Uns blieb keine Asche mehr. Total ausgebrannt!* "We had no more dough. Totally broke." See KALTE ASCHE.

ASCHER, *m.* Ash tray. *Seit wir nicht mehr rauchen, benutzen wir die Ascher nur noch als Untertassen.* "Since we stopped smoking, we just use the ashtrays as saucers."

ASPHALTCOWBOY, *m., youth.* S.o. who hangs out on the streets a lot; city slicker (not pej., as in *Asphaltliterat,* a Nazi term for "cosmopolitan writer not rooted in *Blut und Boden* [blood and soil]"). *Willst wirklich den Anker werfen, alter Asphaltcowboy, du?* "Do you really intend to get hitched, you old urban cowboy?"

AST, *m.* **1.** Tree branch. ***Einen Ast durchsägen.*** To snore. *Ich hab gestern schlecht geschlafen; mein Mann hat wieder einen Ast durchgesägt.* "I slept poorly last night; my husband was sawing wood again." ***Auf dem absteigenden Ast sein.*** To go downhill. *Sein einst blühendes Geschäft ist auf dem absteigenden Ast.* "His formerly flourishing business is going downhill." ***Den Ast absägen auf dem man sitzt.*** To saw off the branch on which one is sitting. *Lass die Untersuchung, du sägst nur den Ast ab auf dem du sitzt.* "Drop the investigation, you're just digging your own grave." **2.** Knot in wood (pine, etc.). See ASTREIN. **3.** Back; humpback. ***Sich einen Ast lachen.*** To double up with laughter. *Opa fand ihre Witze geschmacklos; wir aber lachten uns einen Ast.* "Grandpa thought her jokes tasteless, but we broke up laughing."

ASTEN. 1. To lug. *Es gab keine Kofferkulis und ich musste alles selber asten.* "There were no baggage carts and I had to shlep everything m.s." **2.** To cram; work hard. *Mensch, hab ich geastet, bin aber trotzdem durchge-*

fallen. "Boy, did I work hard, but I failed anyway." Cf. GEASTE. **3.** To speed. (*E.*) *In ihrem Prunkhobel astet sie durch die Gegend.* "She flits around in her nifty new car."

ASTREIN! Terrific!

ASTREIN. Genuine; aboveboard (lit. [wood] free of knots). *Das war nicht ganz astrein.* "There was s.t. fishy about that." Cf. KOSCHER.

ASTSCHOCKE = ASTREIN.

ÄTZEND, *youth.* Extremely bad/good (lit. corrosive; grating). *Die Fete war echt ätzend.* "The party was a real bummer/drag." or "The party was pure magic." (Only the context will indicate whether pej. or laudatory.)

AU BACKE!/AU BACKE MEIN ZAHN! Oh heck!/Oh my aching back! *Au Backe, nichts zu essen im Haus und die Geschäfte sind zu.* "Darn it! Nothing to eat in the house, and the stores are closed."

AU BULLE! Damn it! (youth sl. version of previous entry).

AUF TURKEY. Off drugs. See TURKEY.

AUFBRUMMEN. To sentence. *Man hat ihm 10 Jahre aufgebrummt.* "He got sent up for 10 years."

AUFDREHEN. To accelerate (lit. to turn on [faucet]). *Nach den ersten verlorenen Runden drehte er auf und gewann den Boxkampf.* "After losing the first rounds, he opened up and won the boxing match."

AUFFLIEGEN. To break/bust up (lit. to fly up). *Ein Kinderpornoring ist aufgeflogen.* "A kiddie porn ring was busted."

(SICH) AUFGEILEN. To get excited. *Er hat sich an den Pornovideos aufgegeilt.* "The porn videos made him horny."

AUFGEKNÖPFT. Chatty, unbuttoned. *Er war weniger verklemmt, etwas aufgeknöpfter als das letzte Mal.* "He was less uptight, more open than the last time."

AUFGESCHMISSEN. Up the creek. *Ohne eure Hilfe sind wir echt aufgeschmissen.* "Without your help, we've had it."

AUFGETAKELT. Garishly overdressed (lit. all decked/rigged out [nautical]). *Ich bin nur 'ne aufgetakelte alte Fregatte; aber wie gerne würde ich mich für den Richtigen nackt ausziehen!* "I'm just an overdressed old bag; but I'd gladly take it all off for the right guy."

AUFGEWECKT. Bright (lit. awake). *Sie haben zwei aufgeweckte Töchter.* "They have two sharp-witted daughters."

AUFGUSS, *m., youth.* Brawling (lit. infusion [tea]). *Zwischen Skins und Hools hat's wieder Aufguss gegeben.* "Skinheads and hooligans were brawling again."

AUFHÖREN. To stop. *Da hört sich doch alles auf!* That's too much! *Werbeplakate im Opernhaus! Aber da hört sich doch alles auf.* "Advertising bills in the opera house. That's the living end!"

AUFLEGEN. To put on. *Eine andere Platte/Rille/Scheibe auflegen.* To put on another record. *Dein Geseire hängt mir zum Halse raus; leg doch 'ne andere Platte auf!* "I'm fed up with your moaning and groaning; put on another record!"

AUFMISCHEN. 1. To stir up. *Die junge Regisseurin hat die Kulturszene aufgemischt.* "The young director has shaken up the cultural scene." **2.** To beat up. (*Youth.*) See ABMISCHEN.

AUFMÖBELN. 1. To improve. *Sie versucht, ihre Spanischkenntnisse aufzumöbeln.* "She's trying to polish up her Spanish." **2.** To cheer up. *Dein lieber Brief hat mich so richtig aufgemöbelt.* "Your dear letter really cheered me up."

AUFMOTZEN. 1. To soup up. *Er hat seine alte Schese aufgemotzt.* "He's souped up his old jalopy." **2.** To revamp/revise. *Man versucht jetzt diese klassischen Theaterstücke aufzumotzen.* "They're now trying to revamp those classical plays."

(SICH) AUFMOTZEN. To get all dolled up. *Sie hatte sich aufgemotzt, um den Millionär zu kapern.* "She got all dolled up to get her hooks into the millionaire."

AUFMUCKEN/AUFMUCKSEN. To protest. *Man wollte die Gebühren anheben, und die Studenten mucksten auf.* "They wanted to raise fees and the students kicked up a fuss."

AUFMÜPFIG. Rebellious. *Sie war ein aufmüpfiges Kind.* "She was a rebellious child."

AUFPÄPPELN. To nourish; nurse back to health. *Sie versuchen, das kränkelnde Kind aufzupäppeln.* "They're trying to restore the sickly child's health."

AUFPEPPEN. To pep up. *Wenn Fritz nur hier wär, würde er dich aufpeppen.* "If only Fritz were here, he'd pep you up."

AUFPUTZEN. To decorate; dress up. *Ihr putzt euch moralisch auf, aber ihr seid nur Heuchler.* "You put on a show of morality, but you're just hypocrites."

AUFREIßEN, *youth.* **1.** To pick up s.o. (lit. to tear open; open up). *Gehen wir Tussis aufreißen.* "Let's go pick up chicks." **2.** To get. *Sie hat einen tollen Job aufgerissen.* "She landed a terrific job." **3.** To make plans for a party/s.t. new. *Elfi will 'ne Megaparty aufreißen.* "Elfi's planning a super party."

AUFRISS, *m., youth.* Breaking the ice for personal contact; pickup. Cf. AUFREIßEN. *Wir haben einen irren Aufriss gemacht.* "That was some pickup we made."

AUFSCHAUKELN. To gather momentum (as on a swing). *Drei Tage hat die Gewalt aufgeschaukelt, dann explodierte sie.* "For three days violence built up, then it exploded."

AUFSCHNEIDER, *m.* Braggart. *Dieser Aufschneider hat die ganze Geschichte aus der Luft gegriffen.* "That show-off made up the story out of whole cloth."

AUFZIEHEN. To tease (lit. to pull/wind up). *Warum habt ihr sie mit solchen Witzen aufgezogen?* "Why did you tease her with jokes like that?"

AUGE, *n.* Eye. ***Ins Auge gehen.*** To cause hurt. *Wenn man die Umwelt nicht respektiert, kann das ins Auge gehen.* "Not respecting the environment can bring harmful consequences."

AUGEN ZU UND DURCH! Just take the plunge!/Just close your eyes and run the gauntlet! *Mit Augen zu und durch geht's nicht; die Sache musst du gründlich vorbereiten.* "Just plunging in won't do it; you'll have to prepare the matter carefully."

AUS DAFFKE, *Berlin.* Just for the hell/fun of it. *Er hat's nur aus Daffke gemacht.* "He only did it for the hell of it."

AUS UND EIN GEHEN. To visit frequently. *Was geht's dich an, wer bei mir aus und ein geht?* "What business is it of yours whom I see?"

AUSBADEN. To take the consequences for. *Die Dummheiten, die du angerichtet hast, muss ich jetzt ausbaden.* "Now I've got to pay the price for all the dumb things you did."

AUSBALDOWERN. To scout/spy out (from Hebr. via ROTWELSCH). *Die Ganoven hatten vor, den Laden auszubaldowern.* "The crooks planned to case the joint."

AUSBLASEN. See LICHT.

AUSBOOTEN. To get rid of (lit. to unload a boat; to disembark in boats). *Seine Geschäftspartner hat er zuerst ausgebeutet, dann ausgebootet.* "He exploited, then ditched his business partners."

AUSFLIPPEN = ABHEBEN; AUSKLINKEN.

AUSGEBEN. To distribute. ***Einen ausgeben.*** To treat to a drink/drinks. *Gibst mir einen aus, Süßer?* "Will you buy me a drink, sweetie?"

(ETWAS) AUSGEFRESSEN HABEN. To get into trouble/mischief (lit. to have devoured s.t.). *In meiner Heimatstadt hab ich etwas ausgefressen.* "I got into trouble in my home town."

AUSGEHEN. To go out. ***Auf Bauernfang/Dummenfang***

ausgehen. To be on the lookout for suckers. *Als Werbe-texter musste ich immer auf Bauernfang ausgehen.* "As an advertising copywriter, I was always trying to put one over on the gullible."

AUSGEKOCHT, *usually pej.* Sly (lit. cooked through). *Du bist ja ein ausgekochtes Schlitzohr!* "You're a real shrewdie!" Cf. ABGEBRÜHT.

AUSGEMACHT. Complete. *Du bist 'n ausgemachter Idiot!* "You're a complete idiot!"

AUSGEPICHT. Crafty. *Der ist aber ein ausgepichter Kerl!* "He's a sly one!"

AUSGEPOWERT, *youth. Nach dem Rennen war ich total ausgepowert.* "I was completely wasted after the race." See POWER.

AUSGEPUMPT = **AUSGEPOWERT.**

AUSGERECHNET. Of all times/places/people/things. *Warum musste ausgerechnet hier, und augerechnet uns so was passieren?* "Why did s.t. like that have to happen here, of all places, and to us, of all people?" *Ausgerech-net Bananen!* Wouldn't you know it!/Just what we needed! (from the Ger. version of the 20s hit song, "Yes we have no bananas"). *Er wird nur atonale Mucke spie-len. Ausgerechnet Bananen!* "He's only going to play atonal music. Ugh, we're in for it."

AUSKLAMÜSERN. To figure/work out. *Wer kann so was ausklamüsern?* "Who can figure out anything like that?"

AUSKLINKEN, *youth.* **1.** To flip/freak out; lose control; go into a blackout. *Hier ist der Bär los! Ich klink echt aus!* "This party's ecstasy! I'm getting carried away!" **2.** To flip one's lid. *Brauchst nicht gleich auszuklinken.* "You don't have to hit the ceiling right away." **3.** To clear out; throw in the towel. *Es ist Zeit auszuklinken.* "It's time to split."

(SICH) AUSKOTZEN. To give vent/expression to (lit. to throw up everything). *Jetzt hab ich alles ausgekotzt und 's geht mir besser.* "I've gotten all that off my chest and feel better now."

AUSPOWERN. 1. To exploit; impoverish (from Fr. *pauvre* and pron. as in Fr.; less used than **2**). *Die Arbeiter wurden von den Bonzen rücksichtslos ausgepowert.* "The workers were ruthlessly exploited by the bosses." **2.** To exhaust (from Eng. "power" and pron. as in Eng.). See AUSGE-POWERT.

AUSPUSTEN. See LICHT.

(SICH) AUSQUATSCHEN. To say all one has to say. *Zwei Stunden warst du an der Quasselstrippe; hoffentlich habt ihr euch jetzt endlich ausgequatscht, wenigstens eine Zeitlang.* "You were on the phone for two hours; I hope you've emptied your chatterbox, at least for a while."

AUSRASTEN. To go haywire (lit. to disengage, snap; rel. to *Raste* [notch], not *Rast* [rest]). *Er verlangte noch mehr Geld; da bin ich aber ausgerastet!* "He asked for even more money, and I blew my top."

AUSREIßEN. 1. To tear out. ***Sich den Arsch ausreißen.*** To try very hard/go to great trouble. *Ich reiß mir den Arsch aus, dir zu helfen und du scheißt nur drauf.* "Here I am bustin' my balls to help you, and you don't give a shit." ***Sich kein Bein ausreißen.*** Not to strain o.s. unduly. *Bei deiner vermeintlichen Hilfe hast du dir auch kein Bein ausgerissen.* "You didn't exactly bust a gut with your so-called help." **2.** To run away; split. *Tim riss von zu Hause aus und wurde Stricher.* "Tim ran away from home and became a prostitute." Cf. REIßAUS.

(SICH) AUSSCHEIßEN. See SCHEIß DICH AUS!

AUSSI, *m., youth.* Pej. for *Ausländer* (foreigner). *Die Aussis will er rausschmeißen.* "He wants to throw out the foreigners."

AUSSIBUDE, *f., youth, pej.* State-provided residence for foreigners (lit. foreigners' hut/dump). *Man baut hier noch 'ne Aussibude.* "They're building more housing for foreigners here."

AUSSPRACHE, *f.* Pronunciation. ***Eine feuchte Aussprache haben.*** To spray spittle as one speaks. *Komm mir* *nicht so nahe; du hast 'ne feuchte Aussprache und geduscht hab ich gerade.* "Don't come so close to me; you give me a shower, and I've just had one."

(SICH) AUSSÜLZEN. To go on and on. *Wann wirst du endlich ausgesülzt haben?* "Are you ever going to stop slicing all that baloney?"

AUSTAKTEN, *E., youth.* **1.** To disorient (*Takt* = rhythm). *Ihm macht's Spaß, alle auszutakten.* "He likes unsettling people." **2.** To trick. See AUSTRICKSEN.

AUSTICKERN. To lose control. (Cf. AUSRASTEN. Both rel. to disturbances in technology. TICKERN = to telex. Not rel. to TICK [tic] or *ticken* [to tick; understand].) *Nicht gleich Austickern!* "Don't lose your cool right away!"

AUSTRICKSEN. To trick. *Der Präsident hat allen alles versprochen und dabei nur sich selber ausgetrickst.* "The president promised all things to all people, and just out-smarted h.s."

AUSZIEHEN. To take off. *Einem/jmdm. die Schuhe/Socken/Stiefel ausziehen.* To be too much to take (lit. to take one's/s.o.'s shoes/socks/boots off). *Mit meiner Rock-band zieh ich meinen Alten die Socken aus.* "I drive my parents up the wall with my rock band."

AZUBI, *m., f.* From *der/die Auszubildende* (trainee; apprentice). *Ich war Azubi; sollte Kfz-Mechaniker werden.* "I was an apprentice auto mechanic."

BABY-KIDS. See BONSAI; FRISCHLING; JUNGGE-MÜSE.

BACH, *m.* **1.** Brook. *Einen Bach/ein Bächlein machen.* To urinate. *Musst du ein Bächlein machen, Kleiner?* "Do you have to pee, little lad?" *Etwas/jmdn. den Bach runterspülen.* To get rid of s.t./s.o. (lit. to throw s.t./s.o. into the brook). *Spül's doch den Bach runter, statt dir Depressi-Einheiten reinzuziehen!* "Just let it go, instead of wallowing in self-pity." **2.** To slight/neglect s.o. deliberately. *Versuchst du, mich den Bach runterzuspülen?* "Are you trying to ditch me?"

BACHAB. Downstream. *Etwas/jmdn. bachab schicken = etwas/jmdn. den BACH runterspülen.*

BÄCHLEIN. See BACH.

BACHOTTER, *m., youth.* Ugly girl; bitch (lit. river otter). *Die Olga ist 'n richtiger Bachotter und ihre Schwester ist noch häßlicher.* "Olga's a real dog, and her sister's even uglier."

BACHRATTE, *f., youth.* Ugly girl; bitch (lit. brook/river rat). *Mit der Bachratte soll ich tanzen?* "I'm supposed to dance with that ugly broad?"

BACHRATZ, *m., S.* for BACHRATTE.

BACHSTELZE, *f.* Wagtail/water thrush. Cf. BACHRATTE.

BACKE, *f.* Cheek. *Sich etwas von der Backe putzen kön-*

nen. To have to give up on s.t. *Wird die Arbeit nicht bald fertig, kannst du dir die Urlaubspläne von der Backe putzen.* "If the job doesn't get done soon, you can kiss your vacation plans good-bye." *Über beide (alle vier) Backen grinsen/strahlen.* To be overjoyed (lit. to grin/radiate from both cheeks [facial] or from all four cheeks [facial and anal]). *Als sie den ersten Preis gewann, strahlte sie über alle vier Backen.* "She was overjoyed when she won first prize." See AU BACKE!

BACKFISCH, *m., dated.* Teenage girl (lit. fried fish). See ZIERFISCH.

BACKPFEIFE. Slap in the face. See PFEIFE **4.**

BACKPFEIFENGESICHT, *n.* Face that cries out for a fist in it. *Wenn ich dieses Backpfeifengesicht sehe, kann ich mich kaum mäßigen.* "I can scarcely control m.s. when I see that mug of his."

BADEN. To bathe. *Baden gehen.* To go down the drain. *Es ist fast niemand gekommen und die Feier ist baden gegangen.* "Almost no one came, and the celebration was a washout." Cf. FLÖTEN.

BAFF. Flabbergasted. *Opa trat als Fummeltrine auf, und wir waren alle baff.* "Grampa appeared as a drag queen, and we were all flabbergasted."

BAGGERN. To excavate, dredge. See ABGEBAGGERT; AN-BAGGERN.

BAHNHOF, *m.* Railroad station. See VERSTEHEN.

BALKEN, *m.* Beam. *Dass sich die Balken biegen.* Like all get-out. *Es wird gestrichen, dass sich die Balken biegen.* "They're making drastic cuts." Cf. *dass die FETZEN fliegen; dass die WÄNDE wackeln.*

BALKONIEN. See URLAUBSMUFFEL.

BALLABALLA. Crazy. *Die müssen alle ballaballa sein.* "They must all be bananas."

BALLERMANN, *hum.* Revolver. *Genug der Ballerei! Tut die Ballermänner weg!* "That's enough stupid shooting.

Put your rods away!"

BALLERN. 1. To shoot/fire away. *Im Film wird zu viel geballert.* "There's too much bang-bang in the movie." ***Jmdm. eine ballern.*** To sock s.o. *Der Schriftsteller hat dem Kritiker eine geballert.* "The writer socked the critic." **2.** To have a drink. *Grad noch Zeit, einen zu ballern.* "Just enough time to belt one down."

BAMBULE, *f., youth.* Trouble; fighting (from *bambalon,* Bantu for "drum" and Fr. *bamboula* [fiesta]). Ger. doesn't use it in the sense "party." For some, unfortunately, brawling is partying. Cf. "big blast/bash" and KLOPFKONZERT. A recent bio. of New Orleans born composer Louis Moreau Gottschalk is titled *Bamboula!* ["dance; party"]). ***Bambule anfetzen.*** To start a fight. *Wenn ihr hier Bambule anfetzen wollt, kommt ihr gleich auf eure Kosten.* "If you want to start s.t., you'll get what's coming to you right away." ***Bambule machen.*** To brawl. *Hools und Skins haben wieder Bambule gemacht.* "Hooligans and skinheads were brawling again." Cf. KLOPFKONZERT.

BANANE. 1. Banana. ***Warum ist die Banane krumm?*** How should I know? Quit asking silly questions! (lit. why is the banana curved?). See AUSGERECHNET BANANEN! **2.** Penis. *Lass mal sehen, was für 'ne Banane du hast.* "Let's see what kind of meat you've got."

BANGBÜX, *f., N.* Fearful person. *Du wirst's nie wagen, alte Bangbüx!* "You'll never dare, you chicken!"

BÄR, *m.* Bear. ***Da ist der Bär los!/Da geht der Bär ab!*** We'll have a ball! ***Hier geht der Bär ab!*** "Ain't we got fun!" Cf. ELEFANTÖS; HOTTE.

BÄRIG, *S.* Wonderful. *Beim Alpenrockfest ging's bärig zu.* "The ambiance was spirited at the Alpine rock festival."

BATZEN, *m.* Money (lit. lump; batz [old silver coin]). *Wir haben einen ganzen/schönen Batzen für das Grundstück hinlegen müssen.* "We had to shell out a tidy sum/a pretty penny for the property."

BAUCH, *m.* Stomach. ***Aus dem Bauch.*** By instinct. *Die Entscheidung hab ich aus dem Bauch heraus getroffen.* "I made the decision acting on a gut feeling." ***Aus dem hohlen Bauch.*** Off the top of one's head. *Aus dem hohlen Bauch hatte ich's für eine gute Idee gehalten.* "Off the top of my head, I thought it was a good idea." ***Etwas im Bauch haben/spüren.*** See URIN.

BAUCHMENSCH, *m.* Person guided more by feeling than by intellect. *Meine Frau ist Kopfmensch; ich bin eher Bauchmensch.* "My wife's a cerebral type; I'm more instinctive."

BAUEN. To cause (lit. to build). ***Mist/Scheiße bauen.*** To make a mess; screw up (lit. to create dung/shit). *Du hast Scheiße gebaut und im Knast gesessen; schau zu, dass du jetzt wieder keinen Mist baust.* "You screwed up and got sent to the slammer; see to it that you don't get into trouble again."

BAUER, *m.* Farmer. ***Was der Bauer nicht kennt, frisst er nicht.*** (*Prov.*) The farmer won't eat what he's unfamiliar with. *Die gegrillten Zikaden behältst du für dich. Was der Bauer nicht kennt, frisst er nicht.* "You keep those grilled locusts for y.s. I'm not interested in culinary newness." ***Kalter Bauer.*** Semen stains. *Sie hat den kalten Bauer von ihrem Cocktailkleid nicht entfernt.* "She didn't remove the semen stains from her cocktail dress."

BÄUERCHEN, *n.* Little farmer. ***Bäuerchen machen.*** To burp. *Wenn das Baby Bäuerchen macht, ist es mir lieber als wenn es schreit.* "I like the baby better when it burps than when it cries."

BAUERNFANG = **BAUERNFÄNGEREI.** See AUSGEHEN.

BAUERNFÄNGER, *m.* Con man. *Diesem Bauernfänger sind wir auf den Leim gegangen.* "We fell for that con man's line."

BAUERNFÄNGEREI, *f.* Swindle. *Ich hatte den richtigen Riecher und wusste gleich, dass es Bauernfängerei war.* "I sensed right away that it was phony."

BAULÖWE, *m.* Real-estate speculator (lit. construction lion). *Der Baulöwe hat pleite gemacht.* "The building tycoon went bankrupt."

BAUM, *m.* Tree. ***Bäume ausreißen können.*** To be full of beans (lit. to be able to pull out trees). *Einst glaubte ich, Bäume ausreissen zu können; jetzt ist mir selbst das Jäten im Garten zu viel.* "Once I thought I could move mountains; now even pulling weeds in the garden is too much for me." ***Bäume wachsen nicht in den Himmel.*** (*Prov.*) There are limits to everything (lit. trees don't grow in heaven). *Er hat eingesehen, dass Bäume nicht in den Himmel wachsen.* "He's realized that some things aren't possible."

BAUMANBETER/BAUMKNUTSCHER/BAUM-SCHÜTZER/BAUMSCHWÄRMER, *m., pej.* Environmentalist (lit. tree worshiper/cuddler/protector/enthusiast). *Ihr Baumschützer seht in jedem Baum Yggdrasil, die Weltesche.* "You tree huggers see Yggdrasil (the sacred tree) in every tree."

BEAMEN, *youth.* To be wonderful. *Ihre Technomucke beamt voll.* "Their techno music's a total turn-on." See ANBEAMEN.

BECHERN. To drink a lot. *Als Student becherte ich in dieser Kneipe.* "I knocked 'em back in this tavern when I was a student."

BEDRIPST, *N.* Crestfallen. *Da stand ich bedripst da.* "I stood there dumbfounded."

BEDRÖHNT. Drunk; stoned; crazy. *Auf der Fete waren alle voll bedröhnt.* "Everybody was spaced out at the party."

BEHÄMMERT = **BEKLOPPT.**

BEHUMPSEN, *E.* To cheat. *Dieser Westhai hat uns vielleicht behumpst!* "That W. Ger. shark really screwed us!"

BEIN, *n.* Leg. ***Die Beine in die Hand nehmen/unter den Arm nehmen.*** To move fast; clear out. *Nehmt euch die Beine unter 'n Arm!* "Hurry it up now!" ***Jmdm. (lange)***

Beine machen. 1. To throw out. *Lasst das Brüllen oder ich mach euch Beine!* "Quit yelling or I'll throw you out." **2.** To get s.o. to move faster. *Mach ihm lange Beine, sonst trödelt er hinterher.* "Hurry him up, or else he'll lag behind."

BEINHART. 1. Intense, extreme. *Die Mannschaft hat beinhart gespielt.* "The team gave its all to the game." **2.** Terrific; solid; dependable. *Die sind alle beinharte Kerle.* "They're all regular guys."

BEIßEN. 1. To bite. *Sich in den Arsch/Hintern beißen können.* To feel like kicking o.s. (lit. to bite o.s. in the ass/behind). *Ich könnte mich in den Hintern beißen, die Gelegenheit versäumt zu haben.* "I could kick m.s. for missing out on the opportunity." **2.** To eat. *Wir haben selbst kaum genug zu beißen.* "We've hardly enough to eat ourselves."

BEIßERCHEN, *pl.* Teeth. *Beißerchen jetzt schön putzen!* "Give your teeth a good brushing now." *Sich etwas zwischen die Beißerchen schieben.* To eat. *Kommt, wir wollen uns was zwischen die Beißerchen schieben.* "Come, we want to get a bite to eat."

BEIßSTANGERL, *Aust.* = GLIMMSTENGEL.

BEKAKELN, *N.* To talk over at some length. *Bekakeln wir das zuerst 'n bisschen.* "Let's talk about that a bit."

BEKASPERN = **ANBLÖKEN.** Cf. KASPER; SPRUCHKASPER.

BEKIFFT. Under the influence of drugs. *Bist ja total bekifft.* "You're totally stoned."

BEKLOPPT, *N.* Crazy. *Was? Ihr seid ja alle bekloppt. Beknackte Vollidioten seid ihr!* "What? You've all gone nuts! You're all round the bend!"

BEKLOPPTE, *m.,f.* Crazy person (*klopfen* = to knock; hit; thus s.o. who's been hit over the head too often). *Was will diese Bekloppte von uns.* "What does that nut case want from us?"

BEKLOPPTOMANIE, *f., hum.* Insanity. *Solltest wirklich* *deine Beklopptomanie behandeln lassen.* "You really need psychiatric help."

BEKLUNKERT. Very rich (KLUNKER = jewel, "rock"). *Die ist steinreich, echt beklunkert.* "She's very rich, loaded."

BEKNACKT. Crazy. *Euer beknacktes Gelaber hör ich mir nicht länger an.* "I'm not listening to any more of your lunatic drivel."

BEKOCHEN. To cook for. *Seine Alte bekocht ihn bis zum Gehtnichtmehr.* "His old lady lays on the food till he bursts."

BELÖFFELN = BEKASPERN; BESCHNARCHEN 2.

BEMOOST. 1. Moss covered. *Bemoostes Haupt.* (*Student sl.*) Mossyhead (perennial university student). *Dieses bemooste Haupt hat sein Herz an Heidelberg verloren.* "That life-long Joe College type has lost his heart to Heidelberg." **2.** Rich. *Ja, der ist voll bemoost und kann sich's leisten; sollte aber doch jüngeren Studenten Platz machen.* "Yes, he's loaded and can afford to do that, but he ought to make room for younger students." Cf. MOOS.

BENGALTIGER. See GEHEN.

BENIMM, *m.* Manners. *Dir sollte man Benimm beibringen.* "S.o. should teach you manners."

BENIMMREGEL, *f.* Rule of etiquette. *Du und deine Benimmregeln können mir gestohlen bleiben.* "You and your rules of etiquette can get lost."

BEÖLEN. To tease; dupe (from *ölen,* to lubricate). *Der hat dich wieder beölt, Doofi!* "He put one over on you again, dummy!"

(SICH) BEÖLEN, *youth.* To die laughing. *Bei der Sendung haben wir uns echt beölt.* "We cracked up during the broadcast."

(SICH) BEPISSEN. 1. To get blind drunk (lit. to piss on o.s.). *Du hast dich wieder voll bepisst. Ich will dich nie wieder sehen. Verpiss dich!* "You got soused again. I never want to see you again. Piss off!" **2.** To laugh up-roariously. See (SICH) BEÖLEN.

BERÄDETER DÜSENJET = **VIERRADJET.**

BERAFFEN. To understand. *Hast es jetzt endlich berafft?* "Do you finally get it now?"

BERAPPEN. To cough up money. *Für diese schönen Pferde mussten wir viel Geld berappen.* "We had to shell out quite a bit for those beautiful horses."

-BERGER. See DRÜCKEBERGER; SCHLAUBERGER.

BERGFEX, *m.* Mountain-climbing enthusiast. *In meiner Jugend war ich 'n richtiger Bergfex, 'n Klettermax.* "In my youth I was a real mountain-climbing freak."

BEROTZT. Stupid (lit. snot covered). *Du berotztes, beschlabbertes Windei! Bist ja zum Kotzen!* "You stupid idiot wimp, you make me want to throw up."

BESCHEIßEN. To do dirt to (lit. to shit on). *Der Bürgermeister hat uns richtig beschissen.* "The mayor really screwed us."

BESCHICKERT = **SCHICKER.**

BESCHISS, *m.* Swindle. *Als Werbetexter hab ich nur mit Beschiss zu tun.* "As an advertising copywriter everything I deal with is phony."

BESCHISSEN. Lousy (lit. shitty). *Wenn's dir besonders beschissen geht, parfümier dir Geist und Leib reichlich.* "When everything's particularly lousy, perfume body and spirit liberally." See HÜHNERLEITER; PRAHLEN.

BESCHLABBERT, *youth.* Stupid; crazy (lit. slobbered over). *Mann, bist du echt beschlabbert!* "Man, you're a real retard."

BESCHNARCHEN. 1. To ponder (lit. to snore on). *Lass mich das noch 'n bisschen beschnarchen.* "Let me mull that over a bit." **2.** To importune repeatedly; to talk s.o. to death. *Dein Beschnarchen geht mir auf den Sack.* "Your going on/harping about that is getting on my case."

BESCHUPSEN = **BEHUMPSEN.**

BESEN, *m.* **1.** Broom. ***Einen Besen fressen.*** To eat one's hat. *Wenn dem wirklich so ist, fress ich einen Besen.* "If that's really the way it is, I'll eat my hat." **2.** Old hag; battle-ax. *Diesen bösen Besen willst du heiraten? Sie hat dich wohl verhext!* "You want to marry that old battle-ax? She must have hexed you."

BESENGT = **BESCHLABBERT.**

BESENSTIEL, *m.* **1.** Broomstick. ***Einen Besenstiel verschluckt haben.*** To be stiff as a board. *Er tanzt als hätte er einen Besenstiel verschluckt.* "He dances very stiffly." Cf. VERSCHLUCKT. **2.** Large penis. *Ja, den Besen heirat ich, weil sie meinen Besenstiel richtig zu reiten weiß.* "Yes, I'm marrying that hag because she really knows how to ride my rod."

BESPITZEN = **ANSPITZEN.**

BESSER. Better. ***Besser als in die hohle Hand geschissen.*** Better than nothing (lit. better than shit in the empty hand). *Nur 50 Euros hab ich für den Blechhaufen bekommen—na, besser als in die hohle Hand geschissen.* "I only got 50 euros for the old jalopy—still, better than nothing."

BESSERWESSI, *m., pej., E.* Smart aleck from the former W. Ger. *Diese Besserwessis wollen uns nur ausnutzen.* "Those smart-aleck W. Gers. just want to exploit us."

BESSERWISSER, *m.* Smart aleck. *Solche Besserwisser brauchen wir nicht.* "We don't need know-it-alls like that."

BESTECK, *n.* Cutlery. ***Das Besteck hinschmeißen/hinwerfen*** = ***den Löffel hinschmeißen/hinwerfen.*** See LÖFFEL **1.**

BESTUSST = **BEKLOPPT.**

BESÜLZEN = **ANSÜLZEN.**

BETBRUDER, *m.*/BETSCHWESTER, *f., pej.* Churchly person. *"Jetzt hilft nur noch beten," seufzte der Betbruder.* " 'Only prayer can help now,' sighed the Holy Joe."

BETRÖPST. Stupid. *Da stehste (stehst du) betröpst und tust nichts.* "You just stand there like a dummy and do nothing."

BETRÜGEN. To deceive. ***Den Arsch betrügen.*** To belch (lit. to deceive the ass [deprive the ass of its flatulent due]). *Schön, betrüg nur weiter den Arsch; mir lieber als wenn du weitermiefst.* "Good! Keep belching. Better you let it out that end instead of farting again."

(SICH) BETTEN. To make one's bed. ***Wie man sich bettet, so liegt man.*** (*Prov.*) As you make your bed, so you must lie on it. ***Sich weich betten.*** To feather one's nest. *Du hast dich weich gebettet und uns im Regen gelassen.* "You looked out for yourself and left us out in the cold."

BETTENBURG, *f., pej.* Big hotel (lit. bed fortress). *Von der Mietskaserne wieder in eine der Bettenburgen am Strand? Nein! Machen wir lieber Urlaub auf'm Bauernhof!* "From our tenement to one of the tourist factories on the shore again? No! Let's vacation on a farm."

BETTGESCHICHTE, *f.* Sexual relationship; one-night stand. *Diesmal will ich mehr als 'ne Bettgeschichte.* "I want s.t. more than sex this time."

BETTHASE, *m.* Sexpot (lit. bed rabbit). *Mit diesem Betthasen würde ich gern ins Bett steigen.* "I'd like to get into bed with that sexpot."

BETTZEUG, *n.* Bed linen. ***Am Bettzeug knabbern.*** (*Youth.*) To sleep (lit. to nibble on the bedding). *Steh auf! Hast schon lang genug am Bettzeug geknabbert.* "Get up! You've been in the sack long enough." Cf. MATRATZE.

(SICH) BETÜTERN, *N.* To get slightly drunk. *Sie hatten sich alle schön betütert, als die schlechte Nachricht ankam.* "They were all feeling quite happy when the bad news arrived."

BETÜTERN, *N.* To care for; coddle. *Ich lass mich gern von meiner Frau betütern.* "I like my wife to look after me."

BEURGRUNZEN, *hum.* To scrutinize. *Das muss ich mal näher beurgrunzen.* "I'll have to take a good, long look at that."

BEUSCHELREIßER, *m., Aust.* Cigarette (lit. lung ripper). *Diesmal will ich wirklich die Beuschelreißer den Bach runterspülen.* "This time I'm really going to ditch cigarettes for good." Cf. LUGENTORPEDO.

BEZECHT. Drunk. *Völlig bezecht warst du, und ich musste die Zeche zahlen.* "You were dead drunk, and I had to foot the bill."

BEZIEHUNG. See VITAMIN.

BEZIEHUNGSDRAMA, *n.*/**BEZIEHUNGSKOMÖDIE,** *f.* Movie/play centering on interpersonal relations, often a troubled love affair (lit. relationship drama/comedy). *Die Beziehungskomödie war nicht besonders spaßig.* "That comedy wasn't very funny."

BEZIEHUNGSKISTE, *f.* Love affair; committed relationship. *Wenn 'ne Beziehungskiste mir zur Prokrusteskiste wird, zieh ich Leine.* "When a relationship gets to be too confining, I hit the road."

BH, *m.* Abbr. of *Büstenhalter* (bra). *Dieser BH drückt mich.* "This bra's too tight on me."

BI. Short for *bisexuell* (bisexual). *Meine Geschwister und ich sind alle bi.* "My brothers and sisters and I are all bi."

BIBBERN. To tremble. *Er bibbert um seinen Job.* "He's afraid of losing his job."

BIBERLN = PIPERLN.

BIEGE, *f.* Curve. ***Eine Biege drehen/gehen.*** To go for a walk. *Drehen wir 'ne Biege.* "Let's stretch our legs." ***Eine Biege fahren/fliegen.*** To go for a short drive/flight. *Willst 'ne Biege fahren in meinem neuen Hobel?* "Want to go for a spin in my new car?" ***Die Biege machen.*** To disappear; die. *MacHeath weiß, schnell die Biege zu machen.* "MacHeath knows how to disappear fast."

BIENE, *f.* **1.** Bee. ***Eine Biene drehen/machen.*** To buzz off. Cf. FLIEGE. **2.** Winsome girl (usually used with an adj., such as *flott, kess, flink, scharf;* see FLOTT **2**). *Deb ist 'ne fleißige Biene.* "Deb's a hard-working chick."

BIENENSTICH, *m., youth.* Lady-killer (lit. bee sting; almond cake). In youth sl., s.o. who gets his "stinger" into a BIENE. **2.** Cf. STECHER. *Ja sogar als Grufti war Goethe noch 'n richtiger Bienenstich.* "Even when he was ancient, Goethe was a real ladies' man."

BIG MÄC, *m.* **1.** Large McDonald's hamburger. **2.** Big chief. See OBERMACKER.

BILDUNGSFIMMEL, *m.* Obsession with higher education. *Der Junge will gar nicht auf die Uni, aber die Eltern haben einen Bildungsfimmel.* "The boy doesn't want to go to college, but his parents are hung up on higher education."

BILDUNGSPROTZ, *m.* Conceited, overeducated individual. *Dieser Bildungsprotz ist gar nicht so gescheit.* "That education snob isn't really very smart."

BINDE, *f.* Necktie (old). ***Sich einen hinter die Binde gießen/kippen.*** To knock back a drink. See LAMPE.

BINGO, *n.* Bingo. ***Alles Bingo!*** Everything's in great shape!

BIOLADEN, *m.* Health food store (heard more often now than the grimmer-sounding *Reformhaus*). *Das ist alles Biokost aus dem Bioladen.* "All this is whole food from the health food store."

BIRNE, *f.* Head (lit. pear; lightbulb). ***Eine weiche Birne haben.*** To be soft in the head. *Der hat 'ne weiche Birne.* "He's a dimwit." ***Jmdm. an die Birne pinkeln.*** To put s.o. on (lit. to piss on s.o.'s head). *Versuch nur nicht, mir an die Birne zu pinkeln.* "Just don't try to put anything over on me." ***Ein Blatt vor der Birne haben.*** To be slow on the uptake. *Nix hat er gepeilt; er hat 'n Blatt vor der Birne.* "He didn't get it at all; he's not bright."

BLASEN. To blow. ***Jmdm. einen blasen.*** To fellate. *Tu nicht so blasiert und komm blas mir einen.* "Quit being so blasé and come blow me." Cf. ABLUTSCHEN.

BLASROHR, *n.* Condom (lit. blowpipe). *Ohne Blasrohr bläst sie mein Wunderhorn nicht.* "She won't blow my magic horn (penis) without a rubber."

BLASSACK, *m.* Wind instrument. *Gehst mir auf den Sack mit deinem Blassack.* "You and your horn are bugging me."

BLATT, *n.* Leaf. ***Kein Blatt vor den Mund nehmen.*** Not to mince words (lit. not to take [put] a leaf in front of one's mouth). *Sie nahm kein Blatt vor den Mund und schimpfte auf die Statuen mit Feigenblatt; in allem will sie nur die ganze, nackte Wahrheit.* "She didn't mince words and complained about the statues with fig leaves; she wants the whole, naked truth about everything." ***Auf einem anderen Blatt stehen.*** To be s.t. quite different. *Ob sie ihre Versprechungen halten, das steht auf einem anderen Blatt geschrieben.* "Whether they keep their promises or not, that's another ball game." ***Das Blatt wenden.*** To turn the tide. *Die Mannschaft spielte mit harten Bandagen, um das Blatt noch zu wenden; trotzdem verloren sie.* "The team played a rough game trying to turn the tide, but they lost anyway." ***Ein Blatt raushaben.*** To be crazy (lit. to be lacking a leaf). *Der Macker hat 'n Blatt raus.* "That guy's not playing with a full deck."

BLAU. 1. Blue. ***Mit einem blauen Auge davonkommen.*** To get off relatively easy (lit. to get off with one black eye). *Wir sind mit einem blauen Auge davongekommen.* "We got off easy." **2.** Drunk. See VEILCHEN.

BLAUE, *m.* **1.** 100-mark note, = **BLAUE FLIESE. 2.** Cop, = **BLAUMANN 3.**

BLAUE FLIESE, *f.***/BLAUER LAPPEN,** *m.* Hundred-mark note. (Lit. blue tile/rag. The 100-DM note is blue.) When the euro enters general circulation in 2002, sl. speakers will no doubt "coin" new color coordinated expressions. The 20-euro note is blue. *Mit den blauen Fliesen wollte er nicht rausrücken.* "He wouldn't cough up the dough."

BLAUER BRIEF, *m.* Letter or notice bringing bad news. *Als ich den blauen Brief sah, erlebt' ich mein blaues Wunder.* "I was floored when I saw the pink slip."

BLAUHELM, *m.* UN soldier (lit. blue helmet). *Im Krisen-*

gebiet sollen die Blauhelme den Frieden sichern. "UN troops are supposed to keep the peace in the crisis area."

BLAUMACHEN. To skip work/school. *Diese Woche hat er Montag und auch Freitag blaugemacht.* "This week he took Monday off, and Friday too."

BLAUMACHER, *m.* S.o. who often takes a day off. *Die Blaumacher sollen alle blaue Briefe bekommen.* "The chronic no-shows are going to be laid off."

BLAUMANN, *m.* **1.** Mechanic; repairman (lit. overalls, cf. blue collar). *Mein Mann ist Vollidiot; ich hätte gleich einen Blaumann anrufen sollen.* "My husband's a complete idiot; I should have called a repairman right away." **2.** 100-mark note. See BLAUE FLIESE.

BLAUMÄNNER, *pl., youth.* Police. *Die Blaumänner waren auf der Lauer.* "The cops were lurking."

BLECH, *n.* **1.** Sheet metal. *Aufs Blech hauen.* See AUF DIE PAUKE HAUEN. **2.** Money. *Der Blechbläser ist pleite und hat seine Blechblasinstrumente verpfändet, um Blech zu bekommen.* "The brass player's broke, and he's pawned his brass instruments to get some dough." **3.** Nonsense. *Red kein Blech!* "Cut the crap!" **4.** Mil. decorations. *Ja, er hat viel Blech auf der Brust aber nix in der Hose.* "Yes, he's got a chest full of fruit salad, but not much in his pants."

BLECHEN. To fork over money. *Kannst du die Mäuse dafür blechen?* "Can you cough up the dough for that?"

BLECHHAUFEN, *m.*/**BLECHKISTE,** *f.* Old car. *Die Blechkiste ließ ich einfach in der Blechlawine stehen.* "I just abandoned the old crate in the big traffic jam."

BLECHLAWINE, *f.* Big traffic jam (lit. sheet-metal avalanche). See BLECHHAUFEN.

BLEIFUß, *m.* **1.** Lead foot. *Mit Bleifuß fahren/Bleifuß machen.* (*Youth.*) To drive with one's foot glued to the gas pedal. *Mach Bleifuß, Dussel!* "Step on it, idiot!" **2.** Dumb hulk. *Der Bleifuß war in sie verknallt, und sie wusste ihn auszunutzen.* "That dumb hulk was nuts about her, and she knew how to exploit him."

BLENDER, *m.* Fraud (lit. dazzler). *Nimm dich in acht vor diesem Blender!* "Don't trust that phony!"

BLICKEN, *youth.* To understand (lit. to see; glance). *Davon haben die Gruftis nix geblickt.* "The old farts didn't catch any of it." Cf. DURCHBLICKEN.

BLINDFUCHS, *m., youth.* **1.** New recruit; new university fraternity member (lit. blind fox). *Die Blindfüchse haben noch viel zu lernen.* "The new recruits still have a lot to learn." **2.** Dummy. *Aus dem Blindfuchs ist 'n schlauer Fuchs geworden.* "That mental midget's turned into a sly fox."

BLINDGÄNGER, *m.* Dud. *Was willst du mit diesem Blindgänger?* "What do you want with that deadbeat?"

BLITZ, *m.* Lightning. *Das ging wie der geölte Blitz.* "That went off like greased lightning."

BLITZEN. To run naked (lit. to flash; take flash photos). *Die Studenten blitzten, flitzten splitterfasernackt an den guten Bürgern vorbei.* "The students streaked butt naked past the worthy middle-class citizens."

BLITZER, *m.* Streaker; mooner; flasher. *Die Blitzer sagten, sie hätten nur ihr Jogging gemacht.* "The streakers said they were just out jogging."

BLITZMERKER, *m., ironic.* Dimwit (lit. s.o. who notices lightning). *Dieser Blitzmerker hat wieder nichts gehört oder gesehen.* "Once again, that dummy didn't see or hear anything."

BLÖDEL, *m.* Stupid/clumsy fool. *Die schöne Blondine ist kein Blödel.* "That beautiful blonde's no dummy."

BLÖDELN. 1. To fool/mess around. *Hör doch auf zu blödeln!* "Will ya quit screwin' around!" **2.** To tell (usually idiotic) jokes. *Er kann das Blödeln nicht lassen.* "He can't stop telling silly jokes."

BLÖDHAMMEL/BLÖDIAN/BLÖDMANN = BLÖDEL

BLÖDLER, *m.* S.o. who tells silly jokes. *Seine blöden Witze kenn ich alle, aber der Blödler kann die Klappe nicht hal-*

ten. "I've heard all his dumb jokes, but that joker can't keep his trap shut."

BLÖDLING = **BLÖDEL.**

BLUBBER-BLUBBER, *m., N., youth.* Blah-blah/babble. *Die ist schon echt scharf; sollte aber weniger Blubber-Blubber rauslassen.* "She's a looker alright; if she'd only quit babbling so much." Cf. PLÄTSCHER-PLÄTSCHER.

BLUBBERKOPF, *m.* Dummy, bubblehead. *Was will der Blubberkopf schon wieder?* "What does that airhead want now?"

BLUBBERN. To gabble; mumble. *Was diese Quasselstrippen blubbern, tangiert mich nicht.* "I pay no attention to the cacklings of those old windbags."

BLÜMERANT. Queasy. *Mir wird blümerant.* "I'm feeling queasy."

BLUNZE = **PLUNZE.**

BLUSE, *f.* **1.** Blouse. ***Etwas in/unter der Bluse haben.*** To have a nice set (of breasts). *Lulu hat aber etwas in der Bluse.* "Lulu's really stacked." ***Jmdm. an die Bluse gehen.*** To paw a girl's breasts. *Der Macker ging mir gleich an die Bluse.* "That guy went right for my boobs." See PRALL. **2.** Big-bosomed girl. *Mann, ist Lana 'ne Bluse!* "Man, Lana's one bosomy broad."

BLÜTE, *f.* Counterfeit bank note (lit. blossom). *Kannst du die Blüten unter diesen Hündis identifizieren?* "Can you identify the counterfeits among these 100s?"

BLUTWURST, *f.* Blood sausage. ***Rache ist Blutwurst!*** Revenge is sweet! See LEBERWURST.

BOCK, *m.* **1.** Horny guy (lit. buck; billy goat). *Tim ist 'n richtiger Bock.* "Tim's really randy." **2.** Interest; desire. ***Keinen Bock/null Bock auf etwas haben.*** Not to be interested in s.t. *Ich hab keinen Bock auf dein blödes elektronisches Spiel.* "I'm not interested in your stupid electronic game."

BOCK-, *youth.* An intensifier, as in *bockgeil; bockhart;*

bockmäßig; bockstark. Ihre neue Prunkprotzkutsche ist bockgeil! "Her fantastic new car is mind-blowing!"

BOCKMIST, *m.* Bullshit. ***Bockmist machen.*** To screw up (lit. to make buck dung). *Mach mir keinen Bockmist!* "Don't screw things up for me!"

BODENTURNER, *m.* Dummy (lit. floor exerciser). *Musst dich halt durchbeißen; bist ja kein Bodenturner.* "You'll just have to struggle through; you're no dimwit."

BODYPIERCING, *n., youth.* Piercing (from Eng.). *Euer Bodypiercing und Branding könnt ich vielleicht eher peilen, wenn's in einem schamanistischen Zusammenhang wär.* "I might understand your piercing and branding better if it were in a shamanic context." See BRANDING **2.**

BOGEN, *m.* Curve; arch; detour. ***Einen großen Bogen um jmdn./etwas machen.*** To keep well clear of s.o/s.t. *Seit ich Transi bin, machen viele einen großen Bogen um mich.* "Since I became a transsexual, many go out of their way to avoid me." ***Große Bogen spucken.*** To be pretentious/self-important. *Laß ihn nur große Bogen spucken; wir werden ihn schon kleinkriegen.* "Just let him puff h.s. up; we'll soon bring him around."

BOHNE, *f.* Bean. ***Nicht die Bohne.*** Not at all. *Das alles interessiert uns nicht die Bohne!* "We're not remotely interested in all that."

BOHREN, *youth.* **1.** To understand; cope (lit. to bore, drill). *Dieser Beträpste bohrt nichts davon.* "That dimwit doesn't get it at all." ***Dicke Bretter bohren müssen*** (lit. to have to drill through thick boards). To have to deal with difficult problems. *Von heut auf morgen geschieht's nicht; da müssen noch viele dicke Bretter gebohrt werden.* "It's not going to happen overnight; there are still many tough nuts to crack." Cf. DÜNNBRETTBOHRER. **2.** To work hard. *Genug gebohrt! Wir machen Feierabend.* "That's enough work. We're calling it a day." **3.** To drive fast. *Bohren wir 'n bisschen durch die Pampa.* "Let's burn up the road in the boonies."

BOMBASTICO = **BOMBIG.**

BOMBENFIGUR, *f.* Wonderful figure. *Die Tussi hat echt 'ne Bombenfigur.* "That chick's got a terrific figure."

BOMBENSICHER. Absolutely certain (lit. bombproof). *Der DNA Test gilt als bombensicher.* "The DNA test is considered foolproof."

BOMBIG, *youth.* Wonderful, terrific. *Der Pizzabäcker hat einen Bombenerfolg; alles bei ihm schmeckt ultrabombig.* "The pizza maker's had a smashing success; everything he makes tastes super scrumptious." (Eng. sl. "to bomb" in the sense "fail; be a dud" is the opposite of Ger. use. Cf. GESCHOSS; GRANATE.)

BONGEN. To ring up. *Haben Sie das richtig gebongt?* "Did you ring that up right?" See GEBONGT SEIN.

BONSAI, *m., youth.* Runt; 12–15-year-olds. (From Japn. *bonsai* [dwarf tree art]). *Warum hängst du noch mit diesen Bonsais rum?* "Why do you still hang around with those half-pints?" Cf. FRISCHLING; GRÜNZEUG.

BONZE, *m., pej.* Big boss (orig. from Japn. for Buddhist priest). *Mit Bonzen, ob Partei-, Industrie- oder Gewerkschaftsbonzen haben wir nichts am Hut.* "We have nothing in common with big bosses, whether they're party, industry, or union bosses."

BOOMEN. To boom. *In der Disco boomte es brutal.* "Things were really booming in the disco."

BORDSTEINSCHWALBE, *f.* Prostitute (lit. sidewalk swallow). *Oma meint, es gibt zu viele Bordsteinschwalben in der Stadt.* "Granny thinks there are too many streetwalkers in town." Cf. PARKDROSSEL.

BRANDING, *n., from Eng.* **1.** Coming up with brand names; advertising jargon. *Wenn's um's Branding geht, ist Uli echt 'n Brandmeister.* "Uli's a master at coming up with brand names." **2.** Branding names/drawings on the body with hot irons (a step beyond tattooing in body art). See sent. for BODYPIERCING. (In stand. Ger. *die Marke* means brand name; *das Brandzeichen* is a brand on cattle. "Branding" is thus leaving a mark on a product or on flesh.)

BRANDMEISTER, *m.* Advertising executive who specializes in inventing brand names. See BRANDING **1.**

BRATEN, *m.* Roast. ***Den Braten riechen/schmecken.*** To smell a rat. *Die Gangster hatten den Braten gerochen und gingen nicht in die Falle.* "The gangsters smelled a rat, and didn't fall into the trap." ***Dem Braten nicht trauen.*** To be suspicious of s.t. *Er will, dass ich Geld in sein Unternehmen anlege, aber ich trau dem Braten nicht.* "He wants me to invest money in his firm, but I'm leery of that."

BRATKARTOFFEL. See DAHER DER NAME BRATKARTOFFEL.

BRATKARTOFFELTREND, *m.* Trend toward home cooking (lit. home-fries trend). *Vom Bratkartoffeltrend will ich nichts wissen; auf meine Feinschmeckerkost verzicht ich nicht.* "Don't talk to me about home cooking; I'm not giving up my gourmet fare."

BRATKARTOFFELVERHÄLTNIS, *m.* Meal-ticket relationship. *Ich weiß, für ihn ist's nur ein Bratkartoffelverhältnis; aber ich bin total in ihn verknallt.* "I know it's just a convenient domestic arrangement for him, but I'm madly in love with him."

BRAUT, *f.* **1.** Girl; girlfriend (lit. bride). *Die Schlampe ist jedermanns Braut.* "That broad's everyone's bride." **2.** Girl who hangs out with a rock band. See TUNTE **2.**

BREAKEN. To engage in break dancing. *Wir machen noch Hip-Hop, aber wir breaken weniger, da alle in der Band in die Jahre gekommen sind.* "We still do hip-hop but less break dancing, because everybody in the band's gotten older."

BREI, *m.* Oatmeal; mush. ***Jmdn. zu Brei schlagen.*** To beat s.o. to a pulp. *Die Hools haben ihn zu Brei geschlagen.* "The hooligans beat him to a pulp."

BREIT. Drunk; stoned (lit. broad). *Die Kiffer waren alle breit.* "The potheads were all stoned."

BRETTERN, *S.* To ski; to speed in a vehicle. *Im neuen Mercedes sind wir durch die Alpen gebrettert.* "We sped through the Alps in the new Mercedes."

BRILLE, *f.* **1.** Eyeglasses. ***Etwas durch eine gefärbte/ rosarote Brille sehen.*** To see s.t. subjectively/through rose-colored glasses. *Du siehst alles durch die gefärbte Brille deiner Eitelkeit.* "You see everything from the vantage point of your vanity." **2.** Toilet seat. *Diesmal kauf 'ne Brille aus Kunststoff.* "This time buy a plastic toilet seat."

BRILLENSCHLANGE, *f., pej. or hum.* Four-eyes (someone who wears glasses). *Man nannte mich 'ne Brillenschlange, aber trotz Dorothy Parkers Witzelei versuchten die Jungens oft mich anzumachen.* "They called me 'four-eyes,' but despite Dorothy Parker's quip, the boys often made passes at me."

BRILLI, *m.* **1.** Diamond. *Von meinen Mackern will ich echt viele Brillis geschenkt bekommen.* "I want my guys to give me lots of rocks." **2.** Namby-pamby who wears glasses (*youth*). *Diesem Brilli werd ich die Fresse polieren.* "I'm gonna beat up that four-eyed creep."

BRÖCKCHEN, *n.* Chunk. ***Bröckchen husten.*** To vomit (lit. cough up little chunks). *Zu viel Fusel und du hustest wieder Bröckchen.* "Too much hooch, and you'll be barfing again."

BRUCHBUDE, *f., pej.* Dump; hovel. See BUDE; KOTZBUDE.

BRUDER, *m.* Homosexual. See KLOSTERBRUDER; WARMER BRUDER.

BRUDER LEICHTFUß/BRUDER LUSTIG. Happy-go-lucky fellow. *Dieser Bruder Leichtfuß hat seine Frau und Kinder im Stich gelassen.* "That joker left his wife and children in the lurch." Cf. LUFTIKUS.

BRÜLLAFFE, *m.* Loudmouth (lit. howling monkey). *Halt's Maul, du Brüllaffe.* "Shut your trap, loudmouth."

BRÜLLEN. To roar. ***Zum Brüllen sein.*** To be very funny. *Es war zum Brüllen, als ihm die Hose platzte.* "It was a scream when his pants split."

BRUMMEN. 1. To buzz; drone, hum (motor); rumble. ***Wann's Arscherl brummt, ist's Herzl g'sund.*** (*S. prov.*) When your arse is farting, your heart's happy. Cf. BRUMMI; BRUMMSCHÄDEL. **2.** To grumble. *Ich lass ihn nur brummen, mein Alter.* "I don't let my old man's grousing get to me." **3.** To serve a prison sentence. *Er brummt schon 7 Monate.* "He's been in the slammer seven months now." **4.** To be kept after school. *Wenn ich wieder brummen muss, leg ich den Sherif um.* "If I have to stay after school again, I'll knock off the teach."

BRUMMI, *m.* Truck. *Wegen der Brummis haben wir die Autobahnausfahrt verpasst.* "We missed the highway exit because of the trucks."

BRUMMIKUTSCHER, *m.* Truck driver (lit. truck coachman). *Viele Brummikutscher müssen auch nachts fahren.* "Many truckers have to drive nights too."

BRUMMSCHÄDEL, *m.* Hangover (lit. rumble skull) = **KATER; KATZENJAMMER.**

BRUTAL, *youth.* Wonderful (lit. brutal). *Ihre neue Rille ist brutal!* "Her new record's terrific!"

BRUTALINSKI/BRUTALO, *youth.* **1.** Big bruiser. *Nur Masochisten poofen mit dem Brutalo.* "Only masochists sleep with that bully." **2.** Bodybuilder. *Dieser Brutalinski steckt immer in der Folterkammer.* "That fitness freak's always in the gym."

BUCKEL, *m.* Humpback; back. *Ich hab schon genug auf'm Buckel.* "I already have enough (work) on my plate." ***Den Buckel runterrutschen/raufsteigen.*** To slide down/climb up one's back (used to tell s.o. to get lost). *Ich soll's machen? Kannst mir den Buckel runterrutschen!* "You want me to do it? Go jump in the lake!" ***Jahre auf dem Buckel haben.*** To be old. *Der hat schon voll 90 Jahre auf dem Buckel; ist aber noch gesund und munter.* "He's a good 90 years old, but he's still chipper."

BUDDEL, *f., N.* Bottle. *Trinkste (trinkst du) noch 'ne Buddel Bier?* "Will you have another bottle of beer?"

BUDDELN. To dig. *Es wird noch vielerorts in Berlin gebuddelt.* "There's still a lot of construction site digging in Berlin."

BUDE, *f.* Hut; room; dump. ***Jmdm. fällt die Bude auf den Kopf.*** To get cabin fever. *Gehen wir auf die Piste; mir fällt die Bude aufn Kopf.* "Let's go out on the town; I need a change of scenery." See PENNBUDE.

BÜGELN, *youth.* **1.** To beat up (lit. to iron [clothes]). *Die Hools haben ihn ganz schön gebügelt.* "The hooligans really laid into him." **2.** To speed. *Geil, auf seinem Motorrad mit ihm durch die Gegend zu bügeln.* "It's sensational speeding around with him on his motorcycle."

BULLEN, *pl.* Police. *Die Bullen haben ihn geschnappt.* "The cops nabbed him." See AU BULLE!

BULLENÄRSCHE, *pl.* Police (lit. cop assholes). *Die Bullenärsche haben auf uns geballert.* "The fuckin' fuzz shot at us."

BULLENBEIßER, *m.* Nasty, pugnacious person (lit. bull biter [dog]). *Die Liebe hat den alten Bullenbeißer besänftigt.* "Love has tamed that old curmudgeon."

BULLENHITZE, *f.* Very hot weather. *Bei der Bullenhitze ging auch noch die Klimaanlage kapores.* "The air conditioner also conked out during the heat wave."

BULLIG. **1.** Brawny. *Lass mich deine Muskeln streicheln, du bulliger, geiler Bock.* "Let me feel your muscles, you beefy, horny devil." **2.** Sweltering. *Wenn's heute wieder so bullig ist, geh ich nicht vor die Tür.* "If it's so boiling hot again today, I'm not setting foot out of the house."

BUMFIEDELN. See GEBUM(S)FIEDELT; VERBUMFIEDELN.

BUMMELANT, *m.* Lazybones; slowpoke. *Für Bummelanten gibt es keinen Platz hier.* "There's no room for goldbrickers here."

BUMSEN. **1.** To bang; crash; thump. *Wenn du nicht aufhörst, bumst es gleich!* "If you don't quit that, I'll sock you!" **2.** To copulate. *Die nebenan bumsen Tag und*

Nacht; warum bumst mich keiner? "The couple next door screws night and day; why isn't anybody humping me?"

BUMSKNEIPE, *f.*/**BUMSLOKAL,** *n.* Low dive. *Er ist Milliardär, fühlt sich aber in Bumskneipen am wohlsten.* "He's a billionaire, but feels most at home in low dives."

BUMSMUSIK, *f.* Loud, blaring music. *Stell doch deine verdammte Bumsmusik leiser!* "Tune down your damned noisy music!"

BUMSVOLL. Very crowded. *Die Disko war wieder bumsvoll.* "The disco was packed to the rafters again."

BUNKERN. 1. To stockpile. *Hier hat er seine Hamsterkäufe für die Jahrtausendwende gebunkert.* "Here's where he's piled up the stuff he's hoarded in fear of the new millennium." **2.** To hide. *Die Gangster haben den Kies gut gebunkert.* "The gangsters stashed the dough safely." See WEGBUNKERN; ZWISCHENBUNKERN.

BURGFRIEDE(N), *m.* Truce (lit. castle precincts). *Wir brauchen einen wahren Frieden, nicht bloß einen Burgfrieden.* "We need a real peace, not just a truce."

BÜRONAFFEL = **KRAGEN 2; KRAWATTEN-DJANGO.**

BÜRSTELN = **BÜRSTEN 2.**

BÜRSTEN, *youth.* **1.** To beat up (lit. to brush). Usually used with the prefixes *ab-, nieder-, weg-, zu-, zusammen-.* See NIEDERBÜRSTEN. **2.** To have sex. *Wir bürsteten so oft wir konnten.* "We screwed whenever we could."

BUSCHTROMMEL, *f.* Word of mouth (lit. bush drum). *Bei uns im Dorf gibt's wenige Geheimnisse, denn die Buschtrommel funktioniert sehr gut.* "There are few secrets in our village, because the grapevine's very effective."

BUSSELN = **BUSSERLN.**

BUSSERL = **BUSSI.**

BUSSERLN, *S.* To kiss. *I(ch) mag a bisserl (ein bisschen) busserln vorm Bumsen.* "I like a little bussing before screwing."

BUSSI, *n.* Kiss. *Sie liest ein Buch über die Münchener Bussi-Bussi Schickeria.* "She's reading a book about Munich's kissy-kissy smart set."

BUTSCHER = **BUTTJE/BUTTJER.**

BUTTEL = **BUDDEL.**

BÜTTEL, *m., pej.* Policeman (lit. bailiff). *Die Büttel haben ihn geschnappt.* "The pigs nabbed him."

BUTTJE/BUTTJER, *m., N.* Boy; kid. *Bist dieses Jahr ein gutes Stück gewachsen, mein Buttje.* "You've grown quite a bit this year, my lad."

BÜX/BUXE, *f., N.* Pants. *Siehst schneidig in der neuen Büx aus.* "You look dashing in those new pants."

CHAOT, *m.* **1.** Anarchist. *Während ihrer Chaostage tobten die Chaoten in Hannover.* "During their 'Chaos Days' the radical agitators went wild in Hanover." **2.** Disorganized/sloppy person. *Diesem Chaoten werd ich schon die Flötentöne beibringen.* "I'm going to lay down the law to that ditsy dude." **3.** Individual who is both a disciple and master of all things chaotic; master mayhem maker. *Du bist der coolste aller Chaoten.* "You're the coolest anarchist cat of all." Cf. ANARCHO; DOKTOR CHAOS.

CHAUVI, *m.* Male chauvinist. *Im Bett ist dieser Exzuchthengst 'ne Null geworden; trotzdem bleibt er nach wie vor Chauvi.* "That ex-stud's a dud in bed; but he's still the same male chauvinist pig."

CHECKEN. 1. To check (used as in Eng.). *Die Zöllner checken nichts mehr.* "The customs agents don't examine anything anymore." **2.** To understand (*youth*). *Hast du was davon gecheckt?* "Did you get any of that?" Cf. EXPRESSCHECKER; GECHECKT SEIN; NULLCHECKER.

CHESSENKO(H)L, *historical.* Thieves' slang. From the Hebr. letter *cheth,* and Hebr. *kôl,* voice. See KESS; KESSENLOSCHEN; ROTWELSCH.

CHESSENLOSCHEN = KESSENLOSCHEN.

CHIP, *m., youth.* Chip (esp. potato chip or computer chip). ***Bei jmdm. ist ein Chip locker/Einen Chip locker haben.***

To have a screw loose. *Bei dem ist ein Chip locker!* "He's off his rocker."

CHIP-INFARKT, *m., youth.* Mental breakdown; craziness (lit. (computer) chip coronary [thrombosis]). *Geil dich ab, Mann! Ich glaub, du bekommst 'n Chip-Infarkt.* "Calm down, man! I think you're going over the edge." Cf. ELEKTRONIK; FLOPPY; PROGRAMMABSTURZ; SYSTEMAB-STURZ.

CLARO! Of course! *Claro will ich mit.* "Of course I want to come along." Cf. LOGO.

CLEAN, *youth.* **1.** Drug-free (as in Eng.). **2.** Really good/trustworthy. *Den neuen Trainer mag ich gern leiden; er ist ganz clean.* "I really like the new coach; he's really cool/neat."

COMPUTERN. To use a computer. *Zuerst konnte sie den Computer nicht verknusen, aber jetzt computert sie unaufhörlich.* "First she couldn't stand computers, but now she's at her computer constantly."

CONTROLETTI, *m., N., youth, pej.* Policeman; monitor. *Der Verkehrscontroletti hat ihn geschnappt.* "The traffic cop nabbed him."

COOL, *youth.* **1. *Cool bleiben.*** To keep one's cool. *Trotz allem blieben wir cool.* "Despite everything we kept our cool." **2.** Fair. *Die beiden sind coole Dealer.* "Both dealers are on the level." **3.** Wonderful, outstanding. *Die Band machte eine ganz coole Mucke.* "The band's music was terrific."

COOLMAN. See JOHNNY COOLMAN.

CRUSTIE/CRUSTY, *m., youth.* Grungy, gruff semibum (from Brit. sl.). *Warum hat die elegante Lili diesen Crusty geheiratet?* "Why did elegant Lili marry that crud?"

CUTTEN. To cut (movies/tapes). *Den Film hätte ich anders gecuttet.* "I would have done the film cutting differently."

DACH, *n.* Head (lit. roof). ***Jmdm. etwas aufs Dach geben/Jmdm. aufs Dach steigen.*** To reprimand s.o./to rap s.o.'s knuckles. *Er hat die Arbeit versaut und die Chefin ist ihm aufs Dach gestiegen.* "He screwed up the job, and the boss bawled him out." ***Eins aufs Dach kriegen.*** To be raked over the coals. *Es ist höchste Zeit, dass du eins aufs Dach kriegst.* "It's high time you were put in your place."

DACHS, *m.* Fellow (lit. badger). ***Frecher Dachs.*** Impertinent young man. ***Junger Dachs.*** Whippersnapper; greenhorn. *Der ist 'n frecher Dachs, 'n junger Dachs, aber man kann ihm nicht böse sein.* "He's a nervy greenhorn, but you can't get mad at him."

DACHSCHADEN, *m.* Mental illness (lit. damage to the roof [head]). *Der hat wohl einen kleinen Dachschaden.* "He's probably not quite right upstairs."

DACKEL, *m.* Jerk (lit. dachshund). *Ihr Mann ist 'n richtiger Dackel.* "Her husband's a real idiot."

DACKELN, *youth.* **1.** To undulate (like a dachshund); walk slowly. *Musst du immer wackeln und dackeln, wenn du gehst?* "Do you always have to swing and sway when you walk?" **2.** To cringe/creep. *Das Dackeln ist deine, nicht meine Sache.* "Kowtowing is your sort of thing, not mine."

DAHER DER NAME BRATKARTOFFEL! Oh, I get it now!/So that's why! (lit. That's why they're called home fries!). *Daher der Name Bratkartoffel! Die beiden steckten unter einer Decke.* "So that's why! The two of them were in cahoots!"

DAHERLABERN/DAHERREDEN = **LABERN.**

DAHERSANDELN, *S.* To shuffle along. *Einst war er echt zackig; jetzt sandelt er nur so daher.* "Once he used to be dynamic; now he just shuffles along." Cf. SANDLER.

DALK, *m., Aust.* Jerk; clumsy oaf. *Sie liebt diesen Deppen, diesen Dalk.* "She loves that idiot, that dope."

DALKET/DALKERT, *Aust.* Idiotic. *Solch dalkete Ideen hob i (habe ich) mei' Lebtag net (nicht) kört (gehört).* "I've never heard such foolishness in all my born days."

DALLES, *m.* Poverty. *Im Dalles sein.* To be flat broke. *Damals waren wir im Dalles.* "We were destitute then."

DALLI! Hurry it up! (from Pol.) *Dalli machen.* To make it snappy. *Mach nur 'n bisschen dalli!* "Just get a move on."

DÄMEL = **DÄMLACK.**

DAMISCH, *S.* 1. Nutty. *Damisch wird man davon.* "That'll drive you batty." 2. Dizzy. *Beim Volksfest wurde es mir damisch.* "I felt giddy/dizzy at the folk festival." 3. Extremely (*youth*). *Die Band hat damisch wild gespielt.* "The band's music was wild, out of this world!"

DÄMLACK, *m.* Jerk. *Was findest du an dem Dämlack anfangen?* "Why do you bother with that dummy?"

DAMMELN, *N.* To hang around/out. *Nur ans Dammeln denkst du.* "All you think about is hanging out."

DAMPFNUDEL. See NUDEL.

DANCEFLOOR, *m., youth.* Really hot dance music (not *Tanzboden,* dance floor). *Mit ihrem Hip-Hop macht diese Band Dancefloor.* "That band really revs things up with its hip-hop." Cf. PARKETT.

DANEBENE, *n., youth.* Marginal doings/lifestyle. *Das Danebene, das ist dein Element, und du bist noch stolz drauf!* "The antisocial is your thing, and you're even proud of it!"

DASTEHEN. To stand there. *Wie steh ich jetzt da?* "Just what kind of a chump do I look like now?" ***Dastehen wie bestellt und nicht abgeholt/wie der Ochs vorm Berg.*** To be left high and dry. *Er verließ uns und wir standen da wie bestellt und nicht abgeholt.* "He left us to stand there like wall hangings."

DAUERBRENNER, *f.* Enduring success (lit. slow-burning oven). *Wir hofften auf einen Dauerbrenner; 's war aber nur ein Strohfeuer.* "We were hoping for a long run, but it was just a flash in the pan."

DAUMEN, *m.* Thumb. ***Jmdm. den/die Daumen halten/drücken.*** To wish s.o. good luck. *Drück die Daumen für mich, dass ich Weltmeisterin im Schi werde.* "Keep your fingers crossed for me so that I become a world skiing champion." ***Den Daumen auf etwas drücken.*** To insist on s.t. *Die Behörden drücken den Daumen darauf, dass diese Formulare ausgefüllt werden.* "The authorities insist on these forms being filled out." ***Über den Daumen peilen.*** To make a rough estimate. *Über'n Daumen gepeilt, ist die Sammlung 5.000 Euros wert.* "Roughly speaking, the collection's worth 5,000 euros." See PER DAUMEN.

DAVONSPRITZEN, *youth.* To scram (lit. to squirt off). *Er konnte nicht schnell genug davonspritzen; die Bullen schnappten ihn.* "He couldn't clear out fast enough; the cops nabbed him."

DECKEL, *n.* Head (lit. lid). ***Jmdm. eins auf den Deckel geben.*** **1.** To whack s.o. *Dein Vater wird dir eins auf 'n Deckel geben.* "Your father'll give you a shot in the head." **2.** To bawl out. *Mutti hat mir eins auf den Deckel gegeben.* "Mom gave me a chewing out." Cf. DACH.

DEFTIG. 1. Hearty. *Mein Mann ist Vegetarier und findet Rosenkohl und Grünkohl deftige Gerichte; ich steh eher auf 'ne deftige Bratwurst.* "My husband's a vegetarian and finds Brussels sprouts and curly kale hearty; but a juicy sausage is more my sort of thing." **2.** Crude. *Auch meine Witze findet er zu deftig.* "He also thinks my jokes are too raunchy." **3.** Powerful. *Deine Aussage hat einen deftigen Streit vom Zaune gebrochen.* "Your statement let loose a whale of an argument."

DEICHSELN. To wangle; finagle; manage to do s.t. difficult. *Keine Bange! Dieser Trickdieb wird's schon deichseln.* "Don't worry, that con artist will swing it."

DELI, *E., youth.* Pleasant. *Das Essen war alles andere als deli.* "The meal was anything but a delight."

DENKSTE!, *N.* That's what you think! *Ich soll's bezahlen? Denkste!* "I'm supposed to pay for it? No way!"

DENKZETTEL, *m.* Rebuke, warning. See VERPASSEN.

DENKZWERG, *m.* Mental midget. *Er ist 'n Denkzwerg, hat aber 'ne Riesenkarotte.* "He hasn't got much upstairs, but he's got a giant carrot (big dick)."

DEPP, *m., S.* Jerk. *Was willst du mit dem alten Deppen?* "Why do you want to bother with that old idiot?"

DEPPERT, *S.* Idiotic. *Wenn du nur net (nicht) so deppert wärst!* "If only you weren't such a dunce!"

DEPRESSE, *f., youth.* Woman who's often depressed. *Du verstehst keinen Spaß; bist 'ne richtige Depresse.* "You have no sense of humor; you're always depressed."

DEPRESSI, *m., youth.* **1.** Frequently depressed man. *Der Depressi bläst immer Trübsal.* "That Gloomy Gus is always singing the blues." **2.** Depression. ***Sich Depressi-Einheiten geben/reinziehen.*** To wallow in melancholy. *Statt sich immer Depressi-Einheiten zu geben, sollte Uwe 'n bisschen Mumm zeigen.* "Instead of always being down in the dumps, Uwe should show a little courage."

DEPRESSO = DEPRESSI.

DEPRI, *m.* = **DEPRESSI 1, 2.** ***Einen Depri schieben.*** To be down in the dumps. *Ulla schiebt wieder einen Depri.* "Ulla's got the blues again."

DICHT. 1. Dense; thick. ***Dicht an dicht.*** Very dense. *Die Autos schoben sich dicht an dicht durch die Stadt.* "Cars moved bumper-to-bumper through the city." **2.** Watertight; airtight. ***Nicht ganz dicht sein.*** To be mentally unbalanced. *Manchmal glaub ich, du bist oben nicht ganz dicht.* "Sometimes I think you're off your rocker."

DICK. 1. Fat; thick. ***Jmdn. dick haben.*** (*Youth.*) To be fed up with s.o. *Solche Dummsülzer wie dich hab ich dick.* "I've had it up to here with blabbermouths like you." **2.** Very much; good. *Sie sind dicke Freunde.* "They're fast friends."

DICKE EIER. See EIER.

DICKE KOHLE. See KOHLE.

DICKE LUFT, *f.* Strained relations (lit. thick air). *Es gibt dicke Luft zwischen ihnen.* "There's tension between them."

DICKERCHEN, *n.* Fatty. *Sie ist in ihr Dickerchen verknallt.* "She's nuts about her chubby guy."

DICKKOPF, *m.* Obstinacy; stubborn person. *Diesmal wirst du deinen Dickkopf nicht durchsetzen.* "This time your pigheadedness isn't going to get you anywhere."

DICKSACK = FRESSSACK.

DICKWANST = FETTWANST.

DIENST, *m.* Service. ***Dienst ist Dienst, und Schnaps ist Schnaps.*** Business and pleasure don't mix. *Hast du vergessen, Dienst ist Dienst, und Schnaps ist Schnaps?* "Have you forgotten there's a time and place for everything?" See GAMMELDIENST.

DING, *n.* **1.** Thing. ***Ein Ding mit 'nem Pfiff.*** (*N.*). S.t. unusual/extraordinary. *Dieser Computer kann dir auch die Zähne putzen. Dett iss (das ist) 'n Ding mit 'nem Pfiff!* "That computer can also brush your teeth. It's really s.t!" **2.** Job; caper. ***Das Ding drehen.*** To pull a job. *Im Knast träumte ich nur davon, das große Ding zu drehen.* "All I dreamt about in jail was pulling off the big caper/heist." **3.** Penis. *Der hat ein Ding zum Dichten schön.* "He's got a thing you could write poetry about." **4.** Clout. ***Jmdm. ein Ding verpassen.*** To whack s.o. *Wenn du mir weiter von Kant sprichst, verpass ich dir 'n Ding.* "If you talk any more about Kant, you'll get it/get s.t. from me."

DINGS/DINGSBUMS/DINGSDA, *m., f., n.* Unknown/unspecified person or thing; thingamajig. *Wie heißt denn das Dings?* "What do you call that doohicky?" *Aber vor Jahren hab ich doch die Erlaubnis vom Bundesdingsbumsamt bekommen.* "But years ago I did get an authorization from some federal agency or other."

DINGSDA/DINGSKIRCHEN. Unknown/unspecified place. *Wann kommen denn deine Verwandten aus Dingsda?* "When are your relatives from, where is it, coming?"

DINK, *m., f.* Working couple with no children (from Eng. "double income, no kids"). *Die Soziologin schreibt über die Dinks.* "The sociologist is writing about working couples without children."

DINNERN, *youth.* **1.** To dine (for *dinieren*). **2.** To grab a quick bite to eat. *Auch meine Dinos dinnern mal beim Mc.* "My parents sometimes eat at McDonald's too." (Dinieren (to dine) is high-toned. Dinnern is not.)

DINOS, *pl.* Parents ("old fossils," but usually not pej. Cf. FOSSIL). *Meine Dinos haben mir die Kohle dafür gegeben.* "My folks gave me the dough for it."

DIPLOMALKER, *m.* Confirmed alcoholic. *Ja ja, du Diplomalker, ich mach schon die Pulle auf.* "Yes, yes, super lush, I'm opening the bottle."

DIPLOMDRÖHNER, *m.* Out-and-out junkie. *Er ist auf dem besten Weg, Diplomdröhner zu werden.* "He's well on the way to being totally hooked."

DIPLOMMÜLLOLOGE, *m., hum.* **1.** S.o. wise in the ways of sorting garbage for pickup and recycling—a major Ger. preoccupation (lit. "certified garbageologist"). *Ach, wenn ich nur diesen Diplommüllologen rausschmeißen könnte!* "Oh, if only I could throw out that garbage smartass!" **2.** Person expert at unloading (mental) garbage on s.o. else. *Dieser Diplommüllologe kann mir gestohlen bleiben.* "That guy can go unload his garbage on s.o. else." Cf. ABMÜLLEN.

DIPLOMWINDEI, *n.* Super good-for-nothing/dud. *Wie hat sie dieses Diplomwindei heiraten können?* "How could she marry that super zero?"

DIPLOMZYNIKER Arch-cynic. *Allen ging's unter die Haut, nur dir nicht, du Diplomzyniker.* "All but you were deeply moved, you old cynic."

DIPPE, *E.* = **DÖGE.**

DIREX, *m., youth.* School principal. *Der neue Direx ist voll beschlabbert!* "The new principal's a nut case."

DIRNE, *f.* Prostitute. (not to be confused with *N. Deern* or *S. Dirn/Dirndl,* young girl). *Bevor ich im Puff landete, arbeitete ich als Dirne/Strassendirne.* "Before I wound up in the whorehouse, I worked as a streetwalker."

DJANGO, *m., youth.* **1.** Guy; tough guy (a common Gypsy first name; also poss. influence of *Shango,* a Yoruba [West African] warrior king and later deity). *Mit dem Django hab ich 'n paar Mal gepennt, aber heiraten will ich ihn nicht.* "I've slept with that dude a few times, but I don't want to marry him." **2.** Joker; jerk. *Auf den Django kann man nicht bauen.* "You can't count on that joker." Cf. KRAWATTENDJANGO. **3.** Drunkenness/drug influence. ***Einen Django in der Birne haben.*** To be drunk/spaced out. *Hast wohl einen Django in der Birne.* "You must be freaked out." See DREAM-DJANGO.

DODEL/DÖDEL, *m.* Jerk. (The "doodle" in *Yankee Doodle* is rel.) *Du hast dich selber zum Dodel gemacht.* "You made a fool of y.s."

DÖGE, *f., N.* Cigarette. *Deine verdammten Dögen bringen dich noch um.* "Your damned cigarettes'll kill you."

DÖHNKES, *pl., N.* Anecdotes. *Wir waren alle ganz Ohr, als der Seemann seine Döhnkes erzählte.* "Everyone was all ears when the sailor told his yarns."

DOKTOR CHAOS = **CHAOT 3.**

DOKTOR EASYMAN, *m.* Laid-back guy (from Eng. "Easy, man!"). *Mein letzter Macker war total durchgeknallt; ich seh mich jetzt nach einem Dr. Easyman um.*

"My last boyfriend was really freaked out; I'm looking for a cool dude now." Cf. JO(H)NNY COOLMAN.

DOKTOR EISENBART, *m.* Quack doctor (from an old students' song). *Ja, er war der leibhaftige Dr. Eisenbart, kurierte die Leute nach seiner Art, bis man ihn einlochte.* "Yes, he was a real charlatan, cured people in his fashion, until they locked him up."

DOKTOR MÜLL = DIPLOMMÜLLOLOGE.

DOLL! = TOLL!

DOLLPUNKT = KNACKPUNKT.

DONNERBALKEN, *m.* Communal toilet, latrine (lit. thunder beam). *Eine Bombe schlug in den Donnerbalken ein.* "A bomb hit the latrine."

DONNERSCHLAG, *m.* Thunderclap. ***Aus einem Furz einen Donnerschlag machen.*** To make a mountain out of a molehill (lit. to make a thunderclap out of a fart). *Du kennst ihn ja, aus jedem Furz macht er 'n Donnerschlag.* "You know him, he carries on about everything."

DÖNTJES = DÖHNKES.

DOOF, *N.* Stupid. ***Doof bleibt doof.*** Incurably stupid. *Hast es wieder getan! Doof bleibt doof.* "You did it again. There's no help for you." Cf. PILLE. ***Doof auf beiden Backen sein.*** To be a complete idiot. *Mensch, bist du denn aber auf beiden Backen doof.* "Man, you're a real nitwit." Cf. DUMMBEUTEL.

DOOFI, *m.* Dummy. (Cf. Eng. sl. "doofus/doof" and "dope.") ***Aussehen/dastehen wie Klein Doofi (mit Plüschohren).*** To look like a real jerk (like a silly looking stuffed animal with furry ears); to be a sad, simple soul. *Ich will dich umschulen, damit du nicht immer wie Klein Doofi dastehst.* "I'm going to reeducate you, so you won't always look like such a dumb cluck."

DOOFKOPP, *N./***DOOFMANN = DOOFI.**

(SICH) DOPEN. To take drugs (from Eng. "dope"). *Der Arzt behauptete, die Sportler hätten sich alle gedopt.* "The doctor said the athletes had all taken drugs."

DOPPELNULL. Intensifies NULL **2.**

DÖSCHEN, *n.* Female genitalia. *Ich denke oft an dein turbotraumhaftes Döschen.* "I often think of your terrific little twat."

DOSE, *f.* Female genitalia (lit. box; socket [*Steckdose*]). *Meine Dose steckt voller Elektrizität und Musik.* "My box is full of electricity and music."

DÖSI, *m.* **1.** Dummy. Cf. DUSSEL. **2.** Daydreamer. *Du wirst bald den Ernst des Lebens kennen lernen, du Dösi, du.* "You'll soon find out about what life's really like, you sleepyhead." Cf. DÖSPADDELIG.

DÖSPADDELIG, *N.* Mentally fogged. *Ich bin zu döspaddelig, dem Laberfritzen noch länger zuzuhören.* "I'm not thinking straight and don't want to listen to that windbag any longer."

DRACHEN. See HAUSDRACHEN.

DRACULENE/DRACULOTTE, *youth.* A girl that is unattractive and vampirish, cryptlike, etc. *Lass dich nur nicht von dieser Draculene küssen!* "Just don't let that bitch from the crypt kiss you!"

DRAUF. On it. ***Etwas drauf haben.*** To be an ace/whizz at s.t.; to have s.t. down pat. *Ich glaubte die Rolle drauf zu haben; trotzdem patzte ich mehrmals.* "I thought I really had the part under my belt, but I made many goofs."

DRAUF SEIN. 1. To feel (lit. to be on it; very widely used now, with no drug association). *Heute ist er wieder cool drauf; gestern war er total ungeil drauf.* "Yesterday he blew his cool totally, but he's cool again today." **2.** To be totally competent/incompetent. *Die Mannschaft war wieder absolut beschissen drauf.* "The team played a super shitty game again."

DRAUFLEGEN. To lay out extra money. ***Eins drauflegen.*** To go one better. *In der Jugendsprache wird oft versucht, eins draufzulegen.* "Young people often try to push the language far out."

DREAM-DJANGO, *m.* Drug addict. *Warum musste sie sich*

in diesen Dream-Django vergaffen? "Why'd she have to fall for that junkie?"

DRECK, *m.* **1.** Dirt/filth. *Der letzte Dreck.* The lowest of the low. *Er hat mich wie den letzten Dreck behandelt.* "He treated me like dirt." *Sich einen Dreck um etwas scheren.* Not to give a shit about s.t. *Er schert sich einen Dreck um deine so geschätzten Vorschriften.* "He doesn't give a shit about your precious regulations." **2.** S.t. junky/insignificant. *Was siehst du dir für einen Dreck an im Fernsehen?* "What's that trash you're watching on TV?"

DRECKIG. Dirty. *Dreckig gehen.* To be/feel miserable. *Es geht ihm ganz schön dreckig, seit seine Frau ihn verlassen hat.* "He's been in a bad way since his wife left him."

DRECKKERL = **DRECKSKERL.**

DRECKNEST, *n.* Nasty little town. *In diesem Drecknest halt ich's nicht länger aus.* "I can't stand this lousy burg anymore."

DRESCHEN. 1. To thresh. *Leeres Stroh dreschen.* To talk a lot of hot air. *Wie lange wirst du noch leeres Stroh dreschen?* "How much more claptrap are you going to hand us?" **2.** To thrash, beat. *Auf die Tasten dreschen.* To pound the piano. *Er hat 'n bisschen auf die Tasten gedroschen.* "He thumped the piano a bit." Cf. EIN-DRESCHEN.

DROGENSZENE, *f.* World of drugs. *Seine Tochter ist in die Drogenszene geraten.* "His daughter's gotten involved with drugs."

DROGI, *m., f., youth.* Teenage drug addict. *Diese Schule steckt voller Drogis.* "That school's full of junkies."

DRÖHNEN. 1. To roar; boom. *Jmdm. eine dröhnen.* To give s.o. a clout. *Er wollte mir eine dröhnen, war aber zu besoffen.* "He wanted to sock me, but he was too drunk." *Um sich dröhnen.* To behave in a rowdy manner. *Die Schlachtenbummler dröhnten um sich.* "The itinerant sports fans were drunk and disorderly." **2.** To get drunk; take drugs/get high on drugs. *Mensch, wie das dröhnt,* *das Grass, das du auf Jamaika gekauft hast!* "Man, I really got high on that grass you bought in Jamaica!"

DRÖHNER, *m.* Drug addict. *Meine Schwester ist keine Dröhnerin.* "My sister's no pothead."

DRÖHNUNG, *f.* Drug fix/high. *Die Dröhnung dauerte nur kurz.* "The high didn't last long."

DROSSEL. See PARKDROSSEL; SCHNAPSDROSSEL.

DRÜCKEBERGER, *m.* Shirker. *Hier ist kein Platz für Drückeberger!* "No room for goldbricks here!"

DRUCKSEN. To hem and haw. *Genug gedruckst! Raus mit der Sprache!* "That's enough hemming and hawing. Spit it out now!"

DSCHONNY = JO(H)NNY.

DSCHUNGELKASERNE, *f., youth, pej.* School (lit. jungle barracks). *In der Dschungelkaserne gibt's jeden Tag Klopfkonzerte.* "There's violence every day in blackboard jungle land."

DUDELN. To drone; blare. *Damals dudelte dieser Schlager aus jedem Radio.* "At that time, that hit song blared from every radio."

DUFTE. Wonderful. *'S hat alles dufte geschmeckt!* "Everything tasted great."

DUHN, *N.* Drunk. *Der ist immer duhn.* "He's always plastered."

DUKATENKACKER/DUKATENSCHEIßER, *m.* S.o. made of money (lit. ducats shitter). *Verdammt nochmal, ich bin ja kein Dukatenkacker!* "God damn it, I'm not made of money!" Cf. MÜNZANSTALT.

DULLI, *Aust., youth.* Marvelous. *In der Disko geht's immer voll dulli zu.* "We always have a blast in the disco."

DULLIÄH, *m., Aust.* Tipsy condition. *Im Dulliäh sagte er, er wollte mich heiraten.* "When he was in his cups, he said he wanted to marry me."

DUMM. Stupid. ***Jmdm. ist/wird etwas zu dumm.*** S.t. is/gets to be too much for s.o. *Deine faulen Fische werden mir*

zu dumm. "I've had it with your lame excuses."
Dumm/dämlich wie Schifferscheiße sein. To be incredibly stupid (lit. dumb as sailor shit). *Mensch, bist ja dumm wie Schifferscheiße.* "Man, you've got shit for brains."

DUMMBACH = DUMMSDORF.

DUMMBART(EL)/DUMMBEUTEL, *m.* Dumbbell. *Such dir einen Dummbeutel aus; dafür bin ich nicht zu haben.* "Go find some dummy; I'm not game for anything like that."

DUMMENFANG. See AUSGEHEN.

DUMMERCHEN, *n.* Silly billy/silly goose. *Damals war ich nur noch 'n blutjunges Dummerchen.* "I was so young and foolish then."

DUMMERJAN, *m.* Dummy. *Geh doch weg, du Dummerjan!* "Get away, you idiot!"

DUMMERL = Aust. variant of DUMMERCHEN.

DUMMERLING/DÜMMLING, *m.* Birdbrain. *Er ist 'n lieber Kerl, aber ein regelrechter Dümmling.* "He's a sweet guy, but a real airhead."

DUMMKOPF = DUMMBEUTEL.

DUMMRIAN = DUMMERJAN.

DUMMSDORF. "Dumbville." *Nicht aus Dummsdorf sein.* Not to be born yesterday. *Wir sind ja nicht aus Dummsdorf, aber reingefallen sind wir trotzdem.* "We're not exactly dummies, but we fell for it (the scheme) anyway."

DUMMSÜLZEN, *youth.* To babble on and on. *Dieser Sabbelheini hat uns voll und ganz dummgesülzt.* "That yakety-yakking babbler laid on his baloney real thick."

DUMPFBACKE, *youth* = DUMMBEUTEL.

DUN = DUHN.

DÜNN. Thin. *Sich dünn(e) machen* = (SICH) VERDÜNNISIEREN.

DÜNNBRETTBOHRER, *m.* Dimwit. (Lit. thin-board driller). *Was findest du an dem Dünnbrettbohrer?* "What do you see in that mental midget?" Cf. BOHREN.

(SICH) DÜNNMACHEN = (SICH) VERDÜN-NISIEREN.

DÜNNPFIFF, *m.* Euph. for DÜNNSCHISS (diarrhea). *In Frankfurt haben wir zu viel Äppelwoi (Apfelwein) gesoffen und den Dünnpfiff gekriegt.* "We guzzled too much cider in Frankfurt and got the runs."

DÜNNSCHISS, *m.* Diarrhea (lit. thin shit). *Alles, was er laberte, war nur Dünnschiss.* "Everything he babbled was just a crock of shit."

(SICH) DURCHBEIßEN. To cope successfully (lit. to bite one's way through). *Ich werde mich schon durchbeißen.* "I'll get through all right/I'll swing it."

DURCHBLICK, *m.* Perspicacity, insight. **Den Durchblick haben.** To have smarts/know what's what. *Von dem, was mich anmacht, hast du keinen Durchblick.* "You haven't got a clue as to what turns me on."

DURCHBLICKEN. To understand. *Kaum jemand blickt noch durch beim Steuerrecht.* "Hardly anybody understands the tax laws."

DURCHBLICKOLOGE, *m.* **1.** Person quick on the uptake. **2.** S.o. slow on the uptake; dummy (ironic use of **1**). *Hältst du dich etwa für den Durchblickologen vom Dienst hier?* "Do you take y.s. for the resident smartass here?" Cf. EXPRESSCHECKER.

(SICH) DURCHBOXEN. To get s.t. by fighting hard for it. *Ich musste mich wirklich durchboxen, um die Rolle zu bekommen.* "I really had to go all out to get the part."

DURCHBRENNEN. 1. To burn out. See SICHERUNG. **2.** To abscond. *Mein Geschäftspartner ist mit der Kohle und meiner Frau durchgebrannt.* "My business partner ran off with the money and my wife."

DURCHCHECK = DURCHBLICK.

(SICH) DURCHFRETTEN, *S.* **= (SICH) DURCH-BEIßEN.**

(SICH) DURCHGAUNERN = (SICH) DURCHMOGELN.

DURCHGEDREHT. Confused; spaced out. *Er war gestern abend echt durchgedreht.* "He was really out of it last night."

DURCHGEKNALLT. Freaked/flipped out. *Beim Rave war er schon durchgeknallt.* "He'd already freaked out at the rave."

DURCHHÄNGER, *m., youth.* Dark mood; blackout; total inactivity. *Gestern hatte sie einen Superdurchhänger.* "She was really down yesterday." Intensifies HÄNGER **2.**

DURCHKNETEN. To beat up (*kneten* = to knead). *Die Punks haben ihn richtig durchgeknetet.* "The punks beat him to a pulp."

(SICH) DURCHLAVIEREN, *S.* = **(SICH) DURCH-BEIßEN.**

(SICH) DURCHMOGELN. To brazen s.t. out. *Diesmal wirst du dich nicht durchmogeln können.* "This time your crooked finagling isn't going to get you through."

(SICH) DURCHSCHLAGEN = **(SICH) DURCH-BEIßEN.**

DURCHTICKEN, *youth.* To understand. *Zuerst konnte ich's nicht voll durchticken.* "At first I couldn't really understand it."

(SICH) DURCHWABERN, *N.* = **(SICH) DURCH-BEIßEN.**

DUSEL, *m.* **1.** Luck. *Du hast mehr Dusel als Verstand.* "You've got more luck than brains." **2.** Dizziness; nausea (*N.*). *Ich hatte einen Dusel.* "I felt dizzy."

DUSELIG. 1. Drowsy; dizzy. *Mir wurde ganz duselig.* "My head started to swim." **2.** Tipsy. *Keinen Schnaps mehr; ich hab schon ein duseliges Gefühl.* "No more booze; I already feel under the influence."

DÜSELIG, *N.* = **DUSELIG.**

DUSELN. To doze. *Statt aufzupassen hast du geduselt.* "Instead of paying attention, you dozed."

DÜSEN. 1. To fly in jet planes (*Düsenflugzeug* = jet plane).

Sie düsen durch die Welt. "They're jetting around the world." **2.** To dash. *Ich muss jetzt schnell nach Hause düsen.* "I've got to hurry home now." Cf. ABDÜSEN; RUMDÜSEN.

DÜSENJET = **VIERRADJET.**

DUSSEL, *m.* Doofus, dummy. *Was will der Dussel wieder?* "What does that airhead want again?"

DUSSELEI, *f.* Stupidity. *So eine Dusselei!* "What a dumb thing!"

DUSSELTIER, *n.* = **DUSSEL.**

DUZFUß. See FUß.

EASY, *youth.* Easy (from Eng.). *Nur nicht ausklinken, Mann! 'S ist ja alles echt easy.* "Just don't freak out, man. Everything's cool." Cf. DOKTOR EASYMAN.

EBBE, *f.* Low tide. ***Ebbe im Geldbeutel/Portemonnaie.*** Short on funds (lit. low tide in the wallet). *Einst lebten sie in Saus und Braus; jetzt ist Ebbe im Portemonnaie.* "Once they lived high on the hog; now their finances are at a low ebb."

ECHT, *youth.* Really (lit. genuine). *Ihr Sound ist echt voll geil.* "Their sound's really awesome."

ECHT VERSCHÄRFT, *youth.* **1.** Really sensational (lit. genuinely intensified/aggravated). *Echt verschärft ihr Sound!* "That band's sound is really terrific." **2.** Really too much. *Echt verschärft, so was von mir zu verlangen!* "That's really pushing it, asking me to do s.t. like that."

ECKE, *f.* Corner. ***Jmdm. nicht um die Ecke trauen.*** Not to trust s.o. very far. *Ich trau ihm nicht um die Ecke.* "I'd trust him about as far as I could throw a 10-foot pole."

EDELFLITZER, *intensifies* FLITZER.

EDELNUTTE, *f.* Expensive prostitute (lit. noble whore). *So 'ne Edelnutte ist nichts für dich.* "That high-class whore is out of your range."

EGAL. See SCHEIßEGAL; WURSTEGAL.

EGALO, *youth.* **1.** All the same. *Uns ist das totalo egalo.* "We couldn't care less about it." **2.** *m., f., youth.* Person with a couldn't-care-less attitude. *Den Lernfuzzis sind die Streber lieber als die Egalos.* "Teachers like eager beavers better than those who've tuned out."

E-GITARRE, *f.* Electric guitar. *Sie spielt die klassische und die E-Gitarre.* "She plays the classical and the electric guitar."

EHEFRÄULEIN, *n.* Frigid wife (lit. married miss). *Wenn er nur wüßte, mich richtig anzumachen, wär ich alles andere als ein Ehefräulein.* "If he only knew how to turn me on right, I'd be anything but frigid."

EHEKNECHT/EHESTANDSKRÜPPEL, *m.* Extremely henpecked husband (lit. marriage slave/cripple [stronger than PANTOFFELHELD; TOFFEL]). *Er macht ihr's nie recht, dieser Eheknecht.* "He never does anything to suit her, that wedded wimp."

EHETROTT, *m.* Marital routine. *Ich such einen Scheich, um dem Ehetrott zu entfliehen.* "I'm looking for a lover to escape from a boring marriage."

EHRLICH, *youth.* Really (lit. honest; honorable) = **ECHT.**

EI! = **EY!**

EI, *n.* **1.** Egg. ***Das Ei des Kolumbus.*** Simple, ideal solution previously overlooked. *Vielleicht ist ihre Erfindung das Ei des Kolumbus.* "Maybe her invention is just what's needed." **2.** ***Ein (dickes) Ei sein.*** To be s.t. wonderful. *Mensch, war das ein (dickes) Ei, den ersten Preis zu gewinnen!* "Boy, that was marvelous, winning the 1st prize!" **3.** To be s.t. awful, problematic. *Pass auf, das ist vielleicht 'n Ei!* "Watch out, that might cause trouble."

EI/EI EI MACHEN, *children.* To pet a child/animal. *Nicht so mit dem Kätzchen spielen, mach schön ei.* "Don't play like that with the kitty; pet it nicely."

EIER, *n., pl.* **1.** Eggs. ***Sich um ungelegte Eier kümmern.*** To worry about s.t. that might happen (lit. to worry about unlaid eggs). *Kümmre dich nicht um ungelegte Eier!* "Don't cross that bridge til you get to it." **2.** Testicles. ***Jmdm. auf die Eier gehen.*** To importune s.o. greatly. *Hör doch auf, mir auf die Eier zu gehen!* "Will ya quit bustin' my balls!" Cf. SACK. **3.** ***Jmdm. die Eier polieren.*** To thrash s.o. *Dir polieren wir die Eier, wenn du petzt.* "We'll beat the shit out of you, if you snitch." ***Jmdm. die Eier schleifen.*** To drill s.o. rigorously (lit. to grind s.o.'s balls). *Die Bundeswehr wird dir die Eier ganz schön schleifen.* "The army'll put you through your paces." ***Dicke Eier.*** Venereal disease (lit. swollen testes). *Als ich bei der Fremdenlegion war, hatte ich mehrmals dicke Eier.* "I copped a dose several times when I was in the Foreign Legion." **3.** Money. *Kannst du mir 50 Eier pumpen?* "Can you lend me 50 marks/bucks/euros (etc.)?"

EIERN. To wobble/stagger. *Eiernd verließ er die Kneipe.* "He staggered out of the tavern."

EIGENTOR, *n.* Own goal. ***Ein Eigentor schießen.*** To do s.t. contrary to one's interests. (*Eigentor* and *Steilvorlage* are soccer terms. The object is to kick the ball into the opposing team's goal, not into one's own.) *Der Parteivorsitzende hoffte auf eine Steilvorlage, schoss aber ein Eigentor.* "The party chairman hoped for a winning play, but instead he shot h.s. in the foot."

EIMER, *m.* Bucket. ***Im Eimer sein.*** To be in the toilet/garbage. *Nach dem Skandal war das Image des Senators im Eimer.* "After the scandal, the senator's image was ruined."

(SICH) EINBRINGEN. To commit o.s. (lit. to bring o.s. in). ***Sich bei jmdm. einbringen.*** To communicate with s.o.; to commit to s.o. *Alles versuch ich, mich bei dir einzubringen, aber du bist von dir selbst zu sehr eingenommen; manchmal glaub ich Männer können sich überhaupt nicht einbringen.* "I try everything to get m.s. across to you, but you're too taken up with y.s. Sometimes I think men are incapable of making a commitment." ***Sich bei etwas einbringen.*** To make a commitment to s.t. *Sie hatten sich bei der Partei voll eingebracht.* "They'd made a total commitment to the party."

EINBROCKEN. To crumble. *Sich/jmdm. eine Suppe/ Scheiße einbrocken.* To land o.s./s.o. in the soup/shit. *Diese Scheiße hast du dir selber eingebrockt.* "You got y.s. into that deep doo-doo."

EINBUCHTEN. To lock up. *Den hätte man längst schon einbuchten sollen.* "They should have put him away long ago."

EINBUDDELN. To bury. *Mir ist es egal, wo man mich einbuddelt.* "I don't care where they bury me."

EINDRESCHEN. To lambaste. *Du brauchst nicht so auf mich einzudreschen.* "You don't have to jump on my neck like that."

EINEN ABHABEN/EINEN WEGHABEN. To be drunk. *Wenn er einen abhat, legt er sich mit allen an.* "When he's had one too many, he picks fights with everybody."

EINKAUFSBUMMEL, *m.* Shopping tour. *Wir wollten einen Einkaufsbummel machen, allein die Geschäfte waren zu, aus Angst vor den Schlachtenbummlern.* "We wanted to go shopping, but the stores were closed, all afraid of marauding sports fans."

(SICH) EINLASSEN = (SICH) EINBRINGEN.

EINLOCHEN. To put behind bars (lit. to put in a hole). *Diesen Hool hätte man viel früher einlochen sollen.* "They should have locked up that hooligan much earlier."

EINPENNEN. To fall asleep. *Bei seinen Vorlesungen pennen alle ein.* "Everybody falls asleep during his lectures."

(SICH) EINPFEIFEN, *youth.* **1.** To wolf down food or drink (lit. to pipe in). *Hast aber grad Fritten eingepfiffen.* "But you just got through shoveling in french fries." **2.** To consume/take in. *Wir wollen uns ihren neusten Film einpfeifen.* "We're going to catch her latest movie."

EINSCHNAPPEN. To take offense (lit. to click shut). *Bitte, nicht gleich einschnappen!* "Please don't get huffy right away."

EINSEIFEN. To deceive (lit. to soap up). *Man hat dich ganz schön eingeseift.* "They really conned you." Cf. ANSCHMIEREN.

EIN UND AUS GEHEN = AUS UND EIN GEHEN.

EINWERFEN = EINPFEIFEN.

EKSTASY/EKSI, *n., youth.* Ecstasy (drug). ("Ecstasy" is *die Ekstase*). *Die ist Eksiabhängig.* "She's hooked on ecstasy."

ELBKÄHNE, *pl.* Clodhoppers (lit. Elbe barges). *Schmeiß doch die alten Elbkähne raus.* "Throw out those old clodhoppers."

ELCH, *m.* Elk. ***Ich denk, mich knutscht/küsst ein Elch!*** "I can't believe my eyes!" (Lit. "I think an elk is smooching/kissing me.") Or, ***Zum Elch werden.*** To be flabbergasted. *Du, hier? Ich werd gleich zum Elch!* "You, here? I'll be a monkey's uncle!" Cf. Mich tritt ein PFERD; KNUTSCHEN; ROTKEHLCHEN; STREIFEN.

ELCH-, *youth.* Extremely (an intensifier, like *end-, riesen-, spitzen-, turbo-*). *Die Fete war elchscharf.* "The party was super fabulous."

ELEFANT. Elephant. *Benimm dich nicht wie ein Elefant im Porzellanladen.* "Don't behave like a bull in a china shop." See NACHTRAGEND.

ELEFANTENHOCHZEIT, *m.* Megamerger. *Das Kartellamt hat die Elefantenhochzeit gebilligt.* "The antitrust office approved the megamerger."

ELEFANTÖS, *youth.* Tremendous, wonderful. *Die Ganeschafeier war voll elefantös.* "The Ganesha (Hindu elephant god) celebration was totally overwhelming."

ELEKTRONIK, *f., youth.* Electronics. ***Einen Schaden in der Elektronik haben.*** To be crazy (lit. to have defective electronic circuits). *Hast wohl einen Schaden in der Elektronik.* "You must be nuts."

EMANZE, *f.* Woman's libber (from *Emanzipierte,* liberated woman). *Tim will keine Emanze heiraten; er sucht eher* *ein Heimchen am Herd.* "Tim doesn't want to marry a feminist; he's looking for a submissive little homebody."

E-MUSIK, *f.,* from *ernste Musik.* Serious music. *Was du E-Musik nennst, ist für mich auch U-Musik.* "What you call serious music is also easy listening for me."

END-, *youth.* Intensifying prefix. Cf. Eng. "living end" and "be all end all." *Die Band hat 'n endgeilen Sound.* "The band's sound is totally awesome."

ENTSAUERN. To calm s.o. down. *Er war sauer, dass ich mit 'nem anderen getanzt hatte, aber ich wusste, ihn zu entsauern.* "He was ticked off at my dancing with s.o. else, but I knew how to get around him."

ENTSIFFEN. To clean. *Selbst die Reinigung konnte den Pulli nicht entsiffen.* "Even the dry cleaners couldn't get the sweater clean." Cf. SIFFKOPF.

ERBSE, *f.* **1.** Pea. *Erbsen im Kopf haben.* To be stupid. *Der hat Erbsen im Kopf.* "He hasn't got a brain in his bean." *Erbsen zählen.* To work. *Hast heute nicht viele Erbsen gezählt.* "You didn't work very hard today." **2.** Dummy. *Was kann man mit der Erbse anfangen?* "What can you do with that idiot?" See KICHERERBSE.

ERGEIERN, *youth.* To get one way or another (*Geier* = vulture). *Keine Bange, die Mäuse ergeir' ich schon.* "Don't worry, I'll get the dough if I have to beg, borrow, or steal." Cf. KLAUEN; KLAUFEN; KRALLEN.

ERST. First. *Erster von hinten sein.* To rank lowest (lit. to be the first from the rear). *In Geschichte war er immer erster von hinten.* "He was always at the bottom of his class in history." See SAHNE.

ERWISCHEN. See KALT ERWISCHEN.

ERZEUGER, *m., pej.* Father (lit. generator). *Mein Erzeuger ist er zwar, aber ein Vater war er mir nie.* "He sired me alright, but he was never a father to me."

ERZEUGER, *pl., pej.* Parents. *Tust du immer alles, was dir die Erzeuger sagen?.* "Do you always do what your parents tell you?"

ES, *n.* **1.** E-flat major (music). **2.** Id (psychology). *Er glaubt, seinem Es näherzukommen, jedes Mal, das er Mozarts Symphonie 39 in Es Dur hört.* "He thinks he gets closer to his Id every time he hears Mozart's Symphony #39 in E-flat major."

ES, *m.* Austrian schilling. *Ich will meine Es nicht gegen Euros umtauschen.* "I don't want to change my shillings for euros."

ES HABEN MIT JMDM. To be getting it on with s.o. *Opa hat es mit der Briefträgerin.* "Grandpa's making it with the mail carrier."

ES HABEN MIT/AN ETWAS. To have a problem with s.t. *Er hat es jetzt mit dem Herzen.* "He's got heart trouble now."

ESEL, *m.* Donkey, ass. ***Ein Esel schilt den anderen Langohr*** *(prov.).* That's a case of the pot calling the kettle black.

EULALIE, *f.* Hum. for EULE **2.**

EULE, *f.* **1.** Owl. ***Eulen nach Athen tragen.*** To carry coals to Newcastle. (The owl, emblem of Pallas Athena, Goddess of Wisdom, figured on Athenian coinage.) *Samoware nach Moskau schicken, hieße Eulen nach Athen tragen.* "Sending samovars to Moscow would be like carrying coals to Newcastle." Cf. ***HOLZ in den Wald tragen.*** **2.** Ugly woman. *Die Eule ist voll geil auf mich.* "The ugly old bag's really got the hots for me." **3.** Prostitute. *Wo warst du gestern abend? Hast wohl 'ne Eule.* "Where were you last night? You're probably seeing some whore."

EUMEL, *m., N., youth.* **1.** Thingamajig. *Wozu dient der Eumel?* "What's that gizmo for?" **2.** Sap. *Mann, bist du 'n Eumel.* "Man, you're some dope!"

EUTER, *n., pl.* Sagging breasts (lit. udders). *Als er meine Euter sah, verging ihm die Lust.* "When he saw my droopy boobs, he didn't feel like it anymore."

EVERGREEN, *m.* Old favorite song. *Bisjetzt hat er keine*

Evergreens mit seinem Computer komponiert. "So far he hasn't composed any golden oldies with his computer."

EX! Down the hatch!/Bottoms up!/Down in one!

EX. 1. *Etwas ex trinken.* To drink s.t. down without pause. *Wie immer, trank er seinen Whisky ex.* "As usual he knocked back his whiskey in one gulp." **2.** Dead. *Die sind alle ex.* "They've all croaked."

EXPRESSCHECKER, *n., youth.* **1.** Shrewdie; s.o. quick on the uptake. **2.** Dummy; smarty-pants. *Dieser Express-checker muss immer seinen Senf dazu geben.* "That smart aleck always has to put in his two cents."

EX UND HOPS GEHEN = **HOPSGEHEN 2.**

EY!, *youth.* Hey! *Ey, Mann, schmeiß mir mal 'n paar Hugos rüber!* "Hey, man, lemme have some cigarettes/joints."

F, in the expression *Nach Schema F. Routine* (lit. something done routinely, from *Frontrapporten* [front reports] that always followed a set format; cf. NULLACHTFÜNFZEHN, also of mil. origin). *Mein Leben verlief zu sehr nach Schema F; da brannte ich mit einem Stripper durch.* "My life was in too much of a rut, so I ran off with a stripper."

FACHCHINESISCH, *n.* Technical jargon (lit. "subject Chinese"). *Die Computerhacker laberten ihr Fachchinesisch.* "The computer hackers droned on in their technical jargon."

FACKELN. To burn, torch. ***Nicht lange fackeln.*** Not to be slow to act. *Da wurde nicht lange gefackelt.* "Action was taken quickly."

FACKEREI = **FAULER FISCH.**

FADISIEREN, *Aust., youth.* To bore. *Faszinierst mi' grad' net; fadisierst mi' aber wen'ger wie die andern.* "You don't exactly fascinate me; but you bore me less than the others."

FAHRLAPPEN, *m., youth.* Driver's license. *Diesem Ausgeflippten sollte man den Fahrlappen entziehen.* "That guy's freaked out, and they ought to take his driver's license away."

FAHRLAPPENFRISCHLING, *m., youth.* S.o. who's just obtained a driver's license. *Dieser Fahrlappenfrischling hat schon einen Unfall gehabt.* "He just got his driver's license but has already had an accident."

FAHRT, *f.* Trip. ***Fahrt in etwas bringen.*** To put some life into s.t. *Der Skandal hat endlich ein bisschen Fahrt in die Wahlkampagne gebracht.* "The scandal finally put a little life into the electoral campaign."

FALLE, *f.* Bed (lit. trap). *Ab mit euch in die Falle!* "Off you go to bed now!"

FANTASTICO = BOMBASTICO.

FASCHO, *m., pej., youth.* Fascist. *Ihre Fossilien sind Faschos.* "Her parents are Fascists."

FASELHANS = LABERFRITZE; SABBELHEINI.

FATZKE, *m.* Pretentious fool; hotshot (ironic). *Nichts interessiert diesen blöden Fatzke mehr als seine Klamotten.* "Nothing interests that stuck-up dork more than his outfits."

-FATZKE = FRITZE; FUZZI.

FAULEN. To loaf. *Dieses Wochenende will ich nur faulen.* "I don't want to do a damned thing this weekend."

FAULER FISCH, *pl.* Lame excuse (lit. spoiled fish). *Das sind nur faule Fische.* "Those are just lame excuses."

FAXENHEINI, *m.* Jokester. *Gehst mir vielleicht auf den Keks, du Faxenheini; treib deine Faxen anderswo.* "You really get on my nerves, cowboy; go horse around someplace else."

FEEZ/FE(E)TZ, *f.* Party (youth sl. variants of FETE, influenced by FETZEN and FETZIG). *'S war 'ne voll geile Feetz.* "The party was a real big blast."

FEGEN. 1. To sweep; clean. ***Sich einen fegen.*** To have a quick drink. *Fegen wir uns einen!* "Let's have a snort." **2.** To race. *Wir sind durch die Innenstadt gefegt.* "We dashed around downtown."

FEGER, *m.* **1.** Sweeper, brush. See LUNGENFEGER. **2.** Fast car. *Da kam er angepest in seinem neuen Feger.* "He drove up in his fast new car." **3.** Dynamic person. *Nina ist echt 'n Feger.* "Nina's a real live wire." Cf. STRASSENFEGERIN.

FELL, *n.* Fur; hide. ***Jmdn. das Fell bügeln/gerben/ putzen/versohlen.*** To tan s.o.'s hide. *Sei ruhig oder ich* *gerb dir's Fell.* "Be quiet or I'll tan your hide." ***Jmdm. das Fell über die Ohren ziehen.*** To deceive s.o. *Der Schwindler hat ihm das Fell über die Ohren gezogen.* "The swindler took him for a ride." ***Dir/dich juckt das Fell.*** See JUCKEN.

FENSTER, *n.* Window. *Ich hab mich schon zu weit aus dem Fenster für Sie gelehnt.* "I've already stuck my neck out too far for you."

FERKELEI, *f.* Mess; dirty joke; s.t. sordid. *Von solchen Ferkeleien will ich nichts wissen; ich interessiere mich nur für das Hehre und Erhabene.* "I don't want to hear about such filthy things; I'm only interested in the sublime and uplifting."

FERKELN, *youth.* **1.** To be pregnant; give birth (lit. to farrow [have a litter of piglets]). *Ulla hat wieder geferkelt.* "Ulla's pushed out another brat." **2.** To make a mess. See VERFERKELN. **3.** To tell dirty jokes. *Meine Alten kommen; nicht weiter ferkeln!* "My parents are coming; don't tell any more dirty jokes." See RUMFERKELN.

FERTIG. Finished. ***Und fertig ist der Lack/die Laube!*** There you are!/That's it!/Voilà! (Lit. the paint job/summerhouse is done.) *Hier noch der letzte Schliff, und fertig ist die Laube!* "Now the finishing touch, and there you are!"

FESTEN, *youth.* To party. *Heut abend festen wir.* "We're partying tonight."

FETE, *f.* Party (from Fr. *fête*). *Sie feiern wieder eine Fete.* "They're throwing a party again."

FETT. Fat. ***Das macht den Kohl/das Kraut/die Suppe auch nicht fett!*** Fat lot of good that will do! (Lit. "that won't make the cabbage/soup fat." In pre cholesterol-conscious times, to "live off the fat of the land" or "high on the hog" was considered desirable.) *Behalt deine miesen zehn Euros; die machen das Kraut auch nicht fett.* "Keep your measly 10 euros; they're not going to make much difference."

FETTFLECK/FETTSACK/FETTWANST, *m.* Fat slob/lard ass. *Dieser Fettsack glaubt, keine Frau könne ihm widerstehen.* "That tub o' guts thinks no woman can resist him."

FETZEN, *m.* Rag; scrap. ***Dass die Fetzen fliegen.*** Like all get-out. *Dieses Wochenende wollen wir feiern, dass die Fetzen fliegen.* "This weekend we're going to party like mad." Cf. BALKEN; WÄNDE.

FETZEN, *youth.* **1.** To be mind-blowing (lit. to rip). *Ihr Sound fetzt unheimlich.* "Their sound (rock, etc.) is really mind-blowing." **2.** To have a ball. *Gehen wir heut abend einen fetzen.* "Let's have a blast tonight."

(SICH) FETZEN. To quarrel. *Sie haben sich ordentlich gefetzt.* "They really tore into each other."

FETZIG, *youth.* Marvelous. *Ihre neue Rille ist turbofetzig.* "Her new disc is super sensational."

FEUCHT. Moist. ***Jmdm. einen feuchten Dreck/Lehm/ Kehricht/Schmutz/Staub angehen.*** To be no one's damned business. *Und wenn ich mit ihm getanzt habe? Das geht dich einen feuchten Kehricht an!* "So what if I danced with him? What's it to you?"

FEUCHTFRÖHLICH. Jolly and alcoholic. *Es war 'n feuchtfröhlicher Abend.* "Everyone consumed lots of spirits and was in good spirits that evening."

FICK, *m.* Sexual congress. *Es geht nichts über einen guten Fick.* "There's nothing better than a good fuck."

FICKEN. To fuck. *Mein Klapsdoktor hielt mich für verklemmt und wollte mit mir ficken, aber ich ließ mich nicht von ihm ficken.* "My shrink thought I was sexually uptight and wanted to fuck me, but I wouldn't let him."

FICKEREI, *f.* Coition, copulation. *Er ist der endlosen Fickerei müde geworden und sucht jetzt einen Guru im Himalaya.* "He's grown tired of endless humping and is now looking for a guru in the Himalayas."

FICKFACK, *m.*/**FICKFACKEREI,** *f.* = FAULER FISCH.

FICKRIG. 1. Fidgety; nervous. *Warum bist du so fickrig?* "Why're you so jumpy?" **2.** Randy. *Her zu mir, fickriges Ding; bei mir kannst du dich abgeilen.* "Come to me, you horny thing; I'll calm you down."

FILMRISS, *m., youth.* Blackout (lit. tear/break in movie film). *Deinen Shit kiff ich nicht mehr; gestern hatt ich dabei einen Filmriss.* "I'm not smoking your dope anymore; I blacked out on it yesterday."

FIMMEL, *m.* Obsession. *Du hast wohl 'n Fimmel!* "You must be hung up/have a mania." See BILDUNGSFIMMEL; PUTZFIMMEL; SAUBERKEITSFIMMEL.

FINANZFRITZE/FINANZHEINI, *m.* Financial advisor. *Mein Finanzfritze hat mir vom Kauf abgeraten.* "My financial advisor told me not to buy."

FIRLEFANZ, *m.* Useless trifles. *Der Chef will ein neues Gebäude ohne Firlefanz.* "The boss wants a new building without frills." ***Firlefanz machen.*** To clown around. *Mach keinen Firlefanz!* "Don't fool around!"

FISCHKOPF, *m., N.* Dummy. *Archie Bunker nannte seinen Schwiegersohn oft Fischkopf!* "Archie Bunker often called his son-in-law 'Meathead.' "

FISIMATENTEN, *pl.* Empty pretexts. *Mach keine Fisimatenten!* "No lame excuses!"

FISSELN, *N.* To drizzle. *Es fisselt.* "It's drizzling."

FIX UND FERTIG. 1. Completely ready. *Endlich ist die Arbeit fix und fertig.* "At last, the job's all done." **2.** Thoroughly exhausted. *Nach dem Rennen waren wir fix und fertig.* "We were all done in after the race."

FIX UND FOXI. *Youth sl. var. of prev. entry* (from the comic book characters "Fix" and "Foxi").

FIXE, *f.* Needle. *Wirf doch die Fixe weg!* "Throw away that needle!"

FIXEN. To shoot drugs. *Sie fixt aber nur mit Einwegfixen.* "She's a hard drug addict, but uses only disposable needles."

FLACHKOPF = DUMMKOPF.

FLACHKRAM, *m.* Nonsense. *Spar mir deinen Flachkram.* "Don't lay that load o' malarkey on me."

FLACHMANN, *m.* Hip flask. *Ohne meinen treuen Flachmann hätte ich die Kälte beim Fußballspiel nicht aushalten können.* "Without my trusty hip flask, I couldn't have stood the cold at the football game."

FLACHS, *m.* Joke (lit. flax). *Das war doch nur Flachs.* "I was only kidding."

FLAPS, *m.* **1.** Rascal; impertinent person. *Such dir andere Freunde als diese Flapse.* "Get y.s. other friends instead of those jokers." **2.** Faux pas; error. *Das war aber ein schriller Flaps.* "You really put your foot in it that time." **3.** Joke. *Das war 'n toller Flaps.* "That was some joke!"

FLAPSIG. Sloppy; sassy; offhand. *Warum hast du mich zuerst so flapsig angeredet?* "Why'd you talk so fresh to me at first?"

FLASCHE, *f.* Wimp (lit. bottle). *Diese Flasche solltest du wegwerfen.* "You should get rid of that wimp."

FLATTER, *f.* Shorter version of FLATTERMANN. **1. *Die Flatter kriegen.*** To get the jitters. *Als ich mit ihm allein in der Bude war, kriegte ich die Flatter.* "I got scared when I was alone with him in his pad." **2.** To scram, in *die Flatter machen* (flattern = "to flutter"). *Die Bullen kommen; machen wir schnell die Flatter.* "The cops are coming; let's hit the road fast."

FLATTERMANN, *m.* **1.** Nervous person. ***Einen Flattermann haben.*** To have the jitters. *Bevor ich auftreten sollte, hatte ich einen Flattermann.* "I had stage fright before the performance." **2.** Roast chicken, *hum. Hat dieser Flattermann frei laufen können?* "Was this fluttery fellow a free-range chicken?"

FLAUTEN, *youth.* **1.** To lounge around. *Flauten willst du nur.* "All you want to do is hang out." **2.** To bore. *Willst uns wieder mit dem alten Gelabere flauten—wa?* "Why the hell do you want to bore us with that old crap again?" (Both meanings stem from *die Flaute,* orig. a nautical term for "becalmed waters," later "slack period of economic activity," and "feeling of apathy.")

FLÄZ, *m.* Lout. *Warum lädst du immer wieder diesen Fläz ein?* "Why do you keep inviting that oaf?"

FLÄZEN. To lounge/hang around. *Faulen und Fläzen, nur das kannst du.* "Lazing and lounging around is all you can do."

FLEBBE, *f.* Identification. *Der Spion hat sich neue Flebben machen lassen.* "The spy had new ID papers made for h.s."

FLECK, *m.* Spot. ***Am falschen Fleck.*** In the wrong place. *Ja, viel Energie hast du, aber immer am falschen Fleck.* "Yes, you've got lots of energy, but it's always misplaced."

FLENNEN, *pej.* To cry; bawl. *Flenn nicht, ich penn schon mit dir.* "Don't weep, I'll sleep with you."

FLENNEREI, *f.* Bawling, blubbering. *Hör doch auf mit der Flennerei!* "Stop blubbering!"

FLIEGE, *f.* **1.** Fly. ***Die Fliege/'ne Fliege machen.*** To beat it. *Mach 'ne Fliege!* "Buzz off!" Cf. BIENE; MÜCKE. **2.** Flirtatious girl. *Mimi ist 'ne Fliege; sie weiß, es gibt so viele Macker und so wenig Zeit.* "Mimi flits around; she knows there's so little time and so many men."

FLIEGEN. To be thrown out (lit. to fly). *Tu's wieder und du fliegst.* "Do it again and you're out."

FLIESEN, *pl.* Banknotes (lit. tiles). *Steck doch die Fliesen weg.* "Put that money away." See BLAUE FLIESE.

FLIMMERKASTEN, *m./***FLIMMERKISTE,** *f.* TV set (lit. flicker box). *Er ist vom Flimmerkasten nicht wegzukriegen.* "You can't get him away from the boob tube."

FLINTE, *f.* Penis. (lit. shotgun). *Hol doch deine Flinte endlich aus der Hose!* "C'mon now, open your fly and let's see your rod!"

FLIPPEN, *youth.* **1.** To be crazy. *Mann, du flippst ja.*

"You're nuts, man." **2.** To hang out; wander around. *Geh'n wir flippen, vielleicht Tussis anmachen.* "Let's look around, maybe pick up chicks."

FLIPPERN. To play pinball. ***Eine heiße Kugel flippern.*** To be an ace pinball player. *Ich schwänze die Schule, weil's mir wichtiger ist, 'ne heiße Kugel zu flippern.* "I play hooky from school because being an ace pinball player's more important."

FLIPPIG. 1. Hip; snazzy. *Wo hast du den flippigen Fummel her?* "Where'd you get that snazzy outfit?" **2.** Unconventional. *Viele halten sich für flippig.* "Many think they're unconventional."

FLIPPY, *m., youth.* **1.** S.o. down and out; drug addict. *Du gammelst nur mit Flippys rum.* "You just bum around with deadbeats." **2.** Someone antisocial. *Er ist weniger Flippy als er es sich einbildet.* "He's less unconventional than he thinks."

FLITSCHERL. Aust. variant of FLITTCHEN.

FLITTCHEN, *n.* Slut. *Das Flittchen will er jetzt heiraten.* "He wants to marry that floozie now."

FLITZER, *m.* **1.** Sleek car; sports car. *Wie wär's denn mit einer Probefahrt in dem superaffengeilen neuen Flitzer?* "How about a trial run in your awesome new sports car?" Cf. EDELFLITZER; WAHNSINNSFLITZER. **2.** Streaker = BLITZER.

FLOCKE, *f.* **1.** Jokester (lit. flake, incl. sl. sense; every snowflake is unique and jokesters can be unique to the point of eccentricity). *Spiel hier nicht die Flocke!* "Quit being a clown/flake." **2.** Caressable, foolish girl (feminists deplore the macho ideal of the "flaky-piecrust-tender-girl who's also not too bright"). *Elfi ist vielleicht 'ne Flocke.* "Elfi's some appealing chick!"

FLOCKEN, *pl.* Money (lit. flakes). See FLÖHE.

FLOCKIG, *youth.* Relaxed. *Der ist nicht mehr so ganz flockig.* "He's not as laid back as he used to be."

FLOH, *m.* Flea. ***Jmd. einen Floh ins Ohr setzen.*** To give s.o. a foolish idea. *Wer hat dir diesen Floh ins Ohr gesetzt?* "Who put that bee in your bonnet?" ***Einen Floh im Ohr haben.*** To be crazy. *Der hat wohl 'n Floh im Ohr.* "He must be batty." ***Die Flöhe husten/niesen hören.*** Know it all (s.o. who can hear the fleas cough/sneeze). *Dieser Klugscheißer will immer die Flöhe husten hören.* "That smart-ass thinks he's a real pundit."

FLÖHE, *pl.* Money. *Nur her mit den Flöhen!* "Just hand over the dough!"

FLOHKISTE, *f.* Bed (lit. flea box). *Sie liegen noch in der Flohkiste.* "They're still in the sack."

FLOPPEN. To flop. *Sein letzter Song hat chartmäßig gefloppt.* "His last song flopped on the charts."

FLOPPY, *f., youth.* Head/brains (*from* "floppy disc"). *Bei dir ist wohl die Floppy ausgeflippt.* "You must be off your rocker."

FLOSSE, *f., youth.* **1.** Hand (lit. fin; flipper). *Reich mir die Flosse, Genosse!* "Shake, pal!" ***Frostige Flossen kriegen*** (youth sl. var. of ***kalte Füße kriegen***). To get cold feet. *Dabei wirst du nur frostige Flossen kriegen.* "You'll only get cold feet." **2.** Leg. ***Die Flossen schwingen.*** To shake a leg. *Schwing die Flossen oder sie schnappen uns.* "Step on it or they'll nab us." ***Die Flossen unter den Arm klemmen = die Beine unter den Arm nehmen.*** See BEIN.

FLÖTEN. 1. To speak affectedly (lit. to play the flute). *Flöt nicht mehr lange! Raus mit der Sprache!* "Don't give me a song and dance any more. Out with it!" **2.** To fellate. *Die ist noch 'ne Jungfrau aber aufs Flöten versteht sie sich bestens.* "She's still a virgin, but she gives great head." ***Flöten gehen.*** To go down the drain. *Er hatte viele Schulden und seine Firma ist flöten gegangen.* "He had lots of debts and his firm went down the drain." Cf. BADEN.

FLOTT. 1. Speedy, brisk. ***Der flotte Heinrich/Oskar/Otto.*** Diarrhea. *Esst nicht so viele Kirschen, sonst kriegt ihr* *noch den flotten Otto.* "Don't eat so many cherries or you'll get the runs." (The names are usually male; feminists might prefer s.t. like *die flotte Lotte.* In any case, females get equal treatment in: KATHARINA.) **2.** Stylish, snappy; pert, attractive (often used to describe young girls as in *flotte Bienen/Hasen/Häschen/Käfer/Mädchen/Motten/Zierfische,* see HASE **2**). *Fritz Kreisler hatte eine flotte Spielart.* "Fritz Kreisler's playing was sprightly." **3.** Fast living. ***Ein flotter Dreier/Vierer, usw.*** Sexual threesome, foursome, etc. *Sie führen ein flottes Leben und sind jederzeit für einen flotten Vierer zu haben.* "They like fast living and are game for group sex anytime."

FLOTTEN = FLOTTIEREN.

(SICH) FLOTTEN/(SICH) FLOTTIEREN. 1. To rush off (cf. ABFLOTTIEREN). **2.** To get all dolled up (cf. FLOTT **2**). *Willst du dich nicht zuerst 'n bisschen flottieren?* "Don't you want to put on a little war paint first?"

FLUNDER. See PLATT.

FLUNKERN. To fib. *Er flunkert gern.* "He likes to tell tall stories."

FLUNSCH, *m.* Pouting expression. ***Einen Flunsch ziehen/machen.*** To pull a long face. *Zieh bloß keinen Flunsch, nur weil ich dir die Wahrheit gesagt habe.* "Don't pout just because I told you the truth."

FLUPPE, *f., youth.* Cigarette. *Ihm hängt immer 'ne Fluppe in der Fresse.* "A cigarette's always dangling from his mug."

FLUPPEN. To speed. See LOSFLUPPEN.

FLÜSTERN, *youth.* To say, tell (lit. whisper). *Lass dich nicht mit dem Schlachtschiff ein, das kann ich dir flüstern!* "Don't get involved with that battle-ax, I'm telling you good." Cf. ZISCHEN **1**.

FOLTERKAMMER, *f.* Gym; exercise room (lit. torture chamber). *Wir brauchen keine Folterkammer; mit Mozart und Yoga im Wohnzimmer halten wir uns fit.* "We don't need a gym; we keep fit listening to Mozart and doing yoga in our living room."

FOSE, *f.* Prostitute. *Er verkehrt nur mit Fosen.* "He just hangs out with whores."

FOSSIL, *n., youth.* Authority figure (as in LERNFOSSIL); parent (lit. fossil). *Deine Fossilien peilen's nie.* "Your old parents will never understand." Cf. DINOS.

FOSSILIO = **FOSSIL.**

FOTZE, *f.* **1.** Female genitalia. *Ein Gott hat deine Fotze gesegnet!* "A god has blessed your pussy!" **2.** Female. *Was will die alte Fotze von mir?* "What does that old cunt want from me?" **3.** Mouth, *S. Halt die Fotz' oder ich stopf sie dir.* "Shut your trap or I'll shut it for you."

FÖTZEL, *m., Swiss.* No good. *Was willst du mit dem Fötzel anfangen?* "Why do you bother with that bum?"

FOTZEN, *S.* To slap. *Er hat mir so eine gefotzt.* "It hurt when he slapped me."

FRACK, *m.* Tails (male evening dress). ***Sich in den Frack machen.*** To shit one's pants (out of fear). *Satchmo machte sich in den Frack, als er den Alligator sah.* "Satchmo shit his pants when he saw the alligator." ***Jmdm. den Frack voll hauen.*** To beat s.o. up. *Lass ihn in Ruhe, oder ich hau dir den Frack voll.* "Leave him alone or I'll beat the shit out of you."

FRACKSAUSEN, *n.* **Fracksausen haben.** To be afraid (lit. to have a rumbling in one's pants. Cf. AFTERSAUSEN; MUFFENSAUSEN, and previous entry). *Du hast gleich Fracksausen gehabt.* "You got scared right away."

FRANSE, *f.* Loose thread; strand. **In Fransen gehen.** To go to pieces. *Der Gigolo kam in die Jahre und seine schöne Welt ging in Fransen.* "The gigolo got older, and his wonderful world fell apart."

FRAß, *m.* Lousy food (lit. animal food). *Diesen Fraß kannst du selber fressen.* "You can eat this swill y.s."

FRAUENSCHWARM, *m.* Man whom women adore. *Mit*

fünfzig ist dieser Schauspieler immer noch ein Frauen-schwarm. "At 50 that actor's still a heartthrob."

FRECH. Impudent. *Frech wie Schifferscheiße.* Unbeliev-ably sassy (lit. insolent as sailor shit). *Frech wie Schiffer-scheiße wie er ist, verlangte er, dass ich die Zeche bezahle.* "He's got more nerve than brains and asked me to foot the bill."

FREGATTE, *f.* **1.** Woman who wears lots of makeup/jewels (lit. frigate; cf. AUFGETAKELT). *Er will die reiche alte Fre-gatte heiraten.* "He wants to marry the rich, gaudy, old broad." **2.** Brawny female/tough broad (*youth*). *Mit der Fregatte ist nicht gut Kirschen essen.* "Better not mess around with that battle-ax." Cf. SCHLACHTSCHIFF **1.**

FREI NACH SCHNAUZE. As one feels like; unsystemati-cally; off the top of one's head. *Ich hab's frei nach Schnauze gemacht und das Ergebnis kann sich sehen lassen.* "I played it by ear, and the result is quite pre-sentable."

FREMDGEHEN. To be unfaithful. *Ich glaub, mein Mann geht fremd.* "I think my husband's got s.t. going on the side."

FRESSALIEN, *pl.* Grub. *Fressalien gab's in Hülle und Fülle.* "There were lots of great eats."

FRESSE, *f.* **1.** (animal) Mouth. *Halt die Fresse!* "Shut your trap!" *(Ach, du) meine Fresse!* (Well) I'll be damned! *Meine Fresse, was hast du da angerichtet!* "My God, what have you done there!" **2.** (animal) Face. See POLIEREN.

FRESSEN. To eat like an animal; devour. *Die Kilometer fressen.* To burn up the road. *Du brauchst die Kilometer nicht zu fressen.* "You don't have to burn up the road." *Zum Fressen gern haben.* To like s.o. enough to eat. *Ich hab dich zum Fressen gern.* "I'm so nuts about you, I could eat you up." *Einen Affen/Narren an etwas/jmdm. gefressen haben.* To be mad about s.t./s.o. *Schon als Teenager hat er einen Narren an der Fliegerei gefressen.*

"He was already nuts about flying when he was a teenager." ***Etwas endlich gefressen haben.*** To finally understand. *Hast's jetzt endlich gefressen?* "Have you finally caught on now?" See FRISS.

FRESSER, *m.* Ravenous eater. *Natürlich hab ich abgetrieben; Fresser gibt's schon genug im Haus.* "Of course I got an abortion; there are already enough hungry mouths to feed in the house." See JUDENFRESSER; KOMMUNISTENFRESSER; MENSCHENFRESSER.

FRESSLEISTE, *f. youth.* Mouth; teeth; false teeth; head. *Ich hab dem Alten seine Fressleiste geklaut.* "I swiped the old fogey's choppers."

FRESSSACK, *m.* Glutton. *Dieser Fresssack hat nichts für die anderen übrig gelassen.* "That hog left nothing for the others." Cf. FETTSACK.

FRIEDE, FREUDE, EIERKUCHEN. Peace and harmony (lit. peace, joy, pancakes). *Es herrscht wieder Friede, Freude, Eierkuchen—aber wer weiß, wie lange.* "Everything's rosy, peachy again—but who knows for how long?"

FRIKASSIEREN, *youth.* To beat up (lit. to fricassee). *Die Skins haben ihn echt frikassiert.* "The skinheads made hash out of him."

FRISCHLING, *f.* Greenhorn (lit. young wild boar; used by older teenagers for 10–16-year-olds). *Was suchen diese fiesen Frischlinge hier?* "What's that damned small-fry want here?" See FAHRLAPPENFRISCHLING.

FRISS, VOGEL, ODER STIRB! Sink or swim!/Do or die! *Ich musste es tun. Friss, Vogel, oder stirb!* "I had to do it. Beggars can't be choosers."

FRITTEN, *f., pl.* French fries (from Fr. *frites*). *Jetzt kann man heiße Fritten auch im Automaten bekommen.* "You can now get hot french fries in vending machines too."

-FRITZE = **-HEINI.**

FROMMS, *m., pl.* Condoms (from a brand name; *fromm* = pious). *Er kauft gewissenhaft Fromms.* "He religiously buys condoms."

FROST, *m., youth.* Fear (lit. frost). *Dich wird wieder nur der Frost packen!* "You'll just get cold feet again."

FROTTIEREN = **FRIKASSIEREN.**

FROTZELEI, *f.* Teasing; teasing remark. *Hör auf mit den Frotzeleien!* "Stop that teasing!"

FROTZELN. To kid. *Habt ihr jetzt genug über mich gefrotzelt?* "Have you had enough fun at my expense now?"

FRÜCHTCHEN, *n., pej.* Rascal; good for nothing (lit. little fruit; has no homosexual connotation in Ger.). *Du bist mir aber ein nettes Früchtchen!* "You're some piece of work, you!"

FRUPPIE, *m., youth.* from Eng. "frustrated urban professional" (nontrendy, less consumerist, ex-yuppies wandering on "boulevards of broken dreams"). *Fruppies sind wahre Spaßverderber.* "Fruppies are real killjoys." Cf. YIFFIE.

FRUST, *m.* Frustration (from *Frustration, f.*). *Lass deinen Frust nur nicht an mir raus!* "Just don't take your frustration out on me."

FRUSTEN. To frustrate; deceive; tire out. *Du hast alles getan, mich zu frusten.* "You did everything you could to bug me."

FRUSTIG. Frustrating (for stand. *frustrierend*). *Frustig war damals meine Lage.* "I was in a frustrating situation then."

FUCHS/FUX, *m.* New member of a university fraternity; new army recruit. See BLINDFUCHS.

FUFFI/FUFFILEIN, *N.* Fifty-mark note. *Mit nur einem Fuffilein kann ich nicht viel anfangen; wär's nur 'n Euro!* "Not much I can do with a 50-mark note; if only it were a euro!"

FUMMEL, *m.* Woman's outfit. *Aber ich hab dir erst letzte Woche 'n neuen Fummel gekauft.* "But I bought you a new outfit only last week." ***Im Fummel.*** In drag. *Im Fummel sah er umwerfend aus.* "He looked stunning in drag."

FUMMELEI, *f.* Petting; groping (lit. fidgeting). *Nichts ist zwischen uns passiert. Nur 'n bisschen Fummelei.* "Nothing happened between us. Just a little petting."

FUMMELN. 1. To mess around. *Hast du an meinem Computer gefummelt?* "Did you fiddle around on my computer?" **2.** To dribble a football. *Hör doch auf zu fummeln, spiel mir den Ball zu!* "Quit fumbling and send the ball my way."

FUMMELTRINE, *f.* Drag queen. *Der Exfußballer ist Fummeltrine geworden.* "The former football player's become a drag queen."

FUNDI, *m., f.* Hard-liner. *Die Fundis müpfen auf.* "The strict party-liners are balking."

FUNKEN. 1. To transmit (radio); emit sparks. *Zwischen uns beiden hat's gleich gefunkt.* "The chemistry between us kicked in right away." ***Bei jmdm. funken.*** To catch on. *Endlich hat es bei ihr gefunkt, dass er sie nur ausnutzen will.* "She finally realized that all he wanted was to exploit her." **2.** To clout. *Ich funk dir bald eine.* "I'm gonna clobber you."

FUNKSTILLE, *f.* Radio silence. *Zwischen den Geschäftspartnern herrsch jetzt Funkstille.* "He and his business partner aren't on speaking terms now."

FUNZEL = TRANFUNZEL 1.

FURZ, *m.* Fart. ***Einen Furz gefrühstückt haben.*** To be crazy (lit. to have had a fart for breakfast). *Du hast wohl 'n Furz gefrühstückt.* "You must be off your rocker." ***Einen Furz im Arsch haben.*** To have some minor ache or pain (lit. to have a fart in one's ass). *Hast wieder 'n Furz im Arsch?* "Is your big toe bothering you again?" ***Furz/Fürze im Kopf haben.*** To be off one's rocker (lit. to have a fart/farts in one's head). *Warum brüllst du uns so an? Hast wohl Fürze im Kopf.* "Why are you yelling at us like that? You must be nuts." ***Aus einem traurigen Arsch fährt kein fröhlicher Furz.*** When things are bad, you're not up to rejoicing (lit. from a depressed arse no jolly fart will depart). *Stolz furzen würd ich schon gern, wie es Franklin rät, aber meine Tochter ist schwerkrank. Aus einem traurigen Arsch fährt eben kein fröhlicher Furz.* "I'd love to fart proudly, as Franklin advised, but my daughter's seriously ill, and it's no use my trying to be hearty and farty." See BRUMMEN **1**; DONNERSCHLAG; GARDINENSTANGE.

FUSEL, *m.* Hooch. *Diesen Fusel kannst du selber saufen.* "You can drink that rotgut y.s."

FUß, *m.* Foot. *Mit etwas/jmdm. auf (dem) Duzfuß stehen.* To be very familiar with s.o./s.t. (using the *du* [intimate] form). *Mit 14 Jahren stand sie schon mit dem Rauschgift auf Duzfuß.* "At 14 she was already deeply into drugs." *Mit etwas/jmdm. auf dem Kriegsfuß stehen.* To be on the outs with s.o.; to have trouble mastering s.t. (lit. to be on a war footing with s.t./s.o.). *Mit der Grammatik steht sie auf dem Kriegsfuß.* "She and grammar just don't get along."

FUTSCH. Lost; gone; busted (from Fr. *foutu*). *Futsch ist futsch und hin ist hin.* "It's lost and gone forever; no use crying over spilt milk."

FUTSCHIKATO. Slangier, pseudo It. var. of FUTSCH.

FUX = FUCHS.

FUZZI, *m., youth.* **1.** Joker. *Mit dem Fuzzi brauchst du nicht aufzukreuzen.* "Don't show up (go) with that cowboy." **2.** Nonsense. *Für heute hast du schon genug Fuzzi gesülzt.* "You've sliced enough baloney for today."

-FUZZI, *sometimes pej. youth sl. suffix for "man/guy/dude."* See KONSUMFUZZI; LERNFUZZI; PIZZAFUZZI; SPORTFUZZI; SPRACHFUZZI. Cf. colloquial -FRITZE; -HEINI.

GABEL, *f.* Fork. ***Die Gabel aus der Hand geben.*** (*Youth.*) Cf. LÖFFEL.

GALAKTISCH/GALAXOMÄßIG, *youth.* Galactic. See URST.

GALLE, *f.* Gallbladder; bile. ***Jmdm. kommt die Galle hoch.*** S.o. is infuriated. *Wenn ich an sein Verhalten denke, kommt mir die Galle hoch.* "When I think of the way he behaved, it makes my blood boil."

GAMMEL, *m.* Junk. *Was willst du mit dem ganzen Gammel?* "What do you want with all that junk?"

GAMMELDIENST, *m., mil.* Cushy assignment. *Olaf pennt mit dem Oberfeld und schiebt nur Gammeldienst.* "Olaf's sleeping with the sergeant and always gets easy duty."

GAMM(E)LIG. Decrepit; spoiled (food); old. *Schmeiß doch deine gammligen Klamotten alle raus!* "Throw out all your tattered old clothes."

GAMMEL-LOOK, *m.* Scruffy, run-down appearance. *Aber der Gammel-Look ist gerade das, was ich will.* "But it's precisely the dropout look that I want."

GAMMELN. 1. To go bad. *Der Fisch gammelt schon.* "The fish is already spoiled." **2.** To bum around. See RUMGAMMELN; VERGAMMELN.

GAMMLER, *m.* Lazy hippie; dropout. *Willst wirklich diesen Gammler heiraten?* "Do you really want to marry that shiftless guy?"

GANEFF = GANOVE.

GANG. Step; walk. See ZULEGEN.

GANOVE, *m.* Crook (from Hebr.). *Die Ganoven gingen auf Bauernfang aus, aber die pfiffigen Dorfbewohner trickstern sie aus.* "The thieves tried to make fools of the rubes, but the shrewd villagers outsmarted them."

GARDINE. See SCHWEDISCHE GARDINEN.

GARDINENPREDIGT, *f.* Scolding (lit. curtain sermon). *Wenn ich voll nach Hause komm, hält sie mir 'ne Gardinenpredigt.* "When I come home plastered, she chews me out."

GARDINENSTANGE, *f.* Curtain rod. *Hin und her rasen/sausen wie ein Furz auf der Gardinenstange.* To run around hectically (lit. to race/roar about like a fart on a curtain rod). *Brauchst nicht hin und her zu rasen wie 'n Furz auf der Gardinenstange.* "You don't have to run around like a chicken without a head."

GARTENZWERGE, *pl., youth, pej.* Police (lit. garden dwarves; colorful statues of elves are found in many Ger. gardens). *Lass dich von den Gartenzwergen nicht greifen.* "Don't let the cops get you." Cf. TANGOBRÜDER; TRACHTENGRUPPE.

GAS, *n.* Gas. *Gas geben.* To step on the gas; make an effort. *Die Schule ödete mich an, aber ich musste Gas geben, um die Versetzung zu schaffen.* "School bored me, but I had to hustle to get promoted."

GAUDEE. Aust. variant of GAUDI.

GAUDI, *f., n. S.* Pleasure (from the Lat. *gaudium,* joy). *Beim Oktoberfest auf der Wiesen, doh (da) wird's a (eine) Hetz un' a (eine) Gaudi ge'n (geben).* "During the Octoberfest on the meadow (e.g. Munich's *Theresienwiese*), everyone will have a high old time."

GAUDIWURM, *m., S.* Carnival procession. *Die Kinder folgten dem Gaudiwurm.* "The children followed the carnival procession."

GAUNER = GANOVE.

GAUNERSPRACHE = ROTWELSCH.

GEASTE, *n.* Hard work. *Immer nur Geaste!* "Always the same grind." Cf. ASTEN **2.**

GEBEN. To give. *Es (gar) nicht geben.* To be unthinkable (lit. not to exist). *Erst jetzt denkst du an diese Möglichkeit? Das gibt's (doch gar) nicht!* "Only now that possibility occurs to you? You've got to be kidding!/I don't believe it!"

GEBONGT SEIN. To have taken due note of (lit. to be rung up). *Alles klar, ist gebongt!* "OK, gotcha!/Righto!/Will do!"

GEBLUBBER = BLUBBER-BLUBBER; GELABER; GESÜLZE.

GEBÜGELT. 1. Ironed. *Gestriegelt und gebügelt.* All dressed up (lit. groomed and ironed). *Der Geck ist immer gestriegelt und gebügelt.* "That clotheshorse is always dressed to the nines." **2.** Dumbfounded. See GEPLÄTTET. **3.** Beaten up. See BÜGELN. **4.** Exhausted. *Nach der Arbeit war ich total gebügelt.* "I was all done in after work."

GEBUMSE, 1. Noise. *Lasst das Gebums!* "Quit that racket!" **2.** Sex. *Ihr Gebumse geht mich nichts an.* "Their screwing is none of my business." Cf. BUMSEN.

GEBUM(S)FIEDELT, *hum.* Honored. *Die Chefin hat mir gelächelt; da sollt ich mich vielleicht gebumsfiedelt fühlen.* "The boss smiled at me; I suppose I should feel flattered." See VERBUMFIEDELN.

GECHECKT SEIN = GEBONGT SEIN.

GECK, *m.* Dandy. *Zorro spielte den Geck.* "Zorro played the fop."

GECKO, *m., youth.* **1.** Same as GECK (lit. lizard). **2.** Clown, zany. *Was will dieser Gecko hier?* "What does that jokester want here?"

GEDÖNS, *n.* Fuss. *Warum so viel Gedöns über 'ne solche Kleinigkeit?* "Why so much fuss over such a little thing?"

GEDRÖHNE, *n.* **1.** Droning on. See GELABER. **2.** Drinking bout; drug session. *Gestern gab's das geilste aller*

Gedröhne. "Yesterday was the biggest blast ever." Cf. DRÖHNEN **2**.

GEFINKELT. 1. Sly. *Du bist ein echt gefinkelter Kerl.* "You're a real shrewdie." **2.** Nasty. *Dieser Schlaumeier hat sich wieder was ganz Gefinkeltes ausgeheckt.* "That finagler's cooked up s.t. quite nasty again."

GEGIPSE, *n.* Put-on. *'S war alles nur Gegipse.* "It was all just a put-on." Cf. GIPSEN.

GEHEN. To go. *Für einen kleinen Bengaltiger/Uralbären gehen.* To have to urinate. *Zapf mir noch 'ne Molle; ich geh für einen kleinen Uralbären.* "Draw me another beer; I've got to take a leak." *Für einen großen Bengaltiger/Uralbären gehen.* To have to defecate. *Ich kann nicht länger warten, ich muss für 'n großen Bengaltiger gehen.* "I can't wait any longer, I've got to dump." *Jmdm. geht die Kimme/Muffe/der Ofen.* See KIMME.

GEHTNICHTMEHR, *n.* Surfeit, excess. *Bis zum Gehtnichtmehr.* **1.** Ad nauseam. *Das hab ich bis zum Gehtnichtmehr erklärt.* "I've explained that till I'm blue in the face." **2.** Till one can't take it anymore. *Gestern hab ich bis zum Gehtnichtmehr geschoppt.* "I shopped till I dropped yesterday."

GEIER, *m.* Vulture. *Hol's der Geier!* Devil take it! *Hol's der Geier, jetzt muss ich's auf meine Kappe nehmen.* "Damn it! I've got to assume responsibility for it now." *Weiß der Geier!* Who in the world knows? *Wo sind sie jetzt, die alten Schulkameraden? Weiß der Geier!* "Where are they now, my old school chums? Who knows?" Cf. PLEITEGEIER.

GEIERWALLY, *f., S.* Bitch. *Lass diese Geierwally in ihren eigenen sauren Säften schmoren.* "Let that Nasty Nelly stew in her own sour juices."

GEIGEN. 1. To play the violin. *Jmdm. die Meinung geigen.* To give s.o. a piece of one's mind. *Meinem Makler hab ich die Meinung gegeigt.* "I gave my broker a piece of my mind." **2.** To have sex. *Mit ihrem Gigolo hätt ich gern gegeigt, aber sein Preis war mir zu hoch.* "I'd have loved to get it on with her gigolo, but his price was too high." Cf. ORGELN 1.

GEIL! *youth.* Fantastic!/Neat!/Mind-blowing! See GEIL 3.

GEIL. 1. Lascivious; horny. *Auf jmdn. geil sein.* To lust after s.o. *Mann, bin ich geil auf die Ute!* "Man, have I got the hots for Ute!" *Geil wie Schifferscheiße sein.* To be horny as hell (lit. as sailor shit). *Jan ist geil wie Schifferscheiße.* "Jan's a real gash hound." **2.** Luxuriant (vegetation). *Die hat einen üppigen Vorbau und 'n geilen Garten.* "She's got a lavish balcony and a luxuriant garden." See VORBAU. **3.** Terrific, wonderful. (*Youth.*) *Deine Musik find ich total geil.* "I think your music's orgasmic." Cf. ABGEILEN; ANGEILEN; AUFGEILEN.)

GEILO = GEIL.

GEIST, *m.* Spirit; intellect. *Jmdm. auf den Geist gehen.* To get on s.o.'s nerves. *Sein Gesülze ging mir gewaltig auf den Geist.* "His stupid babbling really bugged me." *Im Geist.* Mentally. *Im Geiste haben sie uns schon abgeschrieben.* "They've already made up their minds to write us off."

GEKNÜPPELT VOLL = GERAMMELT/GERAPPELT VOLL.

GELABER(E), *n.* Jabbering. *Sein Gelabere ödete mich an.* "His babbling bored me."

GEMAUSCHEL, *n.* Conniving. *Wir haben das ganze Gemauschel gleich durchschaut.* "We saw through that scheming right away." See MAUSCHELN 3.

GEPLÄTTET. Floored. *Wir waren alle total geplättet.* "We were all flabbergasted."

GERAMMELT/GERAPPELT VOLL. Jam-packed. *Die Disko war gerammelt voll.* "The disco was packed to the rafters."

GERÄT, *n., youth.* **1.** Penis (lit. appliance; device; equipment). *Mann, ist das echt 'n Gerät!* "Man, that's some tool!" **2.** Female as sex object. *Ich bin ein Mensch, eine Frau, kein Gerät.* "I'm a human being, a woman, not a piece of ass."

GERN(E). Gladly. *Der kann mich mal gern haben.* "He can go to hell."

GERNEGROß, *m.* Would-be big shot. *Du billiger kleiner Gernegroß!* "You cheap little fake!"

GESALBE, *n.* Stupid chatter. *Von eurem Gesalbe halt ich nichts.* "I have a low opinion of your foolish babbling." Cf. SALBEN.

GESCHNIEGELT UND GEBÜGELT. All spruced up. See GEBÜGELT **1.** Cf. MISTER SCHNIEGELMANN.

GESCHOSS, *n., youth.* Stunningly attractive/ugly girl (lit. projectile; missile). *Ist die aber ein scharfes Geschoss!* "Hers is a face to remember!" Cf. **GRANATENMÄßIG.**

GESCHWABBEL = **GELABERE; GESALBE; GE-SÜLZE.**

GESEICH = **GELABERE.**

GESEIER(E), *n.* **1.** Babbling. Cf. GELABERE. **2.** Whining, complaining. *Was soll das ganze Geseire?* "What's the use of all that bellyaching?"

GESÖFF, *n.* Swill; lousy beer. *Dieses Gesöff hat man nicht nach dem deutschen Reinheitsgesetz gebraut.* "This piss wasn't brewed in accordance with the German Purity Law." (A regulation, dating from 1516, that allows only hops, malt, and water for beer brewing.)

GESTELL, *n.* **1.** Skinny person (lit. rack; frame). *Sie ist nur 'n dünnes langes Gestell.* "She's a giant scarecrow, just skin and bones." **2.** Legs. *Mit 'nem solchen Gestell wirst du Karriere machen, wie die Marlene.* "With gams like that you'll go far, like Marlene."

GESÜLZE, *n.* Stupid talk, twaddle. *Hör du noch sein Gesülze an; ich hab's satt.* "You go on listening to his drivel. I've had it."

GESUNDHEITSAPOSTEL, *m.* Health nut. *Der alte Säufer ist Gesundheitsapostel geworden.* "The old drunk's turned into a health nut."

GETRIEBESCHADEN, *m.* Tick; mental defect (lit. gearbox damage/defect in the mechanism). *Mensch, hast du 'n Getriebeschaden, oder was denn?* "Have you got a screw loose, man, or what?" Cf. DACHSCHADEN; SCHALT-FEHLER.

GETÜDDEL, *n., N.* = **GESÜLZE.**

GEWÄSCH, *n.* Nonsense. *Solches Gewäsch hör ich mir nicht länger an.* "I'm not listening to garbage like that anymore."

GEWIEFT. Crafty. *Sie ist eine gewiefte Taktikerin.* "She's a shrewd tactician."

GFRAST, *n., S.* Fluff; trifle. *'S ganze Gfrast nutzt mir nix.* "All that junk's of no use to me."

GFRETT, *n., S.* Worry. *Mit dem Lausbuben hab I' schon so viel Gfrett kappt (gehabt).* "That rotten kid's given me so much grief."

GFRIEß, *n., S., pej.* Face. *Dem möcht ich ins Gfrieß spucken.* "I'd like to spit in his face."

GICKGACK, *n., youth.* Babbling, chattering. *Das Gick-gack der alten Wachteln konnte er nicht mehr ab.* "He couldn't take the old bags' cackling anymore."

GICKS. See WEDER.

GIEPER, *m., N.* Desire. **Einen Gieper auf etwas haben.** To have one's sights set on s.t. *Das Kind hatte einen Gieper auf die Puppe.* "The kid really wanted the doll."

GIEPERN, *N.* To crave. *„Gewinn eins für die Stripperin," flüsterte sie dem Fußballer. Auch er gieperte nach einem großen Sieg.* " 'Win one for the stripper,' she whispered to the soccer player. He too, hungered for a big win."

GIERLAPPEN, *m.* Money-hungry person. *Stinkreich ist er geworden, aber ein Gierlappen geblieben.* "He's become filthy rich, but still can't get enough bread." Cf. LAPPEN.

GIEßEN. To pour. **Sich einen hinter den Schlips/hinter die Binde/Krawatte/Schürze gießen.** To belt down a drink. See LAMPE.

GIEßKANNE, *m.* Penis (lit. watering can). **Sich die**

Gießkanne verbiegen/verbeulen. To contract gonorrhea (lit. to dent one's watering can). *,,Seid vorsichtig und verbeult euch die Gießkanne im Hafen nicht, Jungs!" riet der Kapitän!"* " 'Watch where you stick your wickets and don't catch the clap in port, boys,' the captain advised."

GIFTNUDEL, *f.* **1.** Cigarette (lit. poison noodle). *Schmeiß deine Giftnudeln weg und lerne richtig atmen!* "Throw away your coffin nails and learn how to breathe right!" **2.** Vituperative woman. *Seine Alte ist 'ne richtige Giftnudel.* "His wife's a real shrew."

GIFTSACK/GIFTSPRITZE = GIFTNUDEL 2.

GIFTZAHN, *m.* **1.** Fang. ***Jmdm. die Giftzähne ausbrechen.*** To draw s.o.'s fangs. *Dem hab ich die Giftzähne ausgebrochen; jetzt ist er mir hörig.* "I've drawn his fangs; now he does what I want." **2.** = GIFTNUDEL **2.**

GIGA-, *youth.* Gigantic (lit. a billion times a specific unit). *Du gigadummes Dusseltier, ich lieb dich doch.* "You dumbest of dumb jerks, I love you anyway."

GIGANTISCH, *youth.* Wonderful (lit. gigantic). *Dein neuer Megacocktail schmeckt gigantisch.* "Your new megacocktail tastes great!"

GIPSEN. To fool (lit. to apply plaster). *Der will dich nur gipsen.* "He's just putting you on."

GLATT. Complete; outright (lit. smooth). *Er sprach von ewiger Liebe und was dabei rauskam war das glatte Elend für mich.* "He talked of everlasting love, and the result was total misery for me."

GLATTEIS, *n.* Thin ice. ***Jmdn. aufs Glatteis führen.*** To dupe s.o. *Die Schauspielerin führte die Reporter aufs Glatteis.* "The actress took the reporters for a ride."

GLIMMSTENGEL, *m.* Cigarette (lit. glow stalk). *Auf dein Gelaber vom inneren ewigen Licht fahr ich nicht ab; ich brauch meine Glimmstengel.* "Your babbling about the inner, eternal light doesn't do it for me; I need my cigarettes." Cf. LUNGENFEGER.

GLOCKE, *f.* Bell. *Auf die Glocke hauen.* To beat the drum for o.s. *Urs wird nie müde auf die Glocke zu hauen.* "Urs never tires of blowing his own horn." *Die Glocke läuten hören, aber nicht wissen, wo sie hängt.* To keep on talking even when one doesn't know what one's talking about. *Du hörst die Glocke läuten, weißt aber nicht, wo sie hängt.* "You haven't got a leg to stand on, but you keep running your mouth." *Etwas an die große Glocke hängen.* To tell the whole world. *Ich bin schwanger, aber häng's nicht an die große Glocke.* "I'm pregnant, but don't broadcast it."

GLOCKEN, *pl.* Testicles (lit. bells). *Die Glocken läuten lassen* (*youth*). To get one's rocks off. *Du willst nur deine Glocken läuten lassen.* "You just want to ring your chimes."

GLOTZE, *f./***GLOTZKASTEN,** *m./***GLOTZKISTE,** *f./***GLOTZOPHON,** *n.* Television (*glotzen* = to stare at). *Er sitzt den ganzen Tag vor der Glotze.* "He sits in front of the boob tube all day."

GLÜCK AB!, *aviation.* Happy landings!

GLÜCK AUF!, *miners.* Good luck!

GLÜCKSRITTER, *m.* Adventurer; get-rich-quick schemer. *Glücksritter haben windige Termingeschäfte gemacht.* "Money hunters made shady deals in commodity futures."

GNATZ, *m.* Bad temper. *Wenn ich nicht so sanftmütig wär, könnt ich meinen Mann und seinen Gnatz nicht ertragen.* "If I didn't have such a sweet disposition, I couldn't endure my husband and his nasty nature."

GODEMICHÉ, *m., from Fr.* Dildo. *Sie hat 'ne reiche Auswahl an Godemichés in verschiedenen Grössen und Farben.* "She has a large selection of dildos in various sizes and colors."

GODERL, *n., Aust.* Diminutive of *Goder* (double chin). *Jmdm. das Goderl kratzen.* To soft-soap s.o. *Sie weiß, ihm das Goderl zu kratzen, wenn sie etwas will.* "She

105

knows how to butter him up when she wants s.t."

GOF, *m., n., Swiss.* Nasty brat. *Ihrem Gof gehört der Arsch versohlt.* "Their brat deserves a good hiding."

GO-IN, *n., invented Eng.* Planned disruption of an assembly. *Sie half mir das Go-in zu veranstalten.* "She helped me to organize the protest."

GONZO, *m., from It.* Slightly crazy guy. *Was will der Gonzo wieder?* "What's that zany want now?"

GÖR, *n., N.* Kid (of either gender); brat. *Im Flughafen hatte ich die Hände voll mit den Gören.* "I had my hands full with the kids in the airport terminal."

GÖRE, *f.* Little girl. *Die Göre wird die Macker einst verrückt machen.* "Some day that little girl will drive the guys crazy."

GORILLAMÄßIG = **ELEFANTÖS; KROKOFANTÖS.**

GOSCHE, *f., S.* Mouth. *Hal' (halte) dei' dumme Gosch'.* "Shut your stupid trap."

GÖTZ!/GÖTZ VON BERLICHINGEN!/(DAS) GÖTZZITAT. The hell with you! You can kiss my ass!/Damn you! *Jmdn. mit Götz/Götz von Berlichingen/dem Götzzitat beschimpfen.* To use profanity to s.o. *Sie hätten ihn aber nicht gleich mit Götz von Berlichingen beschimpfen sollen.* "You didn't have to lay obscenities on him right away." Cf. POTZ.

GRABBELHEINI, *m.* Guy who paws women. *Tanz du mit dem Grabbelheini; ich hab's satt.* "You dance with that groper; I've had enough."

GRABBELN, *N.* **1.** To grope; rummage. *Auf dem Grabbeltisch gab's nichts Interessantes mehr zu grabbeln.* "There was nothing interesting worth rummaging for on the cheap goods counter." **2.** To come on to; to chatter; pester with chatter (*youth*). *Das ganze Grabbeln nutzt doch nichts.* "What good's all that hot air?"

GRABSCHE, *f.* Hand. *Wasch deine Grabschen, dann komm*

massier und schmier mich gut ein! "Wash your paws and then come give me a good massage and greasing up."

GRABSCHEN/GRAPSCHEN. To grab; hold. *Ich möchte dich grapschen und küssen.* "I'd like to take hold of you and kiss you."

GRANADA, *f., Aust., youth.* Fight (prob. from GRANATE; poss. infl. of US milit. action in Grenada in 1983). *Die Skins haben wieder Granada gespielt.* "The skinheads were brawling again."

GRANATE, *f.* Grenade; shell. *Voll wie eine Granate.* Roaring drunk. *Der war voll wie 'ne Granate.* "He was smashed out of his mind."

GRANATENMÄSSIG. Sensational. *Wo sie auch hingeht, schlägt die scharfe Lola granatenmäßig ein.* "Wherever bombshell Lola goes, she makes a tremendous impression."

GRANATENVOLL. Thoroughly plastered. *Die waren alle granatenvoll.* "They were all smashed." See VOLL **2.**

GRANT, *m., S.* Ill humor. *Ich merkte ihm sofort seinen Grant an.* "I could see right away he was in a bad mood."

GRANTIG, *S.* Irritable. *Nur nicht so grantig!* "Just don't be so touchy!"

GRAPSCHER, *m.* Masher. *Während der Stoßzeit werden die Grapscher in der U-Bahn sehr aktiv.* "The subway mashers are very active during rush hour."

GRAPSEN, *Aust.* To steal. *Oliver und die anderen Buben grapsten, was sie konnten.* "Oliver and the other boys pinched what they could."

GRASS, *n.* Marijuana. (From Eng. and pronounced as in Eng.). *Auf einer Insel in der Karibik wollte er sich viel Grass kaufen.* "He wanted to buy lots of grass on an island in the Caribbean."

GRÄTSCHE, *m.* Straddling. *Die große Grätsche machen.* To die. *Der Neffe wartet darauf, dass der Alte die große Grätsche macht.* "The old man's nephew is waiting for him to kick the bucket."

GREIFER, *m.* Shoplifter. *Eine Bande Greifer arbeitet für Hedi.* "A gang of shoplifters works for Hedi."

GREIFTRUPP, *m.* Riot squad; police in general. *Sie wurden fast alle von der Greiftrupp geschnappt.* "The cops nabbed most of them."

GREINEN, *N.* Whining. *Sein boshaftes Grienen ist mir lieber als sein Greinen.* "His malicious grinning is easier to take than his whining."

GRELL, *youth.* **1.** Outstanding (lit. glaring; gaudy; shrill). *Die Band ist die grellste.* "That band's the most fabulous." **2.** Very unpleasant. *'S war 'n voll greller Film.* "It was a really horrible movie."

GRETCHENFRAGE, *f.* Crucial question (Gretchen to Faust: "How do you feel about religion?"). *Ob die neuen Maßnahmen greifen, das ist die Gretchenfrage.* "Will the new measures be effective? That's the $64,000 question."

GRIFF, *m.* Grip, grasp. ***In den Griff kriegen/Im Griff haben.*** To get/have under control. *Wann kriegst du den Umgang mit dem Computer in den Griff?* "When are you going to get a handle on the computer?" ***Ein Griff in die Kasse tun.*** To steal from the cash register. *Einer von euch hat einen Griff in die Kasse getan.* "One of you has been dipping into the till." ***Ein Griff ins Klo.*** Failure; wasted effort (lit. reaching into the toilet). *Wir haben ihn verklagt; 's war aber nur 'n Griff ins Klo.* "We sued him, but the suit went down the toilet." ***Griffe kloppen/klopfen.*** To do rifle practice. *Lange hab ich Griffe gekloppt, hab aber nie ins Schwarze getroffen.* "I did lots of rifle practice but never hit a bull's eye."

GRIFFEL, *m.* Finger (lit. slate pencil). *Griffel weg!* "Keep your paws off!"

GRIFFELN, *youth.* **1.** To grab; toss. *Griffel mir 'n paar Hugos rüber.* "Hand/toss me a few cigarettes." **2.** To be grasping/greedy. *Kohle kann er nie genug griffeln.* "He's always anxious to get his hands on money."

GRINGO, *m., youth.* Greenhorn. (Said to come from Sp.,

though not so used in Sp.) *Die alte Fregatte ist echt geil auf Gringos.* "The old bag's really horny for callow youth." See GRÜNSCHNABEL; GRÜNZEUG.

GRIPS, *m.* Common sense; savvy. *Streng doch mal deinen Grips an!* "Come on, use your noodle now!"

GRÖFAZ, *hum.* Big chief. *Ich lass ihn den Gröfaz spielen.* "I let him play the big cheese."

GROOVE, *m., youth.* Groove; pleasing, easy rhythm. ("Groovy" and "in the groove" are dated in Eng., but not in Ger. sl. "Groove" is rel. to "grave." "Digging" [music, etc.], and finding "groovy," are lively activities and prob. derive from grooves on a record that enthusiasts "dig" into and play repeatedly. Cf. RILLE [groove of a record]. *Grooven* [to groove] and *groovig* also exist.) *Diese Band machte einst einen groovigen Sound aber jetzt spür ich den Groove nicht mehr.* "That band used to make a groovy sound, but now I don't feel the beat anymore." Cf. RILLE.

GROßKOTZ = **PROTZ,** but coarser.

GRUFTI, *m., f., youth.* 1. Old (over 30) person (*Gruft* = crypt; grave). *Meine Fossilien und ihre Freunde sind alle echte Gruftis.* "My parents and all their friends are ready for the glue factory." Cf. KOMPOSTI; VORGRUFTI. 2. Devil worshipper. *Diese Gruftis sollen tolle Zombies geschaffen haben.* "They say those Satanists have created some terrific zombies."

GRUFTIG, *youth.* Ancient. *Sie hören noch gerne die gruftigen Schlager der Sechziger.* "They still enjoy listening to the prehistoric hit tunes of the sixties."

GRUNDEIS, *n.* Thin/ground ice. ***Jmdm. geht der Arsch mit Grundeis/auf Grundeis.*** To be scared shitless. *Deine Protzereien nützen mir nichts; dir wird dabei nur der Arsch auf Grundeis gehen.* "Your boasting's no use to me; you'll just shit your pants." ***Mit den Zotten auf Grundeis sein.*** See ZOTTEN.

GRUNDI, *f.* Basic training (from *Grundausbildung*). *Nach der Grundi war ich echt ausgepowert.* "After basic training I was really wasted."

GRÜNE TRUPPE = **GRÜNSCHNÄBEL.**

GRÜNSCHNABEL, *n.* Greenhorn (lit. green beak). *Viellicht weiß doch der Grünschnabel besser als du.* "Maybe that young whippersnapper knows better than you."

GRÜNSCHNÄBEL, *pl., youth.* Police. (Ger. police wear green uniforms. Cf. BLAUMÄNNER.) *Die Grünschnäbel kamen angetanzt.* "The greenies showed up."

GRÜNZEUG, *n., youth.* Juvenile(s) (lit. green vegetables). *Du gehst mir tierisch auf den Keks, du Grünzeug.* "You really bug me, you twirp." Cf. BONSAI; FRISCHLING; JUNGGEMÜSE.

GRUSICAL, *n.* Comic/inept horror film. *Der Gruselfilm war eher ein Grusical; die vermeintlichen Ungeheuer waren nur blöde Fieslinge.* "The horror film was more like a comic routine; the supposed monsters were merely stupid creeps."

GRÜTZE, *f.* Groats. ***Grütze im Kopf haben.*** To be brainy. *Urs hat keine Grütze im Kopf.* "Urs hasn't got a brain in his head."

GSCHAFTLHUBER, *m., Aust.* Busybody. *Dieser Gschaftlhuber tät besser, sich um seine eigenen Sachen zu kümmern.* "That busybody would do better to look after his own affairs."

GSCHAMIG, *Aust.* Shy. *Mei' Gspusi is' a bisserl (ein bisschen) gschamig.* "My boyfriend's a bit bashful."

GSCHERT, *S.* Rude; stupid. *Bist immer so gschert?* "Are you always so uncouth?"

GSCHNAS/GSCHNASFEST, *n., Aust.* Costume party. *Beim Gschnas hat Eisenstein seine eigene Frau net (nicht) erkannt.* "Eisenstein didn't recognize his own wife at the masked ball."

GSPAßIG, *S.* Amusing. *Gspaßig wird's sein.* "It'll be lots of fun."

GSPUSI, *n., Aust.* (from It. *sposa/sposo,* bride/bridegroom, and Ger. *Gespons,* still used hum. for spouse). **1.** Love affair. *Was wär das Leben ohne a (ein) Gspusi un' a (einen) Wein?* "What would life be without love and wine?" **2.** Lover; sweetheart. *Die braucht jed's Jahr a (ein) neues Gspusi.* "She needs a new lover every year."

GUCKEN. To look. ***Dumm aus dem Anzug/aus der Wäsche gucken.*** To look dumbfounded. *Tu doch was, statt dazustehen und dumm aus der Wäsche zu gucken.* "Do s.t. instead of standing there like a dumb jerk."

GUCKER, *pl.* Eyes. *Öffne die Gucker weit!* "Peel your peepers now!"

GÜLLEHÜLLE, *f.* Condom (lit. liquid-manure fertilizer wrapper). *Vergiss die Güllehüllen nicht!* "Don't forget the scumbags."

GUMMI, *m.* Condom (lit. rubber). *Nur ein Dummi macht ohne Gummi.* "Only a dummy does it without a rubber."

GUMMIADLER, *m., hum.* Tough roast chicken (lit. rubber eagle). *Vielleicht hilft ein bisschen Ketschup diesem Gummiadler.* "Maybe a little ketchup'll help this rubbery chicken."

GUMMIHANDSCHUH, *m.* Condom (lit. rubber glove). *Er hat mich zuerst mit Glacéhandschuhen behandelt; wollte aber spater keinen Gummihandschuh benutzen.* "He treated me with kid gloves at first, but later didn't want to use a rubber."

GUMMILUTSCHER, *m.* Condom (lit. rubber lollipop; baby pacifier). *Die Nutte bewahrt die Gummilutscher für Kunden mit besonderen Geschmacksrichtungen.* "That whore saves the rubbers for customers with particular tastes."

GUMMIMANTEL, *m.* Condom (lit. rubber overcoat). *Ohne Gummimantel mach ich's nicht.* "I won't do it without a rubber."

GUMMIRÖHRCHEN, *n.* Condom (lit. little rubber pipe). *Zieh dir doch schnell 'n Gummiröhrchen rüber!* "Put on a rubber fast now."

GUMMIZELLE, *f., youth.* Gym (lit. padded cell). *Die Gummizelle hass ich.* "I hate gym."

GUNSTGEWERBE, *n., hum.* Prostitution (lit. trade in favors). *Für einige hat auch das Gunstgewerbe goldenen Boden.* "For some, hooking is a very profitable trade." Cf. HANDWERK . . . BODEN.

GUNSTGEWERBLERIN, *f.* Prostitute. *Auch die Gunstgewerblerinnen verlangen jetzt ihre sozialen Rechte vom Staat.* "Those practicing the world's oldest profession are now also asking for social benefits from the state."

GURGEL, *f.* Throat, gullet. **Sein ganzes Geld durch die Gurgel jagen.** To squander all one's money on drinking. *Meine Alten jagen ihr ganzes Geld durch die Gurgel; mir wird nichts bleiben.* "My parents blow all their money on booze; there won't be anything for me." **Sich die Gurgel schmieren/ölen.** To drink alcohol. *Der Pfarrer schmiert sich gern die Gurgel.* "The pastor likes to wet his whistle."

GURKE, *f.* **1.** Big nose (lit. cucumber). *Sein Bruder hat 'ne noch größere Gurke.* "His brother's got an even bigger schnoz." **2.** Old car. *Er will die Gurke doch reparieren lassen.* "He wants to have that beat-up old jalopy repaired after all." **3.** Penis. See GURKENFOLIE.

GURKEN. To drive slowly. *Opa gurkt noch 'n bisschen durch die Gegend.* "Grandpa still drives around a little."

GURKENFOLIE/GURKENGUMMI/GURKENTÜTE, *f.* Condom (lit. cucumber wrapper). *Ohne Gurkenfolie gibt's gar nichts bei mir.* "Nothing doing without a rubber."

GURTMUFFEL, *m.* Person who doesn't wear/won't wear a seat belt. *Pass auf, dass du nicht erwischt wirst, du Gurtmuffel.* "Watch out they don't catch you, you seat belt hater."

GUSCHE = GOSCHE.

GV. *Geschlechtsverkehr,* sexual intercourse. *Nur GV und sonst nichts will er.* "All he wants is sex."

HAAR, *n.* Hair. ***Jmdm. aufs Haar gleichen.*** To resemble closely. *Sie gleichen sich aufs Haar.* "They're the spitting image of each other." ***Sich in die Haare kriegen/geraten.*** To quarrel. *Die Partner kriegen sich oft in die Haare.* "The partners often get into each other's hair." ***Sich in den Haaren liegen.*** To be at odds with. *Seit langem liegen sie sich in den Haaren.* "They've been at loggerheads for some time."

HABERN, *Aust.* To eat. *Wir haben nix zu habern kappt (gehabt).* "We had nothing to eat."

HACKE, *f., Aust.* Work (lit. garden hoe; axe). *Endlose Hacke und sonst nix.* "Nothing but an endless grind."

HACKE, *f.*/**HACKEN,** *m.* Heel. ***Einen am/im Hacken haben.*** To be drunk. *Zackig wollte er die Hacken zusammenklappen, allein er hatte einen im Hacken und konnte nicht.* "He wanted to click his heels snappily but couldn't, because he'd tied one on."

HACKEN. 1. To chop. ***Holz auf sich hacken lassen.*** To be long suffering. *Lange ließ er Holz auf sich hacken, aber endlich krümmte sich der Wurm.* "He put up with an awful lot, but finally the worm turned." **2.** To do computer hacking; play electronic games. *Er denkt nur ans Hacken und Surfen im Internet.* "All he thinks about is hacking and surfing the Internet."

HAHN, *m.* Rooster. ***Nach etwas/jmdm. kräht kein Hahn.***

No one gives a hoot about s.t./s.o. *Der Alte schreibt seine Memoiren, aber danach kräht kein Hahn.* "The old man's writing his memoirs, but no one cares." **Wenn der Hahn kräht auf dem Mist, ändert sich das Wetter, oder es bleibt, wie es ist.** (*Prov.*) When the cock crows on dung, the weather will change or stay the same. **Vom Hahn beflattert/betrampelt sein.** To be crazy (lit. fluttered/trampled on by the rooster). *Fallschirmspringen und Bungeejumping in deinem Alter? Bist wohl vom Hahn beflattert!* "Parachuting and bungee jumping at your age? You're batty!"

HAHNEMANN = HANNEMANN.

HALLÖCHEN! "Hi there!"

HALODRI, *m., S.* Boisterous party goer; jerk. *Alle wissen, dass er ein Halodri ist, glauben aber, dass er seinen Job gut macht.* "Everybody knows he's a good-time Charlie, but they believe he does his job well."

HAMMEL, *m.* Oaf (lit. castrated ram; mutton). *Warum hat sie diesen Hammel geheiratet?* "Why'd she marry that mutton head?"

HAMMELBEINE, *pl.* Ram's legs. **Jmdm. die Hammelbeine langziehen.** To bawl s.o. out; discipline. *Einige machten ein Arbeiterdenkmal und der Vorarbeiter musste ihnen die Hammelbeine langziehen.* "Some workers were goofing off, and the foreman had to tell them to shape up." **An/bei den Hammelbeinen kriegen/nehmen.** To censure severely. *Wenn Mutti uns erwischt, wird sie uns ganz schön an den Hammelbeinen kriegen.* "If Mom catches us, she'll give us a real chewing out."

HAMMER, *m.* **1.** Hammer. **Ein Hammer sein.** To be overwhelmingly horrible or wonderful. *Die beiden haben ihre Schulkameraden abgeknallt. Das war ein Hammer!* "The two of them gunned down their classmates. That was a bombshell!" **Einen Hammer haben.** To be off one's rocker. Cf. BEHÄMMERT; BEKLOPPT. *Dass sie an Thor und Schango glaubt, heißt keineswegs, dass sie einen Hammer hat.* "Her belief in Thor and Shango certainly doesn't mean she's crazy." **2.** Bad error. *Mach nicht so viele Hammer das nächste Mal!* "Don't make so many bloopers/boners next time."

HAND, *f.* Hand. ***Jmdm. die Hände schmieren/versilbern.*** To bribe s.o. *Der Bürgermeister hat sich vom Baulöwen die Hände schmieren lassen.* "The real estate speculator greased the mayor's palm." See BESSER; HINTER HAND; VORBEREITEN.

HANDWERK HAT GOLDENEN BODEN, *prov.* Learn a trade and your future's made. *Vergiss die Malerei, und alle brotlosen Künste; Handwerk hat goldenen Boden.* "Don't become a starving artist; learn a trade and you'll have a solid future."

HANDY, *n.* Cellular telephone. *Viele wichtigtuerische Arschlöcher saßen mit ihren Handys im Restaurant und wir wurden oft gestört.* "Many self-important assholes sat there in the restaurant with their cell phones, and we were often disturbed."

HÄNGER, *m., youth.* **1.** Lazybones (lit. loose-fitting coat). *Du solltest dir andere Freunde aussuchen, statt dieser Hänger.* "You should choose other friends instead of those layabouts." **2.** Exhaustion; blackout. *Ich hab 'n tierischen Hänger, bin voll ausgepowert.* "I'm really down, totally played out." See DURCHHÄNGER. **3.** Bore, wimp. *Lad solche Hänger nie wieder ein.* "Don't invite deadbeats like that again."

HÄNGER, *m., pl.* Pendulous breasts. *Solche Hänger passen in keinen BH.* "Deep-dropping knockers like that won't fit into any bra."

HÄNGOLIN, *n., hum.* Substance alleged to diminish sex drive. *Im Internat glaubten wir alle, es gab Hängolin im Essen. Aber wenn ja, nutzte es gar nichts.* "In boarding school we all believed there was limp-dick-powder (saltpeter) in the food. But if so, it was totally useless."

HANNEMANN GEH DU VORAN. You'd better go first! After you, Alphonse."

HANS NARR/HANS TAPS/HANS WURST, *m.* Fool; oaf (from a stock figure in old comedies). *Du bist 'n richtiger Hans Taps.* "You're a real dumb jerk."

HAPPY END/HAPPYEND, *n.* Happy ending. *Er liebt nur Filme mit Happyend.* "He just likes movies with a happy ending."

HÄRTEPREIS, *m., youth.* Exorbitant price. *Karten fürs Konzert sind nur zu Härtepreisen zu haben.* "Tickets for the concert are available only from scalpers."

HASCH, *n.* Hashish. *Hier hast du Hasch vom Feinsten.* "Here's top-quality hash for you."

HÄSCHEN, *n.* Bunny. See HASE 2.

HASCHEN. 1. To catch. *„Hasch mich, ich bin der Frühling," rief die alte Fregatte.* " 'I'm all yours,' cried the dolled-up old bag." **2.** To smoke hashish. *Man hat uns beim Haschen in der Disko erwischt.* "They caught us smoking hash in the disco."

HASCHER, *m.* Hashish smoker. *Meine Schwester ist Hascherin.* "My sister's into hash."

HASCHERL, *n., S.* Pitiable creature. *Das arme Hascherl tat mir leid.* "I felt sorry for the poor thing."

HASE, *m.* **1.** Rabbit. *Wissen wie der Hase läuft.* To know which way the wind is blowing. *Nimm dich in Acht, du weißt ja, wie hier der Hase läuft.* "Watch out, you know which way the wind is blowing here." **2.** Attractive girl. *Auf Hasenjagd(Häschenjagd)/aufs Hasenjagen (Häschenjagen) gehen.* To set out to pick up girls (lit. to go rabbit hunting). *Bei so vielen flotten Häschen in der Stadt, war das Hasenjagen ein Klacks.* "What with so many nifty numbers in that town, picking up chicks was a cinch."

HASENREIN = ASTREIN.

HAUBITZE, *f.* Howitzer. See VOLL **2.** Cf. GRANATENVOLL.

HAUEN. To beat; hit. *Jmdn. vom Stuhl/Hocker hauen.* To knock s.o. for a loop. *Der Geizhals lud mich ein und* *bezahlte alles—das haute mich vom Hocker.* "That skin-flint invited me and paid for everything. I was flabbergasted." **Sich ins Bett hauen.** To hit the hay. *Ich muss mich unbedingt ins Bett hauen.* "I've got to get some shut-eye." See ABHAUEN; HINHAUEN; UMHAUEN.

HAUSDRACHEN, *m.* Nasty woman. *Der Hausdrachen von nebenan schimpft immer auf unsere laute Mucke.* "The battle-ax next door is always complaining about our loud music."

HAUSDRACHEN, *pl., youth.* Parents (lit. house dragons). *Oft denk ich, 's wär total turbogeil, meine Hausdrachen zu killen.* "Sometimes I think it'd be mind-blowing to kill my parents."

HAUSMANN, *m.* Husband who does the housework (newly coined counterpart of the classic *Hausfrau*). *„Mit Babywickeln, Kochen, Staubsaugen, und dergleichen bin ich fix und fertig," klagte der Hausmann.* " 'What with changing diapers, cooking, vacuuming and such, I'm all done in,' complained the househusband."

HAUSSEGEN, *m.* House blessing. **Der Haussegen hängt schief.** Household relations are strained (lit. the house blessing sign is hanging crooked). *Bei ihnen hängt der Haussegen schief.* "Relations are strained between them."

HAUT. Skin. **Unter die Haut gehen/dringen.** To be moved by (lit. to go under the skin). *Ihre rührende Geschichte ging uns wirklich unter die Haut.* "Her touching story really got to us."

HAXE, *f., S.* Foot; leg (lit. animal's leg/joint). *Haxen abkratzen!* "Wipe your feet!"

HEIL! Hail! See BERG HEIL!; PETRI HEIL!; SKI HEIL!; WEIDMANNSHEIL!

HEINI, *m.* **1.** A diminutive of Heinrich (Henry). **2.** Guy, dude (sometimes pej.). *Was will dieser Heini?* "What does that guy want?" **3.** Simpleton. *Dieser Heini ist zu nichts nutzi.* "That nerd's no good for anything." Cf. FRITZE.

-HEINI. Sometimes pej. suffix for guy/dude. See SPEKU-LANTENHEINI; VERSICHERUNGSHEINI.

HEINZELMÄNNCHEN, *n.* Household appliance; robot programmed to do housework (lit. "brownie [benevolent household sprite]"; *Hein* is rel. to *Heim* [home]. *Von wegen Heinzelmännchen, ich hab immer weniger Zeit!* "What do you mean, helpful appliances! I've got less and less time." Cf. KLABAUTERMANN.

HEIßE MÜHLE, *youth* = **HEIßER OFEN.**

HEIßER OFEN, *youth.* **1.** Fast set of wheels, motorbike, souped-up car (lit. hot oven). *Turbogeil dein heißer Ofen!* "Your bike's superfantastic!" Cf. WARMWASSERGEIGE. **2.** Sexy girl. *Dein Zierfisch ist kein heißer Ofen.* "Your coy girlfriend's no hot number."

HEIßER REIFEN/HEIßES SCHIFF = **HEIßER OFEN.**

HEIZEN, *youth.* To speed (lit. to heat). *Die Rocker heizten durchs Dorf.* "The rockers hot-rodded through the village."

(ETWAS) HERAUSHABEN/DEN BOGEN HERAUSHABEN. To have gotten the hang of s.t. *Jetzt hab ich's endlich heraus, wie ich mit dem Computer umgehen soll.* "I've finally gotten the hang of the computer." Cf. MASCHE **2.**

HERAUSMOGELN. See RAUSMOGELN.

(SICH) HERAUSPUTZEN. To get all dolled up. *Für ihn hab ich mich 'n bisschen herausgeputzt.* "I got a bit dressed up for him."

HERUMFOTZEN. To fumble. *Hör doch auf herumzufotzen und hilf mir!* "Quit putzing around and help me!"

HERUMKASPERN. To play the fool. *Hör doch auf herumzukaspern!* "Quit your stupid clowning."

HERUNTERPUTZEN = **RUNTERPUTZEN.**

HETZ, *f., S.* Laugh. *War dös (das) aber eine Hetz!* "Boy, was that fun!"

HEULPETER, *m.* Crybaby. *Sei doch kein Heulpeter!* "Don't be such a crybaby." Cf. WINSELTÜTE.

HEULSUSE, *f.* Crybaby. *Die Schauspielerin wird von der Kritik als Heulsuse abgetan.* "The critics dismiss that actress as a tearful type."

HEY! = **EY!**

HIGH/HIGHLIGER GEIST, *youth.* High; high spirits (lit. Holy Ghost). *High sein, highliger Geist und die ganze Bandbreite aller Geister törnen uns an.* "Getting high and the whole range of spirits are a turn-on for us."

HIMMEL, ARSCH UND WOLKENBRUCH! Goddamn it! (lit. Heaven, ass, and cloudburst!). *Himmel, Arsch und Wolkenbruch, der Typ kotzt mich an!* "Damn it to hell, that guy disgusts me!"

HIMMEL, ARSCH UND ZWIRN! Goddamn it! (lit. Heaven, ass, and yarn!). *Himmel, Arsch und Zwirn, der Wagen springt nicht an!* "Goddamn it, the car won't start!"

HIMMEL, SACK, ZEMENT! Damn it! *Himmel, Sack, Zement, fahr doch endlich los!* "For God's sake, get started, will you!"

(SICH) HINHAUEN. To hit the hay. *Ich muss mich hinhauen oder ich fall um.* "I've got to hit the hay or I'll collapse."

HINKELN. To work very hard. *Die Götter gaben diesen Völkern die Kraft und den Glauben, Hinkelsteine zu versetzen, aber Hinkeln ist nicht meine Sache.* "The Gods gave those people the strength and faith to move menhirs; but slaving away isn't my thing."

HINSCHMEIßEN. 1. To throw away; chuck it all. *Das Studium hat er hingeschmissen.* "He gave up his studies." **2.** To pay. *Schmeiß mal die Fuffis/Hündis hin!* "Come on, out with the dough!"

HINSPUCKEN. See WO MAN HINSPUCKT.

HINTER VORGEHALTENER HAND. Behind the scenes. *Hinter vorgehaltener Hand sagen einige, er sollte sich zurückziehen.* "Off the record, some are saying he should retire."

HINTERHERTRÖDELN. To lag behind; dawdle. *Mein Bruder trödelt immer hinterher.* "My brother always lags behind."

HINTERN, *n.* Behind. ***Hummeln/Pfeffer im/unterm Hintern haben.*** To have ants in one's pants (lit. to have bumblebees/pepper in/under one's buttocks). *Hast heiße Höschen oder nur Hummeln unterm Hintern?* "Have you got hot pants, or are you just fidgety by nature?" ***Mit dem Hintern nicht aus dem Bett können.*** To have trouble getting up. *Morgens kann er nicht mit dem Hintern aus dem Bett.* "He has trouble getting his ass in gear in the morning." ***Sich etwas/nichts an den Hintern zu hängen haben.*** To have s.t./nothing to wear. *Sie sagt, sie hätte sich nichts an den Hintern zu hängen, hat aber 'nen Schrank voll Klamotten.* "She says she hasn't got a thing to wear, but she's got a closet full of clothes." ***Auf den Hintern setzen.*** To be bowled over. *Du wirst dich auf den Hintern setzen, wenn du die Wahrheit erfährst.* "You'll be floored when you learn the truth." See ABWISCHEN; BEIßEN; KRIECHEN; NACKT; TRETEN. Cf. ARSCH.

HIPPE, *f.* Nasty woman (from a dialect word for she-goat. Cf. ZIEGE). *Seine Frau ist 'ne richtige Xanthippe, 'ne Hippe.* "His wife's a real shrew, a bitch."

HIRNAMPUTIERT. Really stupid (lit. brain-amputated). *Du hirnamputierter Schwachkopf!* "You brain-damaged retard!"

HIRNI, *m., youth.* **1.** Brainy, antisocial person. **2.** Dummy. **3.** Killjoy. *Hirnis wie du verstehen keinen Spaß.* "Eggheads/jerks/wet blankets like you have no sense of humor."

HIRNVERBRANNT. Scatterbrained (lit. "brain-burned"). *So was Hirnverbranntes hab ich nie gehört.* "I've never heard anything so screwy."

HIWI, *m., f.* Lab/library/departmental assistant. *Ohne die Hiwis wäre die Arbeit nicht zustande gekommen.* "Without the assistants the work would never have been created."

HOBEL, *m.* **1.** Plane; vegetable cutter. ***Seinen Hobel ausklopfen.*** To retire; die (lit. to shake out [the sawdust from] one's plane). *Wenn's so weit ist, klopf ich meinen Hobel aus und sag der Welt Ade.* "When it's time, I'll hang up my boxing gloves and say good-bye to the world." **2.** Anus. ***Jmdm. am Hobel blasen können/den Hobel blasen.*** To kiss s.o.'s ass. *Ich soll's bezahlen? Ihr könnt mir am Hobel blasen.* "I should pay for it? You can kiss my ass." **3.** Wonderful car/vehicle (*youth*). *Für so 'n Hobel würde ich alles tun.* "For a sensational set o' wheels like that, I'd do anything."

HOBELN. 1. To plane; to work hard. ***Wo gehobelt wird, da fliegen auch Späne.*** (*Prov.*) You can't make an omelette without breaking eggs (lit. planing makes wood shavings fly). **2.** To speed/go for a fast turn in a car/motorcycle. *Willst mit mir 'n bisschen durch die Gegend hobeln?* "Want to go out for a spin with me?"

HOCH. High. ***Jmdn. hoch bringen.*** To infuriate s.o. *Du freust dich, mich hoch zu bringen.* "You enjoy infuriating me." ***Einen hoch haben.*** To have an erection. *Er hatte immer wieder einen hoch. Hoch die Liebe! Hoch das Leben!* "He got it up again and again. Hurray for love and life!" Cf. STEHEN. ***Einen hoch bringen.*** To get an erection. *Jetzt bringt er keinen mehr hoch.* "He never gets it up anymore now."

HOCH DIE GLÄSER!/HOCH DIE TASSEN! "Bottoms up!"

HOCHDEUTSCH MIT STREIFEN. Imperfect Ger. (lit. High Ger. with streaks). *Sie schnackt lieber Platt und spricht so ein Hochdeutsch mit Streifen.* "She speaks flawed High Ger. and would rather use Low Ger."

HOCHPÄPPELN = **AUFPÄPPELN.**

HOCHPOKERN. To take a great risk. *Sie hat hochgepokert und gewonnen.* "She took quite a risk, and won."

HOCHPROZENTIGES, *n.* Hard liquor. *Möchten Sie Wasser, Wein oder Hochprozentiges?* "Do you want water, wine, or s.t. stronger?"

HOCHTOUR, *f.* Full capacity/speed. ***Jmdn. auf Hochtouren bringen.*** To get s.o. going. *Man gab dem Jazzer immer mehr Schnaps, um ihn auf Hochtouren zu bringen.* "They gave the jazz musician more and more booze to get him going."

HOCKER, *m.* Stool. See HAUEN; LOCKER.

HOF, *m.* Court; courtyard; barnyard. ***Vom Hof reiten.*** To scram. *Ich wollte nur vom Hof reiten.* "I just wanted to blow that hole."

HOHL, *pej., youth.* Boring; stupid; passé (lit. hollow, empty). *Die Pennbude find ich total hohl.* "I find school totally stupid." ***Hohl drehen.*** To freak out. *Er hatte 'ne totale Dröhnung und drehte hohl.* "He was really stoned and flipped out."

HOLEN. See RUNTERHOLEN.

HOLTERDIPOLTER. Helter-skelter. *,,Holterdipolter,'' schrieben die Kultkiller.* " 'Helter-skelter,' wrote the cult killers."

HOLZ, *n.* Wood. ***Holz vor der Hütte/Tür/Herberge haben.*** To have big breasts (lit. to have wood [stacked up] in front of the cabin/door/hostel). *Mensch, hat die Holz vor der Hütte!* "Man, is she stacked!" Cf. LUNGENFLÜGEL; MÖPSE; VORBAU; VORSTEVEN. ***Holz in den Wald tragen.*** To carry coals to Newcastle. *Stäbchen nach Schanghai schicken, hieße Holz in den Wald tragen.* "Sending chopsticks to Shanghai would be like carrying coals to Newcastle." Cf. EULE **1.** See HACKEN **1.**

HOLZAUGE, *n.* Wooden eye. ***Holzauge, sei wachsam!*** Keep your eyes peeled!/Be careful, you battered old thing!

HONIGPUPPE = **ZUCKERPUPPE.**

HOOL/HOOLIGAN, *m.* Hooligan. *Nicht alle Schlachtenbummler sind Hools.* "Not all traveling sports fans are hooligans."

HOPFEN, *m.* Hops. ***An/bei jmdm. ist Hopfen und Malz ver-***

loren. S.o. is past helping (lit. hops and malt are lost on s.o.). *Urs ist wieder durchgefallen; bei ihm ist Hopfen und Malz verloren.* "Urs has failed again; he's a hopeless case."

HOPPNEHMEN. To arrest. *Man hat sie alle hoppgenommen.* "They all got busted."

HOPSGEHEN. 1. To lose. *Ihm ist wieder sein Regenschirm hopsgegangen.* "He's lost his umbrella again." **2.** To die. *Die Kumpels sind alle im Scheißkrieg hopsgegangen.* "All my buddies bought it in that damned war."

HOPSNEHMEN = **HOPPNEHMEN.**

HÖREN. To hear. ***Wer nicht hört, muss fühlen.*** (*Prov.*) Those who won't listen to reason, need to have it spelled out on their hide.

HÖRIG. Sexually dependent. *Ich war ihm lange hörig.* "I was his sex slave for some time."

HORROR, *m., youth.* Horror. *Allein mit ihm, 's war der totale Horror! Nur dran denken bekomm ich einen Horror!* "Being alone with him was absolute horror. Just thinking of it makes me shudder!" (Note uses with articles.)

HOSE, *f.* Pants. ***In die Hose gehen.*** To go down the drain (lit. go into the pants). *Die ganze Arbeit ist in die Hose gegangen.* "All the work's in the toilet." ***Die Hosen (gestrichen) voll haben.*** To be very afraid. *Du hattest die Hosen voll.* "You were scared shitless." See RUNTER-LASSEN; STRAMM; TOTE HOSE.

HOSENBODEN. See STRAMM.

HOSENMATZ, *m.* Tiny tot/lad. *Du kleiner Hosenmatz, gib Oma noch 'n Küsschen!* "You little darling, give granny another little kiss."

HOSENSCHEIßER, *f.* Timid person (lit. pants shitter). *Nichts hast du getan, du Hosenscheißer!* "You did nothing, you chicken!"

HOTTE, *f., youth.* Hot time. *Bei den Hottentotten da geht voll die Hotte ab.* "The Hottentots know how to have a high old time."

HOTTEHÜ, *n., children.* Horse; pony. *Willst mit aufs Hottehü?* "You want to get on the horsey with me?"

HOTTEN, *youth.* To play/dance hot jazz/rock; to party. *Mann, kann Bix vielleicht hotten!* "Man, Bix can sure heat things up when he plays." Cf. HOTTE.

(SICH) HOTTEN, *youth.* To have a hot/exhilarating time; get hot, esp. when dancing. *In allen Diskos auf der Piste haben wir uns toll gehottet.* "We burned up the dance floor in all the discos on the strip."

HOTTO = **HOTTEHÜ.**

-HUBER, *S.* See KRAFTHUBER; VEREINSHUBER. Cf. MEIER.

HUCKE, *f.* Back; basket carried on one's back. ***Jmdm. die Hucke voll hauen/schlagen.*** To beat s.o. up. *Sie hat ihm wieder die Hucke voll gehauen.* "She beat him up again." ***Jmdm. die Hucke voll lügen.*** To tell s.o. a pack of lies. *Sie haben uns die Hucke voll gelogen.* "They told us a pack of lies." ***Sich die Hucke voll saufen.*** To get very drunk. *Er wollte das Kind huckepack tragen, allein er hatte sich die Hucke voll gesoffen und konnte nicht.* "He wanted to give the kid a piggyback ride, but was too soused and couldn't."

HUDELN, *S.* To do sloppy work. *Du sollst diesmal Nägel mit Köpfen machen, nicht hudeln.* "Do a good job this time and don't muck it up." ***Nur nicht hudeln!*** Just don't rush things! Take it easy!

HUFE, *pl.* Feet (lit. hooves). ***Die Hufe schwingen/wetzen.*** (*Youth.*) To get a move on (lit. to swing/sharpen one's hooves). *Schwing die Hufe oder sie schnappen uns.* "Shake a leg or they'll nab us." ***Die Hufe nach oben drehen.*** To die. *Pass auf, dass du die Hufe nicht nach oben drehst.* "Watch out you don't go belly up." ***Die Hufe in die Hand nehmen*** = *die* BEINE *in die Hand nehmen.*

HUFLATTICH, *m.* Coltsfoot (a medicinal herb). ***Da wird mir der Huflattich zum Spargel!*** I can't believe my ears/eyes! (lit. The coltsfoot's turning into asparagus!).

HUFPARTY, *f., youth.* Dance (lit. hoof party). *Ute hat 'ne tolle Hufparty veranstaltet.* "Ute threw a fantastic dance party."

HUGO, *m., youth.* Cigar; cigarette; joint. Prob. for Dr. Hugo Eckener, inveterate cigar smoker, associate of Count Zeppelin, and instructor to the Ger. army in the military use of the zeppelin. In Fr. sl., zeppelin is "large cannabis joint." *Die Hugos sind alle.* "The joints are all gone." Cf. ZIGARRE **2.**

HUHN, *n.* Chicken. ***Das Ei unterm Huhn verkaufen müssen.*** To be financially strapped (lit. to have to sell the egg from under the chicken). *Wir sind noch nicht pleite aber wir müssen schon das Ei unterm Huhn verkaufen.* "We're not bankrupt yet, but the wolf is at the door."

HÜHNCHEN, *n.* Pullet. ***Ein Hühnchen mit jmdm. zu rupfen haben.*** To have a bone to pick with s.o. *Ich hab noch ein Hühnchen mit dir zu rupfen.* "I've got one more bone to pick with you."

HÜHNERLEITER, *f.* Chicken ladder. ***Das Leben ist eben nur eine Hühnerleiter, kurz und beschissen.*** (*Prov.*) Life's just a ladder in a chicken coop, short and shitty.

HÜLSE, *f.* Hull; pod. ***Hülsen schlürfen.*** (*E.*) To get drunk. *Jeden Abend gehst Hülsen schlürfen.* "You go out boozing every night."

HUMPTA, *n.* Oompah music. *Oma und Opa lieben Humpta.* "Grandma and grandpa like oompahpah."

HUND, *m.* Dog. ***Getroffene Hunde bellen.*** The truth hurts (lit. hit dogs bark). *Du schreist mich an, weil du dir die Wahrheit gesagt habe. Getroffene Hunde bellen.* "You're yelling at me because I told you the truth. The shoe fits and it's pinching." ***Wie Rockefeller/Rothschild sein Hund.*** In the lap of luxury. *Die Bardame träumt davon, einen Milliardär zu heiraten und wie Rothschild sein Hund zu leben.* "The bar hostess dreams of marrying a multimillionaire and living in luxury." ***Hätt' der Hund nicht gekackt, hätt' er den Hasen gepackt.*** You and your

125

ifs (lit. if the dog hadn't taken a crap, he would have caught the rabbit). *Da wird der Hund in der Pfanne verrückt!* That's mind-boggling! *Du hast trotzdem den ersten Preis bekommen? Da wird ja der Hund in der Pfanne verrückt!* "You won first prize anyway? That's mind-boggling!"

HÜNDI, *m.* Hundred-mark note. *Er hatte einen Stapel Hündis.* "He had a pile of hundred-mark notes."

HUNDSFOTT, *m.* SOB. *Dieser Hundsfott soll sich zum Teufel scheren.* "That bastard can go to hell."

HÜRCHEN, *n.* Little whore. *Dich und dein Hürchen will ich nie wieder sehen.* "I never want to see you and your little whore again."

HURENBOCK, *m.* Pimp; fornicator. *Ich hab dich mit diesem Hurenbock gesehen.* "I saw you with that fucker."

HURENMENSCH = MENSCH *n.*

HURENSOHN, *m., pej.* SOB. *Diesen Hurensohn lad ich nie wieder ein.* "I'll never invite that bastard again."

HUSCH (HUSCH) GEHEN. To do rapidly. *Bei dir muss alles immer husch gehen, aber das geht nicht so husch, husch!* "You want everything done fast, but this simply can't be rushed."

HUSCH! Quickly now!/Away with you!/Shoo!

HUSCHER, *m.* **1.** Quick little kiss. *Nur einen halbherzigen Huscher gab er mir.* "All he gave me was a half-hearted little kiss." **2.** Brief shower. *Abgesehen von einem kleinen Huscher war der Wettergott uns gnädig.* "Except for a little shower, the weather cooperated." **3.** Craziness. *Einen Huscher haben.* To be crazy. *Wir werden sehen, wer hier einen Huscher hat!* "We'll see who's the loony here!"

HUSTEN. 1. To cough. *Auf etwas husten.* To not give a damn for s.t. *Auf meine Gefühle hustet er.* "He doesn't give a damn for my feelings." **2.** To talk; whisper. *Jmdm. etwas husten.* To tell s.o. where to get off. *Ihm hab ich ganz schön was gehustet.* "I sure told him what he could do."

HUT, *m.* Hat. ***Mit etwas nichts am Hut haben.*** To have nothing to do with. *Mit der Sado-Maso Szene haben wir nichts am Hut.* "We have nothing to do with the S&M scene." ***Jmdm. geht der Hut hoch.*** S.o. flies off the handle. *Er braucht nur den Präsidenten im Fernsehen zu sehen, da geht ihm schon der Hut hoch.* "All it takes is the sight of the President on TV for him to get hot under the collar." ***Jmdm. eins auf den Hut geben.*** To give s.o. a clout. *Halt's Maul oder ich geb dir eins auf den Hut.* "Shut your trap or I'll give you a shot in the head."

HUTZEL. See HUTZELWEIBCHEN.

HUTZELMÄNNCHEN/HUTZELWEIBCHEN, *n.* Shrivelled old man/woman (lit. gnome; crone). *Mann, dieses Hutzelmännchen hat mich echt überrascht! So was von Turbopotenz! Viagra hat er wohl geschluckt.* "Boy, that old bag of bones really surprised me. He was superpotent! Must have gulped Viagra."

-I. Often pej. suffix, esp. in youth sl. See, among others: BRILLI; GRUFTI; GRUNDI; HIRNI; LASCHI; KOMPOSTI; SCHIRI; SCHLAFFI; SCHUFTI; TRABBI.

IGEL, *m.* **1.** Curmudgeon. (lit. hedgehog). *Dieser Igel soll mir nur kommen; ich zieh ihm schon die Stachel aus!* "I'll take on that porcupine and dequill him!" **2.** Crewcut (from *Igelschnitt*). *Wo sind deine geilen Locken? Der Igel sieht scheußlich aus!* "Where are your lovely locks? The crewcut looks awful!"

IGITT!/IGITTIGITT! Yuck!/Ugh! *Brokkoli schon wieder? Igitt!* "Broccoli again? Yuck!"

-INSKI. *Youth sl. suffix.* See BRUTALINSKI; RADIKALINSKI; TOTALINSKI.

INTELLELL, *m., often pej.* From *Intellektueller* (intellectual); also adj., from *intellektuell*. *Der hält sich für'n Intellell.* "He thinks he's an intellectual." *Die ist mir zu intellell.* "She's too brainy for me."

INTELLIGENZLER, *m.* Egghead. *Du bist zu sehr Intelligenzler um mich zu lieben.* "You're too much of an egghead to love me."

INTERNIERUNGSANSTALT, *f., hum.* Boarding school. *In der Internierungsanstalt wurden wir mit Mysteriengelaber und einem unbekannten Fleisch abgefüttert.* "In boarding school we were fed mystery meat and drivel about religious mysteries."

IRGENDWIE/IRGENDWO. Somehow/somewhere. (Both are much used fillers; seen by some as symptomatic of muddled thinking.) *Ich weiß nicht, aber irgendwie mein ich, das wär vielleicht doch irgendwo, irgendwie richtig.* "I don't know, but somehow or other, you know, I feel that might be right."

IRRE/IRRSINNIG = **WAHNSINNIG.**

ISCHE, *f.* **1.** Female; girlfriend (from Hebr. for woman). *Er hat 'ne neue Ische.* "He's got a new girlfriend." **2.** Bitch. *Schwirr ab, Ische!* "Buzz off, bitch!"

ITAKER, *m., pej.* Italian. *Hol mir 'ne Pizza vom Itaker um die Eck.* "Get me a pizza from the dago around the corner."

JACKE, *f.* Jacket. ***Jmdm. die Jacke voll hauen/schlagen** = **Jmdm. die** HUCKE **voll hauen/schlagen. Sich die Jacke voll saufen** = *sich die* HUCKE *voll saufen.*

JÄGERLATEIN, *n.* Hunter's tall story; any "fish" story (lit. hunter's Latin). *Er hat uns wieder sein Jägerlatein aufgetischt.* "He laid it on thick again."

JAPPEN/JAPSEN, *N.* To pant. *Sie japste nach dem Rennen.* "She was panting after the race."

JENISCH. Gypsy (from the Romany for "to know"). Cf. ZIGEUNERN. *Jenische Familien aus der ganzen Welt treffen sich in der Camargue in Südfrankreich.* "Gypsy families from all over meet in the Camargue in Southern France."

JESSAS/JESSASNA!/JESSES!/JESUS!/JESUS MARIA!/JESUS MARIA UND JOSEF! *S.* My goodness!/Heavens!/Ye Gods! (lit. Jesus, Mary, and Joseph!) *Jesses! Meine Schlüssel sind wieder futsch!* "Christ! My keys are lost again!"

JETTEN. To jet/fly. *Jedes Wochenende jetten sie irgendwo hin.* "Every weekend they fly off to somewhere or other." Cf. DÜSEN **1.**

JO(H)NNY COOLMAN, *youth.* Laid back guy. *Nichts nervt ihn; er bleibt immer Johnny Coolman.* "Nothing bugs him; he's always a cool dude."

JUBEL, *m.* Rejoicing. ***Jubel, Trubel, Heiterkeit.*** Rejoicing, hubbub, merriment. *Da gab's Jubel, Trubel, Heiterkeit.* "Things were really popping there."

JUBELGREIS, *m.* Spunky oldster. *Manch Jubelgreis hat noch Appetit auf Junghühner.* "Many a spry old geezer still fancies a bit of spring chicken."

JUBELJAHR, *n.* Jubilee year. *Alle Jubeljahre ruft sie an.* "She calls once in a blue moon."

JUCKEN. To itch; scratch. ***Lass jucken!*** Let's get cracking! ***Das juckt mich nicht!*** That's no skin off my nose. ***Wen's juckt, der kratze sich!*** If that rubs someone the wrong way, he/she should speak up. ***Jmdm./Jmdn. juckt der Buckel/das Fell.*** S.o. is looking for a beating. *Du treibst dauernd Faxen, dir/dich juckt wohl das Fell.* "You keep horsing around; you must be looking for a hiding."

JUDENFRESSER, *m.* Rabid anti-Semite (lit. devourer of Jews). *Ezra Pound bereute es, Judenfresser gewesen zu sein.* "Ezra Pound regretted having been a rabid anti-Semite."

JUNGE, *m.* Boy. ***Schwerer Junge.*** Serious offender. *In dem Knast sitzen nur schwere Jungs.* "Only hardened criminals are serving sentences in that prison." ***Harter Junge.*** Tough guy. *Er ist 'n harter Junge, hat aber 'n warmes Herz.* "He's a tough guy, but he has a warm heart."

JUNGGEMÜSE, *n.* Girls in their early teens (lit. young [spring] vegetables). *Auf der Fête gab's nur Junggemüse; ich suchte eher 'ne Nutte.* "There was just jailbait at the party; I was really looking for a whore."

JUNGHÜHNER, *pl.* Young girls (lit. young [spring] chickens). *Junghühner sind zu kompliziert und knifflig; folge Franklins Rat und lass dich nur mit den Älteren ein.* "Young chicks are too complicated and problematic; take Franklin's advice and just get involved with older women."

KABÄUSCHEN, *n.* Small room/house. *Willst du auf mein Kabäuschen?* "You want to come to my place?"

KABBELIG, *N.* Choppy (seas). *Kabbelig war das Meer, aber desto inbrünstiger unsere Umarmungen.* "The sea was choppy, but our embraces were all the more passionate for it."

(SICH) KABBELN. To squabble. *Die Rabbiner kabbelten sich um die Auslegung der Kabbalah.* "The rabbis bickered about the interpretation of the Cabalah."

KABUFF, *n.* Dingy little room. *Die Studenten wollten Lolas Kabuff kennen lernen.* "The students wanted to get to see Lola's little room."

KABUSE/KABÜSE, *f., N.* **1.** Ship's galley. *Der Schiffskoch lässt nur den Kapitän in seine Kabüse.* "The ship's cook permits only the captain to enter his galley." **2.** = **KABUFF.**

KACKBRAUN. Shit brown. *Kein Gentleman trägt braun oder khakifarben, geschweige denn kackbraun.* "No gentleman wears brown or khaki, to say nothing of shit brown."

KACKE, *f.* Excrement. ***Die Kacke ist am Dampfen!*** The shit's hit the fan! (lit. the shit's steaming!). *Meine Alten haben's erfahren. Da ist jetzt aber die Kacke voll am Dampfen.* "My parents found out. The shit's really hit the fan now." Cf. KAKTUS 3; OBERKACKE.

KACKEGAL = **SCHEIßEGAL.**

KACKEN. To defecate. *Wenn Ihr Köter wieder auf meinem Rasen kackt, wird's Krach geben!* "If your mutt shits on my lawn again, there's gonna be trouble!"

KACKER, *m.* SOB (lit. shitter). *Verpiss dich, Kacker.* "Piss off, shitbag!"

KACKFIDEL. Happy and farty. *Die Stripperin hatte ihn ausgezogen, trotzdem war er kackfidel.* "The stripper fleeced him, but he was still happy as all get out."

KACKSTELZEN = **SCHEIßSTÄNDER.**

KADI, *m.* Judge (from Arabic). ***Zum Kadi laufen.*** To go to court. *Er will wieder zum Kadi laufen.* "He wants to litigate again."

KÄFER, *m.* **1.** Beetle; VW. *Er hängt noch an seinem alten Käfer.* "He's still very fond of his old VW beetle." **2.** Young girl. *Jeder wollte mit dem flotten Käfer tanzen.* "Everyone wanted to dance with that attractive chick."

KAFF, *n.* **1.** Hick town. (From Hebr., with Romany [Gypsy] influence, via ROTWELSCH. See KAFFER.) *Aus dem alten Kaff ist fast 'ne Metropole geworden.* "The old hick town's almost turned into a metropolis." **2.** Trash; idle chatter, *N.* (of Germanic origin; rel. to "chaff"). *Dein Kaff will ich mir nicht länger anhören.* "I don't want to listen to your babbling anymore."

KAFFER, *m., pej.* Dummy (from Hebr. for "farmer; rural"). *Du hast's ihm geglaubt? Du bist 'n richtiger Kaffer.* "You believed his story? You're a real stupid idiot."

KAHN, *m.* **1.** Small boat. ***Einen im Kahn haben.*** To be drunk. *Ich wollte darüber reden, aber er hatte schon einen im Kahn.* "I wanted to talk about it, but he was already plastered." **2.** Jail. *Er sitzt im Kahn.* "He's in the can." **3.** Clodhoppers. See ELBKÄHNE.

KAISER, *m.* Emperor. ***Da wo selbst der Kaiser (von China) allein hingeht.*** The toilet (lit. where the Emperor [of China] goes alone). *Ich muss da, wo selbst der Kaiser allein hingeht.* "I've got to do s.t. you can't do for me."

133

KAISERIN, *f.* Empress. ***Und ist die Kaiserin ach so schön, muss sie doch zur Toilette geh'n.*** Do the rich put their pants on any differently from us? (Lit. The empress may be oh so beautiful, but she still goes to the toilet.)

KAKAO, *m.* Cocoa. ***Jmdn. durch den Kakao ziehen.*** To run s.o. down. *Diese Kabarettisten nehmen kein Blatt vor den Mund und ziehen Präsidente und Päpste durch den Kakao.* "Those cabaret artists pull no punches and dump on presidents and popes."

KAKELN, *N.* To chatter; gossip. *Habt ihr jetzt genug gekakelt?* "Have you chewed enough fat now?"

KAKTUS, *m.* **1.** Crew cut/s.o. with a crew cut (lit. cactus). *Lass mich deinen Kaktus streicheln; 's soll Glück bringen.* "Let me rub your crew cut; it's supposed to bring good luck." **2.** Curmudgeon. *Ist meine Alte aber 'n totaler Kaktus geworden!* "My old lady's really become very bristly." Cf. IGEL; KRATZBÜRSTE. **3.** Excrement. ***Einen Kaktus pflanzen/setzen.*** To defecate (euph. for KACKE). *Hoffentlich setzt Ihr Köter nie wieder einen Kaktus vor meine Tür.* "I hope your damned dog won't ever drop another load in front of my door."

KAKTUSKOPF = **KAKTUS 1.**

KALBEN, *youth.* To give birth (lit. to calve). *Lili kalbt bald.* "Lili's due soon."

KALBERN. To mess/fool around. *Hör doch mal auf, hier zu kalbern!* "Quit horsing around here, will you!"

KALK, *m.* Lime; whitewash. ***Bei jmdm. rieselt der Kalk.*** To be getting senile (lit. s.o.'s lime is crumbling). *Einst hauten auch meine Dinos gern auf den Putz; jetzt aber rieselt schon der Kalk bei ihnen.* "My parents used to like to let it all hang out too; but now they're gaga."

KALKLEISTEN, *pl., youth.* Parents; old people (*verkalkt* = suffering from atherosclerosis). *Meine Kalkleisten schlucken oft Kräutertees wie Ginseng und Ginkgo biloba.* "My old fossils often drink herbal teas such as ginseng and Ginkgo biloba."

KALOSCHENSPRACHE = **KOCHEMER LOSCHEN.**

KALT ERWISCHEN. To catch off guard. *Der Sturm hat uns kalt erwischt.* "The storm surprised us."

KALTE ASCHE. Zilch; no action (lit. "cold ashes"). *Im Kaff ist nichts los, total kalte Asche.* "That burg's a real cemetery." Cf. TOTE HOSE.

KALTER BAUER. See BAUER.

KAMELLEN, *pl.* Low Ger. for *Kamille* (chamomile). *Alte/olle Kamellen.* Old hat. *Der Senator hat nichts als olle Kamellen dahergelabert.* "The senator just droned on about the same old stuff." Cf. ALTE KLAMOTTEN.

KANAKE, *m., pej.* Damned foreigner; gook (lit. South Sea Islander; from Polynesian *kanaka,* human being). *Die Kanaken will er alle rausschmeißen; seine Eltern waren aber auch Aussis.* "He wants to throw out all the foreigners; but his parents were foreigners too." Cf. KATZELMACHER.

KANAL, *m.* **1.** Canal. *Den Kanal voll haben.* To be fed up; drunk. *Hör auf damit, wir haben den Kanal schon voll.* "Stop that; we've already had a snoot full of it!" *Sich den Kanal voll laufen lassen.* To get totally drunk. *Er ist nur zu ertragen, wenn er sich den Kanal voll laufen lässt.* "Nobody can stand him until he's tied one on." **2.** TV channel. *Auf einem anderen Kanal senden.* To be on another wavelength (lit. to transmit on another channel). *Der peilt nichts davon; sendet ja halt auf einem anderen Kanal.* "He doesn't understand any of it; after all, he's on another wavelength." *Den Kanal wechseln.* (*Youth.*) To change the subject. *Wechsle doch endlich den Kanal, verdammt nochmal!* "Will you put on another record, damn it!" Cf. AUFLEGEN.

KANNE, *f.* Saxophone (lit. can; pail). *Bill kann auch die Kanne spielen.* "Bill can play the saxophone too."

KANONE, *f.* **1.** Ace (lit. cannon). *Alle hielten den Quacksalber für 'ne Kanone.* "They all thought the quack was a genius." Cf. STIMMUNGSKANONE. **2.** Revolver. *Vor* *dem Gangstertreff mussten alle ihre Kanonen ablegen.* "Before the gangster get-together, they all had to check their rods." **3.** Norm, description. *Unter aller Kanone.* Indescribably bad. *Die Mannschaft hat wieder unter aller Kanone gespielt.* "The team played a lousy game again."

KANTE, *f.* **1.** Edge. *Etwas auf der hohen Kante haben.* To have s.t. (money) put by. *Wir haben nichts auf der hohen Kante, und nun diese Krise!* "We have no money saved, and now this crisis!" *Kante geben.* (*Youth.*) To speed; go all out. *Sie hat dem Schlitten Kante gegeben.* "She opened up the throttle." **2.** Wonderful girl. (*Youth.*) *Ist Tina vielleicht 'ne tolle Kante.* "Tina's some terrific chick!"

KAPEE, *n.* Understanding. *Bist du aber schwer von Kapee!* "You're really slow on the uptake."

KAPIEREN. To understand. *Kapierst jetzt endlich?* "Do you finally get it now?"

KAPIERT?/KAPITO? Is that understood?/You get it? (From the It. *capito.*) *Du sagst meinen Alten, ich war bei dir, kapito?* "You'll tell my parents I was at your place, got that?"

KAPORES = **KAPUTT.**

KAPOTTE, *f.* Old-fashioned/funny hat. *Opa ist Fummeltrine und hat 'nen ganzen Schrank voll Kapotten.* "Grandpa's a drag queen and has a whole closet full of weird hats."

KAPOTTHUT, *m.* = **KAPOTTE.**

KAPPE, *f.* Head (lit. cap). *Auf seine Kappe nehmen.* To assume responsibility for. *Er hat die Schuld für den Verlust auf seine Kappe genommen.* "He assumed responsibility for the loss." *Auf jmds. Kappe gehen.* To assume responsiblity. *Die nächste Runde geht auf meine Kappe.* "The next round's on me." *Neben der Kappe sein.* To be off one's rocker. *Du bist ganz neben der Kappe.* "You haven't got your head on straight."

KAPUTT. 1. Busted. *Der Wagen ist kaputt.* "The car's broken down." **2.** Wonderful (*youth*). *Ist Ralf aber 'n kaputter Typ!* "Ralf's some swell guy!" Cf. KAPUTTO.

KAPUTTGEHEN. 1. To go on the blink/fritz. *Der Fernseher ist wieder kaputtgegangen.* "The TV conked out again." **2.** To die. *Er setzte sich nach Kanada ab, weil er keine Lust hatte, als Kanonenfutter im Vietnamkrieg kaputtzugehen.* "He went to Canada because he didn't want to kick the bucket as cannon fodder in Vietnam."

KAPUTTMACHEN. To break. *Sie hat sich kaputtgelacht, nachdem sie meine stoßsichere Uhr kaputtgemacht hat.* "She nearly died laughing after busting my shock-proof watch."

KAPUTTNICK. *Einen Kaputtnick haben.* (*Youth.*) To be cracked. *Du hast wohl 'n Kaputtnick!* "You must be off your rocker."

KAPUTTO. *Youth sl.* for KAPUTT **1.** *Nach dem Rave war ich echt kaputto.* "I was really burned out after the rave/big blast."

KARACHO. Great speed (from Sp. *Carajo!* [Shit!/Prick!/Damn it!]). *Sie fuhren mit Karacho gegen die Telefonzelle.* "They crashed into the telephone booth at top speed."

KARNICKEL, *n., hum.* Scapegoat (lit. rabbit). *Immer bin ich das Karnickel!* "Everybody always blames me!"

KARO, *n.* Square. ***Karo einfach/Karo trocken.*** Slices of (square cut) bread with nothing on them. *Wir nagten am Hungertuch und meistens gab's nur Karo trocken.* "We were starving and usually had nothing to put on our bread."

KAROSSE. See LUXUSKAROSSE.

KAROTTE, *f.* Penis (lit. carrot). *Von wegen Riesenkarotte! 'ne Kinderkarotte hat er.* "What do you mean giant cock! All he's got is a baby carrot."

KARRIERO, *m., pej., youth.* Career oriented person. *Für uns sind Karrieros nur Beknackte!* "Career creeps are just crazies to us."

KARTOFFEL, *f.* 1. Potato. *Die Kartoffeln abgießen.* To urinate. *Alle zehn Minuten goss er die Kartoffeln ab.* "Every 10 minutes he took a leak." 2. Nose. *Sie will sich die Kartoffel korrigieren lassen.* "She wants to get a nose job." 3. Large hole in socks. *Seine Socken sind voller Kartoffeln, aber er trägt sie dennoch.* "His socks are full of holes, but he wears them anyway."

KARTOFFELKOPF, *f.* Jerk (lit. potato head). *Könnt ihr nichts Besseres, ihr Kartoffelköpfe?* "Can't you do anything better than that, you blockheads?"

KARTOFFELWASSER. *Das/sein Kartoffelwasser abgiessen/abschütten.* To urinate (lit. to drain the potato water). *Nachdem ich mein Kartoffelwasser im Garten abgegossen hatte, sagte eine entrüstete Stimme: „Das ist hier keine öffentliche Bedürfnisanstalt!"* "After I took a leak in the garden, an angry voice said: 'This is no public comfort station.' "

KÄSE, *m.* Nonsense (lit. cheese). *Das ist ja alles nur Käse.* "That's all crap."

KÄSEBLATT, *n.* Local/low-end newspaper. *Was, du liest dieses Käseblatt?* "What, you read that rag?"

KÄSEFÜßE, *pl.* Smelly feet. *Er riecht immer nach Knoblauch; hat auch Käsefüße.* "He always reeks of garlic and also has smelly feet."

KÄSIG. Pale (lit. cheesy). *Plötzlich ist sie ganz käsig geworden.* "She suddenly turned white as a sheet."

KASPAR/KASPERLE/KASPERLI = KASPER.

KASPER, *m.* Buffoon. (One of the Three Wise Men and a comic figure in puppet theater.) *Du alberner Kasper, lass mich in Ruhe!* "Leave me alone, you idiot clown!" See RAUSLASSEN 1; SPRUCHKASPER. Cf. HANS WURST; LARIFARI; PICKELHERING.

KASPERN = HERUMKASPERN.

KASSENKNÜLLER, *m.* Box office smash. *Ihr neuer Film ist 'n Kassenknüller.* "Her new movie's a box office smash."

KASSIBER, *m.* Letter smuggled out of jail; secret/coded message (from Hebr. for "to write"). *Er sitzt im Knast, aber Kassiber bekomme ich oft von ihm.* "He's in the slammer, but I often get kited letters from him."

KASTEN, *m.* **1.** Box, crate. See KISTE **1, 5, 6**; FLIMMERKASTEN; KLAPPERKASTEN; KLIMPERKASTEN; TASTENKASTEN. **2.** Big, brawny man. *Der Boxer ist 'n richtiger Kasten.* "That boxer's some hulk." **3.** Head. *Etwas auf dem Kasten haben.* To be brainy. *Der hat nicht viel auf dem Kasten.* "He's not very bright."

KATANGA, *f., E., youth.* Thin/ugly girl. *Von wegen Katanga! Sie hat sich zu einer Kirsche gemausert.* "No way is she an ugly duckling! She's turned into a peach!"

KATER, *m.* Hangover (lit. tomcat). *Morgen hast du nur einen Kater.* "Tomorrow you'll just have a hangover." Cf. VERKATERT.

KATERSTIMMUNG, *f.* Melancholy. *Die Regierung gewann; bei der Opposition herrscht Katerstimmung.* "The government won; gloom prevails among the opposition."

KATHARINA/KATHRIN. Diarrhea. *Wenn du in der Schlürfbude isst, holst du dir gleich die schnelle Kathrin.* "Eat in that joint and you'll get the shits fast."

KÄTHE, *f., E.* Attractive girl (lit. Kathy, dim. of Katharina). *Ist die ehrlich 'ne scharfe Käthe!* "She's some gorgeous chick!"

KATTUN, *m.* Cotton; calico cloth. *Jmdm. Kattun geben.* (*Youth.*) To beat s.o. up. *Hör auf oder ich geb dir ganz schön Kattun.* "Quit it or you're going to need medical attention."

KATZELMACHER, *m., S.* Italian. *Wörter wie „Kaffer," „Katzelmacher" und „Kanacken" verbiet ich mir.* "I won't tolerate words like 'nigger,' 'wop,' and 'damned foreigners.'"

KATZENJAMMER = KATER.

KATZENMACHEN/KATZENFICKEN, *n.* Cat making/

fucking. ***Wie's Katzenmachen/Katzenficken gehen.*** To happen very fast. *Schon mit der Reparatur fertig? Das ging ja wie's Katzenmachen!* "Already done with the repair job? That was fast work!"

KAUDERN/KAUDERWELSCHEN. To talk gibberish/ jargon. *Die Computerhacker kauderwelschten und wir rafften gar nichts.* "The computer hackers were talking double Dutch, and we understood zilch."

KAVENTSMANN, *m., N.* **1.** Giant wave. *,,Je mehr Kaventsmänner, desto besser," behauptete die Surferin.* " 'The more giant waves, the better,' declared the surfer." **2.** Corpulent, imposing man. *Ja, Kaventsmann ist er, aber es steckt nichts dahinter; innerlich hohl ist er.* "Yes, he's a whale of a fellow, but hollow within."

KECKERN. 1. To snarl, growl, complain. See MECKERN. **2.** To talk nonsense. See QUARKEN.

KEHRICHT. See FEUCHT.

KEILEN. 1. To fight; push and shove (lit. to wedge). *Er kann das Keilen nicht lassen.* "He can't keep his fists to h.s." **2.** To recruit/rope in. *Lass dich nicht für diese Burschenschaft keilen.* "Don't get roped into joining that dueling fraternity."

KEILEREI, *f.* Brawl. *Er ist in eine allgemeine Keilerei gekommen.* "He got into a free-for-all."

KEKS, *m., youth.* **1.** Head (lit. cookie). ***Einen weichen Keks haben.*** To be soft in the head. *Mein Alter hat 'n weichen Keks.* "My old man's dim-witted." ***Jmdm. auf den Keks gehen.*** To get on s.o.'s nerves. *Gehst mir andauernd auf'n Keks.* "You give me a permanent headache." **2.** Breast. *An Ullas tollen Keksen würde ich gern mal knabbern.* "I'd love to nibble on Ulla's jugs sometime."

KENNEN. To know. ***Seine Pappenheimer kennen.*** To know with whom/what one is dealing. *Sie werden's nie schaffen. Ich kenne meine Pappenheimer.* "They'll never manage it. I know what I'm talking about."

KESS. Sassy; jaunty; snappy (from Hebr. *cheth*; see KESSEN-

LOSCHEN). *Eine kesse Sohle aufs Parkett legen.* See PAR-KETT. *Des Wahnsinns kesse Beute sein.* See WAHNSINN. See also KESSER VATER.

KESSENLOSCHEN, *n.* Thieves' slang. (From the Hebr. letter *cheth* used as an abbr. of *chochem* [cunning/shrewd] and Hebr. *lâschôn* [language].) *Keiner verstand ihr Kessenloschen.* "Nobody understood their thieves' slang." Cf. KOCHEMER LOSCHEN; ROTWELSCH.

KESSER VATER, *m.* **1.** Butch. *Dein Kumpel ist 'n kesser Vater.* "Your buddy's a tough guy." **2.** Dominant lesbian. *Macker träumen davon, diesen kessen Vater zu bumsen, aber bei ihr kommt keiner an.* "Guys dream of screwing that bull dyke, but they get nowhere with her."

KEULE, *f., Berlin.* **1.** Bottle containing hard liquor (lit. club, cudgel). *Gib mir noch 'n Schluck aus der Keule.* "Give me another slug o' whiskey." **2.** Tough, brawny woman. *Lass dich von der Keule nicht kleinkriegen.* "Don't let that tough broad walk all over you."

KEULEN. **1.** To beat up. *Die Bande hat ihn gekeult.* "The gang beat him up." **2.** To work hard. *Ihr könnt weiter keulen; ich mach Feierabend.* "You can keep on slaving away; I'm calling it a day." Cf. ASTEN; BOHREN **2**; HINKELN; MALOCHEN; SCHUFTEN; WÖRKEN. **3.** To get drunk. *Wir haben ordentlich gekeult.* "We really tied one on." Cf. KEULE **1.**

KICHERERBSE, *f.* S.o. given to giggling (lit. chickpea; pun on *kichern,* to giggle). *Seid endlich still, ihr Kichererbsen, ihr meine törichten Jungfrauen!* "Will you finally be quiet, you giggling girlies, you foolish virgins!"

KIEBITZ, *m.* Kibitzer; curious onlooker (lit. lapwing [bird]). *Beim Kartenspielen brauchen wir keine Kiebitze.* "We don't need any kibitzers when we're playing cards."

KIEBITZEN. To kibitz; spy on. *Die Kleine wollte auch mit-spielen, nicht nur immer kiebitzen.* "The little girl wanted to play too, not just look on."

KIEKERCHEN, *N.* = **GUCKER.**

KIES, *m.* Money (lit. gravel). *Da ist kein Kies mehr.* "There's no money left."

KIEZ, *m.* **1.** Neighborhood. *Alle im Kiez kennen sie und ihren Hund.* "Everyone in the neighborhood knows her and her dog." **2.** Red-light district. *Ich arbeite in einem Luxuspuff im Kiez.* "I work in a deluxe cathouse in the red-light district."

KIFFE = **KIPPE.**

KIFFEN. To smoke marijuana/hashish (from Arabic for "to feel good"). *Fast alle kifften, sie aber nicht.* "Almost all of them smoked a joint, but not she." Cf. BEKIFFT.

KIFFER, *m.* Smoker of marijuana/hashish; drug addict. *Mit Kiffern hat sie nichts am Hut.* "She has nothing to do with potheads."

KIKI, *m.* Nonsense. *Behalt dir deinen Kiki!* "Keep that foolishness to y.s."

KILLEKILLE, *children.* Tickle-tickle. **Bei jmdm. killekille machen.** To tickle s.o. *Er tut, als ob er bei ihr killekille macht, aber ich fürchte, es handelt sich um etwas Schlimmeres.* "He pretends to tickle her, but I'm afraid it's s.t. worse than that."

KILLEN. To kill. *Der Gangster killte sie alle.* "The gangster killed them all."

KILLER, *m.* Killer; hired killer. *„Wenn ich auch den Partner killen soll, muss ich mehr Kohle bekommen," sagte die Killerin.* " 'If I bump off the partner too, I'll have to get more dough,' said the contract killer."

KIMME, *f.* Cleft between the buttocks; anal sphincter. **Jmdm. geht die Kimme/Muffe/der Ofen.** To be very afraid. *Mir ging ganz schön die Kimme, als die Maschine ins Trudeln geriet.* "I was scared shitless when the plane went into a spin."

KINDERSTUBE, *f.* Upbringing (lit. children's room/nursery). *Wenn ich keine so gute Kinderstube gehabt hätte,* *würde ich Ihnen sagen, was ich von Ihnen denke.* "If I hadn't been so well brought up, I'd tell you what I think of you."

KINKERLITZCHEN, *pl.* Foolish/worthless things. *Von solchen Kinkerlitzchen will ich nichts mehr hören.* "I don't want to hear any more about tomfoolery like that."

KINNLADE, *f.* Jawbone. *Mir klappt die Kinnlade weg!* (*youth*). I'm bowled over (lit. my jawbone's folded on me).

KIPPE, *f.* Cigarette butt. *Der Sandler hob die Kippen auf.* "The vagrant picked up the cigarette butts."

KIPPEN. To topple/dump (lit. to tilt; tip). *Man hat mich als Parteisekretärin gekippt.* "They got rid of me as party secretary." *Einen/ein paar kippen.* To have a drink/a few drinks. *Er wollte noch einen kippen.* "He wanted to knock back another drink." *Aus den Latschen/Pantinen kippen.* To be floored (lit. to topple out of one's slippers/clogs). *Als ich den Jackpot geknackt hab, bin ich aus den Latschen gekippt.* "When I cracked the jackpot, I was knocked for a loop."

KIRSCHBLÜTE, *f., youth.* Sweet, attractive girl (lit. cherry blossom/cherry). *Er hält sie für 'ne Kirschblüte; mir ist sie eine ziemlich saure Kirsche.* "He thinks she's a sweet peach; I find her rather sour."

KIRSCHE, *f.* **1.** Cherry. *Mit jmdm. ist nicht gut Kirschen essen.* It's best not to tangle with s.o. (lit. it's not good to eat cherries with s.o.). *Ja, die Behörden haben dir unrecht getan; aber mit denen ist nicht gut Kirschen essen.* "Yes, the authorities did you wrong, but you'd better not mess with them." **2.** Girl. See KIRSCHBLÜTE.

KIRSCHENBLÜTE = KIRSCHBLÜTE.

KISTE, *f.* **1.** Old car/plane/ship (lit. box, case, crate). *Die Kiste ist mit Mann und Maus untergegangen.* "The old tub sank with all on board." See BLECHKISTE; KLAPPERKISTE. **2.** Relationship. See BEZIEHUNGSKISTE. **3.** Bed; sleeping bag. *Die sind noch in der Kiste.* "They're still in the sack." **4.** Matter; thing. *Mach keine schwere Kiste da-*

raus; 's ist doch nur dieselbe Kiste. "Don't make a big thing of it; it's just the same old story." **5.** Prison. *Er sitzt noch in der Kiste.* "He's still in the clink." **6.** Coffin. *Der Grufti gehört in die Kiste.* "Why doesn't that old thing croak!" *In die Kiste springen.* To die. *Beim Zugunglück ist sie in die Kiste gesprungen.* "She bought it (died) in the train wreck."

KITZELN. To tickle. *Jmdm. das Zwerchfell kitzeln.* To make s.o. laugh (lit. to tickle s.o.'s diaphragm). *Sie weiß, uns das Zwerchfell zu kitzeln.* "She knows how to make us laugh."

KITZLER, *m.* Clitoris. *Du könntest dich auch mal 'n bisschen um meinen Kitzler kümmern.* "You could pay some attention to my clit occasionally."

KIWI, *m., youth.* **1.** Kiwi (fruit/bird/New Zealander). **2.** Mixture of *Kirschwasser* (cherry brandy) or *Kirschlikör* (cherry cordial) with whiskey. *Nach den vielen Kiwis war er voll.* "He was soused after all those kirschwhiskeys."

KLADDERADATSCH, *m.* **1.** Awful mess. *Da haben wir den Kladderadatsch!* "What a mess!" **2.** Scandal. *Das hat 'nen furchtbaren Kladderadatsch gegeben.* "That created a terrible scandal."

KLÄFFER, *m., pej.* Yapping dog. *Ihr Kläffer geht mir auf den Keks.* "Their yapping dog gets on my nerves."

KLAMM. Hard up (lit. numb/stiff [with cold]). *Kohle hab ich keine; bin ja selber klamm.* "I got no dough; broke m.s."

KLAMMHEIMLICH. On the quiet. *Klammheimlich verließ er ihr Zimmer.* "He sneaked out of her room." Cf. STIEKUM.

KLAMOTTE, *f.* **1.** Large rock; big object. *Er spricht liebevoll mit seiner Koseklamotte.* "He talks lovingly to his pet rock." **2.** Lousy play/film. *Bei der Klamotte hat mein Mann geweint.* "My husband wept watching that trash." Cf. ALTE KLAMOTTE(N).

KLAMOTTEN, *f., pl.* Clothes. *Von wegen Mode! Ich trage nur Klamotten, die mir bequem sind.* "What do you mean fashion! I only wear clothes I'm comfortable in."

KLAMOTTENKISTE = MOTTENKISTE.

KLAMÜSERN, *N.* To reflect on. *Wenn ich nur Zeit hätte, drüber 'n bisschen zu klamüsern.* "If I'd only had time to puzzle over it a bit."

KLAPPE, *f.* **1.** Mouth (lit. lid; vent; valve). *Halt die Klappe!* "Shut your trap!" **2.** Bed. *Sich in die Klappe hauen.* To hit the hay. *Haut euch endlich in die Klappe!* "Hit the sack now, will you!" **3.** Site of homosexual encounters (gay bar, park, public toilet). *Gestern war's ganz toll auf der Klappe.* "Yesterday was fabulous in the gay bar."

KLAPPERKASTEN/KLAPPERKISTE, *m.* Rattly old car. *Nach der langen Fahrt in seiner Klapperkiste war ich fix und fertig.* "I was all done in after that long ride in his rattly old buggy."

KLAPPRIG. Shaky. *Meine Eltern werden immer klappriger.* "My parents are getting more and more tottery."

KLAPS, *m.* **1.** Smack. *Ich geb dir gleich einen Klaps.* "I'm gonna clobber you now." **2.** Lunacy. *Einen Klaps haben.* To be crazy. *Der hat 'n Klaps und gehört in die Klapsmühle.* "He's a nutcase and should be in the loony bin."

KLAPSDOKTOR, *m., pej.* Psychiatrist. *Der Klapsdoktor hat ihr eher geschadet als geholfen.* "The shrink did her more harm than good."

KLAPSE, *f.* Youth sl. var. of KLAPSMÜHLE.

KLAPSIG. Crazy. *Voll klapsig ist der.* "He's totally nuts."

KLAPSMÜHLE, *f.* Insane asylum; psychiatric ward. *Der beknackte Klapsdoktor in der Klapsmühle hat ihn für geheilt erklärt.* "That weirdo shrink in the loony bin said he was cured."

KLAR. Clear. *Aber klar!* Yes, of course! *Klar wie Klara/ Klärchen/Klossbrühe/dicke Suppe/dicke Tinte.* As plain as the nose on your face. *Klar wie Klossbrühe wollen wir unsere Rechte geltend machen.* "Of course we want to stand up for our rights." ***Klar Schiff machen.*** **1.** To make everything shipshape. *Dein Zimmer ist ein Schweinestall. Morgen machst du klar Schiff!* "Your room's a pigsty. Tomorrow you're going to clean it up." **2.** To make a clean sweep and set everything in order. *Mein Guru sagt, ich muss in meinem Leben klar Schiff machen.* "My guru says I've got to set my life in order."

KLARKOMMEN. 1. To manage; cope. *Mit meinen Alten kann ich nicht klarkommen.* "I can't get on with my parents." **2.** To get o.s. ready. *Ich muss mich schön machen und es wird 'ne Weile dauern, bevor ich klarkomme.* "I've got to put my face on, and it'll be a while before I'm ready."

KLARO! = **CLARO!**

KLASSE. First class. *Sie hat sich 'n klasse Auto gekauft.* "She bought a top-notch car."

KLASSEFRAU, *f.* Very attractive woman. *Viele halten sie für 'ne Klassefrau.* "Many think she's a looker/stunner."

KLASSEMANN, *m.* Great guy. *Du schimpfst ihn einen Säufer, aber er ist mein Kumpel und ein Klassemann.* "You call him a lush, but he's my buddy and a terrific guy."

KLASSEWEIB = **KLASSEFRAU.**

KLATSCHBASE = **KLATSCHTANTE.**

KLATSCHE, *f., school sl.* **1.** Snitch. *Dieser Klatsche wollen wir die Fresse polieren.* "We're going to beat up that snitch." Cf. PETZE. **2.** Pony, crib sheet. *Ohne die Klatsche wärst du durchgefallen.* "You would have failed without the trot."

KLATSCHEN. 1. To clap. ***Beifall klatschen.*** To applaud. *Alle haben der Sängerin laut Beifall geklatscht.* "Everybody applauded the singer vigorously." **2.** To slap. ***Jmdm. eine/ein paar klatschen.*** Give s.o. a good whack. *Seid endlich ruhig oder ich klatsch euch 'n paar.* "Be quiet, will you, or I'll whack you." **3.** *Youth.* To beat up (from mil. sl, "to open fire." lit. to applaud). Cf. KLOPFKONZ-ERT. *Klatschen, nicht quatschen, ist unser Prinzip.* "We use our fists instead of running our mouths." **4.** To gossip. *Was alles über sie geklatscht wird, interessiert uns nicht.* "We're not interested in all that gossip about them."

KLATSCHMAUL, *n.* Gossip. *Du musst nicht alles glauben, was dieses Klatschmaul sagt.* "You don't have to believe everything that gossip says."

KLATSCHNASS. Wringing wet. *Klatschnass sind wir nach Hause gekommen.* "We came home soaked to the skin."

KLATSCHTANTE, *f.* Gossip. *Dein Onkel ist 'ne richtige Klatschtante.* "Your uncle's a real gossip." Cf. TRATSCHTANTE.

KLATSCHWEIB = KLATSCHMAUL.

KLAUBEN, *S.* To pick; pick out/over. *Genug der Wort-klauberei! Gehen wir Himbeeren klauben!* "Enough quibbling! Let's go pick raspberries."

KLAUEN. To swipe (lit. to claw). *Wer hat meine Uhr geklaut?* Who swiped my watch? See VERSTAND.

KLAUFEN, *youth.* To shoplift. (A composite of *kaufen* [to buy] and *klauen* [to steal]. *Nachmittags klauf ich, abends kiff ich.* "Afternoons I go shoplifting; evenings I smoke pot." Cf. STAUCHEN.

KLAVIER, *n.* Piano. ***Mein Goldfisch/Hase/Krokodil spielt Klavier!*** I'm dumbfounded! (lit. My goldfish/rabbit/crocodile is playing the piano!) Cf. SCHWEIN **1**; STRULLEN; ZWITSCHERN.

KLEBEN. To paste. ***Jmdm. eine kleben.*** To whack s.o. *Ich kleb dir bald eine.* "I'm gonna paste (slam) you one."

KLECKERN. To spill; make a mess. ***Nicht kleckern, sondern klotzen.*** No half measures, but going all out. *Jetzt heißt es, nicht kleckern, sondern klotzen.* "We can't mess this up; we've got to go all out."

KLEINKLECKERSDORF, *n.* Insignificant provincial town. *Als Großstadtmensch konnte sie's kaum in Kleinkleckersdorf aushalten.* "As a big-city person, she could hardly stand it in the provinces."

KLEINKRAM, *m.* **1.** Odds and ends. See KRAM **1. 2.** Chicken feed. *Das alles ist doch nur Kleinkram.* "But all that's just peanuts."

KLEINKRÄMER = **KRÄMER.**

KLEMME, *f.* Tight spot (lit. clip; clamp). **In der Klemme sitzen.** To be in difficulty. *Könnt ihr mir nicht aus dieser Klemme helfen?* "Can't you help me out of this jam?"

KLEMMEN. 1. To wedge; jam. **Hinter die Vorhaut klemmen.** See VORHAUT. **2.** To swipe. *Hedi hat den Brilli geklemmt.* "Hedi swiped the diamond ring."

KLEMMI, *m., youth.* **1.** Uptight bourgeois. *Was willst du mit diesen Klemmis anfangen?* "Why do you want to bother with those squares?" **2.** Sexually repressed person. *Vielleicht könnte dir ein Seelenklempner helfen, alter Klemmi.* "Maybe a shrink could help you, old prude."

KLEMMIG, *youth.* Difficult; unpleasant. *Meine Alten haben's erfahren; da wird's echt klemmig werden.* "My parents found out; things are gonna get real hairy."

KLEMPNERLADEN, *m.* Plumber's store. **Einen Klempnerladen auf der Brust haben.** To have lots of mil. decorations. *Er ist nur Major und hat schon 'n ganzen Klempnerladen auf der Brust.* "He's just a major but already has a chest full of fruit salad."

KLIMBIM, *m.* **1.** Junk. *Was soll ich mi'm ganzen Klimbim?* "What am I supposed to do with all that junk?" **2.** Fuss. *Brauchst nicht so viel Klimbim drum zu machen.* "You don't have to make such a fuss about it."

KLIMPERKASTEN, *m.* Piano (lit. tinkle box). *Wir sind ausgezogen und haben den Klimperkasten zurückgelassen.* "We moved out and left the piano behind." Cf. TASTENKASTEN.

KLIPP-, *youth.* Rotten. *Ich schmiss die Klippschule und* *hab jetzt diesen Klippjob.* "I quit the damned school and now I've got this lousy job."

KLIPP UND KLAR. Unequivocally. *Ich sag's Ihnen klipp und klar—damit will ich nichts zu tun haben.* "I'm telling you straight out—I don't want anything to do with it."

KLITSCHE, *f.* **1.** Run-down rural house. *In der Klitsche wohnten wir ganz glücklich.* "We were happy living in that shack." **2.** Small-time theater; shoestring outfit. *Heute spiel ich in dieser Klitsche aber ich träume davon, ein Weltstar zu werden.* "Today I'm playing in this crummy amateur theater, but I'm dreaming of becoming an international star." **3.** Posh place (ironic use of **1** and **2**). *Wir haben im Ritz übernachtet. Ja, in der Klitsche fühlten wir uns wohl.* "We stayed at the Ritz. Yes, we were right at home in that dump."

KLITSCHNASS. Dripping wet. *Klitschnass tanzten wir um den Tümpel.* "Dripping wet, we danced around the pond."

KLITZEKLEIN. Teeny-weeny. *Sie trug 'nen klitzekleinen Bikini.* "She was wearing a teeny-weeny bikini."

KLO, *n.* Toilet. *Nach dem Fraß kam ich die ganze Nacht nicht vom Klo runter.* "After eating that swill, I spent the whole night on the can." ***Griff ins Klo.*** See GRIFF.

KLÖNEN, *N.* To chat. *Bei Kaffee und Kuchen haben wir übers Klonen geklönt.* "We had a nice chat about cloning over coffee and cake."

KLÖNSCHNACK, *m., N.* Chat. *Für 'n Klönschnack hab ich jetzt keine Zeit.* "I have no time for a chat now."

KLOPFEN. 1. To knock. ***Sprüche klopfen.*** To keep on quoting proverbs. *Statt Sprüche zu klopfen, solltest du was tun.* "Instead of intoning proverbs, you should do s.t." **2.** To beat up. See WEICHKLOPFEN.

KLOPFKONZERT, *n., youth.* Beating; brawl. *Beim Klopfkonzert haben wir sie richtig geklatscht.* "We made mincemeat out of them at the bash."

KLOPFTHERAPIE, *f., youth.* Beating (lit. beating therapy). *Dir hat anscheinend die Klopftherapie von gestern* *nicht gereicht.* "It seems yesterday's beating wasn't enough for you; you need another treatment."

KLOPPE, *f., N.* Severe beating. *Er hat 'ne Kloppe gekriegt.* "He got worked over badly."

KLOPPEN, *N.* for KLOPFEN.

KLOPS, *m.* **1.** Fatty (lit. meatball). *Der Klops wackelt mit dem Po, wenn er Rad fährt.* "That guy's fat ass shakes when he rides a bike." **2.** Head. *Schmeiß doch deinen Klops mal an!* "Use your noodle, will you!"

KLOSTERBRUDER, *m.* Homosexual (lit. monk). *Der pennt nur mit Klosterbrüdern.* "He only goes to bed with gays."

KLÖTZE = **KRÖTEN.**

KLOTZEN. 1. To work hard; go all out. See KLECKERN; RANKLOTZEN. **2.** To put up a building/housing project. *Wo man hinspuckt, wird geklotzt.* "Wherever you look, buildings are going up."

KLUG. Clever. *Nicht klug werden können.* Not to be able to make head or tail of. *Ich hab's mehrmals gelesen, aber daraus kann ich nicht klug werden.* "I've read it over many times, but I can't make heads or tails of it."

KLUGREDEN/KLUGREDNER. Nonvulgar equivalents of KLUGSCHEIßEN/KLUGSCHEIßER.

KLUGSCHEIßEN. To be a smart aleck. *Kluggeschissen hast du genug für heute.* "You've shot your mouth off long enough today."

KLUGSCHEIßER, *m.* Smart-ass (lit. clever shitter). *Klugscheißer wie dich brauchen wir nicht.* "We don't need smarty-pants like you."

KLUGSCHEIßERISCH. Smart (stupid). *Tu nicht so klugscheißerisch!* "Quit being such a wise-ass!"

KLUGSCHNACKEN/KLUGSCHNACKER, *N.* equivalents of KLUGREDEN/KLUGREDNER.

KLUMP, *m., N. for* KLUMPEN (lump). *In/zu Klump fahren.* To smash up a car/bike. *Zu Klump hauen/schla-*

gen. To beat to a pulp. *Nachdem er meinen Wagen zu Klump gefahren hatte, haute ich ihn zu Klump.* "After he smashed up my car, I beat the daylights out of him."

KLUMPATSCH, *m.* Junk. ***Der ganze Klumpatsch.*** The whole shooting match. *Raus mit dem ganzen Klumpatsch!* "Out with the whole kit and kaboodle!"

KLUMPERT, *n.* Aust. for KLUMPATSCH.

KLUNKER, *m.* Jewel (lit. clod). *Die alte Fregatte trug viele Klunker.* "The old bag wore lots of rocks." Cf. BEKLUNKERT.

KLUNKERN, *youth.* To lose money; spend money fast. *Hast ganz schön geklunkert; jetzt biste (bist du) scholle.* "You threw your money around; now you're broke." See WEGKLUNKERN.

KLUPPE, *f.* Clothespin; castrating instrument. ***In der Kluppe sein/sitzen.*** See KLEMME.

KNACKARSCH, *m.* **1.** Jackass. *Was will dieser Knackarsch?* "What's that jerk want?" **2.** Homosexual. *Schwirr ab, Knackarsch!* "Beat it, fag!" **3.** Sexy posterior. *So ein turbogeiler Knackarsch!* "What a supersexy piece of ass!"

KNACKEN. To burgle (lit. to crack, burst). *Damals hab ich viel Scheiße gebaut, Autos geknackt und noch Schlimmeres.* "I got into all sorts of shit then—broke into cars, and worse."

KNACKER, *m.* **1.** Old man. See ALTER KNACKER. **2.** Safe-cracker. *Die Bande braucht 'n tüchtigen Knacker.* "The gang needs a competent safecracker." **3.** Short for *Knackwurst* (sausage that bursts when boiled). *Iss nicht so viele Knacker oder du platzt bald.* "Don't eat so many knockwursts or you'll burst."

KNACKI, *m.* Convict. *Die Knackis verlangten besseres Essen.* "The jailbirds demanded better food." Cf. KNASTBRUDER; VERKNACKEN.

KNACKIG. Appealing; sexy (lit. crisp, fresh). *Wenn ich ihren knackigen Po beim Gehen wiegen seh, verkläre ich.*

"When I see her sexy ass undulate as she walks, I'm transformed."

KNACKPUNKT, *m.* Crucial issue. *Bei den Verhandlungen wollen wir die Knackpunkte vorerst vermeiden.* "We'll leave the crucial issues alone in the early stages of the negotiations."

KNALL, *m.* Bang. *Das war 'n richtiger Knall, als die Nachricht kam.* "It was a real shock when the news came." ***Einen Knall haben.*** To be crazy. *Der hat 'n Knall, 'n solches Risiko einzugehen.* "He's off his rocker taking a risk like that." ***Auf Knall und Fall.*** Suddenly/on the spot. *Wenn du's wieder tust, verlass ich dich auf Knall und Fall.* "If you do that again, I'll waste no time in leaving you."

KNALLEFFEKT, *m.* S.t. sensational/surprising. *Die Enthüllungen der Reporterin hatten einen richtigen Knalleffekt.* "The reporter's revelations came as a real bombshell."

KNALLEN. 1. To explode; slam; shoot. ***Hände hoch, oder es knallt!*** "Hands up, or I'll shoot!" ***Jmdm. eine knallen.*** To clout s.o. *Knall ihm eine!* "Give him a shot in the head!" **2.** To have sex. *Auf dem Strand knallten sie stundenlang.* "They screwed for hours on the beach." **3.** To get drunk. *Wir wollen uns heut abend voll knallen.* "We're gonna booze it up tonight."

KNALLENG. Skin-tight. *Ich brannte darauf, ihr die knallenge Bluse auszuziehen.* "I was hot to take off her skin-tight blouse."

KNALLHART = **BEINHART.**

KNALLIG. Gaudy; loud. *Auf seiner Beerdigung war seine Geliebte auffallend knallig bekleidet.* "His mistress was garishly dressed at his funeral."

KNALLKOPF/KNALLKOP, *m.* Blockhead; nutcase. *Das sieht dir ähnlich, du Knallkopf!* "That's just what I'd expect from you, you dumb dork."

KNALLTÜTE, *f.* = **KNALLKOPF/KNALLKOP.**

KNAPSEN. To skimp. *Mein Mann ist arbeitslos und wir müssen knapsen; wir sind wirklich knapp bei Kasse.* "My husband's unemployed and we have to skimp and scrape; we're really strapped for cash." Cf. KNAUSERN.

KNARRE, *f.* Gun (lit. rattle). *Man sieht ihn nie ohne seine Knarre.* "You never see him without his shooting iron."

KNAST, *m.* Jail. *Die meisten anderen Frauen des Scheichs waren glücklich; mir aber war der Harem ein Knast.* "Most of the sheik's other wives were happy, but the harem was a prison to me."

KNASTBRUDER, *m.* Jailbird. *Mit nur 17 Jahren wurde er mit abgebrühten Knastbrüdern eingelocht.* "He was only 17 when they locked him up with hard-boiled cons." Cf. KNACKI.

KNASTER, *m.* Pungent tobacco. *Deinen Knaster rauchst du draußen!* "You'll have to smoke that foul stuff outside!"

KNASTOLOGE, *hum.* = **KNASTBRUDER.**

KNATSCH, *m.* Trouble. *In der Kneipe hat's wieder Knatsch gegeben.* "There was trouble in the tavern again."

KNAUSER, *m.* Miser. *Mein Alter ist 'n richtiger Knauser.* "My old man's a real skinflint."

KNAUSEREI, *f.* Miserliness. *So was von Knauserei hab ich nie gesehen!* "I've never seen such stinginess."

KNAUSERIG. Stingy. *Sei nicht so knauserig!* "Don't be so tightfisted."

KNAUSERIGKEIT = **KNAUSEREI.**

KNAUSERN. To skimp. *Er knausert mit allem, nur nicht mit Eigenlob.* "He's stingy with everything except self-praise." Cf. KNAPSEN.

KNEIPE, *f., univ. student sl.* Evening of drinking (lit. tavern/bar). *Bei der Kneipe hat sich Rudi wieder ausgezeichnet.* "Rudi really distinguished h.s. again during the drinking bout."

KNEIPEN. To go bar hopping. *Im Urlaub haben wir jede*

Nacht gekneipt. "We went bar hopping every night during vacation."

KNEIPENBUMMEL, *m.* = **KNEIPTOUR.**

KNEIPENWIRT/KNEIPER/KNEIPIER, *m.* Tavern owner (the *-ier* in *Kneipier* is pronounced as in Fr.). *Eine Zeitlang war ich auch Kneipier.* "I was a barkeep for a while too."

KNEIPTOUR, *f.* Bar hopping. *Statt 'ner Kneiptour solltest du eher 'ne Kneippkur machen.* "Instead of going pub crawling you should take Kneipp treatments." (Sebastian Kneipp's hydrotherapeutic system features cold baths and abstinence from alcohol.)

KNEISEN, *Aust.* To notice. *Gekneist hab ich ihn schon, aber ich hab ihn wie Luft behandelt.* "I noticed him, but I ignored him."

KNETE, *f.* Money (*kneten* = to knead). *Hast keine Knete für mich?* "Haven't you got any bread for me?"

KNICK, *m.* **1.** Crack; crease. *Wegen der vielen Skandale hat ihre Karriere manchen Knacks und Knick bekommen; trotzdem ist sie nach wie vor ein Star.* "Her career's been marred by many a scandal but she continues to be a star." *Einen Knick in der Optik haben.* **2.** To see poorly. *Du siehst es nicht? Hast 'n Knick in der Optik?* "You don't see it? Are you blind?" **3.** To be a little crazy. *Der hat wohl 'n Knick in der Optik.* "He's a little off the beam."

KNICKER = **KNAUSER.**

KNIE, *n.* Knee. *In die Knie gehen.* To collapse. *Unsere Aktien sind in die Knie gegangen.* "Our stocks have dropped drastically." *Fick dir bloß nichts aufs/ins Knie!* Don't get your balls in an uproar! (lit. Just don't fuck anything into your knee!)

KNILCH, *m.* Rotten person; jerk; clown. *Ich kann diesen Knilch nicht verknusen.* "I can't stand that idiot."

KNILLE. 1. Drunk; exhausted. *Die Studenten waren alle knille.* "The students were all plastered." **2.** Bankrupt.

Hab keine Kohle mehr; bin total knille. "I have no more money; I'm flat broke."

KNISPELN. To have sex. *Ganz knusperfrisch bin ich nicht mehr; trotzdem wollen viele mich noch knispeln.* "I'm no spring chicken, but many still want to make it with me."

KNITTEL = KNÜPPEL.

KNITTELN = KNÜPPELN.

KNOBELBECHER, *m., mil. sl.* Army boot (lit. dice cup). *Er hatte es eilig und nahm nicht mal seine Knobelbecher ab.* "He was in a hurry and didn't even take off his boots."

KNOBELN. To throw dice. *,,Sag Kopf oder Zahl!" ,,Knobeln wir lieber darum."* " 'Say heads or tails (on a coin).' 'Let's toss for it instead.' "

KNOCHEN, *m.* **1.** Bone. *Jmdm. alle Knochen einzeln brechen.* To break every bone in s.o.'s body. *Dir brech ich alle Knochen einzeln!* "I'll break every bone in your body!" *Auf die Knochen gehen.* To be exhausting. *Jahrelang hab ich unter Tage geschuftet. Das geht auf die Knochen.* "For years I toiled in the mines. That wears you out." *Bis auf die Knochen.* Completely. *Wenn das rauskommt, sind wir bis auf die Knochen blamiert.* "If people find out about that, we'll look like complete idiots." **2.** Lazybones. *Du fauler Knochen!* "You lazybones/lazy lout!" **3.** Large key. *Blaubart gab ihr nicht den Knochen zum verbotenen Zimmer.* "Bluebeard didn't give her the key to the forbidden room."

KNOFEL, *m.* Garlic (for stand. *Knoblauch*). *Ohne Knofel schmeckt's fad.* "It tastes insipid without garlic."

KNÖLLCHEN, *n.* Parking ticket (lit. small tuber). *Was, wieder ein Knöllchen?* "What, another parking ticket?"

KNOLLE, *f.* Big nose (lit. tuber). *Er hat 'ne rote Knolle, ist aber kein Alker.* "He's got a red schnoz, but he's no alky."

KNÖPFE = KRÖTEN.

KNÖPFELN. To have sex. *Die Stimmung war schon aufgeknöpft, aber geknöpfelt haben wir nicht.* "Yes, the mood was rather unbuttoned, but we didn't get it on."

KNÖTTERN, *N.* To blather on. *Nur Knöttern kanste (kannst du); 's steckt nichts dahinter.* "All you do is talk nonsense; there's nothing behind it."

KNUBBELIG, *N.* Roly-poly (lit. lumpy). *Ja, er ist knubbelig, aber süß.* "Yes, he's pudgy, but sweet."

KNUDDELN, *N.* To hug and squeeze. *Sie waren zerstritten, aber jetzt knuddeln sie wieder.* "They were on the outs with each other, but now they're smooching again."

KNUFF, *m.* Nudge; push; blow. *Er hat mir 'nen Knuff gegeben.* "He gave me a poke."

KNUFFELIG. Cuddly. *Mein neuer Macker ist so knuffelig.* "My new boyfriend's so cuddly."

KNUFFEN. To push/nudge. *In der U-Bahn hat mich ein Lümmel in die Rippen geknufft.* "Some lout poked me in the ribs in the subway."

KNUFFI, *m., youth.* Pugnacious sort. *Bist Masochist? Was willst du mit dem Knuffi?* "Are you a masochist? What do you want with that bully?"

KNÜLCH = KNILCH.

KNÜLLE = KNILLE.

KNÜLLER, *m.* Great success. *Ihr erster Spielfilm war 'n Knüller.* "Her first feature film was a sensation."

KNÜPPEL, *m.* Cudgel; billy club. **Jmdm. einen Knüppel zwischen die Beine werfen.** To create difficulties for s.o. *Der Baubehörde macht's Spaß, uns Knüppel zwischen die Beine zu werfen.* "The housing authority enjoys giving us a hard time."

KNÜPPELN. 1. To beat up. *Die Hools haben ihn voll geknüppelt.* "The hooligans beat him brutally." **2.** To kick wildly (*sports sl.*). *Unsere Kickers haben geknüppelt, allein es hat nichts geholfen.* "Our football team kicked up a storm, but it didn't do any good."

KNÜPPELDICK. In excess; hard and fast (lit. cudgel thick). ***Wenn's kommt, kommt's immer gleich knüppeldick.*** (*Prov.*) It never rains but it pours. ***Knüppeldick voll sein.*** **1.** To be full to the rafters. *Die Disko war wieder knüppeldick voll.* "The disco was jam-packed again." **2.** To be very drunk. *Ja, und du warst wohl auch knüppeldick voll.* "And you were probably also soused to the gills."

KNÜPPELTHERAPIE, *f.* = **KLOPFTHERAPIE.**

KNUSPER, *youth.* Attractive; scrumptious; OK, with it (from stand. *knusprig* [crispy, crunchy]). *Hältst du den für ganz knusper?* "Do you think he's an OK guy?" ***Nicht ganz knusper in der Lampe/Waffel sein.*** To be soft in the head. *Er ist nicht ganz knusper in der Lampe.* "He's not quite right in the head."

KNUTSCHEN. To smooch. *Geknutscht haben wir, aber nicht gebumst.* "We petted, but didn't screw." Mich knutscht ein Affe/Bus/Elch/Elefant/Jet/Kamel/Krokodil, etc. See ELCH.

KNUTSCHFLECK, *m.* Love bite. *Sie zeigte stolz ihre Knutschflecke.* "She proudly showed her love bites."

KNUTSCHINSEL, *f.* Lover's lane/place where petting goes on. *Das Autokino, Knutschinsel meiner Jugend, gibt's nicht mehr.* "The drive-in movie, lover's lane of my youth, no longer exists."

KNÜTTEL = **KNÜPPEL.**

KNÜTTELN = **KNÜPPELN.**

KOCHEM, *m.* Thief, crook (from Hebr. *chochem* [cunning]). *Du gehörst in den Knast, du gerissener Kochem.* "You belong in jail, you sly crook."

KOCHEMER KO(H)L = **KOCHEMER LOSCHEN.**

KOCHEMER/KOCHUMER LOSCHEN, *n.* Thieves' slang (from Hebr. *chochem* [cunning; crook] and *lâschôn* [language]). Cf. KESSENLOSCHEN; ROTWELSCH.

KOCHEMER SPIEß, *m.* Crooked innkeeper/fence (from

Hebr. *chochem* and *uschpitza* [innkeeper]). *In der Herberge vom Kochemer Spieß wurden die Gäste oft ausgeraubt oder gar ermordet.* "In that fence's inn, guests were often robbed or even murdered."

KOFFER, *m.* 1. Suitcase. *Die Koffer packen.* To pack one's bags. *Wenn du's wieder tust, kannst du die Koffer packen.* "If you do it again, you're out." *Den großen Koffer bauen.* (*Youth.*) To scram. *Bauen wir den großen Koffer, sonst erwischen sie uns.* "Let's clear out fast or they'll nab us." *Einen Koffer stehen lassen.* To fart. *Wer hat hier 'n Koffer stehen lassen?* "Who's been farting here?" 2. Nonsense. (*Youth.*) *Wer kann so 'n Koffer anhören.* "Who can listen to crap like that?"

KOHL, *m.* 1. Cabbage. *Alten Kohl aufwärmen.* To dredge up the past. *Wärm doch nicht immer wieder den alten Kohl auf!* "Will you quit bringing up all that old stuff!" *Seinen Kohl bauen.* To live quietly. *Man hört nichts mehr von ihr; sie baut irgendwo auf'm Lande ihren Kohl.* "You don't hear any more about her; she's cultivating her garden somewhere in the country." *Das macht den Kohl auch nicht fett.* See FETT. 2. Nonsense. *Der redet nur Kohl, macht immer nur Kohl.* "He's full o' baloney and always just messes around."

KOHLDAMPF SCHIEBEN. To be hungry (lit. to push cabbage steam). *Warum soll der sich voll fressen und ich Kohldampf schieben?* "Why should I starve while he stuffs his face?"

KOHLE, *f.* Money (lit. coal). *Heut abend kriegst du deine Kohle zurück.* "You'll get your dough back tonight." *Dicke Kohle.* Lots of money. *Als Dealer hat er dicke Kohle gemacht.* "He made big bucks as a drug dealer."

KOHLEN. To exaggerate; lie; boast (lit. to smoulder; carbonize). *Lass ihn nur kohlen, aber glaub ihm nichts.* "Just let him go on, but don't believe anything he says."

KOHLENKELLER, *m.* Bank vault (lit. money cellar). *Sie drangen in den Kohlenkeller rein, konnten aber nicht raus.* "They got into the bank vault but couldn't get out."

KOHLENPULVER = KOHLE.

KOKOLORES/KOKOLORUS, *m.* Nonsense; silly fuss. *Ach, mach doch nicht so 'n Kokolores!* "Just stop that foolish carrying on."

KOKS, *m.* **1.** Nonsense (lit. coke). *Du laberst nur Koks.* "That's a lot o' malarkey." **2.** Money. *Her mi'm Koks.* "Gimme the dough."

KOKS, *m.* or *n.* Coke (for *Kokain*). *Er verkauft nur Koks vom Feinsten.* "He sells only top-grade coke."

KOKSEN. To take cocaine. *Auch Freud soll gekokst haben.* "Freud's supposed to have been a snow candy snorter too."

KOKSER/KOKSFATZKE, *m.* Cocaine user. *Sherlock Holmes war auch Koksfatzke.* "Sherlock Holmes was also a snowbird." Cf. SCHNUFFI.

KOLBEN, *m.* **1.** Big nose (lit. piston; gun butt). *Sie findet seinen Kolben schön.* "She thinks his beak is attractive." **2.** Penis. *Mein Macker hatte 'n kräftigen Kolben, bis er defekt wurde.* "My guy had a potent penis before it went on the blink." Cf. FLINTE; GURKE **1, 3;** RÜBE; RÜSSEL.

KOLDERN, *S.* To quarrel; be quarrelsome. *Sie koldern wieder.* "They're on the outs again."

KOMMUNISTENFRESSER, *m.* Rabid anti-Communist (lit. Communist devourer). *Brecht und Eisler wurden von den Kommunistenfressern verhört.* "Brecht and Eisler were interrogated by the rabid anti-Communists."

KOMPI/KOMPOSTI, *m., youth, pej.* Decrepit old person, human compost. *Nur Gruftis und Vorgruftis gab's auf der Kompostiparty.* "Only the dead and nearly dead were at the old fossils' party."

KONDUKTEUR/KONDUKTOR, *m., youth, Aust., Swiss.* Leader of the pack. *Spielst du etwa auf den Kondukteur hier?* "Are you trying to make like the big boss here?"

KONFUSI, *m.* Confused person. *Der Typ war vielleicht 'n Konfusi, bis er Konfutse und Maimonides las.* "That guy was all mixed up till he read Confucius and Maimonides."

KONNÄCKTSCHENS, *youth.* Contacts (translit. of Eng. "connections"). *Kai hat tolle Konnäcktschens zu einem coolen Dealer.* "Kai's got terrific connections to a great (drug) dealer."

KÖNNEN. To be able. *Mich (auch, mal) können.* You know what *you* can do. (Short for the vulgar *am Arsch lecken können* [you can kiss my ass]. See GÖTZ; LECKEN.) *Ihr könnt mich mal, wenn euch meine Zigarre stört.* "You can go to hell if my cigar bothers you."

KONSUMFUZZI, *pej., youth.* Consumerist; plutocrat. *Die meisten Gruftis sind Konsumfuzzis.* "Most oldsters (those over 30) are consumer freaks."

KONSUMI, *pej. youth.* Materialist, consumerist. *Wir Yiffies sind keine Konsumis, wie die Yuppies.* "We yiffies aren't into consumerism, like the yuppies."

KOPF, *m.* **1.** Head. *Du hast's wohl am Kopf.* You need to see a shrink. *Keinen Kopf und keinen Arsch finden/ haben.* To find/have no solid footing. *An deiner Geschichte find ich keinen Kopf und keinen Arsch.* "I can't make head or tails of your story." *Etwas im Kopf nicht aushalten können.* To find incredible. *Wenn ich's dir sag, hältst du's im Kopf nicht aus.* "It'll blow your mind when I tell you." *Sich auf den Kopf spucken lassen.* To let people spit all over one. *Der lässt sich von jedem auf den Kopf spucken.* "He lets everyone walk all over him." *Jmdm. den Kopf waschen.* To tell s.o. off. *Die Chefin hat ihm den Kopf gewaschen.* "The boss gave him a piece of her mind." *Jmdn. einen Kopf kürzer machen.* To take s.o. down a peg or two. *Ich hab diesem Unhold schon mehrmals einen Kopf kürzer gemacht, aber es wachsen ihm immer neue nach.* "I've already cut that creep down to size several times, but he keeps puffing up again." See WACHSEN. **2.** Stubbornness. *Alles muss immer nach deinem Kopf gehen.* "You always have to have your own way." **3.** Person, personage. *Damals trafen sich die geistreichen Köpfe Königsbergs in einer Kürbishütte.* "At that time Königsberg's intellectuals met in a hut filled with pumpkins."

KORINTHENKACKER, *m.* Stickler for detail (lit. currant shitter). *Solche Korinthenkacker gehen mir echt auf den Keks.* "Fusspots like that get on my nerves." Cf. ROSINEN-SCHEIßER.

KORRUPTI, *m., youth.* Corrupt person. *Die Politpopper sind alle Korruptis.* "The politicos are all corrupt."

KOSCHER. On the up-and-up (lit. conforming to Jewish dietary laws). *Der Deal ist absolut koscher, total OK, voll astrein.* "The deal's absolutely straight, totally OK."

KOSMISCH. See URST.

KÖTER, *m.* Mutt. *Ihr Kater und mein Köter vertragen sich nicht.* "Her tomcat and my old mutt don't get along."

KOTZBROCKEN, *m.* Piece of filth (lit. lump of vomit). *Dieser Kotzbrocken soll mir nur nicht vor die Flinte kommen.* "That scuzzball better keep out of my way!"

KOTZBUDE, *f., youth.* Rotten school (lit. "puke hut"). *Wer kann's schon in dieser Kotzbude aushalten?* "Who can stand it in this dump of a school?"

KOTZE, *f.* Vomit. *Kabbelig das Meer und Kotze überall, aber so gefiel mir die Kreuzfahrt.* "The sea was choppy and there was puke everywhere, but that was the way I liked the cruise."

KOTZEN. To vomit. **Zum Kotzen sein.** To be revolting. *Das ist zum Kotzen, wie er der Chefin Honig um den Mund schmiert.* "It's revolting the way he butters up the boss." Cf. (SICH) AUSKOTZEN.

KOTZHÄSSLICH. Hideous (lit. "puke ugly"). *Kotzhässlich ist die; bumst aber toll.* "She's ugly as sin, but a great lay."

KRAFTHUBER/KRAFTMEIER/KRAFTPROTZ, *m., pej.* Muscle man; strongman. *Im Bett ist dieser Kraftprotz nur 'ne Null.* "That muscle man's just a dud in bed."

KRAFTMEIEREI, *f.* Strong-arm tactics. *Wir brauchen Verständnis, keine verbale Kraftmeierei.* "We need understanding, not inflammatory language."

KRAGEN, *m.* **1.** Collar. *Bis jmdm. der Kragen platzt.* Until s.o. is fed up. *Endlich platzte ihm der Kragen.* "He finally blew his top/got fed up." **2.** Stuffed shirt. (*Youth.*) *Dieser Kragen geht mir auf den Zeiger.* "That stuffed shirt pushes all my buttons."

KRÄHE. See NEBELKRÄHE.

KRÄHEN. See HAHN.

KRAKEEL, *m.* Row, racket. *Die Nachbarn machen immer wieder Krakeel.* "The neighbors are constantly having noisy quarrels."

KRAKEELEN. To quarrel. *Ja, jede Nacht krakeelt's bei ihnen.* "Yes, they get into a row every night."

KRAKEELER, *m.* Rowdy. *Auch ihre Kinder sind Krakeeler.* "Their children are also rowdies."

KRAKEL, *m.* Scribble. *Wer kann diesen Krakel lesen?* "Who can read this scrawl?"

KRAKELEI, *f.*/**KRAKELFUß,** *m.* = **KRAKEL.**

KRALLEN. 1. To swipe (lit. to claw). *Das Kind krallt mir all meine Bleistifte.* "That kid makes off with all my pencils." Cf. ERGEIERN; KLAUEN. **2.** To nab. *Die Bullen haben sie gekrallt.* "The cops caught them."

KRAM, *m.* **1.** Stuff; junk. *Den (ganzen) Kram (hin) schmeißen/(hin)werfen.* To chuck it all. *Ich hatte es satt und warf den ganzen Schulkram.* "I was fed up and dropped out of school." **2.** Agenda; business. *Mein letztes Buch passte den Parteibonzen nicht in den Kram.* "My last book didn't fit in with the party bosses' scheme of things."

KRAMBAMBULI/KRAMBIMBAMBAMBULI, *m., univ. students sl.* Any alcoholic drink (orig. a Danzig gin). *Bambule machen? Nein, wir bleiben froh und trinken unsern Krambambuli.* "Go out and riot? No, we stay happy and put away the booze." Cf. POKULIEREN.

KRAMBAMBULIST, *m.* University student devoted to

drinking. *Wir Krambambulisten glauben an leben und leben lassen.* "We boozers believe in live and let live."

KRÄMER, *m.* **1.** Small shopkeeper, general store operator. *Die Engländer seien ein Volk von Krämern, behauptete oft Napoleon.* "Napoleon often said that the English are a nation of shopkeepers." **2.** Petty minded, stingy person. See KRÄMERGEIST/KRÄMERSEELE.

KRÄMERGEIST, *m.*/**KRÄMERSEELE,** *m.* Petty-minded person; skinflint. *Mercator (eigentlich Gerhard Kremer) war keine Krämerseele; seine Karten zeigen die ganze Welt.* "Mercator (real name Gerhard Kremer) wasn't small-minded; his maps show the whole world."

KRAMURI, *f.* Aust. form of KRAM.

KRANKFEIERN/KRANKMACHEN = BLAUMACHEN.

KRASS, *youth.* Wonderful (usually used in compounds such as *hyperkrass; maxikrass; ultrakrass*). *Das Konzert war turbokrass!* "The concert was mind-blowing!"

KRATZBÜRSTE, *f.* Touchy individual (lit. wire brush). *Lass diese Kratzbürste in Ruhe!* "Leave that curmudgeon alone."

KRATZBÜRSTIG. Touchy. *Sei doch nicht so verdammt kratzbürstig!* "Don't be so damned bristly."

KRATZEN. To scratch. *Jmds. Arsch nicht kratzen.* To be a matter of indifference to s.o. (lit. not to scratch s.o.'s ass). *Das soll meinen Arsch nicht kratzen, ob du hingehst oder nicht.* "It's no skin off my butt whether you go or not."

KRÄTZER, *m.* New wine; cheap wine. *So viel Kohle hast du für diesen Krätzer ausgegeben?* "You spent that much for this lousy wine?"

KRAUT, *n.* **1.** Herb, plant. *Gegen den Tod ist kein Kraut gewachsen.* (*Prov.*) Death is inevitable. *Vielleicht gibt's doch ein Kraut gegen den Tod, auf diesem oder einem anderen Planeten.* "Maybe there's an antidote to death growing on this or some other planet." **2.** Herbage, foliage. *Ins Kraut schießen.* To run wild (lit. to go to seed). *Wer wird ihre Nachfolgerin sein? Da schießen sich die*

Spekulationen ins Kraut. "Who'll be her successor? There's no end of speculation about that." **3.** Cabbage. *Das macht das Kraut auch nicht fett.* See FETT.

KRAWALL, *m.* Riot; brawl. *Nächstes Jahr wollen die Chaoten wieder großen Krawall machen.* "The chaos kids are planning to go on a rampage again next year."

KRAWALLBRUDER/KRAWALLMACHER/KRAWAL-LO, *m.* Hooligan. *Warum hängst du mit diesen Krawallos rum?* "Why do you hang out with those rowdies?"

KRAWATTE, *f.* Necktie. *Sich einen hinter die Krawatte gießen/kippen.* See LAMPE.

KRAWATTENDJANGO, *m., pej., youth.* Bureaucrat; official (lit. "tie dude"). *Jetzt ist er Krawattendjango wie sein Vater, aber einst war er Chaot.* "Once he was a hellraiser; now he's a functionary like his father."

KRAWATTENMUFFEL, *m.* Person who doesn't like to wear ties. *Ich weiß, du bist Krawattenmuffel, aber beim Empfang in der Botschaft gibt's Krawattenzwang.* "I know you're hostile to ties, but they're obligatory for the reception in the embassy."

KRAXELN, *S.* To climb laboriously. *Meine alten Haxen kraxeln noch auf die Berge hinauf.* "My old legs still clamber up the mountains."

KREBSGANG, *m.* Regression; reversal (lit. crab's walk). *Einen/den Krebsgang gehen/machen/nehmen.* To decline. *Die Aktien nehmen einen Krebsgang.* "Stocks are declining."

KREMPEL, *m.* Stuff; junk. *Der ganze Krempel, den er gesammelt hatte, wird jetzt von einigen für Kunst gehalten.* "All that junk he collected is now considered art by some." *Den ganzen Krempel (hin)schmeißen/(hin)werfen.* See KRAM.

KREN, *m. Aust.* Horseradish. *Seinen Kren zu etwas geben/in alles seinen Kren reiben.* To put one's two cents in (into everything). *Nix versteht er davon, wird aber gewiss seinen Kren dazu geben.* "He knows nothing about it, but will undoubtedly put in his two cents' worth." Cf. SENF.

KREPIEREN. To croak (lit. to explode). *Wenn er jetzt krepiert, ist's mir scheißegal.* "I gon't give a shit if he drops dead now."

KRIBBELIG. Edgy. *Vorm Exam war ich 'n bisschen kribbelig.* "I was a bit edgy before the exam."

KRIECHEN. To crawl/creep. *Jmdm. in den Arsch/Hintern kriechen.* To be sycophantic. *Sie versuchen alle, der neuen Chefin in den Hintern zu kriechen.* "They're all trying to brownnose the new boss." Cf. ARSCHKRIECHER.

KRIEGEN. To get. *Eine/ein paar kriegen.* To get smacked. *Tu's noch einmal und du kriegst eine von mir.* "Do it again and I'll whack you."

KRIEGSFUß. See FUß.

KRIMSKRAMS = KRAM 1.

KRINGELIG. Crinkly; squiggly. *Sich kringelig lachen.* To die laughing. *Beim Film haben wir uns kringelig gelacht.* "We doubled up with laughter during the movie."

KRINGELN. To curl (hair); make pastry rings. *Zum Kringeln sein.* To be hilarious. *Die Sendung war zum Kringeln.* "The TV show was sidesplitting." Cf. PIEPEN; SCHIEßEN.

KRITIKALO, *m., youth.* Chronic criticizer. *Diesen Kritikalo kann ich nicht ab.* "I can't stand that self-appointed critic."

KROKOFANTÖS, *youth.* Supersensational (a mix of *Krokodil* and *Elefant*). *Krokofantös war die Fete!* "The party was fantabulous!" See ELEFANTÖS.

KRONE, *f.* 1. Crown. *Die Krone aufsetzen.* To take the cake. *Zuerst haut er uns übers Ohr; jetzt verunglimpft er uns. Das setzt der Unverschämtheit die Krone auf!* "First he cheats us; now he's slandering us. That takes the cake for impudence." *Jmdm. fällt keine Perle/kein Stein/ Zacken aus der Krone.* To be no big deal to s.o. *Dir* *würde kein Stein aus der Krone fallen, wenn du 'n bisschen mit Hand anlegtest.* "It wouldn't kill you if you pitched in a little." **2.** Head. *Was ist dir denn in die Krone gefahren?* "What's gotten into you?" ***Jmdm. in die Krone steigen.*** To go to one's head. *Der Sekt ist mir schnell in die Krone gestiegen.* "The champagne went to my head fast." ***Einen in der Krone haben.*** See ZACKEN **1.**

KROPF, *m.* **1.** Goiter. ***Überflüssig wie ein Kropf.*** Totally unnecessary (lit. superfluous like a goiter). *Deine bissigen Bemerkungen waren mir so überflüssig wie ein Kropf.* "I needed your nasty remarks like a hole in the head." **2.** Crop (birds). ***Seinen Kropf leeren.*** To get s.t. off one's chest. *Mein Mann leert oft seinen Kropf bei mir, macht seinem Frust Luft; aber er denkt nie an meine Gefühle.* "My husband often unloads his anger and frustration on me; but he never thinks of my feelings."

KROPPZEUG, *n.* **1.** Bunch of brats. *Was hat das Kroppzeug wieder angerichtet?* "What mischief have those rotten kids gotten into again?" **2.** Rabble. *Mit diesem Kroppzeug haben wir nichts am Hut.* "We have nothing in common with that riffraff." **3.** Junk. *Das ganze Kroppzeug nutzt ja gar nichts.* "That whole pile of junk is worthless."

KRÖTE, *f.* Toad. ***Eine Kröte schlucken.*** To make a concession grudgingly (lit. to swallow a toad). *In den Verhandlungen haben wir eine Kröte nach der anderen schlucken müssen.* "We had to give in on one issue after another in the negotiations."

KRÖTEN, *pl.* Money (lit. toads). *Drück nur schnell die Kröten ab!* "Just hand over the dough, fast."

KRUMME TOUR, *f.* Crooked doings. *Hier läuft 'ne verdammt krumme Tour!* "Some really dirty rotten business is going on here."

KÜBELN. 1. To booze (*Kübel* = bucket, pail). *Mit den Kumpeln in der Kneipe kübeln, nur das kannst du!* "Putting away buckets of booze with the boys in the bar, that's all you're good for!" **2.** To vomit. *Kübelt in der Bar* *oder auf der Straße, aber nicht hier.* "Do your vomiting in the bar or on the street, but not here."

KUDDELMUDDEL, *m., n.* Mess; confusion. *Welch Kuddelmuddel!* "What a mess!"

KUH, *f.* Cow. *Die Kuh ist vom Eis.* A difficult problem is solved (lit. the cow's off the ice). *Beide Seiten haben Kröten geschluckt, und jetzt ist endlich die Kuh vom Eis.* "Both sides made concessions, and the issue's finally settled." *Hier fliegt 'ne Kuh.* See BÄR. *Die Kuh fliegen lassen.* See SAU.

KULI, *m.* Ballpoint pen. *Kulis kommen mir oft abhanden.* "I often lose ballpoints."

KULTIG, *youth.* New; unconventional; unique. *Ihre Skulpturen sind wirklich voll kultig.* "Her sculptures are like no others I've ever seen."

KUMMERSPECK, *m., hum.* Excess weight due to emotion-related overeating (lit. "grief bacon"). *Verknall dich wieder richtig, dann wirst du deinen Kummerspeck abspecken!* "Fall head over heels in love again, then you'll work off the weight you've gained by compulsive eating."

KUPPELINGENIEUR = **KUPPELMACKER.**

KUPPELMACKER, *m.*/**KUPPELMACKERIN,** *f.* Pimp/ procuress (*kuppeln* = to couple). *Wenn du besondere Wünsche hast, bist du bei der Kuppelmackerin an der richtigen Adresse.* "If you have special requests, that madam will fix you up just right."

KUPPELMUTTER = **KUPPELMACKERIN.** Cf. PUFF-MUTTER.

KÜRBIS, *n., youth.* Head (lit. pumpkin). *Jmdm. auf den Kürbis gehen.* To annoy s.o. *Dein Geseire geht mir echt auf den Kürbis.* "Your bellyaching is giving me a headache."

KURVE, *f.* Curve, bend. *Die Kurve kratzen.* To clear off fast; disappear. *Jetzt müssen wir aber die Kurve rapido kratzen.* "Now we've got to get out of here fast."

KURZ. Short. ***Kurz und klein schlagen.*** To beat to a pulp. *Der Besoffene wollte die Kneipe und den Kneipier kurz und klein schlagen.* "The drunk wanted to smash up the tavern and the barkeep."

KURZER, *m.* **1.** Short circuit (for *kurzschluss*). *Ach, schon wieder 'n Kurzer!* "Oh, another short circuit." **2.** Shot glass of hard liquor. *Gib mir noch 'n Kurzen!* "Gimme another short one!" **3.** Shorty; 10–14-year-old. (*Youth.*) *Was wollen diese Kurzen hier in der Disko?* "What do those half pints want here in the disco?"

KURZSCHLUSSHANDLUNG, *f.* Knee-jerk/spontaneous reaction (lit. short-circuit act). *Der Mord war vorsätzlich, keine Kurzschlusshandlung.* "The murder was premeditated, not a crime of passion."

KUSSELPERLE, *f., youth, E.* Kissable, cuddly girl. *Ja, küssen und knutschen will sie nur, meine Kusselperle; aber manchmal tut sie des Guten zu viel.* "Yes, she just wants to kiss and smooch, my cuddle-cutey, but sometimes she overdoes it."

KUTSCHE, *f.* Car (lit. coach). *Hast noch die alte Kutsche?* "Still got that old jalopy?" Cf. PRUNKPROTZKUTSCHE; RETOURKUTSCHE.

KUTTE, *f., youth.* **1.** Hooded monk's robe. ***Aus der Kutte springen.*** To leave a religious order (lit. to jump out of the habit). *Dieser aus der Kutte gesprungene Mönch ist jetzt Freigeist und FKK-Apostel (Freikörperkulturapostel).* "That unfrocked monk's now a freethinker and ardent nudist." **2.** Jacket; coat. *Mann, ist die vielleicht 'ne knallige Kutte!* "Man, that's some sharp jacket!"

LABBERN = LABERN.

LABEL-LADY, *f.* Woman preoccupied with designer fashion. See LACKO.

LABERFRITZE, *m.* Windbag. *Für Laberfritzen und Quasselstrippen hab ich keine Zeit.* "I have no time for windbags and chatterboxes." Cf. SABBELHEINI.

LABERFRITZEN, *pl., youth.* Authority figures. *Ich lass sie nur labern, die Laberfritzen.* "I just let them babble on, the baloney throwers."

LABERN. To talk nonsense. *Gönn dir mal 'ne Labepause und hör auf zu labern.* "Give it a rest and quit babbling."

LACK, *m.* Varnish; lacquer. ***Der Lack ist ab.*** The bloom is off the rose. *Bei dem Macker ist längst schon der Lack ab.* "That guy's seen better days." ***Im Lack sein.*** To be OK. *Bei uns ist wieder alles im Lack.* "We're in great shape again." See FERTIG.

LACKAFFE, *m.* Dandy (lit. lacquered monkey). See LACKO.

LACKEL, *m., S.* Oaf. *Diesen Lackel lad ich nicht ein.* "I'm not inviting that lout."

LACKIEREN. 1. To put on; swindle (lit. to varnish). *Der Heiratsschwindler hat die Witwe ganz schön lackiert.* "The con man really took the widow for a ride." **2.** To beat up. See POLIEREN.

LACKIERTER/LACKIERTE, *m., f.* S.o. who's been taken for a ride. *Am Ende wirst du der Lackierte sein.* "You'll wind up the big chump."

LACKMEIERN = **LACKIEREN 1.**

LACKO, *m., pej., youth.* Dandy (for *Lackaffe*; cf. GECKO **1**). *Dieser Lacko und die Label-Lady sind wie füreinander geschaffen.* "That fashion-plate fop and the label-lady are made for each other."

LADEN, *m.* Store. See SAULADEN.

LAGE. See SCHMEIßEN.

LAHMARSCH, *m.* Slowpoke (lit. lame ass). *Mach dich auf die Socken, du Lahmarsch.* "Get your butt moving, lazy bum."

LAHMARSCHIG. Slow moving. *Seine Filme sind mir alle zu lahmarschig.* "All his films are a drag."

LAMPE, *f.* Lamp. *Sich einen auf die Lampe gießen/Öl auf die Lampe gießen.* To knock back a drink. *Jetzt will ich mir aber einen auf die Lampe gießen.* "I'm going to have a little snort now." *Die Lampe ausschießen.* (*Youth.*) **1.** To get very drunk (lit. to shoot out the lamp). *Er hatte sich die Lampe ausgeschossen.* "He was dead drunk." **2.** To kill. *Sein Gelabere von der inneren Erleuchtung und der unsterblichen Seele törnte mich total ab; ich hatte Lust, ihm die Lampe auszuschießen.* "His babbling about inner illumination and the immortal soul really turned me off; I felt like blowing him away." Cf. LICHT.

LANGER LULATSCH = **LANGES LASTER.**

LANGES LASTER/LANGES REGISTER, *n.* Lanky fellow/tall person. *Sie hat 'nen Zwerg, später 'n langes Register geheiratet.* "She married a dwarf, and later a very tall guy."

LAPPEN, *pl., youth.* Banknotes; money (lit. rags). *Wenn wir nur die Lappen hätten!* "If only we had the bread!" See BLAUER LAPPEN; FAHRLAPPEN; GIERLAPPEN.

LARI/LARIFARI, *m.* Clown. *Mach nicht den Lari bei*

ihnen! "Don't play the fool at their place." See RAUS-LASSEN **1.**

LARIFARI, *n.* Nonsense. *Behalt dein Larifari für dich.* "Keep your foolishness to y.s."

LASCH. Insipid; limp. *Ich esse gern scharf, weil bei meinen Eltern der Fraß immer lasch war.* "I like spicy food because the grub was always tasteless at my parents."

LASCHI, *m., youth.* Wimp. *Sei kein Laschi!* "Don't be such a wimp."

LASS DICH ZUSCHEIßEN! Get stuffed! (lit. Go get covered with shit!). *Deine Hilfe will ich nicht, Siffkopf! Lass dich zuscheißen!* "I don't want your help, shithead! Go flush y.s. down the toilet!"

LÄSSIG = **LOCKER 2.**

LATEIN, *n.* Jargon (lit. Latin). ***Mit seinem Latein am Ende sein.*** To have no further remedy. *Die Ärzte sind jetzt mit ihrem Latein am Ende.* "The doctors don't know what to do now." Cf. JÄGERLATEIN.

LATSCHEN, *m., pl.* **1.** Beat up shoes/slippers. See KIPPEN. **2.** Feet. *Nimm deine Latschen vom Sofa weg!* "Get your big feet off the sofa."

LATSCHEN. To shuffle along. *Latsch nicht so; mach mal 'n bisschen zack!* "Don't drag your feet; snap to it!" Cf. ABLATSCHEN; ANGELATSCHT KOMMEN.

LATTE, *f.* **1.** Lathe; slat; bar. ***Eine lange Latte.*** Tall person. *Aus dem Kleinen ist 'ne lange Latte geworden.* "The little lad's grown very tall." ***Nicht alle auf der Latte haben.*** To be crazy. *Du hast wohl nicht alle auf der Latte.* "You must be nuts." ***Jmdn. auf der Latte haben.*** To be out to get s.o. *Einst stand er bei ihnen hoch im Kurs; jetzt haben sie ihn auf der Latte.* "Once he was in their good books, now they've set their sights on him." **2.** Erect penis. *Beim Duschen hatten die Knastis alle 'ne Latte.* "The jailbirds all had boners when taking a shower." **3.** List; series. *'Ne ganze Latte Wünsche für den Weihnachtsmann hat die Kleine schon.* "She's got a whole string of things she wants Santa to bring her."

LATÜCHTE, *f., hum.* Lamp; light. *Geh mir aus der Latüchte! Dein Vater war kein Glaser.* "Get out of my light. You're not transparent (lit. your father wasn't a glazier)."

LATZ, *m.* Bib; flap. ***Jmdm. eine/einen/eins/ein paar vor den Latz knallen/ballern.*** To sock s.o. *Pass auf, oder ich knall dir eins vor den Latz.* "Watch out or I'll clobber you."

LAU. 1. Mild; tepid (of Germanic origin). *Seine Haltung war ziemlich lau.* "His attitude was rather lukewarm." **2.** Nothing (from Hebr. via Yiddish). *Sie erwarten, dass ich's für lau mache, aber nichts drin!* "They expect me to do it for nothing, but no way!"

LAUAFFE = LAUMANN.

LAUBE. See FERTIG.

LAUFEN. To walk; run. ***Sich voll laufen lassen.*** See KANAL.

LAUFPASS, *m.* Walking papers. *Tu's wieder und du bekommst den Laufpass.* "Do it again and you'll get your walking papers."

LAUMANN, *m.* Weakling. *Harte, kernige Kerls will ich um mich, keine Laumänner!* "I want tough, hearty men around me, not wimps."

LAUS, *f.* Louse. ***Jmdm. ist eine Laus über die Leber gelaufen/gekrochen.*** To be in a foul mood (lit. a louse has crept over s.o.'s liver). *Ihm ist heute wieder 'ne Laus über die Leber gefahren.* "He's gotten up on the wrong side of the bed again today." ***Jmdm./sich eine Laus in den Pelz/ins Fell setzen.*** To harrass s.o./worry o.s. *Wenn du sie verklagst, setzt du dir selber nur 'ne Laus in den Pelz.* "If you sue them, you'll just be creating difficulties for y.s." ***Sich eine Laus über die Nase laufen lassen.*** To get upset (lit. to let a louse walk over one's nose). *Geil ab und lass dir keine Laus über die Nase laufen!* "Just cool off and don't sweat it."

LAUSEKALT. Icy cold. *Lausekalt ist's draußen.* "It's freezing cold outside."

LAUSEN. 1. To delouse. *Mich laust der Affe!* "I'll be a monkey's uncle!" **2.** To fleece. *In dem Nepplokal wird man echt gelaust.* "They really take you to the cleaners in that clipjoint."

LAUSIG. Lousy. *Kinder kauft euch Kämme, die Zeit wird lausig!* (*Prov.*) Get a hold of combs, kiddos, lousy (bad) times are coming!

LEBEN, *n.* Life. *Leben in die Bude bringen.* To liven up the party/place. *Der Exhibitionist hat wenigstens 'n bisschen Leben in die Bude gebracht.* "The exhibitionist at least put a little life in the joint."

LEBERWURST, *f.* Liverwurst. *Die beleidigte Leberwurst spielen.* To pout (lit. to play the insulted liver sausage). *Ja, spiel nur die beleidigte Leberwurst; mir ist's Wurst!* "Go ahead and sulk if you want. I don't care."

LECK MICH!/LECKT MICH! *Abbr. form of* LECK(T) MICH AM ARSCH.

LECK MICH AM ÄRMEL! Kiss my backside!/Go to hell! (*Ärmel* [sleeve] is euph. for *Arsch*).

LECK/LECKT MICH AM ARSCH! Kiss my ass! *Ich soll's bezahlen? Leck mich am Arsch!* "Me pay for it? Go to hell!" Cf. GÖTZ!; KÖNNEN.

LEGEN. To lay/put. *Ein Ei legen* (lit. to lay an egg). **1.** To defecate. *Wartet noch auf mich, ich muss 'n Ei legen.* "Wait for me, I've got to dump." **2.** To produce s.t. laborious and complicated. *Der Bericht des Senatausschusses liegt endlich vor. Sie haben wieder mal ein Ei gelegt.* "The Senate committee's report is finally in. They've produced a big dud/lead balloon again."

LEHM, *m.* Clay, loam. *Jmdm. einen feuchten Lehm angehen.* See FEUCHT.

LEIM, *m.* Glue. *Auf den Leim führen/locken.* To deceive. *Der Schwindler hat sie auf den Leim gelockt.* "The con man took them for a ride."

LEIMEN. To con (lit. to glue). *Du Nullchecker, hast dich richtig leimen lassen!"* "You dummy, you really got taken for a ride."

LEINE, *f.* Rope. *Leine ziehen/die Leine losmachen.* To scram (lit. to cast off). *Zieh Leine, rapido, oder du bekommst eine gezischt.* "Get lost fast, or I'll clobber you."

LEISETRETER, *m.* Creep; timid person (lit. soft walker). *Nietzsche machte sich über Leisetreter und Leisebeter lustig.* "Nietzsche made fun of creeps and Holy Joes."

LENZ, *m.* Spring. *Einen faulen/lauen/ruhigen/sonnigen Lenz haben/schieben.* To loaf (lit. to have a lazy/peaceful/sunny spring). *In der Fastenzeit hat Veronika gar nicht gefastet oder gebüßt; sie schob eher einen sonnigen Lenz in Florida.* "During Lent Veronica did no fasting or mortifying; instead she took it nice and easy in Florida."

LERNFOSSIL = LERNFUZZI.

LERNFUZZI, *m., youth.* Teacher. *Was die Lernfuzzis labern, geht mir echt auf den Sack.* "What the teachers go on about gets on my case."

LESBE, *f., pej.* Lesbian. *Er hat sich in eine Lesbe verknallt.* "He fell for a lez."

LESEMUFFEL, *m.* S.o. who doesn't like to read. *Lise ist Lesemuffel; sie kuckt nur Fernsehen oder geht ins Kino.* "Lise never reads; she just watches TV or goes to the movies."

LICHT, *n.* Light. *Jmdm. das Licht ausblasen/auspusten.* To kill. *Die Fliesen konnte er nicht abdrücken und die Gangster haben ihm das Licht ausgepustet.* "He couldn't come up with the dough, and the hoods rubbed him out." Cf. LAMPE.

LIEBESMÜHE, *f. Vergebliche/verlorene Liebesmühe.* Wasted effort. *Ich versuchte den Staubsauger zu reparieren; 's war aber verlorene Liebesmühe.* "I tried to repair the vacuum, but it was no go."

LIEBESTÖTER, *m., pl., hum.* Long johns (lit. love killers).

Ich trug Reizwäsche und hoffte er würde seine Liebestöter ausziehen. "I wore sexy lingerie and hoped he'd take off his long johns."

LIEGEN. To lie/be situated. ***Richtig/falsch liegen.*** To be on the right/wrong track. *Mit 'nem klassichen schwarzen Kleid liegen Sie immer richtig.* "You can't go wrong with a basic black dress."

LINKEN. To deceive. *Der Ganove hat sie richtig gelinkt.* "That crook conned them good."

LINKE TITTE, *f., pej.* Militant, left-wing woman (lit. left tit). *Die Reporterin sagt die Wahrheit; daher schimpfen sie die Chauvis 'ne linke Titte.* "That reporter tells the truth; that's why male chauvinists call her an aggressive, leftist bitch."

LINKS. Left. ***Links liegen lassen.*** To slight/ignore. *Warum hast du mich links liegen lassen?* "Why'd you give me the cold shoulder?"

LIPPE, *f.* Lip. ***Eine dicke/große Lippe riskieren.*** To run one's mouth; be brazen. *Riskier hier keine große Lippe oder wir machen dir lange Beine.* "Don't shoot your mouth off here or we'll throw you out."

LOCH, *n.* Hole. ***Jmdm. ein Loch in den Arsch/Bauch fragen.*** To pester s.o. with questions. *Du Arschloch, hast mir schon 'n Loch in den Arsch gefragt. Schluss damit jetzt!* "You asshole, you've already torpedoed me with questions. That's enough now." ***Jmdm. ein Loch in den Arsch/Bauch reden.*** To talk s.o.'s head off. *Der hat mir wieder 'n Loch in den Bauch geredet.* "He talked my head off again."

LÖCHERN. To pester. *Hör auf, mich zu löchern!* "Quit bugging me."

LOCKER. 1. Loose. *Sie gehen mit dem Wort locker um.* "You talk freely." ***Locker machen.*** To loosen; make available. *Die Regierung will Krediten für die Förderung der Solarenergie locker machen.* "The government intends to make credits available for the promotion of solar energy."

Locker sitzen. To be freely available (lit. to fit loosely). *Wegen der Wirtschaftskrise sitzt das Geld nicht mehr so locker.* "People don't spend money the way they used to because of the economic crisis." **2.** Casual. *Einst war er verklemmt; jetzt ist er ganz locker.* "He used to be uptight; now he's real cool." *Locker vom Hocker.* Laid back, free and easy. *Diesmal soll's aber locker vom Hocker losgehen.* "This time let's do it in a calm, cool, collected way."

LODDEL, *m., S.* Pimp. *Mein Loddel ist oft recht lieb zu mir.* "My pimp's often very sweet to me."

LÖFFEL, *m.* **1.** Spoon. *Den Löffel abgeben/hinlegen/hinwerfen/fallen lassen/wegschmeißen.* To die (lit. to surrender/put down/throw away/drop the spoon). Cf. AB-NIBBELN; BESTECK. *Sie ist unheilbar krank und will den Löffel abgeben. Ich sag ihr aber, sie soll den Löffel nicht wegschmeißen, denn die Fülle des Lebens ist nie auszulöffeln.* "She's incurably ill and wants to check out/pull the plug. But I tell her it's not yet time to cash it all in, because life's abundance can never be exhausted." *Über den Löffel balbieren.* To swindle. *Er ist nicht der erste, den sie über'n Löffel balbiert hat.* "He's not the first one she's led by the nose." See WEISHEIT. **2.** Ear. *Die Löffel aufsperren/spitzen.* To listen closely. *Spitz nur schön die Löffel! ich sag's nur einmal.* "Listen up good now; I'm just going to say it once." *Jmdm. eins/ein paar hinter die Löffel geben/hauen.* To slap s.o. *Jetzt hau ich dir eins hinter die Löffel.* "I'm going to box your ears now."

LÖFFELN, *youth.* To understand (lit. to ladle). *Die Lebensweisheiten, die Oma mir austeilte, hab ich nie richtig gelöffelt.* "I never really understood the wise sayings Granny kept dishing out to me."

LOKALMATADOR, *m.* Popular local figure (sports, politics, etc.). *Unser Lokalmatador will sich jetzt international versuchen.* "Our local hero wants to try his luck on the international scene now."

LOKUS, *m.* Toilet. *Er verbringt immer mehr Zeit auf dem*

Lokus. "He spends more and more time in the john."

LOOKIST, *m.* S.o. obsessed with how they look. *Sei doch nicht so 'n Lookist!* "Don't be so hung up on externals."

LORE, *f.* Open railroad freight car/open car in a mine (from Brit. Eng. lorry [truck]). *Wie eine Lore Affen.* Like a wagonload of monkeys. *Die Kids haben sich wie 'ne Lore wilder Affen benommen.* "The kids behaved like a wagonload of wild monkeys."

LOSFLUPPEN, *youth.* To speed off/away. *Er schwang sich in seinen Hobel und fluppte los.* "He jumped into his car and sped off."

LOSHÄMMERN = **LOSFLUPPEN.**

LÖWE, *m.* Lion. *Gut gebrüllt, Löwe!* **1.** You said it!/That's tellin' 'em! (lit. well roared, lion!). *Du hast ihm gehörig den Kopf gewaschen. Gut gebrüllt, Löwe!* "You sure told him a thing or too. Good for you!" **2.** Well, aren't you terrifying (ironic use of **1** to belittle s.o.'s threats). *Mit Drohungen hielt er nicht hinterm Berg. Ich lachte ihn nur aus und sagte, „gut gebrüllt, Löwe!"* "He wasn't slow to make threats. I just laughed at him and said, 'My, aren't you the tiger!' " Cf. STOFFLÖWE.

LUDE, *m.* Pimp. *Ich arbeite selbständig; brauch keinen Luden.* "I'm an independent working girl; I don't need a pimp."

LUDENTONI, *S.* var. of **LUDE.**

LUFTBALLON, *m.* Condom (lit. balloon). *Der Luftballon ist geplatzt.* "The bag broke."

LUFTNUMMER, *f.* Hot air; stupid put-on. *Zieh nicht wieder eine deiner hohlen Luftnummern ab!* "Don't try another one of your stupid put-ons again."

LUFTIKUS, *m.* Unreliable fellow; intellectual lightweight. *Auf diesen Luftikus kann man nicht bauen.* "You can't count on that flibbertigibbet." Cf. BRUDER LEICHTFUß.

LULATSCH = **LANGER LULATSCH.**

LULLE, *f., youth.* **1.** Cigarette (lit. baby pacifier). *Die*

Lullen sind alle. "The cigs are all gone." **2.** Wimp. *Mensch, bist du aber 'ne Lulle.* "Man, you're just a chicken liver."

LULLIG, *youth.* Boring. *Mann, war der Film aber lullig!* "Man, that movie was dull!"

LULL UND LALL, *youth.* Completely exhausted. *Beim Konzert ging's mir nur so lala; später war ich total lull und lall.* "I was feeling only so-so at the concert; later I was really wasted."

LÜMMEL, *m.* Penis (lit. lout; rascal). *Er glaubt, sein Lümmel habe seinen eigenen Willen, und ich sei dazu da, ihn zu befriedigen.* "He thinks his dick's got a will of its own and that I exist to satisfy it." Cf. LÜMMELTÜTE.

LÜMMELEI, *f.* Sprawling/lounging. *Genug der Lümmelei! Ran an die Buletten!* "That's enough loafing! Get to work!"

LÜMMELN, *n.* Loafing around. *Die sind ja immer am Lümmeln!* "They're always goofing off."

LÜMMELTÜTE, *f.* Condom (lit. rascal [dick] bag). *Lümmeltüten gibt's überall zu kaufen.* "You can buy condoms everywhere."

LUNGENBRÖTCHEN, *n.*/**LUNGENFEGER/LUNGENTORPEDO,** *m.* Cigarette (lit. lung roll/sweeper/torpedo). Cf. BEUSCHELREIßER. *Mit den Lungenfegern ist mir 's Leben nur 'n Fegefeuer, statt 'ner Hölle.* "Life without cigarettes would be hell, instead of just purgatory for me."

LUNGENFLÜGEL, *pl.* Big breasts (lit. lung wings). *Mit solchen Lungenflügeln wird die gewiss nicht absaufen.* "With gourds like that she certainly won't drown."

LUNGERN. See RUMLUNGERN.

LUSCHE, *f.* Low card; ineffectual/slovenly person. *Mich behandelt er wie 'ne Lusche, damit er mit seinen Leistungen besser auftrumpfen kann.* "He treats me like dirt, so he can blow his own trumpet louder."

LUSTMOLCH, *m., often hum.* Sex fiend; sexy person (lit. lusty lizard). *Im Film spielt er einen impotenten alten Lustmolch.* "In the movie, he plays an impotent old lecher."

LUTSCHEN. See ABLUTSCHEN.

LUTSCHER, *m.* Lollipop; baby pacifier. See LULLE **2.**

LUXESE, *f.* Mix of *Luxus* (luxury) and *Askese* (asceticism); refers to people who are equally at home at the Ritz or in a thrift shop. *Du sprichst von Luxese, aber da ist herzlich wenig Askese dabei.* "You talk of blending luxury and asceticism, but there's precious little asceticism in your mix."

LUXUSDAMPFER, *m., youth.* Wonderful girl, terrific chick (lit. luxury liner). *Ein Luxusdampfer war sie einst; heute ist sie eher ein Trampschiff.* "Once she was a lassie with a classy chassis; now she's more like a battered old tramp steamer." Cf. FREGATTE; SCHLACHTSCHIFF.

LUXUSKAROSSE, *f.*/**LUXUSSCHLITTEN,** *m.* Big, fancy car (lit. luxury coach/sled). *Mit der Luxuskarosse kam er nicht durch die engen Gassen der Altstadt.* "He couldn't get through the old town's narrow streets in his limousine."

MACHEN. 1. To make. *Das macht nichts.* That doesn't matter. **2.** To play; be. *Er macht den Romeo.* "He's playing Romeo."

MACH'S GUT! So long!/Take care!/Good luck! *Mach's gut, und nicht zu oft.* Do it well and not too often! (puns on "to do it [sex]").

MACHULLE. 1. Bankrupt. *Sie wollten hoch hinaus, sind aber jetzt machulle.* "They had big plans, but they're bankrupt now." Cf. PLEITE; SCHOLLE. **2.** Exhausted. *Ich war völlig machulle.* "I was bushed." **3.** Crazy. *Ich denk, du bist machulle.* "I think you're nuts."

MACKE, *f.* **1.** Odd personality trait. *Er versuchte seine Macken zu verbergen und sich von seiner Sonnenseite zu zeigen.* "He tried to conceal his quirks and show his best side." *Eine Macke haben.* To be crazy. *Hast 'ne Macke, Mensch?* "Are you nuts, man?" **2.** Defect. *Der Motor hat 'ne Macke.* "There's s.t. wrong with the motor."

MACKER, *m., youth.* **1.** Guy. *Kennst du den Macker da?* "You know that dude?" *Der letzte Macker.* See MENSCH. **2.** Tough guy. *Mit dem Macker tanz ich nie wieder.* "I'll never dance with that macho guy again." **3.** Boyfriend. *Sie hat 'n neuen Macker.* "She's got a new boyfriend." Cf. KUPPELMACKER.

MACKERIN/MACKERINE, *f., youth.* Female. *Die Mackerine ist echt 'ne Wuchtbrumme, kann ich dir flüstern.* "I can tell you that broad's one tough battle-ax." Cf. KUP-PELMACKERIN.

MALEFIZKERL = **MORDSKERL 3.**

MALEN. To paint. ***Den Teufel an die Wand malen.*** To imagine the worst (lit. to paint the devil on the wall). *Mal doch nicht den Teufel an die Wand! 'S wird schon werden!* "Don't go looking for trouble; things'll work out."

MALESCHE, *f., N.* Unpleasantness. *Du hättest mir die Malesche sparen können.* "You could have spared me that bit of trouble."

MALL, *N.* **1.** Crazy (from a nautical term for variable winds that exasperate sailors). *Der ist megamall.* "He's a super loony." **2.** Exhausted. *Bin total mall; geh nicht auf die Piste.* "I'm bushed; I'm not going out on the town." **3.** Drunk. *Warst gestern voll mall.* "You were soused yesterday."

MALOCHE, *f.* Hard work (from Hebr. for "work," via ROTWELSCH). *Die tägliche Maloche in der Fabrik hängt mir zum Halse raus.* "I've had a bellyful of the daily grind in the factory."

MALOCHEN. To slave away. *Der Urlaub ist zu Ende und jetzt muss ich wieder malochen.* "Vacation's over and I've got to get back to the grind."

MAMPFEN. To munch; eat with one's mouth full. *Gibt's nichts mehr zu mampfen hier?* "Nothing more to nibble on here?"

MÄNNCHEN, *n.* Little man. ***Männchen machen.*** **1.** To grovel (lit. to sit up and beg [like a dog]). *All meine Macker müssen lernen, Männchen zu machen.* "All my guys have got to learn how to do my bidding." **2.** To jump to attention. *Mit der lass ich mich nicht ein; beim Militär hab ich genug Männchen gemacht.* "I'm not getting involved with her; I had to do enough snappy saluting in the service."

MÄNNE, *m.* Hubby. *Ich leb nur meinem Männe.* "I live only for my hubby."

MANNOMANN! Boy oh boy!/Man oh man!

MANSCHETTE, *f.* Cuff, sleeve. ***Manschetten haben.*** To be afraid. *Claro hatte ich vor den Skins mächtige Manschetten.* "Sure, I was real scared of the skinheads."

MANNSTOLL. Crazy about men. *Die Macker mag ich; mannstoll bin ich aber nicht.* "I like guys but I'm no nympho."

MANOMETER! Man alive!/Man oh man! (Lit. pressure gauge.)

MARIE, *f.* **1.** Money. *Ja, die allmächtige Marie macht alles.* "Yes, almighty money does everything." **2.** Marijuana. *Schmeiß mir die Marie rüber.* "Lemme have the grass."

MARILLE, *f., Aust.* Head (lit. apricot). Cf. BIRNE, KÜRBIS, MELONE, PFIRSICH, RÜBE, TOMATE, and other fruits with the sl. meaning "head"). *Mann, hat der Marotten und Grillen in der Marille!* "Man, has he got weird ideas!"

MASCHE, *f.* **1.** Stitch, mesh. ***Eine Masche am Bein/Strumpf laufen.*** To have a run in one's stocking. *Dir läuft 'ne Masche am Bein.* "You've got a run in your stocking." ***Durch die Maschen laufen.*** To get through loopholes. *Diesmal läuft er nicht durch die Maschen des Gesetzes.* "This time he won't find loopholes in the law." **2.** Trick. ***Die Masche raushaben.*** To have found the knack. *Das ist die Masche! Jetzt hast du die Masche raus.* "That's the way/trick! You've found the knack." Cf. HERAUSHABEN. **3.** Fad; craze. *Das Piercing ist ihre neuste Masche.* "Body piercing's her latest fad."

MASCHINE, *f.* Airplane; motorcycle (lit machine; engine). *Hast 'ne tolle Maschine.* "You've got a terrific bike."

MASSEL, *m.* Luck (from Hebr. *mazel* [fate; fortune]; *Schlamassel* is bad luck). *Wenn wir 'n bisschen Massel haben, ziehen wir uns noch aus diesem Schlamassel raus.* "With a little luck we'll get out of this mess." Cf. VERMASSELN.

-MÄßIG. -wise. Used excessively, as in Eng. (e.g. *chartmäßig,* "chartwise," *karrieremäßig,* careerwise; sometimes also tr. as -like, as in GRANATENMÄßIG (bomblike). *Fanmäßig könnte es der Band besser gehen.* "Fanwise the band could be doing better."

MAST, *m.* Penis. ***Matrosen am Mast haben.*** To have pubic lice (lit. to have sailors at the mast). *Nach einer geilen Nacht mit 'ner Hafennutte hatte er wieder Matrosen am Mast.* "After a hot night with a hooker who works the waterfront, he got crabs again."

MATHE, *f.* School sl. for *Mathematik. Mathe liegt mir nicht.* "I have no flair for math."

MATRATZE, *f.* Mattress. ***An der Matratze horchen/Matratzenhorchdienst haben.*** To nap (lit. to listen at the mattress/be on mattress duty). *Ja, er ist zu Hause; aber er horcht an der Matratze.* "Yes, he's home; but he's having a little lie-down." Cf. BETTZEUG.

MATRATZENWALZER, *m.* Sex (lit. mattress waltz). *Ein Matratzenwalzer mit dir? Niemals!* "A roll in the hay with you? Never!"

MATSCH. Exhausted. *Ich fühlte mich total matsch.* "I was really bushed."

MATSCHAUGE, *n.* Black eye. *Wem verdankst du dieses Matschauge?* "Who gave you that shiner?"

MATSCHIG. Slushy. *Bei diesem Matschwetter gehst du barfuß? Bist wohl matschig in der Birne!* "You walk around barefoot in this slushy weather? You must have slush for brains."

MÄTZCHEN, *n., pl.* Antics; tricks (dim. of *Matz,* young boy). *Auf solche Werbemätzchen fallen wir nicht rein.* "We don't fall for advertising gimmicks like that." ***Hände hoch, und keine Mätzchen!*** Hands up, and no tricks!

MAU. Poor, slack. *Das Geschäft geht mau.* "Business is off."

MAUL, *n.* Mouth (of animals, pej. when applied to humans). *Halt's Maul!* "Shut your trap!" ***Das Maul verbrennen.*** See VERBRENNEN.

MAULEN. To complain; be ornery. *Den ganzen Tag mault*

er nur. "All day long he does nothing but grouse."

MAULHELD, *m.* Braggart (lit. mouth hero). *Diesem Maulhelden würd ich gern das Maul verstopfen.* "I'd like to shut that loudmouth's trap."

MAUS, *f./***MÄUSCHEN,** *n.* Sweetie pie (lit. mouse/mousie). Cf. MIEZE **1.** *Gehen wir mauseln, du süße kleine Maus.* "Let's get it on, honeybunch."

MAUSCHELN. 1. To talk Yiddish (from Yiddish for Moses). *Die Professorin ist ein Sprachgenie und kann mauscheln, sächseln, böhmeln und berlinern.* "The professor is a whiz at languages and can talk in Yiddish and the Saxon, Bohemian, and Berlin dialects." **2.** To babble incomprehensibly. *Was hat er da gemauschelt?* "What was he babbling?" **3.** To cheat; engage in crooked deals. *Wenn es ums Mauscheln geht, ist er ein Meister.* "When it comes to shady wheeling and dealing, he's a master."

MÄUSE, *pl.* Money (lit. mice, prob. same origin as MOOS **2**). *Mäuse hab ich keine mehr.* "I've got no more dough."

MAUSELN. To have sex. *Wer hat mit dieser Schlampe nicht schon gemauselt?* "Who hasn't already gotten it on with that slut?"

MÄUSEMELKEN, *n.* Mice milking. *Das ist zum Mäusemelken!* "That'd drive anybody nuts!"

MAUSIG. *Sich mausig machen.* To be insolent. *Mach dich hier nicht mausig!* "Quit being a nuisance!"

MAXI-, *youth.* Super-, ultra-, etc. *Siehst maxigeil aus in deinen neuen Klamotten.* "You look supersexy in your new rags." Cf. GEIL.

MC-JOB, *m., youth.* Part-time, low-paying job (at McDonald's or similar establishments). *Alex Bumstedt hat 'n Mc-Job in der neuen Schlürfbude.* "Alex Bumstedt's got a part-time job in the new fast food joint."

MECKERFRITZE, *m./***MECKERLIESE,** *f.* Chronic complainer. *Ich hör gar nicht hin, was dieser Meckerfritze auch sagt.* "I don't listen, no matter what that belly-aching Billy says."

MECKERN. To complain/grumble. *Ja, er hat immer was zu meckern.* "Yes, he's always got s.t. to grouse about."

MEHL, *n.* Money (lit. flour; bonemeal). *Wenn wir nur's Mehl hätten!* "If only we had the moola."

-MEIER. See KRAFTMEIER; VEREINSMEIER.

MEGA-, *youth.* Intensifies any adj. *Megagrell war die Band.* "The band was orgasmic."

MELONE, *f., youth.* Head (lit. melon; bowler hat). *Ich polier dir gleich die Melone.* "I'm going to knock your block off."

MENSCH, *m.* Human being. *Wie der erste Mensch/wie die ersten Menschen.* Extremely clumsy (lit. like the first human[s]). *Der Herr Professor ist sehr gescheit, aber manchmal benimmt er sich wie der erste Mensch.* "The professor's very smart, but sometimes he acts like he's all thumbs." *Wie der letzte Mensch.* Outrageously bad. *Du hast dich bei meinen Eltern wie der letzte Mensch benommen.* "Your behavior at my parents' was beyond the pale."

MENSCH, *n.* Slut. *Ist die aber ein unverschämtes Mensch!* "She's certainly one brazen trollop."

MENSCH! Wow!/Man!/Boy! (in youth sl., *Mann!* is more frequent). *Mensch, ist der dick geworden!* "Man, has he gotten fat!"

MENSCHENFRESSER, *m.* Cannibal. *Setz dich zu mir, süßes Törtchen, ich bin doch kein Menschenfresser.* "Come sit by me, sweetie pie, I won't eat you."

MENSCHENSKIND! For heaven's sake!

MENSCH MEIER! Man alive!/Gosh! *Mensch Meier, sie haben doch gewonnen!* "Well what d'ya know, they won anyway!"

MESCHUGGE = MACHULLE 3 (both are from Hebr. via Yiddish).

MESSE/ALTE MESSE, *f., youth, E.* Classy, wonderful. *Das Spiel war urst alte Messe!* "The game was really sensational."

META-, *youth.* Intensifies any adj. *Die Fete war metaelefantös.* "The party was mind-blowing."

MICK(E)RIG. Measly; puny. *Die Pflanzen wirken etwas mickrig in diesem grossen Saal.* "The plants seem a bit puny in this big room."

MIEF. See OZON.

MIEFEN. To stink; fart. *Wer hat hier gemieft?* "Who's been farting here?"

MIES. Rotten (from Hebr. for "contemptible"). *Mies machen.* To denigrate; spoil. *Nur weil du 'ne Null bist, machst du die anderen mies; dabei hast du mir auch den Abend mies gemacht.* "Just because you're a dud, you run down the others; you've also ruined my evening."

MIESE. *In den Miesen sein/stehen.* To be in debt. *Die Mäuse sind alle und die Firma steht tief in den Miesen.* "The dough's all gone and the firm's deep in the red."

MIESEPETER, *m.* Grump. *Wie hat ein so fröhlicher Mensch wie sie diesen Miesepeter heiraten können?* "How could such a cheerful person like her marry that grouch?"

MIESMACHER, *m.* Killjoy. *Diesen Miesmacher laden wir nicht ein.* "We won't invite that spoilsport."

MIEZE, *f.* **1.** Pussycat (feline and human); girlfriend. *Bleib noch 'n bisschen, süße Mieze.* "Stay a little longer, sweetheart." **2.** Any female. *Trude ist 'ne geile Mieze.* "Trude's one terrific chick." **3.** Prostitute. *Die Miezen im Puff wollen sich gewerkschaftlich organisieren.* "The whores in the cathouse want to unionize."

MIEZENDOMPTEUR, *m.* Pimp (lit. whore trainer). Cf. MIEZE **3**; KUPPELMACKER. *Den Miezendompteur sollte man einlochen.* "They ought to lock up that pimp."

MIJNHEER, *m., hum.* Dutchman (from Dutch for *mein Herr* [sir]). *Mir hat's Spaß gemacht, bei den Mijnheers zu arbeiten.* "I enjoyed working in Holland."

MIKO, *m.* Inferiority complex (for *Minderwertigkeitskomplex*). *Von wegen Miko! Eingebildet und angeberisch ist* *er.* "What do you mean inferiority complex! He's conceited and boastful."

MIKROFONPROFESSOR, *m., youth.* Vocalist. *Die Band hat 'n tollen Mikrofonprofessor; auch ohne Mikro singt er scharf.* "The band's got a fabulous vocalist; he sings great even without a mike."

MILCHBUBI, *m.* S.o. still wet behind the ears. *Was, dieser Milchbubi will mit in die Disko?* "What, that twirp wants to come along to the disco?"

MILCHTÜTE, *f.* **1.** Underage twirp (lit. milk carton). See MILCHBUBI. **2.** Milquetoast; milksop. *Bist ja immer ausgepowert, du Milchtüte!* "You never have any energy, you wimp!"

MIST, *m.* Manure. ***Auf jmds. Mist nicht gewachsen sein.*** To be s.o. else's work (lit. not to have grown on s.o.'s compost). *Dieser Plan ist nicht auf seinem Mist gewachsen, ich weiß, wer dahinter steckt.* "That plan doesn't bear his trademark; I know who's behind it." ***Kleinvieh macht auch Mist.*** *(Prov.)* It all adds up (lit. small animals leave droppings too). *Unsere Aktien werfen keine großen Dividenden ab, aber Kleinvieh macht auch Mist.* "Our stocks don't pay big dividends, but every little bit helps." See BAUEN.

MISTER SCHNIEGELMANN, *m.* Mr. Squeaky Clean. *Ich weiß, was du wirklich bist. Hör doch auf hier den Mr. Schniegelmann zu spielen.* "I know what you really are; quit coming on like Mr. Super Clean." Cf. GESCHNIEGELT UND GEBÜGELT.

MISTKERL, *m.* SOB/bastard. *Dieser Mistkerl will dir nur ans Portemonnaie.* "That shitbag's just interested in your money."

MISTSTÜCK/MISTVIEH, *n.* Equivalents of MISTKERL, but applicable to either gender.

MIT ANPACKEN. To lend a helping hand. *Beim Neuaufbau unserer Scheune haben die Nachbarn kräftig mit angepackt.* "Our neighbors really pitched in to help us rebuild our barn."

MITGEHEN. To go along. ***Etwas mitgehen lassen.*** To shoplift. *Man hat Hedi geschnappt, als sie im Supermarkt Koteletts und Kaviar mitgehen lassen wollte.* "They nabbed Hedi when she tried to swipe caviar and cutlets in the supermarket."

MITMISCHEN. To take part in; be involved in. *Auf lokaler Ebene hat sie Erfolg, aber sie will auch bei den Großen mitmischen.* "She's successful locally, but she wants to be a major player too."

MITNEHMEN. To take along. ***Jmdn. mitnehmen.*** To affect strongly. *Emotional haben uns die Bilder der Flüchtlinge ganz schön mitgenommen.* "The pictures of the refugees really blew us away."

MITTE, *f.* Center. ***Durch die Mitte abhauen.*** To clear out fast. *Jetzt will ich aber durch die Mitte abhauen.* "I want to head on out now." Cf. ABHAUEN.

MOBBEN. To mob (gang up on a fellow worker to get rid of her/him). *Zuerst haben sie versucht mich zu mobben, aber ich ließ mich nicht kleinkriegen.* "At first they tried to mob me, but I wouldn't be intimidated."

MODEMUFFEL, *m.* S.o. disinterested in fashion. *Meine Frau ist Gott sei Dank Modemuffel.* "My wife's not interested in fashion, thank God."

MOGELN. To cheat. *Wenn du bei der Prüfung nicht gemogelt hättest, wärst du durchgefallen.* "If you hadn't cheated on the exam you would have failed." See RAUS-MOGELN; VORBEIMOGELN.

MOLLE, *f., N.* Glass of beer. *Ich trink gern 'ne Molle.* "I like a glass o' beer."

MOLLENFRIEDHOF, *m., hum.* Beer belly (lit. beer cemetery). *Er hat sich 'n schönen Mollenfriedhof angesoffen.* "He's acquired a sizable beer belly."

MONETEN, *pl.* Money. *Rück nur raus mit den Moneten!* "Come on, fork over the moolah."

MOOS, *n.* **1.** Moss. ***Moos ansetzen.*** To get old/old-fashioned (lit. to gather moss). *Sie halten sich noch für*

Provokids; haben aber schon Moos angesetzt. "They think they're still young revolutionaries; but they've gotten on in years." **2.** Money (from Hebr. for "small change"). *Zuerst hieß es, ,,ohne Moos nix los,'' aber meinem Scharm konnte sie nicht widerstehen.* "First she said, 'no dough, no go'; but she couldn't resist my charm." Cf. BEMOOST.

MÖP, *m., f. Fieser/fiese Möp.* Repellent person. *Diesen fiesen Möp willst du doch nicht heiraten?* "You don't really want to marry that creep, do you?"

MOPS, *m.* Fat person (lit. pug dog; dumpling). *Willst noch 'n Stück Strudel, kleiner Mops?* "You want more strudel, little fatty?"

MÖPSE, pl. of MOPS. **1.** Money. *Her mit den Möpsen!* "Let's have the dough." **2.** Breasts. *Meine Möpse sind üppig und echt.* "My breasts are opulent and genuine."

MOPSEN. To swipe. *Im Supermarkt mopst der Lausbube immer wieder Schokolade.* "That rotten kid always pinches chocolate in the supermarket."

(SICH) MOPSEN. To be bored/annoyed. *In unserem Kabarett mopst sich keiner.* "Nobody's bored in our cabaret."

MOPSIG. Pug-faced. *Sich mopsig machen.* To get uppity. *Wenn du dich wieder mopsig machst, kriegst du eine von mir.* "Start acting up again and I'll whack you."

MORALAPOSTEL, *m.* S.o. holier-than-thou. *Die Moralapostel liefen Sturm gegen ihr letztes Stück.* "The holier-than-thous were up in arms about her last play."

MORDS-. Immense; unbelievable; terrible (used as an intensifier).

MORDSDUSEL, *m.* Great stroke of luck. Intensifies DUSEL **1.**

MORDSGAUDI, *f., S.* Wonderful time. *Beim Jodeln und Schuhplatteln hamma (haben wir) a (eine) Mordsgaudi kappt (gehabt).* "We had a high old time yodeling and doing the *Schuhplattler* (Bavarian folk dance that features thigh whacking)."

MORDSGLÜCK *n.* = **MORDSDUSEL.**

MORDSKERL, *m.* **1.** Huge man. *Der Mordskerl hat 'ne Zwergin geheiratet.* "That hulk married a dwarf." **2.** Great guy. *Ein Mordskerl bist du!* "You're one hell of a guy." **3.** Daredevil. *Ulla will weder 'n Mordskerl noch 'n Schlappschwanz heiraten.* "Ulla doesn't want to marry a go-getter, or a wimp either."

MORDSWENIG. Very little. *Sie hatten mordswenig zu sagen.* "They had precious little to say."

MORGENMUFFEL, *m.* S.o. who is not a "morning person." *Denk an das Sprichwort, „Morgenstund' hat Gold im Mund, wer verschläft sich geht zu Grund," du Morgenmuffel, du.* "Think of the proverb, 'Golden-mouthed are the morning hours; who oversleeps comes to grief,' you morning hater, you."

MORGENSTUND' HAT GOLD IM MUND UND BLEI IM ARSCH/MORGENSTUND' HAT BLEI IM ARSCH/HINTERN, *vulgar var. of the prov. cited in the sent. for the previous entry.* "The morning's got gold in its mouth and lead in its ass."

MÖSE, *f.* Female genitalia. *Meine Möse ist wie eine blühende Rose.* "My nooky is like a blooming rose."

MOSERN. To complain. *Nur mosern und meckern kannst du.* "All you can do is grouse and bellyache."

MOSES = **MOOS.**

MOTTE, *f.* **1.** Attractive, pert, saucy girl. *Diese tolle Motte würde ich zur Miss Universe wählen.* "I'd make that classy chick Miss Universe." **2.** Unattractive girl. *Diese Motte wird 'n richtiges Schlachtschiff werden.* "That broad'll turn into a real battle-ax."

MOTTENKISTE, *f.* Mothproof chest. ***Aus der Mottenkiste/in die Mottenkiste gehören.*** Thoroughly dated/consignable to oblivion. *Solche Schlager von gestern und vorgestern gehören in die Mottenkiste.* "Hit tunes like that, yesterday's cornballs, should be consigned to oblivion."

MOTZEN. To complain. *Motz nicht rum und mach's nur!* "Stop bellyaching and just do it!"

MÖWENDRECK, *m.* Junk; nonsense (lit. gull shit). *'S ist alles nur Möwendreck.* "It's all trash."

MUCK = MUCKS.

MUCKE, *f.* **1.** Dissonant music. *Preisgekrönt ist seine Mucke, aber für mich hat sie null Power.* "His (atonal) music has won prizes, but it doesn't turn me on." **2.** Any music. *Wer hat die Mucke gemacht?* "Who wrote the music?"

MÜCKE, *f.* Gnat. *Mücke machen.* To clear out. *Mach Mücke!* "Beat it!/Buzz off!" *Aus einer Mücke einen Elefanten machen.* To make a mountain out of a molehill. *Aus jeder Mücke macht mein Mann 'n Elefanten.* "My husband makes a big deal out of every little thing."

MUCKEFUCK, *m.* Coffee substitute; rotten coffee. *Wir mussten seine Mucke anhören und dabei seinen Muckefuck trinken.* "We had to listen to his screechy music and drink his lousy coffee."

MUCKEN, *pl.* Moods/caprices. *Jmdm. die Mucken austreiben.* To straighten s.o. out (lit. to drive out s.o.'s whims). *Den Wagen hat er wieder ohne Erlaubnis genommen? Dem werd ich die Mucken austreiben, wenn er zurückkommt.* "He's taken the car without permission again? I'll straighten him out when he gets back!"

MÜCKEN, *pl.* Money (lit. gnats; mosquitos). *Wir würden schon hingehen, wenn wir die Mücken hätten.* "We'd go if we had the dough."

MÜCKENDRECK/MÜCKENSCHISS, *m.* Trifle (lit. gnat shit). *Ein Mückendreck war's nur; sie ist aber doch an die Decke gegangen.* "It was diddly-squat, but she hit the ceiling anyway."

MUCKER, *m.* **1.** Creep; hypocrite. *Spar mir deine Predigt, Mucker!* "Spare me your sermon, creep!" **2.** Musician (*youth*). *Wo sind die Mucker?* "Where are the musicians?"

MUCKS, *m.* Sound. *Ab in die Heia und keinen Mucks mehr!* "Off to bed now and not another word out of you."

(SICH NICHT) MUCKSEN. Not to make a sound; not to say a word. *Er war damit unzufrieden, hat sich aber nicht gemuckst.* "He wasn't satisfied with it, but he didn't open his mouth."

MUCKSER = MUCKS.

MUCKSMÄUSCHENSTILL. Absolutely silent. *Überall im Haus war's mucksmäuschenstill.* "All over the house not even a mouse was stirring."

MUFFEL, *m.* Sourpuss. *Ach, komm mit auf ein Bier, du alter Muffel.* "Come on, let's go for a beer, you old grouch."

-MUFFEL. Person who is indifferent or hostile to s.t. See AKTIENMUFFEL; GURTMUFFEL; KRAWATTENMUFFEL; LESE-MUFFEL; MODEMUFFEL; MORGENMUFFEL; SEXMUFFEL; URLAUBSMUFFEL.

MUFFELIG = MUFFIG 2.

MUFFENSAUSEN, *n.* ***Muffensausen haben/kriegen.*** To be/get scared stiff. *Um Mitternacht im Friedhof kriegten wir das große Muffensausen.* "At midnight, in the cemetery, we got the willies."

MUFFIG. 1. Musty. *Hier ist's muffig.* "It's stuffy here." **2.** Grumpy. *Sei nicht immer so muffig!* "Don't always be such a grouch."

MUFTI, *m., youth.* **1.** Big boss; gang leader (from Arabic, "expounder of Islamic law," usually a civilian). *Diesen Vorgrufti habt ihr zum Mufti gewählt?* "You picked that oldie (s.o. in their 20s) as leader of the pack?" **2.** Wiseguy. *Spiel hier nicht einen auf Mufti!* "Don't try to be a smartass." See OBERHAÜPTLING; OBERMACKER.

MÜLL. See ABMÜLLEN.

MÜLLOLOGE = DIPLOMMÜLLOLOGE.

MÜLLSPRUCH, *m., youth.* Sententious advice (lit. garbage saying). *Lebensweisheiten nennen die Laber-*

fritzen ihre Müllsprüche. "Those bull throwers call their crap 'wisdom for better living.' " See RAUSLASSEN.

MULTIKULTI. For *multikulturell,* multicultural. *Er ist Mufti einer Multikultibande.* "He's the leader of an ethnically mixed gang."

MUMM, *m.* Courage. *Ich bin hier der einzige, der Mumm hat.* "I'm the only one who's got any guts around here."

MUMPITZ! *Dated.* Humbug! *Das ist ja alles nur Mumpitz.* "That's all nonsense."

MÜNZANSTALT, *f.* Mint. *Mein Arsch ist doch keine Münzanstalt!* "Do you think I'm made of money?"

MURRKOPF, *m.* Grouch. *Warum hast du den ollen Murrkopf eingeladen?* "Why'd you invite that old grouch?"

MURKS, *m.* Sloppy work; mess. *So ein Murks!* "What bungling!"

MURKS MACHEN. To bungle. *Hast wieder Murks gemacht.* "You screwed up again."

MURKSEN = **MURKS MACHEN.**

MUSCHE = **MUSCHI.**

MUSCHI, *f.* Pussy (in both senses: small feline and female genitalia). *Du musst lernen, meine Muschi richtig zu streicheln.* "You've got to learn how to pet my pussy properly."

MUSCHKOTE, *m.* **1.** Private (mil. sl., from *Musketier*). *General Patton hat einen Muschkoten geohrfeigt.* "General Patton slapped a private." **2.** Ordinary person. *Ich hätte nie geglaubt, die schöne Bauchtänzerin könnte auf 'n Muschkoten wie mich stehen.* "I'd never have believed that beautiful belly dancer could go for an ordinary Joe like me."

MUSIK, *f.* Music. **Die Musik machen.** To call the tune. *Warum soll nur der immer die Musik machen, den Ton angeben?* "Why is he always the one who says what goes?"

MUSKELPROTZ, *m.* Muscle man who struts his stuff. *Dieser Muskelprotz beeindruckt mich wenig.* "That muscle man doesn't impress me much."

MUSKELTENNE, *youth.* Gym (lit. muscle threshing floor). *Jeden Tag trainiert er in der Muskeltenne.* "He works out in the gym every day."

MUTTERSEELENALLEIN. All alone. *Da saß ich, mutterseelenallein.* "There I sat, all alone, like a motherless child."

MUTZ/MUTZE/MUZE = **MUSCHI.**

MÜTZE, *f.* Head (lit. cap). *Das neue Gesetz geht gar nicht nach meiner Mütze.* "The new law is not at all to my way of thinking." ***Eine Mütze voll Schlaf.*** Nap. *Ich brauch dringend 'ne Mütze voll Schlaf.* "I really need 40 winks." ***Eins/etwas auf die Mütze.*** A scolding; a whack. *Ich hatte die Schule geschwänzt und mein Alter gab mir eins auf die Mütze.* "I played hooky and my old man socked me." ***Sich einen auf die Mütze hauen.*** To belt down a drink. *Hauen wir uns schnell einen auf die Mütze.* "Let's have a quick snort."

NACHTRAGEND. Unforgiving. ***Nachtragend wie ein indischer Elefant/wie ein Wasserbüffel sein.*** To hold a grudge forever. *Statt nachtragend wie 'n indischer Elefant zu sein, denk lieber an Ganescha, der dir alle Hindernisse wegräumen wird.* "Instead of holding a grudge forever, think of Ganesha (Hindu elephant god), who'll remove all your obstacles."

NACKT. Naked. ***Jmdm. mit dem nackten Hintern ins Gesicht springen.*** To be furious (lit. to jump butt-naked into s.o.'s face). *Brauchst mir nicht gleich mit dem nackten Hintern ins Gesicht zu springen!* "You don't have to chew my head off right away!"

NAFFEL, *m., youth.* Square. *Lad doch diesen Naffel nicht ein!* "Don't invite that old bore."

NAFFELBALL/NAFFELFETE/NAFFELPARTY, *f.* Old-fogey ball/party. *Was wolltest du auf der Naffelfete?* "What were you doing at that square party?"

NAFFELN, *youth.* **1.** To be square. *Die Laberfritzen haben mich echt voll genaffelt!* "Those windbags really dumped a lot of garbage on me." **2.** To work. *Was nutzt das blöde naffeln?* "What's the use of work? It's for squares."

NAFFELSACHEN, *pl., youth.* Things squares are interested in. *Oma hängt sehr an ihren Nippsachen; für mich sind's nur Naffelsachen.* "Granny's devoted to her knick-knacks; for me they're just dumb bourgeois clutter."

NAGELN. To fuck. *Die Ute hab ich echt gut genagelt.* "I gave Ute a good plugging."

NAHKAMPFSOCKE, *f.* Condom (lit. close-combat sock). *Die Nahkampfsocke ist keine Waffe im Geschlechterkampf, sondern ein Schild gegen die Krankheit.* "The condom isn't a weapon in the battle of the sexes, but rather a shield against disease."

NAHRUNGSBESCHAFFER, *pl., youth.* Parents (lit. food obtainers). *Den Kies krieg ich schon aus meinen Nahrungsbeschaffern raus.* "I'll get the dough out of my parents."

NARR. See FRESSEN.

NASE, *f.* Nose. ***Sich einen auf die Nase gießen/schütten.*** To have a drink; wet one's whistle. See LAMPE.

NASS. Wet. ***Sich nass machen.*** To get upset. *Mach dich bloß nicht nass!* "Just hold your horses/water!" Cf. (SICH) AN-PISSEN. ***Jmdn. nass machen.*** To beat s.o. badly (sports). *Unsere Kicker haben mit Haken und Ösen gespielt, wurden aber trotzdem nass gemacht.* "Our football team played an all-out game, but they were trounced anyway."

NEBELKRÄHE, *f.* Ugly girl; bitch (lit. hooded crow). *Was macht denn die Nebelkrähe hier?* "What does that dog-faced broad want here?"

NEPP, *m.* Rip-off. *So ein Nepp!* "That's highway robbery!"

NEPP. Fraudulently exorbitant. *Das Restaurant is das Neppste, was es gibt.* "That restaurant's the biggest rip-off going."

NEPPEN. To dupe. *Da wurdest du aber geneppt.* "They really took you for a ride."

NEPPER, *m.* Rip-off artist. *Karten gibt's nur bei Neppern.* "You can get tickets only from scalpers."

NEPPLOKAL, *n.* Clipjoint. *Nur Deppen gehen in dieses Nepplokal.* "Only dorks go to that clipjoint."

NERVEN. To annoy. *Alles nervt mich heute.* "Everything's getting on my nerves today."

NEUTRALO, *m., youth.* **1.** Impartial person. *Hier musst du Flagge zeigen und nicht den Neutralo spielen.* "You've got to commit y.s. on this and not stand aloof." **2.** Umpire. *Der Neutralo muss einen an der Waffel haben!* "The umpire must be off his rocker!"

NICHTSCHEN, *n.* Little nothing. ***Ein goldenes Nichtschen und ein silbernes Warteinweilchen.*** Lots and lots of shiny nothing (lit. a golden little nothing and a silvery wait-a-while). The S. version is "Ein goldenes Nixl un' a silbernes Warteweil." *Was ich dir zu deinem Geburtstag schenke? Ein goldenes Nichtschen und ein silbernes Warteinweilchen!* "What am I going to give you for your birthday? Heaps of brightly wrapped nothing!"

NICKERCHEN, *n.* Nap. *Ich hab 'n kleines Nickerchen gemacht.* "I got a little shut-eye."

NIEDERBÜRSTEN, *youth.* To beat up (lit. to brush down). *Die Hools haben ihn echt niedergebürstet.* "The hooligans really bashed him."

NIEDERKNÜPPELN. Intensifies KNÜPPELN **1.**

NIEDERWAFFELN. To talk to death. *Diese Quasselstrippe kann einen total niederwaffeln.* "That windbag can talk at you till you can't see straight anymore." Cf. WAFFELN.

NIETE. See VOLLNIETE.

NOBELKAROSSE = LUXUSSCHLITTEN; PRUNK-PROTZKUTSCHE.

NORDI, *m.* N. Ger. *Was heißt Ossis, Wessis? Wir Mecklenburger sind Nordis!* "What do you mean E. Gers., W. Gers.! We Mecklenburgers are Northies."

NORMALO, *m., youth.* Square. *Wie hast du's so lange bei so vielen Normalos aushalten können.* "How could you stand it so long with all those squares?" Cf. NAFFEL.

NUCKELPINNE, *f.* Beat-up old car; small car. *Er zieht seine Nuckelpinne dem neuen Mercedes vor.* "He prefers his old jalopy to the new Mercedes."

NUDEL, *f.* **1.** Individual (lit. pasta; noodle). *Eine dicke Nudel.* Fatty. *Udo ist 'ne dicke Nudel und braucht 'n grösseren Stuhl.* "Udo's obese and needs a larger chair." *Eine giftige Nudel* = GIFTNUDEL. *Eine komische Nudel.* A comical character. *Onkel Otto ist 'ne komische Nudel.* "Uncle Otto's a card." Cf. ULKNUDEL.

NUDELDICK. Obese. *Nudeldick bin ich nicht, nur schön mollig.* "I'm not tubby, just pleasingly plump."

NUDELN. 1. To force-feed; overfeed. *Nach der Pute mit allem Drum und Dran waren wir alle genudelt.* "After the turkey with all the trimmings, we were all stuffed." **2.** To rattle off. (*Youth.*) See RUNTERNUDELN.

NULL, *f.* **1.** Zero. *Null Komma Nichts.* Nothing at all. *Von mir kriegst du Null Komma Nichts.* "You'll get zilch from me." *Jmdn. auf Null bringen.* To wipe s.o. out. *Die Rache gelang, und er brachte seinen Rivalen auf Null.* "His revenge succeeded and he demolished his rival." **2.** Nonentity. *Was willst du mit dieser Null anfangen?* "What do you want to bother with that cipher for?" **3.** Nothing; no (for *nichts; kein*). *Ich hab null davon gepeilt.* "I didn't catch any of that." Cf. BOCK.

NULLACHTFUFFZEHN/NULLACHTFÜNFZEHN. Run-of-the-mill; boringly routine. *Das Konzert war total nullachtfünfzehn.* "The concert was certainly nothing to write home about."

NULL-BOCK! "No way!" See BOCK.

NULL-BOCK-GENERATION, *f.* Drop-out generation. *Er sagt, er glaube an nichts und gehöre der Null-Bock-Generation an.* "He says he believes in nothing and belongs to the count-me-out generation."

NULLCHECKER, *m., youth.* Dummy. *Der Schiri ist echt 'n Nullchecker.* "That umpire's super dumb."

NULLERL, *f., Aust.* Insignificant person. *Dieses Nullerl willst du heiraten?* "You want to marry that dud?"

NULLI/NULLINGER, *youth* = **NULL 2.**

NULL-NULL, *n.* Rest room. *Er musste immer wieder aufs*

Null-Null. "He had to go to the john often."

NULLO. Youth sl. var. *of* NULL; substitutes for *kein* (no), as in *nullo Ahnung, nullo Idee, nullo Interesse.*

NULLO PROBLEMO! No problem! *Ich mach's sofort. Nullo Problemo!* "I'll do it right away. No problem!"

NULLSPANNER = **NULLCHECKER.**

NULPE, *f.* Jerk. *Die Nulpe hat mir den Computer vermasselt.* "That nerd screwed up my computer."

NUMMER, *f.* **1.** Number. ***Auf Nummer Sicher gehen.*** To play it safe. *Die Wähler wollten keinen Wechsel und gingen auf Nummer Sicher.* "The voters didn't want a change and played it safe." ***Auf Nummer Sicher sein/sitzen.*** To be in jail. *Der kann's nicht getan haben; er sitzt auf Nummer Sicher.* "He can't have done it; he's in the clink." **2.** Sex; trick. ***Eine Nummer machen/schieben.*** To have sex; to turn a trick. *Heut abend hab ich bisjetzt wenige Nummern geschoben.* "So far, I haven't turned many tricks tonight."

NUMMER NULL = **NULL-NULL.**

NUSCHELN. To mumble. *Er nuschelte etwas.* "He mumbled s.t."

NUSS, *f.* **1.** Head/face (lit. nut). ***Jmdm. eine/eins auf/vor die Nuss geben.*** To clout s.o. *Verpiss dich, oder ich geb dir eins vor die Nuss.* "Piss off or I'll give you a shot in the head." **2.** Dud. ***Taube Nuss.*** S.t. or s.o. utterly useless. *Diese taube Nuss will ich loswerden.* "I want to get rid of that dead loser." **3.** Idiot. *Was willst du mit dieser doofen Nuss anfangen?* "What can you do with that stupid jerk?" **4.** Girl (virgin or difficult conquest). *„Gott gibt die Nüsse, wir aber müssen sie knacken," sangen die Studenten.* " 'God provides the nuts (girls), but we've got to crack them,' sang the students at the banquet."

NUTTE, *f.* Slut. *Sie ist 'ne nette Nutte und macht's manchmal umsonst, oder zumindest auf Pump.* "She's a nice whore and sometimes does it for nothing, or at least on credit."

-O. Suffix popular in young people's sl., but not confined to youth. Occasionally pej., as in: LACKO; KARRIERO; KRITIKALO; NORMALO. Can add a Sp. flavor, as in CLARO; BOMBÁSTICO, or an It. note, as in PALAZZO PROTZO.

OBENAUF. Healthy and in good spirits. *Die ganze Familie ist obenauf.* "The whole family's doing wonderfully."

OBENAUS = **OBENAUF.**

OBEN-OHNE. Topless. *Bei der Sonnwendfeier im Prater tanzten die Priesterinnen oben-ohne.* "The priestesses danced topless at the solstice celebrations in the Prater (park in Vienna)."

OBEN-OHNE-BEDIENUNG, *f.* Topless waitress service. *Im Oben-ohne-Lokal mit Oben-ohne-Bedienung haben wir gut gegessen.* "We ate well in the topless bar with topless waitress service."

OBER-. Prefix with the same intensifying function as *giga-, hyper-, mega-, maxi-, super-, über-, ultra-,* etc.

OBERAFFENGEIL, *youth.* Wonderful; orgasmic. Intensifies **GEIL,** already intensified by **AFFEN-.** *Das nennt ihr oberaffengeil; ich find's aber unter aller Sau.* "You call that mind-blowing; I think it sucks."

OBERANTÖRNER, *m., youth.* Life of the party (from Eng. "turn on"). *Fritz ist vielleicht 'n Oberantörner; hier würd er 'n bisschen Leben in die Bude bringen.* "Fritz sure is a million laughs; he'd pep up this place a little."

OBERFAUL. Extremely suspect. *Es geht da was Ober-faules in dem Laden vor.* "There's s.t. very fishy about what's going on in that outfit."

OBERFELD. (Master) sergeant. *Hallo, Oberfeld! Bleibst lange in der Stadt?* "Hi Sarge! Staying in town long?"

OBERFIESLING, *m.* Archvillain. *Der Schauspieler hatte es satt, immer den Oberfiesling zu spielen.* "That actor was fed up with always playing a super creep."

OBERHÄUPTLING/OBERINDIANER/OBER-JOCKEY/OBERJOHNNY. See OBERMACKER.

OBERKACKE, *f., youth.* Execrably excremental, real shit. *Diese Mucke ist echt Oberkacke.* "That music's super shit."

OBERKLEMMI. See KLEMMI.

OBERMACKER/OBERMOTZ/OBERMUFTI/OBER-NEGER, *youth.* Big cheese/big chief/boss; ringleader; alpha male; leader of the pack. *Er hält sich für den Ober-macker hier.* "He thinks he's the head honcho here."

OBERSTÜBCHEN, *n.* Little room upstairs. ***Nicht ganz richtig im Oberstübchen sein.*** To be crazy. *Wenn er predigt, hör ich gar nicht hin; er ist nicht ganz richtig im Oberstübchen.* "I don't listen when he preaches; he's got s.t. wrong upstairs."

OBERWASSER, *n.* Headwater, backwater (for turning a mill wheel). ***Oberwasser haben.*** To be in a strong position. *Wenn du mir die Kohle pumpst, hätt ich bald wieder Oberwasser.* "If you lend me the money, I'll soon be on top of things again."

OBERWEITE, *f.* Breast measurement. *Tina hat 'ne ganz tolle Oberweite.* "Tina's beautifully busty."

OBERZOTTEL = OBERMACKER.

ÖDEN = ANÖDEN.

ÖDIG, *youth.* Boring. *Oft find ich alles voll ödig, selbst Einkaufen und Ficken.* "Often I find everything devastatingly boring, even shopping and fucking."

OFEN, *m.* **1.** Oven. *Der Ofen ist aus!* It's all over! *Für dich ist der Ofen aus bei mir! Ich lieb 'n anderen; du hast zu lang gewartet.* "You're history. I love s.o. else; you waited too long." *Hinterm Ofen hocken.* To be a stick-in-the-mud. *Mein Mann hockt gern hinterm Ofen; ich geh aber gern auf die Piste.* "My husband's a homebody; but I like to go out on the town." Cf. STUBENHOCKER. *Ein Schuss in den Ofen.* See SCHUSS **1. 2.** Vehicle. See HEIßER OFEN **1. 3.** Girl. See HEIßER OFEN **2. 4.** Anus. *Jmdm. geht der Ofen.* See KIMME.

OFFEN. Open. *Den Arsch offen haben.* To be crazy (lit. to have one's ass open). *Das kann nicht dein Ernst sein! Du hast wohl den Arsch offen!* "You can't be serious! You must have shit for brains!"

OHR, *n.* **1.** Ear. *Sich aufs Ohr hauen/legen.* To have a little rest. *Leg dich 'n paar Stunden aufs Ohr.* "Have a little lie-down for a few hours." *Jmdn. übers Ohr hauen.* To cheat s.o. *Der Brilli ist unecht; man hat euch übers Ohr gehauen.* "The diamond's a fake; you got taken." See LÖFFEL; SCHLACKERN; SCHREIBEN. **2.** Breast. *Mensch, hat die pralle Ohren!* "Man, she's got beautiful bazooms!"

OHRFEIGE, *f.* Box on the ears. *Pass auf, dass ich dir keine Ohrfeige verpasse.* "Watch out or I'll box your ears."

OHRFEIGENGESICHT, *n.* Face you'd like to slap. *Der hat 'n richtiges Ohrfeigengesicht.* "His face cries out for a fist in it."

OHRWURM, *m.* Catchy tune (lit. earworm/earwig). *Paul Lincke komponierte das „Glühwürmchen-Idyll" und viele andere Ohrwürmer.* "Paul Lincke composed the 'Glowworm' and many other catchy tunes."

ÖKOLOZISMUS, *m.* Fervent belief in ecology (from *Ökologie* [ecology] and *Katholizismus* [Catholicism]). *Sie glauben an die Göttin Gaia und den Ökolozismus.* "They believe in the Goddess Gaia and 'ecolocism.' "

ÖLEN. 1. To lubricate. *Wie geölt.* Like clockwork. *Alles lief wie geölt.* "Everything went like clockwork." See BLITZ;

ÖLUNG. **2.** To beat up. *Die Skins haben sie richtig geölt.* "The skinheads beat them up badly." **3.** To cheat; make a fool of. *Warum hast du dich vom ihm ölen lassen?* "Why'd you let them con you?"

(SICH) ÖLEN. To get drunk. *Wir hatten uns voll geölt.* "We got thoroughly soused." See GURGEL.

OLL. Old. *N. for alt. „Je oller, je doller" scheint Opas Devise zu sein.* " 'The older you get the more you should live it up,' seems to be grandpa's motto."

OLLE, *m., N.* **1.** Old man. *Der Olle gefällt mir.* "I like the old guy." **2.** Father. *Sei nett zu deinem Ollen.* "Be nice to your dad/pop." **3.** Boss. *Der Olle murrt wieder.* "The boss is grousing again."

OLLE, *f., N.* **1.** Old woman. *Was will die Olle?* "What's the old bag want?" **2.** Mother. *Meine Olle sagt nein.* "My old lady says no." **3.** Boss. *Hoffentlich wird die Olle zufrieden sein.* "I hope the boss'll be content."

ÖLUNG, *f.* Intercourse (lit. oiling/lubrication). *Hab heiße Höschen und denk oft an die Letzte Ölung; brauch daher regelmäßig 'ne Ölung.* "I've got hot pants and often think of Extreme Unction (the last anointing); that's why I need regular sexual oiling."

OMA, *f.* Grandma. *Oma will mit in die Disko.* "Granny wants to come along to the disco."

OMI = OMA, but more affectionate.

ÖMMELN. See RUMÖMMELN.

ONKEL, *m.* Uncle. ***Der große/dicke Onkel.*** The big toe (prob. a hum. or erroneous rendering of Fr. *ongle* [nail]). *Beim Schwofen trat er mir immer wieder auf den dicken Onkel.* "He kept stepping on my big toe when we were dancing."

ONKELEHE, *f.* Couple living as man and wife, but not legally married so that a widow may continue to collect her late husband's social benefits (lit. uncle marriage). *Sie leben schon seit 10 Jahren in Onkelehe.* "Those oldies have been an unmarried couple for 10 years."

OPA, *m.* Grandpa. *Opa tanzt auch noch gern.* "Gramps also still likes to dance."

OPER, *f.* Opera. ***Opern quatschen.*** To talk on and on; talk nonsense. See OPERN. Cf. ARIE; OPERNARIE. *Quatsch keine Opern!* "Cut the crap!"

OPERETTENSELIGKEIT, *f., pej.* See SELIGKEIT.

OPERN, *youth.* To talk nonsense. *Du hast uns schon voll genug geopert.* "You've already sliced us enough baloney."

OPERNARIE, *f.* Chatter; babble; fuss (lit. opera aria). *Deine Opernarien will ich nicht mehr hören.* "I don't want any more of your song and dance."

ORGELN. 1. To play the organ. ***Georgelt haben, bevor die Kirche angegangen ist.*** To have had sexual congress before holy matrimony. *Die hatten längst schon georgelt, bevor die Kirche angegangen war.* "They were shacked up and making beautiful music together, long before the benefit of clergy." Cf. GEIGEN **2. 2.** To drone on (like a barrel organ). *Jetzt hast aber genug georgelt.* "You've gone on long enough now."

ORGELPFEIFE, *f.* Organ pipe. ***Dastehen wie Orgelpfeifen.*** To stand in a row according to height. *Auf diesen alten Fotos stehen die Kinder da wie Orgelpfeifen.* "On these old photos the children are positioned according to height."

ÖRTCHEN, *n.* Little place. ***Das stille/gewisse/verschwiegene Örtchen.*** (*Euph.*) Toilet. *Er ist noch auf dem stillen Örtchen.* "He's still in the john."

ÖSI, *m., f. Aust.* Austrian. *Einige Ösis interessieren sich jetzt für Isis und Osiris, wie einst Mozart.* "Some Austrians are now getting interested in Isis and Osiris, as Mozart did."

OSSI, *m.* S.o. from former E. Ger. *In nur einer Generation wird man weniger von Ossis und Wessis sprechen.* "In just one generation there'll be less talk of 'Easties' and 'Westies.'" Cf. BESSERWESSI; ZONI.

OSSILAND, *n.* Former E. Ger. *Thüringen nennt sich stolz*

„das grüne Herz Deutschlands" und viele Thüringer und andere nehmen Anstoß am Begriff „Ossiland." "Thuringia proudly calls i.s. 'Ger.'s green heart' and many Thuringians and others take exception to the concept 'Eastie Land.' "

OSTERN, *n.* Easter. ***Wenn Ostern und Pfingsten auf einen Tag fallen/Wenn Ostern, Pfingsten und Weihnachten zusammenfallen.*** Never (lit. when Easter, Pentecost, Xmas occur on the same day). *„Wann rammeln wir?" „Wenn Ostern und Pfingsten auf einen Tag fallen."* " 'When are we going to get it on?'—'When hell freezes over.' "

OZON, *m.* Air (lit. ozone). ***Lieber warmer Mief als kalter Ozon.*** Better a warm and musty room than a cold one. *Lieber warmer Mief als kalter Ozon. Das Fenster bleibt zu!* "Better stale air than that Arctic stuff outside. The window stays closed."

PACKEN. 1. To pack. ***Sich in Watte packen lassen.*** To be overly sensitive (lit. to have o.s. packed in cotton padding). *Du solltest dich in Watte packen lassen.* "My, aren't you the sensitive one." **2.** To manage to do. *Keine Bange, du wirst es schon packen.* "Don't worry, you'll swing it." **3. *Jmdn. packen.*** To get the better of an opponent. *Beim Tennis hat sie mich immer gepackt.* "She always beat me at tennis." **4.** To understand. *Packst du's endlich?* "Do you finally get it?" **5.** To enthrall. *Der Film hat uns gepackt.* "We found the movie gripping."

PALAWATSCH, *m., Aust.* Nonsense; foolish talk (from Hungarian). *Die labert nur Palawatsch!* "Everything she says is drivel."

PALAZZO PROTZO, *m.* Ostentatious mansion (It. *palazzo* [palace] + PROTZ; cf. PROTZBUNKER). *Ja, unser Haus ist groß und schön, aber längst kein Palazzo Protzo.* "Yes, our house is large and beautiful, but it's far from a sumptuous palace."

PALETTI. See ALLES PALETTI.

PAMPA, *f.* The boonies. *Ab in die Pampa mit dem Schiri, diesem Nullchecker!* "Put that jerk of an umpire out to pasture!" Cf. SAVANNE.

PAMPE, *f.* **1.** Rotten food (lit. mud; mush). *Diese Pampe kannst du ja selber fressen.* "You can eat this slop y.s." **2.** Boot. *Wo hast du die Pampen gekauft?* "Where'd you buy those boots?"

PAMPIG. Impudent (lit. mushy, soggy). *Sei nicht so pampig.* "Don't be so sassy."

PANSCHER, *m.* S.o. who adulterates/botches things. *Prinz Charles schimpft auf Amerikanismen und die Panscher der englischen Sprache.* "Prince Charles complains about Americanisms and those who louse up the Eng. language."

PANTINE. See KIPPEN.

PANTOFFEL, *m.* Open-back slipper. ***Unter dem Pantoffel stehen.*** To be henpecked. *Seine Alte führt das Regiment; er steht unterm Pantoffel.* "His wife calls the tune, she's got him under her thumb."

PANTOFFELHELD = **TOFFEL.**

PANTOFFELKINO, *n.* TV at home (lit. slippers cinema). *Immer nur Kartoffeln schälen und Pantoffelkino; ich brauch auch mal Tapetenwechsel.* "It's always just peeling potatoes and watching TV at home; I need an occasional change of scenery too."

PAPPE, *f.* Cardboard. ***Nicht von/aus Pappe sein.*** Not to be chicken feed/insignificant. *Ute ist 'ne glänzende Schwimmerin, aber Patricia ist auch nicht von Pappe.* "Ute's a wonderful swimmer, but Patricia's no slouch either."

PAPPENHEIMER. See KENNEN.

PAPPENSTIEL. See WERT.

PAPPERLAPAPP! Horsefeathers!/Applesauce!

PAPPNASE, *f.* Clown, jerk (lit. fake nose). *Er braucht sich keine Pappnase aufzusetzen; er ist schon eine.* "He doesn't need to put on any false nose, that stupid clown."

PARADEDISZIPLIN, *f.* Showpiece. *Der Stabhochsprung ist eine Paradedisziplin dieses Zehnkämpfers.* "Pole vaulting is a showpiece of this decathlon competitor."

PARAGRAPHENARSCH, *m.* Nasty pedant centered on the letter of the law (lit. paragraph asshole). *Mit dem Paragraphenarsch konnte ich nichts anfangen.* "I couldn't get anywhere with that asshole who does everything by the book."

PARAGRAPHENREITER = PARAGRAPHENARSCH, but not vulgar.

PARISER, *m.* Condom (lit. Parisian). *Diese Pariser sind schön parfümiert.* "These condoms have a nice scent."

PARKDROSSEL, *f.* Prostitute who works parks (lit. park thrush). *Gehst in den Park um die Natur zu genießen, oder 'ne Parkdrossel zu suchen?* "Do you go to the park to enjoy nature or to look for a hooker?" Cf. BORDSTEIN-SCHWALBE.

PARKETT, *n.* **1.** Parquet floor; dance floor. *Eine heiße/kesse Sohle aufs Parkett legen.* To dazzle dance; to put on a bravura performance in anything (lit. to lay a hot/sassy [shoe] sole on the dance floor). *Oma und Opa können noch 'ne heiße Sohle aufs Parkett legen.* "Grandma and grandpa can still dance up a storm." Cf. DANCEFLOOR; (SICH) HOTTEN. **2.** Orchestra seats. *Heut abend sitzen wir Parkett.* "We're sitting in the orchestra tonight." **3.** Milieu. *Auf internationalem Parkett.* In international circles. *Die Chefin kann sich auf jedem Parkett bewegen, auch auf internationalem Parkett.* "The boss is at ease in all circles, internationally too."

PASTETE, *f.* Pie; pâté. *Die ganze Pastete.* The whole schmear. *All seine Sachen hab ich rausgeschmissen, die ganze Pastete.* "I threw out all his stuff, the works!" *Da/jetzt/nun haben wir die Pastete!* That's just what we needed!

PATSCHNASS = PUDELNASS.

PATTE = PINKEPINKE.

PAUKE, *f.* Kettledrum, timpani. *Mit Pauken und Trompeten.* **1.** With much fanfare. *Die Weltmeisterin im Schilauf wurde mit Pauken und Trompeten empfangen.* "The World Champion skier was given the red carpet treatment." **2.** To fail dramatically (ironic use of **1**). *Gepaukt hab ich schon; trotzdem bin ich mit Pauken und Trompe-*

ten durchgefallen. "I did cram; but I still failed miserably." ***Auf die Pauke hauen. 3.*** To brag; blow one's own horn. *Er haut immer auf die Pauke, aber es steckt nichts dahinter.* "He's always blowing his own horn, but there's no substance to it." **4.** To paint the town red. *Heut abend wollen wir ordentlich auf die Pauke hauen.* "We're gonna have a big blast tonight."

PAUKEN. To cram (lit. to drum). *Wir haben zusammen Mathe gepaukt.* "We boned up on math together."

PAUKER, *m.* Teacher (lit. timpanist; drummer). *Diesen voll verkalkten Pauker sollte man in die Pampa schicken.* "They should put that senile teacher out to pasture."

PAUKERHÖHLE, *f., youth.* School (lit. teachers' cave). *Wir wollen alle aus der Paukerhöhle raus.* "We all want to get away from school."

PECH, *n.* Bad luck (lit. pitch). *Der hat wieder Pech gehabt!* "He got a bad break again."

PECHSTRÄNE, *f.* Consecutive misfortunes. *So 'ne Pechsträne! 'S ist wirklich schade.* "What a string of rotten luck! It's really too bad."

PECHVOGEL, *m.* Chronically unlucky person. *Diesen Pechvogel vermeid ich.* "I stay away from that walking disaster area."

PEILEN. 1. To take a bearing on; sound, plumb. ***Die Lage peilen.*** To assess s.t.; see how the wind's blowing. *Bevor wir uns dafür einsetzen, möchten wir zuerst die Lage peilen.* "Before committing o.s., we'd first like to size up the situation." See DAUMEN. **2.** To understand. (*Youth.*) *Selbst der Expresschecker hat's nicht gleich gepeilt.* "Even that shrewdie didn't get it right away."

PEKINESENJO-JO, *n.* Retractable dog leash (lit. Pekinese [dog] yo-yo). *Mit dem Pekinesenjo-jo hat Nero mehr Freiheit als mit der alten Leine.* "The (fishing) reel leash gives Nero more freedom than the old leash."

PELLE, *f.* Skin. ***Jmdm. auf die Pelle rücken.*** To harrass s.o. *Die Paparazzi rückten dem Prinzen zu nahe auf die Pelle* *und er wurde handgreiflich.* "The paparazzi went too far harrassing the prince, and he resorted to fisticuffs."

PELLEN. To peel. ***Wie aus dem Ei gepellt.*** Impeccably dressed. *Die beiden sehen immer wie aus dem Ei gepellt aus.* "The two of them always look like they've stepped out of a bandbox."

PENNBRUDER = PENNER.

PENNBUDE, *f., youth.* **1.** Small room. *Ich musste aus der Pennbude raus.* "I had to get out of my pad." **2.** School. See PENNE 2.

PENNE, *f.* **1.** Flophouse. *Ich halt's nicht länger aus in dieser Penne.* "I can't stand it anymore in this fleabag." **2.** School. *Ich will arbeiten und aus der Penne raus.* "I want to go to work and get away from school."

PENNEN. 1. To sleep. *Kann ich heut abend bei dir pennen?* "Can I crash at your place tonight?" **2.** To have sex with. *Ich möcht mit dir pennen.* "I'd like to sleep with you."

PENNER, *m.* **1.** Tramp, bum. *Dieser Penner war einst Bankpräsident.* "That hobo was once a bank president." **2.** Inattentive person. *Du Pennerin, hättest besser aufpassen sollen!* "You sleepyhead, you should have paid more attention." **3.** Teacher (*school sl.*). *Mann, die Penner haben mich wieder schrill gepiesackt.* "Man, the teachers really bugged me again."

PENUNSE/PENUNZE, *f., from Polish.* Money. *Mit mir pennen? Ja, wenn du dafür die nötigen Penunzen hast.* "Sleep with me? OK, if you've got the dough it takes."

PER ANHALTER FAHREN = PER DAUMEN FAHREN.

PER ARM GEHEN. To walk arm in arm. *Sie gingen per Arm.* "They walked arm in arm."

PER DAUMEN FAHREN/REISEN. To hitchhike. *Was, ihr wollt per Daumen durch Sibirien fahren?* "What, you want to thumb your way through Siberia?" Cf. TRAMPEN.

PERSILSCHEIN, *m., hum.* Certificate of blamelessness (from the detergent **Persil**®). *Einige versuchen jetzt,* *diesem Ganoven einen Persilschein auszustellen.* "Some are now trying to whitewash that crook into a Mr. Clean."

PESEN. To rush. *Mit seinem neuen Sportwagen pest er durch die Gegend.* "He darts around in his new sports car." Cf. ANPESEN **1**.

PETRI HEIL! Good fishing! (St. Peter was a fisherman.)

PETZE, *f., school sl.* Sneak/telltale. *Diese Petze wollen wir richtig weichklopfen.* "We'll make mincemeat out of that snitch."

PETZEN, *school sl.* To tell tales. *Er hat der Lehrerin alles gepetzt.* "He finked to the teacher."

PFAFFENGELABERE, *n., pej., youth.* Sermon (lit. priest/Holy Joe babble). *Im Internat musste ich täglich 'ne geballte Ladung Pfaffengelabere über mich ergehen lassen.* "In boarding school, I had to submit to a big load of religious drivel every day."

PFANNE, *f.* Frying pan. ***In die Pfanne hauen.*** To pan. *Das Stück wurde von der Kritik in die Pfanne gehauen, ist aber ein Publikumserfolg.* "The play was panned by the critics, but it's a popular success." ***Etwas auf der Pfanne haben.*** To have s.t. ready/have s.t. on one's mind. *Der Laberfritze hat seine Müllsprüche immer auf der Pfanne.* "That windbag's always ready to trot out his platitudinous crap." ***Einen auf der Pfanne haben.*** To be about to flatulate. *Wenn du wieder einen solchen auf der Pfanne hast, tritt schnell aus.* "If you feel another fart like that coming on again, leave the room fast."

PFAUCHEN. *S.* for FAUCHEN.

PFEFFER, *m.* **1.** Pepper. ***Jmdm. Pfeffer in den Arsch blasen.*** To incite s.o. to work (lit. to blow pepper up s.o.'s ass). *An die Arbeit, oder ich blas euch Pfeffer in den Arsch.* "Get to work or I'll light a fire under your ass." ***Wo der Pfeffer wächst.*** Hell; any far-off place. *Die können hingehen, wo der Pfeffer wächst.* "They can go to hell." **2.** Pep, dynamism. *Dahinter steckt Pfeffer!* "It's got plenty of zip!" See HINTERN.

PFEFFERN. To season with pepper. ***Jmdm. eine pfeffern.***
To whack s.o. *Pass auf, oder ich pfeffre dir eine.* "Watch
out, or I'll whack you."

PFEIFE, *f.* **1.** Pipe. ***Jmdn. in der Pfeife rauchen.*** To make
short work of s.o. *Bisher hatten unsere Kickers alle Geg-
ner in der Pfeife geraucht.* "Up to now our football team
had all opponents for lunch." **2.** Failure; wimp. *Aber
gestern, dank dieser Pfeife, haben wir das Spiel verloren.*
"But yesterday, thanks to that dumb dork, we lost the
game." **3.** Penis. *Ja, aber er ist 'n knackiger Kerl mit 'ner
Prachtpfeife.* "Yes, but he's a sexy guy with a terrific
dick." **4.** Clout. *Seine Frau wird dir gleich 'ne Pfeife verpassen.* "His wife'll sock you."

PFEIFEN. To whistle. ***Auf etwas pfeifen.*** Not to give a
damn about. *Wir pfeifen auf deine Meinung.* "We couldn't
care less about what you think." ***Auf dem letzten Loch
pfeifen.*** To be on one's last legs. *Seine Firma pfeift auf
dem letzten Loch.* "His firm's had it."

PFEIFENDECKEL! No way! ***Ja, Pfeifendeckel!*** Thanks,
but no thanks!

PFEIFENMANN, *m.* Referee (lit. whistle man). *Beim
Pfeifenmann piept's heute!* "The referee's gone bananas
today!"

PFEIFENPULLOVER, *m.* Condom (lit. pipe [penis]
cover; cf. PFEIFE 3). *Ich weiß, wie sparsam du bist, aber
Pfeifenpullover benutzt man nur einmal.* "I know how
thrifty you are, but condoms are for one-time use only."

PFERD, *n.* Horse. ***Ich denk, mich tritt ein Pferd!*** Well blow
me down!/Well I'll be damned!" Cf. KNUTSCHEN;
STREIFEN. ***Mit jmdm. Pferde klauen/stehlen können.*** To
feel confident/relaxed with s.o. *Mit diesen Kumpels kann
man Pferde stehlen.* "Those chums of mine are the right
stuff; they're game for anything."

PFERDCHEN, *n.* Prostitute working for a pimp (lit. little
horse/filly; cf. ACKERGAUL). *Ich bin nicht arbeitslos; drei
Pferdchen hab ich für mich laufen.* "I'm not unemployed;

I've got three intercourse fillies working for me."

PFIFF, *m.* **1.** Whistle. ***Den Pfiff heraushaben/kennen/ loshaben.*** To have the knack/know the ropes. *Zuerst hatte ich viel Kopfschmerzen mit dem Computer aber ich glaub jetzt den Pfiff rauszuhaben.* "At first the computer gave me a hard time, but I think I've got it down now." **2.** Style; flair; zip. *Wie gewöhnlich hat sie alles mit Pfiff gemacht.* "As usual, she did everything stylishly."

PFIFFIG. Shrewd. *Der ist 'n pfiffiger Kerl.* "He's a shrewdie."

PFIFFERLING. See WERT.

PFIFFIKUS, *m.* Shrewdie. *Spiel hier nicht auf den Pfiffikus!* "Quit trying to be a wiseguy."

PFIRSICH, *m.* Head (lit. peach; cf. BIRNE; KÜRBIS; MARILLE; MELONE). *Dir kullert's wohl im Pfirsich.* "You don't have your head on straight."

PFLAUME, *f.* **1.** Female genitalia/cunt (lit. plum). *Er sagt, meine Pflaume sei ausgetrocknet, aber er irrt sich gewaltig.* "He says my plum's become a prune, but boy is he wrong!" **2.** Jerk. *Du Pflaume, hast wieder alles vermasselt!* "You idiot, you've screwed up everything again!"

PFLAUMEN = ANPFLAUMEN.

PFLAUMENWEICH. Squishy soft. *Der ist ein pflaumenweicher Feigling.* "He's a chicken-livered coward."

PFLÖCKELN. To screw. *Außer den 3 Schwulen hat mich schon die ganze Mannschaft gepflöckelt.* "Except for the 3 gays, the whole team's plugged me."

PFUNDIG. Wonderful. *Das hat er pfundig gemacht.* "He did a terrific job."

PFUNDSKERL/PFUNDSTYP, *m.* Great guy. *Dein Kumpel ist 'n Pfundskerl.* "Your buddy's a swell guy."

PFUNDSSTIMMUNG, *f.* Exhilarated mood. *Im Bierstadel herrschte eine Pfundsstimmung.* "Everyone was in great spirits in the beer barn."

PI, *n.* Greek letter *pi.* ***Etwas Pi mal Daumen/Schnauze machen.*** To do s.t. off the top of one's head; to figure approximately. *Sie hat's zuerst Pi mal Schnauze gemacht, später aber genau ausgerechnet.* "At first she did it very roughly, but later she figured it out exactly."

PICHELEI, *f.* Boozing. *Genug der Pichelei!* "That's enough boozing!"

PICHELN. To drink alcohol. *Sie picheln alle in der Familie.* "The whole family tipples." ***Einen picheln gehen.*** To go out for a drink. *Wir wollten einen picheln gehen.* "We wanted to go out for a snort."

PICHELTOUR, *f.* = **KNEIPTOUR; SAUFTOUR.**

PICHLER, *m.* Boozer. *Schon mit vierzehn Jahren war er Pichler.* "He was already an alkie at 14."

PICKELHERING, *m.* **1.** Clown (lit. pickled herring). Cf. HANS WURST; KASPER; LARIFARI. *Olaf ist vielleicht 'n Pickelhering!* "Olaf's some clown!" **2.** Pimply-faced kid (pun on *Pickel,* pimple). *Dieser Pickelhering wollte mich küssen.* "That kid with all the zits tried to kiss me."

PICKEPACKE VOLL. 1. Extremely full. *Das Programm ist schon pickepacke voll.* "The program's already chock full." **2.** Very drunk. *Er war wieder pickepacke voll.* "He was soused again."

PICKO/PICKO-PICKO, *youth.* Terrific. *Die Fete war echt picko.* "The party was marvelous." Cf. PIEKFEIN.

PICOBELLO. Shipshape; impeccable; wonderful. *Es muss nicht alles immer picobello in Ordnung sein.* "Everything doesn't always have to be in apple pie order."

PIEFIG, *N.* **1.** Stupidly pretentious. *Der Kunsthistoriker ist selber piefig.* "The art historian is stupidly pretentious h.s." **2.** Clever, shrewd (*youth*). *Die Tussi ist mir zu piefig.* "That broad's too shrewd for me."

PIEFIGKEIT, *f.* Narrow-minded stupidity. *Dieser Kunsthistoriker spricht immer wieder von der angeblichen Piefigkeit des Publikums.* "That art historian is always talking about the supposed closed-minded stupidity of the public."

PIEFKE, *m., N.* **1.** Boorish/pretentious fool. *Diesen Piefke kann ich nicht ab.* "I can't stand that pushy jerk." Cf. PIESEPAMPEL. **2.** Kid; pipsqueak; Berlin boy. *Die pfiffigen Piefkes kamen Emil schnell zu Hilfe.* "The clever little lads quickly came to Emil's help." Cf. STEPPKE. **3.** N. Ger. (as used pej. in Aust.). *Die Piefkes fühlen sich wohl bei uns in Österreich; mir san (wir sind) ja halt so g'mütlich und scharmant.* "Pushy Prussians feel right at home with us here in Austria, because we're so charming and convivial." Cf. SAUPREUß.

PIEK-. Select, distinguished. Cf. PICKO; PICOBELLO.

PIEKFEIN. Fancy; excellent. ***Sich piekfein anziehen.*** To get all dressed up. *Sie sind immer piekfein angezogen und wirken manchmal lächerlich.* "They're always dressed to the nines and sometimes seem ridiculous."

PIEKSAUBER. Squeaky clean. *Ich halt's nicht lange bei ihnen aus; 's ist alles so pieksauber.* "I can't stand their place for very long; everything's so squeaky clean."

PIEP, *m.* Peep. *Jetzt keinen Piep mehr!* "Not a peep out of you now." ***Einen Piep haben.*** To have a screw loose. *Du hast 'n kleinen Piep!* "You haven't got all your marbles." Cf. PIEPEN; VOGEL. ***Keinen Piep mehr machen/sagen/tun.*** To be dead. *Er tat keinen Piep mehr.* "He was stone-cold dead."

PIEPE/PIEPEGAL. Of no concern. *Uns ist es piepe, was die Nachbarn treiben.* "We couldn't care less about what the neighbors are up to." Cf. SCHNURZ.

PIEPEN. To squeak; chirp. *Bei dir piept's wohl!* "You must be nuts!" ***Zum Piepen sein.*** To be very funny. *Die Sendung mit den beiden Komikern war zum Piepen.* "The program with the two comedians was hilarious."

PIEPEN, *pl.* Money. *Er schuldet mir noch 200 Piepen.* "He still owes me 200 marks/bucks/euros, etc."

PIEPHAHN, *m., children, rural.* Penis (lit. peeping rooster). *Eines Tages wird dein Piephahn ganz stolz* *krähen.* "One day your cock will crow proudly."

PIEPMATZ, *m., children, hum.* Dickeybird. *Dem Vogelfänger sind all seine Piepmätze entflohen.* "All the bird catcher's birdies got away from him." *Einen Piepmatz haben.* See PIEP/VOGEL.

PIERCING. See BODYPIERCING.

PIESACKEN. To pester. *Hör doch auf, mich zu piesacken!* "Quit bugging me."

PIESELN. To rain; to urinate (a mix of *pissen,* to piss, and *nieseln,* to drizzle). *Wenn's pieselt, pieselt er öfter.* "When it drizzles, he pisses more often."

PIESEPAMPEL, *m.* Narrow-minded, stupid person. *Deine Eltern sind richtige Piesepampel.* "Your parents are real squares." Cf. PIEFKE **1.**

PIETSCHEN, *E.* To have a little drink. *Nach der Arbeit geh ich gern einen pietschen.* "I enjoy a little drink after work."

PIK, *m.* Grudge. *Ich hab noch einen Pik auf ihn, aber ich versuche zu positivieren und mich davon zu befreien.* "I've still got a grudge against him, but I try to be positive and get free of it."

PIKEN. To prick; scratch. *Wer nie sein Brot im Bette aß, weiß nicht wie Krümel piken.* Impossible to figure unless you've experienced it y.s. (lit. Anyone who's never eaten bread in bed, doesn't know how much crumbs can scratch). *Natürlich kann ich da nicht urteilen; wer nie sein Brot im Bette aß, weiß nicht wie Krümel piken.* "Of course I can't make a judgement about it; if you haven't been there y.s., you can't criticize."

PIKO/PIKO-PIKO = PICKO/PICKO-PICKO.

PIKOBELLO = PICOBELLO.

PIKSEN = PIKEN.

PILLE, *f.* Pill. *Da hilft keine Pille mehr.* To be a hopeless case. *Du machst immer wieder denselben Fehler. Da hilft keine Pille mehr.* "You keep making the same mistake. You're past praying for."

PIMMEL, *m.*/**PIMMELCHEN,** *n.* Penis. *Sie war neugierig auf seinen Pimmel.* "She was curious about his dick."

PIMPE, *N.* Indifferent. *Das ist mir pimpe!* "I don't care about that."

PIMP(E)LIG. Wishy washy; affected. *Der ist mir zu pimpelig.* "He's too much of a milksop for me."

PIMPERN. To have sex. *Sie denken nur ans Pimpern.* "All they think about is screwing."

PIMPERLINGE, *pl.* Money. *Ach, die paar Pimperlinge sind nicht der Rede wert.* "Aw, small bucks like that aren't worth mentioning."

PINGELIG. Fussy. *Sei nicht so pingelig!* "Don't be so fussy."

PIMPF, *m.* Kid; brat. *Dieser Pimpf ist jetzt in die Pubertät gekommen.* "That squirt's now pubescent."

PINKE = PINKEPINKE.

PINKEL, *m.* Pretentious, stuck-up person. *Kommt auch dieser feine Pinkel mit?* "Is that piss-elegant fellow coming too?"

PINKELN. To urinate. *Beim Biertrinken muss er oft pinkeln.* "He often has to pump ship when drinking beer." ***Jmdm. ans Bein/an die Birne pinkeln.*** See BIRNE; see also ANPINKELN.

PINKELPAUSE, *f.* Pause to pee. *Ich muss jetzt unbedingt 'ne kleine Pinkelpause machen.* "I've absolutely got to take a break to take a leak."

PINKEPINKE, *f.* Money. *Wer soll das bezahlen, wer hat soviel Pinkepinke?* "Who's gonna pay for that, who's got that much dough?"

PIPAPO, *n.* The works. *Sie will heiraten mit allem Pipapo.* "She wants a wedding with all the frills."

PIPERLN = PICHELN.

PIPIFAX, *m.* Nonsense. *Komm mir nur nicht wieder mit dem alten Pipifax!* "Don't bother me anymore with such trash."

PIPIMÄDCHEN, *n.* Bimbo. *In seinen Memoiren hat er mich wie ein Pipimädchen beschrieben.* "He described me as a dumb broad in his memoirs."

PISSE, *f.* Piss. **Die kalte Pisse kriegen.** Till the cows come home (lit. to get cold piss). *Bis die Behörden was für uns tun, kann man die kalte Pisse kriegen.* "Before the authorities do anything for us, we can wait till hell freezes over."

PISTE, *f.* **1.** Ski run; track. See PISTENSAU. **2.** Street with many bars/discos. **Auf die Piste gehen/Sich auf die Piste schwingen.** (*Youth.*) To go bar/disco hopping. *Gehen wir heut abend auf die Piste.* "Let's go out on the town tonight." **3.** Mattress. *Haut euch endlich auf/in die Piste!* "Hit the hay now, will you!"

PISTENSAU, *f.*/**PISTENSCHRECK,** *m.* Skier you have to watch out for (lit. ski lane hog/terror). *Benimm dich besser 's nächste mal, du Pistensau!* "Behave better next time, you ski hog!"

PITSCH(E)NASS/PITSCH(E)PATSCH(E)NASS   =   **QUATSCHNASS.**

PIZZAFUZZI, *m.* Pizza man. *Wo steckt denn der Pizza-fuzzi? Kalt will ich sie nicht.* "What's happened to the pizza man? I don't want it cold."

PLÄRREN. To howl; blare; blubber. *Dein Plärren macht mich verrückt.* "Your bawling's driving me crazy."

PLASTIKBOMBER, *m.* Slow, smelly, cheap car. *Dein Plastikbomber gehört in eine Giftmülldeponie.* "Your stinky old clunker belongs in a toxic waste dump."

PLASTIKTÜTE, *f.* Condom (lit. plastic bag). *Ich bin altmodisch und hab mit Plastiktüten nichts am Hut.* "I'm old-fashioned and have nothing to do with condoms."

PLÄTSCHER-PLÄTSCHER. Babble-babble. *Für euer Plätscher-Plätscher hab ich keine Zeit.* "I have no time for your boring chatter." Cf. BLUBBER-BLUBBER.

PLÄTSCHERN. See RUMPLÄTSCHERN.

PLATT. Flat. ***Platt sein.*** To be flabbergasted. *Als ich die Nachricht hörte, war ich platt wie 'ne Flunder.* "When I heard the news, I was knocked for a loop."

PLATTE, *f.* **1.** Slab; plate. ***Platte machen.*** To bed down. *Ich muss Platte machen oder ich fall um.* "I'll have to hit the sack or I'll fall over." ***Die Platte putzen.*** To scram. *Putzen wir die Platte!* "Let's make o.s. scarce!" **2.** Record (from *Schallplatte*). *Immer dieselbe Platte.* "Always the same broken record." Cf. RILLE. **3.** Bald pate. *Mit zwanzig hat er schon 'ne Platte.* "He's only 20 but already has a bald spot." **4.** Criminal gang. (*Aust.*) *Er verneint, Mitglied der Platte zu sein.* "He denies being a member of that gang."

PLATZE, *f.* Rage. *Wenn sie das erfährt, kriegt sie die Platze.* "She'll explode when she hears that."

PLATZEN. To burst; fall through. *Ihr Scheck ist geplatzt.* "Their check bounced."

PLEITE, *f.* Bankruptcy. ***Pleite machen/gehen.*** To go bankrupt; fail at s.t. *Er hat wieder Pleite gemacht.* "He went bust again."

PLEITEGEIER, *m.* Threat of bankruptcy (lit. bankruptcy vulture). ***Der Pleitegeier kreist/schwebt.*** The wolf is at the door. *Der Pleitegeier schwebt über seinem Unternehmen.* "His firm is about to go under."

PLEITEN, PECH, PANNEN (UND PROBLEME). A series of disasters. *Die Premiere war ein Knüller aber bei den Proben gab's nur Pleiten, Pech und Pannen.* "The premiere was a smash hit, but during the rehearsals there was one catastrophe after another."

PLEMPE, *f.* Insipid/watery drink. *Deinen neuen Cocktail will ich gern probieren, aber bitte diesmal keine Plempe.* "I'll be glad to try your new cocktail, but please, no dishwater this time."

PLEMPERN = **VERPLEMPERN.**

PLEMPLEM. Crazy. *Bist ja völlig plemplem.* "You're totally nuts."

PLIEREN, **1.** To squint. (*N.*) *Du solltest zum Augenarzt,* *plierst ja ständig.* "You should see the eye doctor, you're always squinting." **2.** To chat (*Swiss;* from Fr. *parler*/It. *parlare*). *Zum Plieren hab ich jetzt keine Zeit.* "I have no time to chat now."

PLIETSCH, *N.* = **PFIFFIG.**

PLINKEN = **PLIEREN 1.**

PLOMBEN, *E.* To swindle. *Wir sind schon zu oft geplombt worden.* "We've been taken for a ride too often."

PLÖRRE, *N.* = **PLEMPE.**

PLÖTZE, *f., youth, N.* Unattractive female (lit. a fish). *Alle halten sie für 'ne Plötze, aber im Bett ist sie 'n süßes Plätzchen.* "Everybody thinks she's a dog, but she's a sweet cookie in bed."

PLUMPSKLO/PLUMPSKLOSETT, *n.* Toilet (lit. outhouse; latrine). *Ist jemand aufm Plumpsklo?* "Is there anybody in the can?"

PLUMPVERTRAULICH. Overly familiar. *Mir ist er zu plumpvertraulich.* "He's too hail-fellow-well-met for me."

PLÜNNEN, *pl., N.* Old clothes; gear. *Hast 'n ganzen Schrank voll Plünnen, die du nicht mehr trägst.* "You've got a whole closet full of clothes you don't wear."

PLUNZE, *f., pej. E.*/**PLUNZEN,** *f., pej., S.* Pudgy/massive female (lit. blood sausage). *Der hat dauernd Angst vor seiner Plunze.* "He lives in fear of his beefy broad."

PO/PODEX, *m., children, hum.* Buttocks. *Benimm dich, oder da gibt's was aufm Po.* "Behave y.s. or I'll whack your bottom."

POFEN = **POOFEN.**

PÖKER, *N.* = **PODEX.**

POKULIEREN. To drink alcohol (*Pokal* = goblet). *Die alten Burschenherrlichkeiten pokulierten viel und sangen Loblieder auf ihren Krambambuli.* "The alumni Joe College types were in their cups and sang the praises of alcohol."

POL, *m.* Pole. *Der ruhende Pol.* Calming influence. *Mutter* *war immer der ruhende Pol in der Familie.* "Mother was always the peacemaker in the family."

POLENTE, *f.* Police. *Selbst in Zivil sah man's ihm an, dass er von der Polente war.* "Even in plainclothes he looked like a cop."

POLI, *m., youth.* Policeman. *Der Poli hat uns nicht gesehen.* "The cop didn't see us."

POLIEREN. To polish. ***Jmdm. die Fresse/Fressleiste/Schnauze/Visage polieren.*** To bash s.o.'s face in. *Singst du den Bullen, polier ich dir die Fresse.* "If you sing to the cops, I'll bash your face in."

POLITPOPPER, *pej., youth.* Square politician (politically correct and correctly dressed; see POPPER). *Die Politpopper lassen nur Müllsprüche raus.* "The politicos just give off garbage."

POLITUR, *f.* Beating. *Dir tut 'ne Politur not.* "You need a fist in your face." Cf. POLIEREN.

POLSTERN. To upholster. *Sie ist gut gepolstert.* "She's got curves in the right places." ***Finanziell gut gepolstert.*** Well-heeled. *Finanziell sind wir nicht mehr so gut gepolstert.* "We're not as secure financially as we once were."

POLTERABEND, *m.* Shower or bachelor party at which crockery is broken (*poltern* = to crash around). *Beim Polterabend hättet ihr meine Schäferin aus Meißner Porzellan schonen können.* "You could have spared my Dresden china shepherdess at the bachelor party."

POLTERN. To celebrate at a shower/bachelor party.

POMADENHENGST, *m.* Dandy (lit. hair cream stallion). *Als Nackedei sieht dieser Pomadenhengst noch lächerlicher aus.* "That clotheshorse looks even more ridiculous with his clothes off."

POMADE SEIN, *Berlin.* To be of no concern. *Ob wir hingeh'n oder nischt (nicht), 's iss (es ist) mir pomade.* "Whether we go or not, I couldn't care less."

POMADIG. 1. Jaded. *Mir ist er zu pomadig.* "He's too blasé for me." **2.** Sluggish. *Die Mannschaft hat wieder pomadig gespielt.* "The team played listlessly again."

POMMES, *f., pl.* French fries. *Geh hol mir Pommes und 'ne Cola.* "Go get me some fries and a coke."

POOFE = PENNE.

POOFEN, *N.* To sleep; sleep with. *Die Hotels waren alle belegt; ich musste im Puff poofen.* "The hotels were all full; I had to sleep in the brothel."

POPEL, *m., pej.* Low class no-good (lit. piece of snot). *Was hat dieser Popel hier zu suchen?* "What's that sleazy lowlife doing here?"

POP(E)LIG. 1. Crummy. *Echt popelig ist ihre Mucke.* "Their music's real lousy." **2.** Narrow-minded. *'S lohnt sich nicht mal drüber zu reden mit so popligen Spießern.* "No point in even discussing it with such squares."

POPELN. See PULEN.

POPO = PO/PODEX.

POPPER, *m., youth.* Smartly-dressed preppy. *Mit Punk und Punkern hat er nichts am Hut, dieser Popper.* "That preppy wants nothing to do with punk and punk rockers." Cf. POLITPOPPER.

POPPIG. 1. Pertaining to pop music/art. *Er macht jetzt poppige Music.* "He's now a pop musician." **2.** Smartly fashionable; flashy. *Poppige Klamotten brauch ich nicht.* "I don't need trendy clothes."

POST, *f.* Mail; post office. ***Jetzt geht die Post ab!*** Now's the time to get going!/Things are going to pop now! ***Da geht die Post ab!*** See BÄR; HOTTE.

POTZ!/POTZ BLITZ!/POTZTAUSEND! Well I'll be gosh-darned!/Holy Moses!

POWER. Poor (from Fr. *pauvre* and pron. more or less as in Fr.) *Der Schmuck sieht power aus.* "The jewelry looks cheap." Cf. AUSPOWERN **1.**

POWER, *f.* Force; energy; strength (from Eng; pron. as in Eng.). *Wenn ich mit meinen Brummikutschern bumse,* *bringen sie mir die Power voll rein.* "When I sleep with my truck drivers, they really energize me." See ANPO-WERN; AUSGEPOWERT **2.**

POWERFRAU, *f.* Dynamic career woman. *Aus dem Zierfisch ist 'ne richtige Powerfrau geworden.* "Once an affected teenager, she's now a boss lady who's really got it together."

POWERN. To get things moving; make dynamic. *Jetzt sollt ihr aber 'n bisschen powern!* "Give it the gun now!"

PRAHLEN. To boast. ***Beschissen wäre noch geprahlt.*** "Shitty" would be high praise. *„Wie geht's dir jetzt, Alter?" „Beschissen wäre noch geprahlt."* " 'How're you doing, old boy?' 'I'm in deep doo-doo, to put it mildly.' "

PRAHLHANS = PROTZ.

PRALL, Full; bulging; fully inflated (often pleonastically used with *total, voll,* as in *prallvoll,* or *voll prall*). *Ihr sülzt nur voll/total prall heute.* "You're all really full of hot air today." ***Eine prall gefüllte Bluse haben.*** To be stacked (lit. to have a tautly filled blouse). *Mensch, hat Ute 'ne prall gefüllte Bluse.* "Man, Ute's really stacked."

PRÄSER, *m.* Prophylactic. *Wenn wir nur vor 20 Jahren Präseraktien gekauft hätten!* "If only we'd bought condom stocks 20 years ago!"

PRESSLUFTHÜTTE, *f., Aust., youth.* Discotheque. *Den Presslufthütten bleib ich jetzt fern und such eher Oasen der Ruhe.* "I stay away from discos now and look for quiet places."

PREUßE, *m.* Prussian. ***So schnell schießen die Preußen nicht.*** Some things just can't be rushed.

PRIESTERLICH. Priestly. ***Auf priesterlich machen/spielen.****(Youth.)* To be a smug know-it-all. *Einst warst du cool, jetzt machst du immer wieder auf priesterlich.* "Once you were cool; now you keep coming on holier-than-thou." Cf. PFAFFENGELABERE.

PRIMA. First rate; fantastic. *Das Essen war prima.* "The meal was great."

PROFI, *m., f.* Pro. *Der Fußballer will nicht Profi werden.* "The football player doesn't want to turn pro."

PROGRAMM, *n.* Program. ***Falsches Programm fahren/haben/laden.*** (*Youth.*) To be crazy (lit. to load/be on a wrong computer program). *Du hast wieder wohl falsches Programm geladen.* "You're going off the deep end again."

PROGRAMMABSTURZ. See ABSTURZ.

PROLL/PROLO, *m., pej.* Blue-collar worker. *Prolls sollte man rapido durch Roboter ersetzten; die machen keine Kinder, wenigstens noch nicht.* "Robots should replace proles right away; robots don't make children, at least not yet."

PROMI, *m.* Prominent person. *Dieser Fotograf ist Promijäger.* "That photographer chases after prominent people."

PROMILLE, *n.* Blood alcohol level. *Sie fährt nur ohne Promille.* "She never drinks and drives."

PROMILLOLOGE, *m., hum.* **1.** Habitual drinker (s.o. whose blood alcohol is always high). *Schon früh morgens sitzen die Promillologen in der Kneipe.* "The alkies start boozing early in the tavern." **2.** Traffic cop who administers breath tests. *Vorsicht, die Promillologen sind auf der Lauer.* "Watch out, the traffic cops are lurking."

PROMOTEN. To promote. *Ich bin hier, mein neues Hip-Hop Album zu promoten.* "I'm here to promote my new hip-hop album."

PROPELLER, *m.* Propeller. ***Etwas am Propeller haben.*** To be crazy. *Du hast was am Propeller.* "You've got a screw loose."

PROPPEN, *m., N.* See WONNEPROPPEN.

PROPPENVOLL. Jam-packed. *Der Saal war proppenvoll.* "The hall was packed to the rafters."

PROTOPRIMA. Youth sl. intensifier of PRIMA.

PROTZ, *m.* Show-off. *Ich kann ihn nicht leiden, diesen Protz.* "I can't stand that show-off."

-PROTZ. Pretentious with respect to s.t. See BILDUNGS-PROTZ; MUSKELPROTZ; SEXPROTZ.

PROTZBUNKER, *m.* Big, showy house or building complex. *Der Anwalt hat da so kräftig abgesahnt, dass es sich mehrere Protzbunker bauen ließ.* "The lawyer's cut was so hefty, he had several mansions built for h.s."

PROTZEN. To show off. *Mit ihren Pelzmänteln protzt sie weniger, seit die Tierschützer sie bespritzt haben.* "She parades around less in her fur coats, ever since the animal rights activists sprayed her."

PROTZEREI, *f.* Showing off. *Hör auf mit deiner blöden Protzerei!* "Stop your stupid showing off!"

PROVO/PROVO KID, *m., youth.* Antiestablishment radical agitator; frequent street demonstrator. *Der Sohn des Bankers ist Provo.* "The banker's son's a professional radical."

PRUNKPROTZKUTSCHE, *f.* Big, showy car. *Der Ganove wohnt in einem Protzbunker und fährt 'ne Prunkprotzkutsche.* "That crook lives in a super mansion and drives a big, flashy car."

PUCKEL = BUCKEL.

PUCKERN. To throb. *Puckert's dir noch im Bauch?* "Do you still have shooting pains in your stomach?"

PUDEL, *m.* **1.** Poodle. ***Wie ein begossener Pudel dastehen.*** To be dumbfounded/crestfallen. *Stehst wie 'n begossener Pudel da und guckst dumm aus der Wäsche.* "You just stand there like a chump and gawk." ***Das ist des Pudels Kern!*** So that's what it's really about!/So that's what's behind it! **2.** Miss in bowling. *Diesmal schieß keinen Pudel!* "Don't miss this time!"

PUDELN, *youth.* To have sex. *Gehen wir pudeln!* "Let's get it on!"

PUDELNACKT. Stark naked. *Pudelnackt schwammen wir im Tümpel; nachher tanzten wir pudelnass und pudelnackt im Mondlicht.* "We skinny-dipped in the pond; afterwards we danced dripping wet and butt-naked in the moonlight."

PUDELNASS. Drenched. See KLATSCHNASS; KLITSCHNASS.

PUDELWOHL. Just great. *Beim Schwimmen und Tanzen fühlten wir uns pudelwohl.* "We felt wonderful swimming and dancing." Cf. the less elegant SAUWOHL.

PUDERANT, *m., Aust.* Horny guy. *Ich hielt ihn für einen Puderanten, aber welche Enttäuschung!* "I thought he was a stud, but what a disappointment!"

PUFF, *m.* or *n.* Brothel. *Im Puff wird nicht nur gebumst; oft plaudern auch wir über Gott und die Welt.* "We don't just screw in the whorehouse; we often talk about God and the world."

PUFFMUTTER, *m.* Madam. *Sie ist die netteste Puffmutter in der ganzen Puffgegend.* "She's the nicest brothel keeper in the whole red-light district."

PUFFSTRAßE, *f.* Brothel street. *Sie zeigte mir die Puff-straßen in Hamburg und Amsterdam.* "She showed me the cathouse streets in Hamburg and Amsterdam."

PÜLCHER, *m., Aust.* No-good. *Warum hat sie diesen Pülcher geheiratet?* "Why'd she marry that bum?"

PULEN, *N.* To drill; pick. *In der Nase pulen.* To pick one's nose. *Hör doch auf in der Nase zu pulen.* "Quit picking your nose."

PULLE, *f., N.* Bottle. *Dieser Säufer hat immer 'ne Pulle bei sich.* "That drunk's always got a bottle with him." *In die Pulle fallen.* To get drunk. *Fall nicht wieder in die Pulle!* "Don't get plastered again." See VOLLE PULLE.

PULLEN/PULLERN, *E.* To urinate. *Der Hund wollte nicht schnell machen und pullerte an jedem Baum.* "The dog didn't want to hurry up and pissed on every tree."

PULLI/PULLOVER, *m.* Sweater. *Zieh den roten Pulli an!* "Put on the red sweater."

PULLUNDER, *m., invented Eng.* Short-sleeved sweater; tanktop. *Er trägt immer 'n Pullunder.* "He always wears a short-sleeved sweater."

PULVER, *n.* 1. Powder, gunpowder. *Sein Pulver ver-*

schossen haben. To have shot one's wad/load. *Er konnte nichts mehr machen, denn er hatte sein Pulver verschossen.* "He couldn't do anything more, because he'd used up all his ammunition/arguments." **2.** Money. *Das Pulver ist alle.* "No more dough left."

PUMMEL, *m.*/**PUMMELCHEN,** *n.* Fatty. *Er pennt nur mit Pummeln.* "He only sleeps with fat girls."

PUMMELIG. Chubby. *Er liebt sie schön pummelig.* "He likes them pleasingly plump."

PUMP, *m.* Credit. *Alles haben wir auf Pump gekauft.* "We bought everything on credit."

PUMPEN. To borrow; lend (lit. to pump). *Willst wieder Piepen bei mir pumpen?* "You want to borrow money from me again?"

PUMPERN = PUPEN.

PUNKIG. Like a punk rocker. *Mit so grell gefärbten Haaren siehst du echt punkig aus, wie 'ne richtige Punkerin.* "With such garishly dyed hair you look like a real punk rocker."

PUP = PUPS.

PUPE, *f., pej.* **1.** Stale beer. *Schade ums Berliner Weißbier, das Pupe geworden ist.* "Too bad about the Berlin wheat beer that's gone flat." **2.** Homosexual. *Mein Mann hat sich in eine Pupe verknallt.* "My husband's fallen for a fag."

PUPEN. To fart. *Iss nicht so viel Pumpernickel, sonst pupst du wieder die ganze Nacht.* "Don't eat so much pumpernickel bread or you'll be farting all night again."

PUPIG. Worthless. *Spar mir deine pupigen Argumente!* "Spare me your worthless arguments."

PUPILLE, *f.* Pupil (eye). *Einen Riss in der Pupille haben = einen KNICK in der Optik haben.*

PUPPE, *f.* Doll. *Ist Nora vielleicht 'ne dufte Puppe!* "Nora's some terrific chick!" *Bis in die Puppen.* Till all hours. *Wir haben bis in die Puppen gefeiert.* "We partied the night away." ***Die Puppen tanzen lassen.*** **1.** To live it up. *Heut abend wollen wir die Puppen tanzen lassen!* "We're going to have a ball tonight." **2.** To liven/stir things up. *Die neue Chefin droht, die Puppen tanzen zu lassen.* "The new boss is threatening to shake things up." See ZUCKERPUPPE.

PUPPENJUNGE, *m.* Young male homosexual (lit. doll boy). *Dem alten Lustmolch macht's Spaß, seinen Puppenjungen zu verwöhnen.* "The old lecher loves pampering his little darling."

PUPS, *m.* **1.** Fart. *Auf einen solchen Pups wären Franklin und Mark Twain stolz gewesen.* "Franklin and Mark Twain would have been proud of a fart like that." ***Einen Pup(s) im Gehirn haben.*** See FURZ. **2.** Trifle. *Die Stasi hörte jeden Pups ab.* "The Stasi (secret police of the former GDR) electronically eavesdropped on even the most trivial things."

PUPSEN = **PUPEN.**

PUPSER = **PUPS.**

PUSSELN. To fuss around; tinker. *Seit mein Mann in Rente ist, pusselt er die ganze Zeit im Haus.* "Ever since my husband's been retired, he fusses around the house all the time."

PUSTE, *f.* Breath. *Dem Tenor ging die Puste aus, der Sopranistin nicht.* "The tenor ran out of breath, but not the soprano."

PUSTE!/PUSTEKUCHEN! Nonsense! No way! Just the opposite (usually preceded by *ja* or *aber*). *Ich wär gern länger geblieben, aber Pustekuchen, ich musste zurück.* "I would have liked to stay longer, but nothing doing; I had to return."

PUSTEN. To blow; puff. *Es pustet ganz schön draußen.* "That's some wind blowing out there." *Pusten müssen.* To have to submit to a breath test. *Der blöde Bulle hielt mich an, und ich musste pusten.* "The dumb cop stopped me, and I had to blow into the bag."

PUTE, *f., pej.* Female (lit. turkey-hen). *Die ist nur 'ne dumme, eingebildete Pute.* "She's just a silly goose, a stuck-up little girlie."

PUTZ, *m.* **1.** Plaster. ***Auf den Putz hauen.*** **A.** To live it up. *Heut abend wollen wir ordentlich auf den Putz hauen.* "We're gonna live it up tonight." Cf. PAUKE. **B.** To kick up a fuss; protest. *Brauchst nicht gleich so aufn Putz zu hauen.* "You don't have to make such a to-do about it." **2.** Quarrel. ***Putz machen.*** To fight. *Der Brutalo will nur Putz machen.* "All that bruiser wants to do is fight." **3.** Finery. *Die Naffel kamen aus der Kirche in ihrem Putz.* "The squares came out of church in their Sunday best."

PUTZEN. See (SICH) HERAUSPUTZEN; HERUNTERPUTZEN.

(SICH) PUTZEN. To clean o.s./dress up. ***Sich nach Mekka putzen.*** (*Youth.*) To hit the road (lit. go off to Mecca). *Macht was ihr wollt; ich putz mich nach Mekka.* "Do what you want, I'm shoving off."

PUTZFIMMEL, *m.* Mania for cleaning. *Craigs Frau hatte einen Putzfimmel.* "Craig's wife had a thing about cleaning."

QUALMEN. To emit smoke; puff away at. *Er qualmt noch wie 'n Schlot.* "He still smokes like a chimney." ***Jmdm. qualmen die Socken.*** To do a lot of running around (lit. s.o.'s socks are steaming). *Ich musste schuften; mir qualmten ganz schön die Socken.* "I had to jump to it what with all those errands to do."

QUANTEN, *pl.* Big, dirty feet. *Ja, studier nur ruhig die Quantenphysik, aber vergiss nicht, deine Quanten mal zu waschen.* "Yes, study quantum physics, but don't forget to wash your feet occasionally."

QUARK, *m.* Nonsense (lit. curd cheese). ***So ein Quark!*** That's a lot of baloney/applesauce! ***Einen Quark.*** Nothing. *Du verstehst 'n Quark davon.* "You don't know beans about it." ***Quark reden.*** See QUARKEN.

QUARKEN. To talk nonsense. *Ja, quark nur weiter, keiner hört hin.* "Just keep up your stupid chatter; nobody's listening."

QUARKLADEN, *m., youth, pej.* School (lit. nonsense store). *Im Quarkladen lernt' ich gar nichts.* "I didn't learn anything at all in school."

QUASSELIG = SABBELIG.

QUASSELN. To babble. *Der quasselt nur dummes Zeug.* "He just drones on and on about nothing."

QUASSELSTRIPPE, *f.* **1.** Telephone (lit. prattle wire). *Meine Tochter ist von der Quasselstrippe nicht* *wegzukriegen.* "You can't get my daughter away from the phone." **2.** Windbag. *Was die Quasselstrippe gackelt, ist mir Wurst.* "That old bag's prattling means nothing to me."

QUATSCH!/QUATSCH MIT SOßE! Nonsense!/Stuff and nonsense! *Ihm soll ich dabei geholfen haben? Quatsch mit Soße!* "I'm supposed to have helped him do it? Applesauce!"

QUATSCHEN. 1. To chatter. *Quatsch nicht so 'n Blödsinn!* "Don't babble on about such nonsense." **2.** To chat. *Wir müssen wieder schön quatschen.* "We'll have to have a nice chat again." See (SICH) AUSQUATSCHEN.

QUATSCHE, *f.*/**QUATSCHI,** *m., youth* = **QUATSCH-KOPF.**

QUATSCHKOPF, *m.* Talkative fool. *Ich hab keine Zeit für den Quatschkopf.* "I have no time for that windbag."

QUATSCHNASS. Drenched. *Sie kamen quatschnass zurück.* "They came back soaked to the skin."

QUECKSILBER, *m.* Mercury. **Quecksilber im Arsch/Hintern haben.** To have quicksilver in one's ass. *Bleib doch sitzen; hast Quecksilber im Hintern?* "Just sit down; have you got ants in your pants?"

QUENGELEI, *f.* Nagging; carping. *Was soll die ganze Quengelei?* "What's the use of all that grousing?"

QUETSCHKOMMODE, *f.* Accordion (lit. squeeze box). *Er ist ein Künstler der Quetschkommode.* "He's an accordion artist."

QUIEK(S)EN/QUIETSCHEN. To squeal/squeak. *Zum Quiek(s)en/Quietschen sein.* To be very funny. *Der Film war zum Quietschen.* "The movie was a howl."

QUIETSCHLEBENDIG. Chipper. *Siehst heute quietschlebendig aus.* "You're looking bright-eyed and bushy-tailed today."

QUIETSCHFIDEL/QUIETSCHVERGNÜGT. Happy as could be. *Das Kind spielte quietschvergnügt.* "The child was playing happy as a clam."

RABATTEN = ROBOTERN.

RABATZ, *m.* Noisy carrying on; shindig. ***Rabatz machen.*** To make a stink. *Die Studenten haben beim Dekan Rabatz gemacht.* "The students kicked up a fuss with the dean."

RABAUKE, *m.* Lout; hoodlum. *Hast dich in diesen Rabauken verknallt?* "You've fallen in love with that roughneck?"

RABE, *m.* Raven. ***Wie ein Rabe klauen.*** To thieve like a magpie. *Hedi klaut immer noch wie ein Rabe.* "Hedi is still pinching everything she can get her hands on."

RABENELTERN/RABENMUTTER/RABENVATER. Bad parents/mother/father. See RABENSTARK **2** for use in sentence.

RABENSTARK, *youth.* **1.** Wonderful. *Suzannes Gemälde ist aber rabenstark!* "Suzanne's painting is marvelous!" **2.** Sexually exciting. *Ich weiß nicht, warum die vielen Macker meine Rabenmutter so rabenstark finden.* "I don't know why so many guys find my rotten mother so exciting."

RABOTTEN = ROBOTERN.

RACHE IST BLUTWURST!/RACHE IST SÜß! Revenge is sweet! See BLUTWURST.

RAD, *n.* Wheel. ***Ein Rad ab haben.*** To be crazy. *Der Macker hat wohl ein Rad ab.* "That guy must have a screw loose."

RADAU, *m.* Commotion; trouble. *Mach keinen Radau hier.* "Don't make such a racket here."

RADAUBRUDER/RADAUMACHER, *m.* Troublemaker, hooligan. *Die Radaubrüder haben 's Geschäft ausgeplundert.* "The rowdies looted the store."

RADFAHRER, *m.* Sycophant (lit. bicycle rider). *Es ist zum Kotzen wie dieser Radfahrer um die neue Chefin schleicht.* "It's revolting how that toady sucks up to the new boss."

RADI, *m., S.* Radish. **Einen Radi kriegen.** To catch hell. *Dafür kriegst bestimmt einen Radi.* "You'll certainly get a chewing out for that."

RADIKALINSKI/RADIKALO, *m., youth.* Extremist. *Gestern war er Rechtsradikalo. Heute ist er Linksradikalinski.* "Yesterday he was a right-wing radical; today he's a left-wing extremist."

RAFFEN. 1. To snatch; grab. *Er denkt nur ans Geldraffen.* "All he's out for is money." **2.** To understand. See BERAFFEN.

RAFFKE, *m.* Money grubber. *Dein Rechtsanwalt ist 'n richtiger Raffke.* "Your lawyer's out to rake in money."

RAMASURI, *f., S.* Total confusion; hubbub. *Sie hat versucht, etwas Zucht und Ordnung in die Ramasuri zu bringen.* "She tried to bring some order and discipline into that chaos." Cf. REMMIDEMI.

RAMBAZAMBA MACHEN. To make a big fuss. *So ein großes Rambazamba um nichts!* "Such a big to-do for nothing."

RAM(M)DÖSIG. Dizzy; dopey. *Sitz nicht so ramdösig da!* "Don't sit there like an idiot!"

RAMMELEI, *f.* **1.** Madding crowd; crush. *Welche Hetz! So 'ne Rammelei beim Schlussverkauf!* "What a hassle! What a mad mob at the clearance sale!" **2.** Sex. *Die Party wurde zu einer Rammelei.* "The party wound up as a screwing session."

RAMMELN. To have sex (lit. to mate [of animals]). *Sie denken nur ans Rammeln.* "All they think about is screwing."

RAN!/RAN AN DEN FEIND!/RAN AN DIE ARBEIT!/ RAN AN DIE BULETTEN! Up 'n at 'em!/Go 'n get 'em! *Jetzt hättest du vielleicht 'ne Chance. Also ran an die Buletten!* "You might have a chance now. So go to it!"

RANBAUEN/RANHALTEN/RANHAUEN/RAN-KLOTZEN. To get going; work hard. *Jetzt müsst ihr aber ranklotzen!* "You've got to step on the gas now."

RANKOMMEN. To approach, get at. *Fast unmöglich an die neue Chefin ranzukommen.* "The new boss is almost inaccessible."

RANLASSEN. To allow to get at. *Jmdn. ranlassen.* To let s.o. in (sexually). *Du glaubst, ich lass jeden ran, aber du irrst dich.* "You think I'm an easy lay, but you're wrong."

RANPADDELN. To paddle up to. *An jmdn. ranpaddeln.* See RANSEGELN.

RANSEGELN. To sail up to. *An jmdn. ransegeln.* To come on to. *Denk bloß nicht dran, an die Tussi ranzusegeln.* "Don't even think of getting anywhere near that broad."

RANSCHMEIßER, *m.* Fast worker. *Bist 'n richtiger Ranschmeißer, schmeißt dich an jede Tussi ran.* "You're a real goer; you throw y.s. at every broad."

RANSCHWIMMEN. To swim up to. *An jmdn. ranschwimmen.* See RANSEGELN.

RANZEN, *m.* Fat belly (lit. satchel; school bag). *Sich den Ranzen voll schlagen.* To stuff one's face. *Wie gewöhnlich, hat er sich den Ranzen voll geschlagen.* "As usual, he pigged out."

RAPIDO, *youth.* Right away. *Mach's aber rapido, subito!* "Jump to it!"

RAPPEL, *m.* Crazy; crazy mood. *Der hat 'n Rappel.* "He's off his rocker."

RAPPELN. To be rattled/crazy (lit. to rattle, jangle). *Bei* *dem rappelt's immer öfter.* "He's flipping out more and more often." See GERAPPELT VOLL.

RAPPELIG. Jumpy. *Alles macht ihn heute rappelig.* "Everything makes him edgy today."

RASANT. Extremely fast; dashing/stylish. *Ute fährt immer rasant. Ist auch 'ne rasante Tussi.* "Ute always speeds. She's a snappy/snazzy chick too." Cf. FLOTT **1, 2.**

RASANTO. Youth sl. for RASANT. *Wir haben uns rasanto weggeschaltet.* "We hit the road fast."

RASPELN. To grate. *Süßholz raspeln.* To sweet-talk (lit. to grind licorice). *Er raspelte mir Süßholz, aber ich ließ ihn nicht ran.* "He fed me a line, but I wouldn't let him in."

RASPUTIN, E. Den Rasputin machen. To have sex. (Grigori Rasputin, deeply committed to making love not war, was renowned for his romantic prowess. Cf. **den TOWARITSCH machen.**) *Uli will immer nur den Rasputin machen.* "All Uli wants to do is screw."

RASTER, *n.* Raster (a rectangular pattern of parallel scanning lines). *Aus dem Raster fallen.* Not to fit into the scheme of things. *Das fällt aber ganz aus dem Raster.* "That's totally at odds with the pattern."

RATTENSCHARF = RABENSTARK.

RATZ, FATZ. Quickly. *Meine Kinder kamen ratz, fatz; drei in drei Jahren.* "My kids came in rapid succession; three in three years."

RATZEKAHL. Completely. *Ratzekahl hat er alles aufgefressen.* "In two shakes of a rat's tail he devoured everything."

RATZEN. To sleep/nap. *Ratzen darfst jetzt nicht!* "No nodding off now!"

RAUSLASSEN. 1. To let out. *Die Sau rauslassen.* To let it all hang out. *Bei der Fete wollen wir die Sau rauslassen.* "We'll have a blast at the party." *Den Kasper/Lari(fari) rauslassen.* To play the clown. *Mann, lass hier nicht den Lari raus!* "Man, don't act the fool here!" **2.** To talk.

Einen Müllspruch/Müllsprüche rauslassen. (*Youth.*) To talk rot. *Hat er was Interessantes abgelassen oder wieder nur Müllsprüche rausgelassen?* "Did he say anything interesting or just throw the same old bull?"

RAUSMOGELN. To worm out of. *Bisher hat sich der Senator aus allen Skandalen rausgemogelt.* "So far the senator's wormed his way out of all the scandals."

RAUSRÜCKEN. To hand over. *Rück nur raus mit den Lappen.* "Just cough up the dough." Cf. ABDRÜCKEN.

RAUSPAUKEN. To get s.o. off the hook. *Ich hab alles versucht, ihn rauszupauken.* "I tried everything to get him off the hook."

(SICH) RAUSSPRENGEN = **(SICH) WEGKLEMMEN.**

RAVE, *m., n., youth.* "Rave" (large dance party of long duration). *Der Rave auf Goa war gigageil.* "The rave on Goa was fantabulous."

RAVEN, *youth.* To dance to techno music intensely and for a long time (pron. as in Eng.). *Wir haben drei Tage lang geravt.* "We techno-partied for three days."

RAVER, *m.* Techno-music dancer. *Der alte Raver ist fast taub und hört jetzt nur Menuette von Mozart und Haydn.* "The old raver's almost deaf and now just listens to minuets by Mozart and Haydn."

REALO! *Youth.* Sure thing!

REALO, *m.* Realist. *Die Realos waren kompromissbereit, die Fundis nicht.* "The realists were prepared to compromise, not the hard liners."

REGENBOGENPRESSE, *f.* Gossip magazines (lit. rainbow press). *Mein Mann suhlt sich in den Sehnsüchten der Regenbogenpresse.* "My husband wallows in the sentimental yearnings of pulp magazines."

REGISTER, *n.* **1.** Official list. ***Ins alte Register kommen*** (*dated*). To get old. *Dieser Kaskadeur wird nie ins alte Register kommen.* "That stuntman will never make old bones." See ALTES REGISTER; LANGES REGISTER. **2.** Organ stop. *Alle Register spielen lassen/ziehen.* To pull out all the stops. *Wir mussten alle Register ziehen, um den Auftrag zu bekommen.* "We had to go all out to get the contract."

REINFÜLLEN. To fill in. *Sich einen reinfüllen.* See REIN-SAUGEN.

REINHÄMMERN = **REINHAUEN.**

REINHAUEN. 1. To bash. *Zieh Leine, oder ich hau dir eine rein.* "Beat it, or I'll clobber you." **2.** To work hard. *Haut jetzt nur richtig rein!* "Go to it now!" **3.** To boast. *Hast aber ganz schön reingehauen.* "You really laid it on thick."

REINKRIECHEN. To creep in. *Jmdm. hinten reinkriechen.* To be s.o.'s ass kisser. *Den Vorgesetzten ist er hinten reingekrochen; den Job aber dennoch nicht bekommen.* "He brownnosed the bosses, but still didn't get the job."

(SICH) REINPFEIFEN = **EINPFEIFEN.**

(SICH) REINZIEHEN. To take in. *Ziehst dir nur Depressi-Einheiten rein, du Depp, und lässt nur Müllsprüche raus.* "All you do is wallow in (let in) depression and talk (let out) a lot of garbage, you nerd."

REINSAUGEN. To suck in. *Sich einen reinsaugen.* To get soused. *Hast dir ordentlich einen reingesaugt.* "You really got tanked up."

REINSAUSEN. To roar in. *Sich einen reinsausen.* See REINSAUGEN.

REIßAUS, *m. Reißaus nehmen.* To clear out. *Die Polente kam und wir nahmen Reißaus.* "The fuzz came, and we cleared out."

REIßEN. *Wenn alle Stränge/Stricke reißen.* If worse comes to worst. *Wenn alle Stricke reißen, verscherbeln wir was noch übrig bleibt und wandern nach Australien aus.* "In the worst case scenario, we'll sell whatever's left and emigrate to Australia."

REIZWÄSCHE, *m.* Sexy underwear. *Ich kaufte Reizwäsche, um meinen Mann anzumachen; 's war aber* *verlorene Liebesmühe.* "I bought sexy lingerie to turn on my husband, but it was no use."

REMISURI = RAMASURI; REMMIDEMMI.

REMMIDEMMI, *n., S.* Row; rumpus; wild party. *Am Wochenende machen wir Remmidemmi, dass die Wände wackeln.* "On the weekend we're really going to raise the roof."

REMPELN = KNUFFEN.

RETOURKUTSCHE, *f.* Tit-for-tat reaction; retort (lit. return coach). *Genug der Retourkutschen! Vergebung und Verständnis tun Not.* "That's enough reactive behavior! Understanding and forgiveness are what's called for."

REVOLVERBLATT, *n.*/**REVOLVERPRESSE,** *f.* Scandal sheet/sensation-mongering press. *Glaubst du alles, was du in diesem Revolverblatt liest?* "Do you believe everything you read in that scandal sheet?"

RHYTHMUSPRÄSIDENT, *m., youth.* Percussionist. *Habt ihr den turbogeilen Rhythmuspräsidenten schon gehört?* "Have you heard that sensational drummer yet?"

RIBBELN, *N.* To put s.o. on (lit. to pinch, rub). *Von dir lass ich mich nicht ribbeln.* "You're not going to pull the wool over my eyes."

RIECHEN. To smell. ***Jmdn. nicht riechen können.*** To be unable to stand s.o. *Diesen pickligen Streber kann ich nicht riechen.* "I can't stand that pimply eager beaver."

RIECHER, *m.* Nose (lit. smeller). ***Den richtigen Riecher haben.*** To have the right instinct. *Beim Aktienkauf hatte sie den richtigen Riecher.* "She made the right choices when buying stocks."

RIECHKOLBEN = KOLBEN 1.

RIESEN-. Gigantic (an intensifier).

RIESENALK, *m.* Huge amount of alcohol. ***Sich einen Riesenalk reinfüllen/reinpfeifen/reinsausen.*** See REIN-SAUGEN.

RIESENHUNGER, *m.* Huge appetite. *Wir hatten einen Riesenhunger.* "We were ravenously hungry."

RIESENKAROTTE. Penis. See KAROTTE.

RIESENHAMMER. Intensifies HAMMER.

RIESENRINDVIEH, *n.* Colossal idiot. *Ach, du Riesenrindvieh!* "You super fool!"

RIESENTRARA, *n.* Big fuss (lit. big trumpet flourish). *Wozu das Riesentrara um diese Null?* "Why so much hullabaloo about that cipher?"

RIESIG. Wonderful (lit. gigantic). *Die Fete war riesig.* "The party was terrific."

RILLE, *f., youth.* Record (lit. groove). *Die Band macht keine Rillen mehr.* "The band isn't recording anymore." See AUFLEGEN.

RINDFLEISCH = BULLEN.

RINGELPIEZ/RINGELPIEZ MIT ANFASSEN, *m.* Hop, square dance (*piez* is from Pol. for "song"). *Beim Ringelpiez ging's hoch her.* "All had a high old time at the hoedown."

RINGELREIGEN/RINGELREIHN, *m.* Ring-around-the-rosy. *Als Kind spielte ich Ringelreigen; jetzt mach ich flotte Vierer.* "As a child I played ring-around-the-rosy; today I have group sex."

RISS, *m.* Tear, crack. ***Einen Riss im Wirsing/in der Birne/Marille/Pupille haben.*** To be crazy, cracked. See PUPILLE.

RITZEN. To scratch; carve. ***Geritzt sein.*** To be OK. *Gib mir 'n Kuss, dann ist alles geritzt!* "Give me a kiss, then everything'll be all fixed up." ***Ist geritzt!*** Roger!/Fine!

RITZER, *m.* Scratch. *„Die paar Ritzer sind nichts," behauptete der Dompteur.* " 'Just a few minor scratches,' declared the animal trainer."

ROBOTERN. To work hard (from Russ.). *Was ist das für 'n Leben, nur Robotern!* "What kind of life is this; just a constant grind."

ROCHUS, *m.* ***Einen Rochus auf jmdn. haben.*** To be out to get s.o. (from Hebr. via ROTWELSCH). *Er tut freundlich, aber ich weiß, er hat einen Rochus auf mich.* "He's all smiles, but I know he's got it in for me."

ROHR, *n.* **1.** Firearm (lit. gun barrel). *Im Western feuerten die Soldaten aus allen Rohren, wurden aber von den Indianern besiegt.* "In the Western, all the soldiers' guns were blazing, but the Indians beat them." ***Ein Rohr brechen.*** To get drunk. *Brechen wir uns ein Rohr.* "Let's tie one on." **2.** Telephone. *Das Rohr klingelte.* "The phone rang." **3.** Penis. ***Ein/sein Rohr verlegen.*** To get one's end in. *Bei mir verlegt keiner sein Rohr heut abend.* "Nobody's getting into me tonight." ***Sich das Rohr verbiegen.*** To get VD. *Warum? Einfach weil wenigstens einer von euch sich das Rohr verbogen hat.* "Why? Because at least one of you's picked up a nail." **4.** Car/motorcycle. *So ein tolles, flottes Rohr möcht ich auch haben!* "I'd like a fast, nifty car like that m.s."

ROLLE, *f.* **1.** Roll. ***Von der Rolle kommen.*** To miss the boat; be edged out. *Du warst nicht auf der Höhe und bist von der Rolle gekommen.* "You weren't on top of things and you missed out." ***Von der Rolle sein.*** To have missed the boat; be in a bad situation. *Seine Frau ist durchgebrannt und er ist ganz von der Rolle.* "His wife's run off, and he's in a bad way." ***Von der Rolle bringen.*** To get pushed off course. *Lass dich nicht von der Rolle bringen.* "Don't get sidetracked!" **2.** Role. ***Keine Rolle spielen.*** To be of no importance. *In dieser Sache spielt ihre Vergangenheit keine Rolle.* "Her past is not a factor in this matter." ***Seine Rolle ausgespielt haben.*** To be of no further importance. *Die Partei hat seine Rolle längst schon ausgespielt.* "For some time the party's ceased to have any relevance." ***Aus der Rolle fallen.*** To make a faux pas. *Ja, er ist aus der Rolle gefallen, aber er hat uns amüsiert.* "Yes, he behaved unsuitably, but he amused us." **3.** Street with discos/bars. See PISTE **2.**

ROSETTE, *f., from Fr.* Anus. ***Ein komisches Gefühl in der Rosette/um die Rosette haben*** (lit. to have a funny feeling in/around the rose window/rosette). **1.** To smell a rat. *Ziehen wir Leine, ich hab so 'n komisches Gefühl um die Rosette.* "Let's scram, I smell a rat." **2.** To have to defecate. *Er hatte ein komisches Gefühl in der Rosette aber* *die Polente liess ihn nicht aufs Klo.* "He had to go, but the cops wouldn't let him use the john."

ROSINE, *f.* Raisin. **Die (größten) Rosinen (aus dem Kuchen) herauspicken/herausklauben.** To skim off the cream (lit. to pick out the [biggest] raisins [from the cake]). *Das Beste ist weg; schwer wird's sein, noch einige Rosinen aus dem Kram rauszupicken.* "The best stuff's gone; it'll be difficult to find any plums/pearls in that mass."

ROSINENSCHEIßER = **KORINTHENKACKER.**

ROTIEREN. To rotate. *Am Rotieren sein.* To be in a whirl, be stressed/agitated. *Setz dich hin, bist am Rotieren. Immer mit der Ruhe.* "Sit down. You're in a dither. Just keep calm."

ROTKEHLCHEN, *n.* Robin red breast. **Mich rammt ein Rotkehlchen!** (*E.*) Well, I'll be a monkey's uncle! (Lit. a robin's ramming me.) *Du hier? Mich rammt ein Rotkehlchen!* "You here? Well, I'll be darned!" Cf. **mich knutscht ein** ELCH**; mich** LAUST **der Affe**; STREIFEN.

ROTWELSCH, *n.* Thieves' cant; crook talk; slang. Cf. JENISCH; KESSEMER LOSCHEN; KOCHEMER KO(H)L/LOSCHEN. *Viele Wörter aus dem Rotwelschen, z.B.* kess*, sind allgemeines Sprachgut geworden.* "Many words from thieves' slang, for example *kess,* are now in general use."

ROTZ, *m.* Snot. **Rotz und Wasser heulen.** To bawl. *Als er mich verließ heulte ich Rotz und Wasser; jetzt lach ich drüber.* "When he left me, I cried my eyes out; now I laugh about it." **Der ganze Rotz.** The whole damned business. *Den ganzen Rotz hab ich schon mehrmals gehört.* "I've heard that whole schmear many times before." **Jmdm. Rotz auf die Backe schmieren.** To flatter s.o. obsequiously (lit. to smear snot on s.o.'s cheek). *Es ist zum Kotzen wie er der neuen Chefin Rotz auf die Backe schmiert.* "It's disgusting the way he brownnoses the new boss."

ROTZBENGEL/ROTZBUB = **ROTZNASE.**

ROTZEN. To blow one's nose loudly; sniff back snot; spit. *Bei uns wird nur gerotzt; alle sind erkältet.* "Everybody's hacking and wheezing here; we've all got colds." Cf. BEROTZT.

ROTZFAHNE, *f.* Handkerchief (lit. snot flag). *Deine Rotzfahne riecht nach Soße.* "Your snot rag smells of come."

ROTZFRECH/ROTZIG. Impudent. *Rotziger als der ist keiner.* "No one's cheekier than he."

ROTZLAPPEN = **ROTZFAHNE.**

ROTZLÖFFEL/ROTZLÜMMEL = **ROTZNASE.**

ROTZNASE, *f.* Impudent kid (lit. snot nose). *Halt's Maul, Rotznase!* "Shut your trap, brat!"

ROTZNIGEL, *Aust.* = **ROTZNASE.**

RÜBE, *f.* **1.** Turnip. *Jmdn. über die Rüben jagen.* To send s.o. packing (lit. to chase s.o. across the turnips). *Sie jagte ihn über die Rüben.* "She gave him his walking papers." **2.** Head. *Eins auf/über die Rübe kriegen.* To get smacked. *Jetzt kriegst eins auf die Rübe.* "You're going to get a good whack now." *Rübe runter!/Rübe ab!* Off with his/her head! *Die Rübe voll schießen/die Rübe glatt machen.* To get totally plastered. *Wir haben uns die Rübe echt voll geschossen.* "We really tied one on." **3.** Nose. *Hör auf in der Rübe zu popeln.* "Quit picking your nose." Cf. GURKE **1.** **4.** Penis. Cf. GURKE **3**; KAROTTE). *Die Tussi ist noch 'ne Jungfrau; isst aber wahnsinning gern Rüben.* "That broad's still a virgin, but she's nuts about eating cock."

RÜBENHALTER, *m.* Condom. *Der Rübenhalter ist geplatzt; hättest aufs Frische-Datum achten sollen.* "The bag broke; you should've paid attention to the sell-by date."

RÜBERREIßEN, *youth.* To understand (lit. to grab across). *Schmeiß deine Nuss an und du wirst's rüberreißen.* "Use your noodle and you'll get it."

RÜBERSCHMEIßEN, *youth.* To pass (lit. to throw across). *Schmeiß mir die Fluppen mal rüber.* "Hand me the cigarettes."

RÜBERWACHSEN. *Etwas rüberwachsen lassen.* (*Youth.*) To give/send/convey s.t. *Lass mir mal die Marmelade rüberwachsen!* "Pass me the jam."

RÜBERZIEHEN. To pull across. *Jmdm. eine rüberziehen.* (*Youth.*) To beat up. *Dem werden wir echt eine rüberziehen.* "We're going to knock his block off."

RUCK, ZUCK! In a jiffy. *Ruck, zuck war alles getan.* "In a flash, everything was done."

RÜCKEN, *m.* Back. *Jmdm. den Rücken freihalten.* To unencumber s.o. *Ihr Mann ist Hausmann und hält ihr den Rücken frei für ihre schöpferisch künstlerische Arbeit.* "Her husband does all the housework and frees her up for her creative artistic work."

RUCKIZUCKI = **RUCK, ZUCK.**

RUHE, *f.* Rest; calm. *Die Ruhe weghaben.* To be completely unflappable. *Ja, er hat immer die Ruhe weg; gerade das nervt mich an ihm.* "Yes, he's always calm and collected; that's just what bugs me about him." *Immer mit der Ruhe!* Don't panic!/Hang loose!

RUHEPOL. See POL.

RÜHRSCHINKEN, *pej.* Intensifies SCHINKEN **2.** Slushy, sentimental play/movie/book. *Wie hast du diesen Rührschinken zu Ende sehen können?* "How could you watch that cornball all the way through?"

RÜLPS = **RÜLPSER.**

RÜLPSEN. To belch. *Aus der Flasche/Pulle rülpsen.* To be drunk. *Der rülpst schon aus der Pulle.* "He's already soused."

RÜLPSER, *m.* Belch. *Hat's euch nicht geschmeckt? Ich hör kaum einen Rülpser oder Furz.* "Didn't you like it? I don't hear much belching or farting."

RUMBRETTERN. See BRETTERN.

RUMDÜSEN, *youth.* To speed. *Wir sind durch die Savanne rumgedüst.* "We peeled some rubber in the boonies."

RUMFERKELN, *youth.* To screw/sleep around with. *Ich*

weiß nicht, mit welchen Nutten er jetzt rumferkelt. "I don't know what sluts he's screwing around with now."

RUMFLIPPEN = **FLIPPEN 2.**

RUMFUMMELN. See FUMMELN.

RUMGAMMELN. To bum around; loaf. *Wie lange willst du noch rumgammeln?* "How much longer do you intend to bum around?"

RUMGONDELN. To drive around; travel about (lit. to sail around in a gondola). *Die gondeln noch irgendwo in der Welt rum.* "They're still off globetrotting somewhere."

RUMHÄNGEN = **RUMLUNGERN.**

RUMKOMMEN. Youth for *rauskommen.* To come out; result. *'S ist nix dabei rumgekommen.* "The result was zilch."

RUMLUNGERN. To hang out; loaf. *Er lungert nur den ganzen Tag rum.* "All he does is hang out all day."

RUMÖMMELN, *youth, N.* To hang out/bum around. *Dieser Lümmel ömmelt nur rum.* "All that guy does is lounge around."

RUMOPERN. See OPERN.

RUMPLÄTSCHERN, *youth.* To shoot the breeze. *Den ganzen Tag haben wir nur rumgeplätschert.* "We just chewed the fat all day."

RUMSALBEN, *youth.* To prattle. *Ihr salbt nur rum; ich hab anderes zu tun.* "All you do is babble on; I've got other things to do." Cf. SALBEN.

RUMSCHNÜREN = **RUMDÜSEN.**

RUMSÜLZEN = **RUMSALBEN.**

RUMWABERN, *youth.* To hover about/hang around. *Warum waberst du immer bei mir rum?* "Why're you always lurking around me?"

RUMWEDELN, *youth.* To throw money around (*wedeln* = to wag [tail]; wave). *Musst du dauernd mit den Hündis rumwedeln?* "Do you have to keep flashing that bankroll of 100-mark notes?"

RUMZICKEN. To be bitchy. *Willst nicht aufhören hier rumzuzicken?* "Won't you please give it a rest?" Cf. ZICKE.

RUND/RUND WIE EINE TONNE. Drunk (lit. round/ round as a barrel). *Er saß im Weinkeller, rund wie 'ne Tonne.* "He sat in the wine cellar, drunk as a lord."

RUNTERHOLEN. To get/bring down. ***Jmdm./sich einen runterholen.*** To jerk s.o./o.s. off. *Ich hab ihm nur schnell einen runtergeholt.* "I just gave him a quick hand job."

RUNTERLASSEN. To lower. ***Die Hosen runterlassen.*** To come clean (lit. to drop one's pants). *Endlich ließ er die Hosen runter.* "He finally came out with the whole story."

RUNTERNUDELN, *youth.* To rattle off; recite by rote. *Jeder nudelte eine Schiller Ballade runter, und ich war voll genudelt.* "Everyone recited a ballad by Schiller, and I was saturated."

RUNTERPUTZEN. To bawl out. *Die Chefin hat mich vielleicht runtergeputzt!* "The boss gave me some bawling out!"

RUPFEN. 1. To fleece (lit. to pluck feathers; pull up weeds). *Im Nepplokal hat man ihn ordentlich gerupft.* "They really took him to the cleaners in that clipjoint." See HÜHNCHEN. **2.** To fight, brawl. (*Youth.*) *Die Hools haben ihn echt gerupft.* "The toughs really gave it to him."

RÜSSEL, *m.* **1.** Nose (lit. elephant's trunk; pig's snout). *Hast in meinen Papieren geschnüffelt. Halt deinen Rüssel raus!* "You've been snooping in my papers. Keep your nose out of them!" **2.** Penis. *Der hat einen Riesenrüssel!* "He's got a huge cock." Cf. GURKE; RÜBE.

SABBELHEINI = **LABERFRITZE.**

SABBELIG, *pej.* Talkative. *Sei nicht so sabbelig!* "Quit running your mouth."

SABBELN, *N.* To talk nonsense (lit. to slobber/drool). *Der sabbelt nur dummes Zeug.* "Everything he says is just drivel."

SABBERMAUL, *n.* Blabbermouth. *Man sollte diesem Sabbermaul das Maul stopfen.* "S.o. should shut up that blabbermouth."

SABBERN = **SABBELN.**

SACHE (MIT EI) SEIN. To be wonderful. *Die Sektfrühstücke auf seiner Jacht, das war Sache mit Ei!* "The champagne breakfasts on his yacht, that was the berries!"

SACK, *m.* **1.** Bag; sack. *Jmdm. den Sack abbinden.* To put an end to s.o.'s activities; cut off funds. *Ich hatte große Erweiterungspläne, aber die Gläubiger haben mir den Sack abgebunden.* "I had great plans for expansion, but my creditors put the kibosh on them." *In den Sack hauen.* To abandon. *Oft hatte ich Lust in den Sack zu hauen, aber ich blieb dran.* "I often felt like chucking it all, but I stuck with it." *Jmdn. in den Sack stecken.* To put s.o. in the shade. *Die Chefin hat die Konkurrenz in den Sack gesteckt.* "The boss ran rings around the competition." **2.** Despicable person. *Diesen Sack kann ich* *nicht riechen.* "I can't stand that bastard." **3.** Testicles (short for *Hodensack* [scrotum]; cf. EIER **2**). ***Jmdm. auf den Sack fallen/gehen.*** To annoy s.o. greatly. *Das Wetter hier geht mir tierisch auf den Sack.* "I find the weather here a real ballbuster." ***Jmdm. auf den Sack treten.*** To give s.o. a hard time; to bawl s.o. out. *Der Chef versucht immer wieder mir auf den Sack zu treten.* "The boss is always trying to bust my balls."

SADO. From *Sadismus.* Sadism. *Mit der Sado-Maso Szene haben wir nichts am Hut.* "We have nothing to doing with the S&M (sadomasochist) scene."

SAFTARSCH = **SAFTSACK.**

SAFTHEINI, *m.* Dumb jerk. *Dieser Saftheini hat wieder alles vermasselt.* "That nerd screwed up everything again."

SAFTLADEN = **SAULADEN.**

SAFTSACK, *m.* Stupid bastard. *Diesem Saftsack werde ich die Fresse polieren.* "I'm gonna bash that bastard's face in."

SAHNE, *f.* Cream. ***Erste Sahne/allererste Sahne.*** Topnotch. *Das Konzert war allererste Sahne.* "The concert was first rate."

SAHNEMÄßIG, *youth.* Wonderful (*sahnig* = creamy). *Echt sahnemäßig damals, als wir tagelang geravt haben.* "It was mind-blowing, orgasmic back then, when we danced for days at raves."

SAHNESCHNITTE, *m.*/**SAHNETÖRTCHEN,** *n.* = **TÖRTCHEN.**

SALAT, *m.* Mess; unpleasantness (lit. salad). *Mach keinen Salat! Wir haben schon genug Zeit.* "Don't get all stirred up. We've got enough time." ***Da haben wir den Salat!*** What a mess! *Du hast Fahrkarten, Kohle, und Kreditkarte vergessen? Da haben wir den Salat!* "You forget the tickets, the money, and the credit card? What a mess!"

SALBEN, *youth.* To prattle, babble (lit. to anoint). Cf. GESALBE; RUMSALBEN. *Der Lernfuzzi hört nie zu salben auf.* "That teacher goes on and on about nothing."

SALM, *m., N.* Psalm. ***Einen langen Salm machen.*** To make a big song and dance. *Mach keinen langen Salm; rück nur mit der Kohle raus.* "Don't go on about it, just come across with the dough."

SALONTIROLER, *m.* Jokester, clown (lit. parlor Tyrolean/parlor yodeler). *Tu nicht so verdodelt, Salontiroler du!* "Stop being such a jerk, cowboy!"

SAND, *m.* **1.** Sand. ***Auf dem Sand sein.*** To be all washed up. *Seit einem Jahr ist er aufm Sand.* "He's been down and out for a year." Cf. SANDLER. **2.** Money. *Der Sand ist weg.* "The money's gone." Cf. KIES; SCHOTTER **1**; STEINE.

SANDELN. See DAHERSANDELN.

SANDLER, *m., S.* Homeless person; bum. *Sandler sieht man jetzt überall.* "You see vagrants everywhere now."

SATT. 1. Drunk (lit. full). *Da sitzt er, satt wie üblich.* "There he sits, soused as usual." **2.** Whopping. *Dieses Modell kostet satte $1.000.* "This model costs a whopping $1,000."

SAU-. 1. Rotten. See SAUKERL; SAUWETTER. **2.** Extremely (good or bad). See SAUBLÖD; SAUGEIL; SAUWOHL.

SAU, *f.* **1.** Sow; pig. ***Die Sau rauslassen/losmachen.*** To let it all hang out. *Auf Mallorca haben wir die Sau richtig rausgelassen.* "We let it all hang out on Mallorca." ***Jmdn. zur Sau machen.*** To run s.o. down. *Lass dich nicht zur Sau machen!* "Don't let them walk all over you!" ***Unter aller Sau.*** Really rotten. *Deine Arbeit ist unter aller Sau.* "Your work is the pits." **2.** Bitch; SOB. *Du alte Sau!* "You dirty bastard!" **3.** Person (usually with *keine*). *Keine Sau interessiert sich für deine Mucke.* "Nobody at all is interested in your music."

SAUBANDE, *m.* **1.** Pack of swine. *Was treibst du mit dieser Saubande?* "What are you up to with that pack of swine?" **2.** No-goods. *Na kommt die Saubande endlich?* "Is that no-good bunch o' bums finally coming?"

SAUBER. 1. Fine/great (lit. clean). ***Etwas sauber hinkriegen.*** To do a good job. *Das hast du sauber* *hingekriegt.* "You did a neat job on that." **2.** Fine (ironic use of **1**). *Ihr seid mir ja saubere Freunde!* "Some friends you are!"

SAUBERKEITSFIMMEL, *m.* Cleanliness hangup. *Felix hatte einen Sauberkeitsfimmel.* "Felix was compulsive about cleanliness."

SAUBERMANN, *m.* Mr. Nice Guy; self-righteous person. *Sein Image als Saubermann hat jetzt einige Kratzer bekommen.* "His image as Mr. Clean has been somewhat tarnished recently."

SAUBLÖD(E)/SAUDUMM. Really stupid. *Warum hast du dich so saublöd benommen?* "Why'd you act like such a stupid idiot?"

SAUER. 1. Sour. *Gib ihm Saures.* Give it to him good!/Let him have it! *Sauer verdient.* Hard-earned. *Die Kohle hab ich sauer verdient.* "I worked hard for that money." **2.** Annoyed. *Die Mannschaft ist sauer aufn Schiri.* "The team's ticked off at the umpire." See ENTSAUERN; STINKSAUER.

SAUERTÖPFISCH, *hum.* Sour-faced. *In ihrer Religion wird gehüpft und getanzt; es geht gar nicht so sauertöpfisch zu wie bei uns.* "In their religion they jump around and dance; things are nowhere near so gloomy as with us."

SAUFBRUDER, *m., pej.* Drinking buddy. *Dich und deine Saufbrüder will ich nicht mehr sehen.* "I don't want to see you and your boozing buddies anymore."

SAUFEN. To guzzle alcohol. *Saufen wie ein Loch/Bürstenbinder.* To drink like a fish. *Er säuft immer noch wie ein Loch.* "He still drinks like a fish." *Sich die Hucke/Jacke voll saufen.* See HUCKE.

SAUFGELAGE, *m.* Session of heavy drinking. *Beim Saufgelage rief er immer wieder „Hoch die Tassen!"* "During the drinking bout he kept saying, 'Bottoms up!' "

SAUFKOPF = SUFFKOPF.

SAUFKUMPAN = SAUFBRUDER.

SAUFRAß. Intensifies FRAß.

SAUFTOUR = KNEIPTOUR; PICHELTOUR.

SAUGEIL. Intensifies GEIL.

SAUHAUFEN = SAUBANDE.

SAUHUND = SAUKERL; SCHWEINEHUND.

SÄUISCH. 1. Obscene (lit. sow-like). *Seine säuischen Witze will ich mir nicht länger anhören.* "I won't listen to his dirty jokes any longer." **2.** Extreme(ly). *Wir haben säuisch viel Glück gehabt.* "We really lucked out."

SAUKERL, *m.* SOB. *Diesem Saukerl verzeih ich nie.* "I'll never forgive that bastard."

SAULADEN, *m.* Dump. *Das ist 'n richtiger Sauladen hier.* "This place is a real dump." Cf. SAFTLADEN; SCHEIßLADEN.

SAUREGURKENZEIT, *f.* Slack period (lit. sour pickle season). *Ich freu mich immer auf die Sauregurkenzeit.* "I always look forward to the lull."

SAUSCHWER. Very difficult. *Sauschwer war die Arbeit.* "That was damned hard work."

SAUSE, *f.* Barhopping; pub crawl. ***Eine Sause machen.*** See KNEIPTOUR; KNEIPENBUMMEL.

SAUSEN. To roar; buzz. ***Einen sausen lassen.*** To fart. *Im Takt der Nationalhymne ließ er einen nach dem anderen sausen.* "He cracked one fart after another to the tune of the national anthem." ***Etwas sausen lassen.*** Not to bother about s.t. *Wir haben's Konzert sausen lassen.* "We didn't bother to go to the concert." ***Jmdn. sausen lassen.*** To drop s.o. *Ich ließ ihn sausen.* "I dropped him." See AFTERSAUSEN.

SAUWETTER, *n.* Rotten weather. *Bei diesem Sauwetter bleiben wir lieber zu Hause.* "We'd rather stay home in rotten weather like this."

SAUWOHL. Really wonderful (stronger than PUDELWOHL). *Wir hatten keine Kohle mehr, fühlten uns aber sauwohl.* "We had no money left, but we felt just great."

SAVANNE, *f.* Savannah; boonies. See PAMPA.

SCHACHTEL, *f.* Box; packet. ***Alte Schachtel.*** Old woman. *Wie viele alte Schachteln, träum ich noch von der großen Liebe.* "Like many old bags, I still dream of romantic love."

SCHAFSKOPF, *m.* Dummy (lit. sheep's head). *Hast es wieder verkehrt gemacht, Schafskopf.* "You got it wrong again, dummy!"

SCHALTFEHLER, *m., youth.* Circuit/gearbox defect. *Hast 'n Schaltfehler, oder wa?* "Are you off your rocker, or what?" Cf. ABSTURZ; CHIP-INFARKT; FLOPPY; GETRIEBESCHADEN, PROGRAMM.

SCHAMOTT, *m.* Stuff; junk. *Für den ganzen Schamott hab ich fast nichts bekommen.* "I got practically nothing for all that junk."

SCHARF. 1. Sexy; horny (lit. sharp). ***Auf jmdn. scharf sein.*** Weaker equivalent of ***auf jmdn.*** GEIL ***sein. Scharf wie sieben Sensen/wie tausend Russen.*** Horny as hell (lit. horny as seven scythes/1,000 Russians). *Er glaubt, er sei scharf wie sieben Sensen; ist auch scharf auf mich. Mich macht er aber gar nicht scharf.* "He thinks he's a sex machine, and he's got the hots for me; but he doesn't turn me on." **2.** Wonderful; beautiful. (*Youth.*) *Ihr Sound ist echt scharf.* "Their sound is fantastic." Cf. GEIL.

SCHARFMACHER, *m.* Rabble-rouser. *Das Land braucht Frieden, nicht Scharfmacher.* "The country needs peace, not rabble-rousers."

SCHARTEKE, 1. Trashy old book. *Die Scharteken kannst du alle rausschmeißen.* "You can throw out all those junky old books." **2.** Old bag/hag. *Ja, aber die Scharteke ist doch millionenschwer.* "Yes, but the old bag's got millions."

SCHATTEN, *m.* Shadow. ***In den Schatten fahren.*** (*Youth.*) To lay low. *Nach dem Banküberfall fuhr er in den Schatten.* "He hid out after the bank robbery." ***Einen Schatten haben.*** (*Youth.*) To be crazy. *Der hat 'n Schatten aber manchmal auch lichte Augenblicke.* "He's crazy, but sometimes has lucid intervals."

SCHATTENSEITE, *f.* Disadvantage; dark side. *Dass alles seine Schatten- und Sonnenseiten hat, wussten schon die alten Taoisten, längst vor Jung.* "Everything has its positive and negative aspects, as the old Taoists knew long before Jung."

SCHATTENVOGEL, *m., pej., youth.* Unattractive girl who dogs s.o.'s tracks (lit. a hovering bird who "shadows" s.o.). *Verflieg dich, Schattenvogel!* "Fly off, dogface."

SCHAUM, *m.* Foam. **Schaum schlagen.** To talk big. *Der Senator hat nur Schaum geschlagen.* "Everything the senator said was just hot air."

SCHAUMSCHLÄGER, *m.* Four-flusher. *Ja, er ist 'n richtiger Schaumschläger.* "Yes, he's a real windbag."

SCHEIBE, *f.* 1. Slice. **Sich von jmdm. eine Scheibe abschneiden können.** To be able to learn from s.o. *Uta arbeitet fleißig; von ihr könntest du dir 'ne Scheibe abschneiden, du Faulpelz.* "Uta's a hard worker; you could take a leaf from her book, you lazybones." 2. Record, disc. (*Youth.*) *Ich sammle all ihre Scheiben.* "I collect all her records."

SCHEICH, *m.* 1. Guy (lit. sheikh [Arab chief; Muslim guru]). *Der Scheich soll mir vom Leibe bleiben.* "That guy'd better stay away from me." 2. Lover. *Mein Hausfrauendasein wär leichter, wenn ich nur 'n Scheich hätt; selbst wenn er nicht aussieht wie Rudolph Valentino.* "My life as a housewife would be easier if I had a lover, even if he doesn't look like Rudolph Valentino." 3. Fat cat, plutocrat. *Einen steinreichen Scheich brauch ich dringend.* "I'm in great need of a sugar daddy."

SCHEISS DICH AUS! "You're full o' shit!/Go to hell!" *Geh scheiß dich aus! Du hast's nötig!* "Go take a shit! You're full of it!"

SCHEISS, *m.* 1. Shit. *Einen Scheiß tu ich für euch!* "I won't do shit/a goddamned thing for you." 2. Foolishness; stupidity. **Scheiß machen.** A. To kid around. *Mach keinen Scheiß!* "Quit fuckin' around." B. To do s.t. wrong/stupid.

Mach keinen Scheiß oder du landest wieder im Knast! "Don't do anything stupid, or you'll wind up in the clink again."

SCHEIßDRECK, *m.* Stronger form of DRECK **1.** *Uns geht das einen Scheißdreck an.* "We don't give a good goddamn/we don't care diddly-squat about that."

SCHEIßE, *f.* Shit. *Diese Stadt ist echt Scheiße.* "This town really sucks." ***Jmdm. steht die Scheiße bis zum Hals.*** To be up to one's neck in difficulty. *Dem Chef steht die Scheiße bis zum Hals.* "The boss is in deep doo-doo." ***Scheiße bringt Glück.*** Shit brings luck. *Sie trat in einen Hundehaufen und erinnerte sich an den Spruch: „Scheiße bringt Glück."* "She stepped in dog shit and remembered the saying, 'Shit brings luck.' " ***Scheiße im Trompetenrohr!*** The shit's really hit the fan! *Sie gehen jetzt auf Distanz? Scheiße im Trompetenrohr!* "They're backing off? Goddamn it to hell!" ***Scheiße bauen.*** See BAUEN.

SCHEIßE! Shit! *Meinen Pass hab ich verloren. Scheiße!* "I lost my passport. Shit!" See VERDAMMTE SCHEIßE!

SCHEIßE MIT REIS! Fuckin' shit! (lit. shit with rice; cf. QUATSCH MIT SOßE!). *Scheiße mit Reis, der Computer ist wieder gestört!* "Damn it to hell, the computer's down again."

SCHEIßEGAL. Thoroughly indifferent. *Was er denkt, ist mir scheißegal.* "I don't give a shit about what he thinks."

SCHEIßEN. To defecate. ***Jmdm. eins/was scheißen.*** To be unwilling to do what s.o. wants (lit. to shit s.t. for s.o.). *Nach der Arbeit soll ich dich noch bedienen? Dir scheiß ich was!* "You expect me to wait on you after I come home from work? You can get lost!" ***Scheiß drauf!*** Forget it! (lit. shit on it). *„Mein Schmuck ist noch drin!" „Scheiß drauf, das Haus brennt!"* " 'My jewels are still inside!' 'Forget about them, the house is on fire!' " Cf. BESCHEIßEN; VERSCHEIßEN; VERSCHEIßERN; ZUSCHEIßEN.

SCHEIßER, *m.* **1.** Asshole (lit. shitter). *Geh doch weg, du Scheißer!* "Get away, you shithead!" **2.** Sweetheart; little rascal. *Komm setz dich zu mir, kleiner Scheißer!* "Come sit by me, little sweet ass."

SCHEIßFREUNDLICH. Excessively friendly. *Ja, er tut immer so scheißfreundlich, aber ich weiß, was er will.* "Yes, he's always sugar-shitass sweet, but I know what he's after."

SCHEIßGASSE, *f.* Shit street. ***In der Scheißgasse sitzen.*** To be in a difficult situation. *Wir haben pleite gemacht und sitzen jetzt in der Scheißgasse, total aufgeschmissen.* "We're bankrupt and up shit's creek without a paddle." See KLEMME.

SCHEIßGEGEND, *f.* Rotten area. *Wie kommt man aus dieser Scheißgegend wieder in die Stadt zurück?* "How do you get back to the city from this goddamned area?"

SCHEIßKERL, *m.* SOB, shithead. *Warum klatscht ihr nicht, ihr Scheißkerle?* "Why don't you clap, you bastards?"

SCHEIßLADEN, *m.* Dump (lit. shit store). *Von diesem Scheißladen hab ich genug.* "I've had enough of this lousy outfit." Cf. SAFTLADEN; SAULADEN.

SCHEIßSTÄNDER, *pl., mil.* Legs (lit. shit stands). *Rühr deine Scheißständer und verpiss dich!* "Stir your stumps and piss off."

SCHEIßVORNEHM. Excessively polite. *In dem Nobelhotel tut das Personal scheißvornehm.* "The staff is really piss-elegant in that fancy hotel."

SCHERBE, *f.* Fragment. *Scherben bringen Glück.* "Broken pieces bring luck." See POLTERABEND; SCHEIßE.

(SICH) SCHEREN. 1. To care about. ***Sich den Henker/Teufel um etwas scheren.*** Not to give a damn. *Er schert sich den Teufel um unsere Geldnot.* "He doesn't give a damn about our being strapped for money." See DRECK. **2.** To clear out. *Wir müssen uns jetzt nach Hause scheren.* "We've got to shove off for home now." ***Scher dich zum Henker/Teufel!*** Go to hell!

SCHERZBOLD/SCHERZKEKS, *m*. Joker/prankster. *Nur ein dummdreister Scherzkeks wie der würde über so etwas scherzen.* "Only an impudent, stupid joker like him would joke about s.t. like that."

SCHESE, *f*. Car. *Du fährst noch die alte Schese?* "You're still driving that old heap?"

SCHESEN = PESEN.

SCHICK. Elegant. *Siehst ganz schick aus in deinem cognac Cocktailkleid.* "You look real chic in your golden-brown cocktail dress."

SCHICKER. 1. Drunk (not rel. to *schicker* [more chic] or *schicken* [to send]; (from Hebr. via Yiddish). *Er behauptet, er trinke nur ein bisschen Rotwein für seine Gesundheit, aber schicker ist er immer.* "He says he just drinks a little red wine for his health, but he's always stewed." **2.** *m*. Drunkenness. **Einen (kleinen/leichten) Schicker haben.** To be (a bit) drunk. *Ihr habt alle schon 'n kleinen Schicker.* "You're all a little plastered already."

SCHICKERIA, *f*. Smart set. *Der Gecko glaubt, er gehöre der Schickeria an.* "That fop thinks he's part of the smart set."

SCHICKERN. To drink alcohol. *Genug geschickert! Raus mit euch!* "Enough boozing! Get going, all of you!"

SCHICKIMICKI, 1. *m., often pej.* Person who's with it; s.o. rich/famous. *Nur Schickimickis verkehren jetzt dort.* "Only the trendy go there now." **2.** Trendy; pretentious. *Die alte Kiezkneipe ist uns zu schickimicki geworden.* "The old neighborhood bar's become too pretentious for us."

SCHICKISCHNÖSEL, *m., always pej. var. of* SCHICKIMICKI. Snooty, trendy person. *Die Schickischnösel können mir gestohlen bleiben.* "Those pretentious snobs can get lost."

SCHIEF. Crooked, lopsided. **Schief gewickelt sein.** To be dead wrong (lit. wrongly packaged). *Da bist du schief gewickelt.* "You've got another guess coming."

SCHIEßBRÜDER, *pl*. Police. See TANGOBRÜDER; WAFFEN-FUZZIS.

SCHIEßEN. To shoot. ***Zum Schießen sein.*** To be very funny. *All ihre Sendungen sind zum Schießen.* "All her shows (TV, radio) are a scream." ***Schießen lassen.*** To abandon. *Das ist aber kein Grund, alles schießen zu lassen.* "But that's no reason to drop everything."

SCHIEßER, *m.* Drug addict who injects narcotics (lit. shooter). *Ihr Sohn ist Schießer.* "Their son's a mainliner."

SCHIET, *m.*/**SCHIETE,** *f.* Excrement (*N.* for **SCHISS/SCHEIßE**). *Komm mir nicht wieder mit dem ollen Schiet!* "Don't give me any more of that old shit."

SCHIETER, *N. Var. of* SCHEIßER.

SCHIFF. See KLAR.

SCHIFFEN. 1. To urinate (lit. to go by ship; steer). *Bestell mir noch 'ne Mass; ich geh schiffen.* "Order me another beer; I'm going to pump ship." **2.** To rain. *Da schifft's schon wieder.* "It's pissing rain again."

SCHIFFERKLAVIER, *n.* Accordion (lit. sailor's piano). *Hein spielt abends so schön auf dem Schifferklavier seine Lieder.* "Evenings Hein strikes up his songs on the accordion." Cf. QUETSCHKOMMODE.

SCHIFFERSCHEIßE, *f.* Extremely (lit. sailor's shit). See DUMM; FRECH; GEIL.

SCHIFFSCHRAUBE, *f., youth.* Unattractive woman. *Mir müsste man Daumenschrauben anlegen, bevor ich mit der Schiffschraube ficke.* "They'd have to apply thumbscrews to me before I'd screw that scarecrow." Cf. SCHRAUBE **2.**

(SICH) SCHIMPFEN. To style o.s. *Er schimpft sich Komponist, aber sein Musical ist nicht sehr musikalisch.* "He calls h.s. a composer, but his music isn't very melodious."

SCHINDEN. To mistreat; stall; pad. *Er schindet nur Zeit, um uns hinters Licht zu führen.* "He's just playing for time so he can put one over on us."

(SICH) SCHINDEN. To slave away. *Ich schinde mich mit dieser Knochenarbeit und du lungerst nur rum.* "I work my fingers to the bone, and you just loaf."

SCHINKEN, *m.* **1.** Fat tome; giant painting (lit. ham). *Solche Schinken sind aus der Mode gekommen.* "Epic canvases like that are no longer fashionable." **2.** Sentimental, kitschy play/movie/book. *Beim Schinken hat Oma geweint.* "Granny wept during that slushy movie." Cf. RÜHRSCHINKEN; SCHMIERENKOMÖDIANT.

SCHIRI, *m.* Umpire. *Die Zuschauer wollten den Schiri weichklopfen.* "The spectators wanted to beat up the umpire."

SCHISS, *m.* **1.** Shit. **Den Schiss kriegen.** To get the shits (diarrhea). *Gleich nach'm Festessen kriegten wir 'n Schiss.* "We got the shits right after the banquet." **2.** Fear. **Schiss haben.** To be afraid. *Du hast gleich Schiss gehabt vor den Skins.* "The skinheads scared you shitless right away." **Schiss kriegen.** To get scared. *Du hast auch Schiss gekriegt.* "You got scared too." Cf. SCHISSER; SCHISSHASE.

SCHISSER, *m.* Timid person (lit. shitter). *Du hast mich im Stich gelassen, du Schisser!* "You left me in the lurch, you chicken!"

SCHISSHASE, *m.* Vulgar var. of stand. *Angsthase* (timid rabbit). See SCHISSER.

SCHLABBERFOTZE, *f.* Slobbery cunt; talkative woman. *Sie schimpfen mich 'ne alte Schlabberfotze, aber bumsen wollen sie mich doch noch alle.* "They call me a slobbery old cunt, but all of them still want to hump me."

SCHLABBERSACK, *m.* Baggy/sloppy man's suit jacket. *Wirf doch den alten Schlabbersack weg und kauf dir was Poppiges.* "Throw away that old burlap bag and get s.t. hip."

SCHLACHTENBUMMLER, *m.* Sports fan who follows a team (usually soccer) to other cities/countries. *Die Schlachtenbummler zogen grölend durch die Straßen.* "The sports fans went rumbling through the streets."

SCHLACHTSCHIFF, *n.* **1.** Battle-ax (lit. battleship). See FREGATTE **2. 2.** Limousine. *Da kam der Bonze in seinem*

Schlachtschiff angepest. "The big boss drove up in his big limousine." Cf. STRAßENKREUZER.

SCHLACKERN. To shake; flap. ***Mit den Ohren schlackern.*** To be dumbfounded. *Wenn du vom neuesten Skandal hörst, wirst du mit den Ohren schlackern.* "When you hear about the latest scandal, you won't believe your ears."

SCHLAFFI/SCHLAFFNASE, *m.* Wimp. *So 'n Schlaffi kommt nie auf einen grünen Zweig.* "A wimp like that will never make a go of anything." Cf. SCHLAPPSACK.

SCHLAKS, *m.* Gangling, lanky person. *Dieser Schlaks hat mir beim Schwof die Füße wund getreten.* "I've got sore feet after dancing with that clumsy guy."

SCHLAKSIG. Gangling, gawky. *In seinem Alter sind sie alle schlaksig.* "At his age, they're all awkward."

SCHLAMASSEL. See MASSEL.

SCHLAMPAMPE/SCHLAMPE, *f.* Slut; slovenly/disorderly female. *Geh, deine Schlampe wartet auf dich!* "Go, your slut's waiting for you!"

SCHLAMPEN. To do a sloppy job. *Bei der Untersuchung wurde voll geschlampt.* "The inspection was anything but thorough."

SCHLAMPENGIRLIE = SCHLAMPAMPE.

SCHLAMPEREI, *f.* Sloppy work. *Was ist das aber für 'ne Schlamperei!* "What kind of a rotten mess is that!"

SCHLAPP. Slack; flabby; worn out. *Schlappe fünf Mark kostet das.* "That costs a measly five marks." ***Schlapp machen.*** To conk out. *Auf der Autobahn hat der Motor schlapp gemacht.* "The motor conked out on the highway."

SCHLAPPE, *f.* Setback. *Noch 'ne Schlappe wie diese und 's ist mit der Partei aus.* "Another setback like that and the party's done for."

SCHLAPPEN. To shuffle along; be too wide/baggy. *Da schlappt er in seinen Latschen.* "There he goes, flip-flopping in his old shoes."

SCHLAPPI = **SCHLAFFI**.

SCHLAPPSACK/SCHLAPPSCHWANZ, *m.* Wimp; sad sack; dumb jerk (lit. limp bag/limp dick). *Wenn er nicht so 'n Schlappschwanz wär, hätt er die Wahl gewonnen.* "If he weren't such a drip, he would have won the election." Cf. SCHLAFFI/SCHLAFFNASE.

SCHLARAFFENLAND, *n.* Land of peace and plenty. *Im Krieg nagten wir am Hungertuch; träumten aber vom Schlaraffenland.* "In the war we starved, but dreamed of the land of the land of milk and honey."

SCHLAUBERGER, *m.* Wise guy; smart aleck. *Du Schlauberger, das sieht dir ähnlich.* "You shrewdy, that's just the sort of thing you'd do."

SCHLAUBERGEREI, *m.* Know-it-all attitude. *Wir verlangen mehr ehrliche Arbeit und weniger Schlaubergerei von dir.* "We want you to be less of a wise guy and do more honest work."

SCHLAUCH, *m.* **1.** Hose; inner tube. ***Auf dem Schlauch stehen.*** To be uncertain; be at loose ends. *Seit sie ihn verlassen hat, steht er auf dem Schlauch.* "He's been at loose ends ever since she left him." **2.** Tough job; grind. *War das 'n Schlauch!* "That was some tough job."

SCHLAUCHEN. 1. To slave away. *Den ganzen Tag hab ich geschlaucht, aber du gönnst mir keine Ruhe.* "I've been slaving away all day, but you won't let me rest." ***Jmdn. schlauchen.*** To drive s.o. hard. *Bei der Grundi hat der Spieß uns echt geschlaucht.* "During basic training the sergeant really put us through our paces." **2.** To mooch. *Bei mir gibt's nichts zu schlauchen, weder Kies noch Hugos.* "I've got nothing for you to mooch, neither money nor cigarettes."

SCHLAUFUCHS/SCHLAUKOPF = **SCHLAUBERGER**.

SCHLAULE, *n., S.* = **SCHLAUBERGER**.

SCHLAUMEIER = **SCHLAUBERGER**.

SCHLAWINER, *m.* Trickster; rogue. *Der Schlawiner hat all meine Pläne zunichte gemacht.* "That joker wrecked all my plans."

SCHLEIMBEUTEL, *m.* **1.** Condom (lit. slime bag). *Gestern im Bett platzte der Schleimbeutel und jetzt platzt mir der Teebeutel!* "The bag broke in bed yesterday, and now the tea bag breaks on me!" **2.** Sleazeball; servile flatterer. *Mit diesem Schleimbeutel hab ich nichts am Hut.* "I have nothing to do with that scuzzball."

SCHLEIMI, *m., youth* = **SCHLEIMBEUTEL 2.**

SCHLIPS, *m.* Necktie. ***Jmdm. auf den Schlips treten.*** To step on s.o.'s toes. *Ich wollte Ihnen nicht auf den Schlips treten.* "I didn't want to step on your toes." ***Sich einen hinter den Schlips gießen*** = ***sich einen auf die*** LAMPE ***gießen.***

SCHLITTEN, *m.* Car (lit. sled). *Auch ich hab 'n Schlitten.* "I've got wheels too." Cf. AMISCHLITTEN; LUXUSSCHLITTEN.

SCHLITZOHR, *n.* Sly fox; finagler. *Der Senator ist Schlitzohr und Frauenheld.* "The senator's a shrewdy and a ladykiller."

SCHLOTTERBEIN/SCHLOTTERHOSE = **TANTE SCHLOTTERBECK** (*schlottern* = to shake; tremble).

SCHLUCKEN. To booze (lit. to swallow; gulp). *Genug geschluckt! An die Arbeit!* "Enough boozing! Get to work!"

SCHLUCKSPECHT, *m.* Boozer (lit. guzzling woodpecker). *Von morgens früh bis abends spät steht der Schluckspecht an der Theke.* "From early in the morning till late at night, he's at the bar guzzling." Cf. SCHNAPSDROSSEL.

SCHLÜRFBUDE, *f., youth.* Fast-food restaurant (lit. slurp dump). *Die Schlürfbude hat pleite gemacht.* "That snack bar folded."

SCHLUSS, *m.* End. ***Schluss mit lustig!*** No more Mr. Nice Guy. *Jetzt ist aber Schluss mit lustig!* "Things have gone far enough now!"

SCHLÜSSEL, *m.* Penis. ***Der Schlüssel passt.*** Sexual compatibility (lit. the key fits). *Bislang hat mir keiner der vielen Schlüssel voll und ganz gepasst.* "So far, none of numerous penis keys has succeeded in completely unlocking my box."

SCHLUSSLICHT, *n.* Taillight. ***Das Schlusslicht sein.*** To be in last position. *Im Bündnis sind wir nicht die Vortänzer, aber auch nicht das Schlusslicht.* "We're not the front-runners in the alliance, but we're not at the bottom of the pile either."

SCHMACKES, *pl.* Smacking. ***Mit Schmackes.*** Forcefully. *Er knallte den Maßkrug mit Schmackes auf die Theke.* "He slammed the beer stein on the bar."

SCHMÄH, *m., Aust.* **1.** Put-on; con. ***Einen Schmäh führen.*** To kid; tell jokes. *Man weiß nie, wann er einen Schmäh führt.* "You never know when he's putting you on." **2.** Sardonic humor. *Zuerst lernte ich seinen Wiener Scharm kennen, später seinen Wiener Schmäh.* "First I noted his Viennese charm, then his sarcastic Viennese sense of humor."

SCHMÄHTANDLER, *m., Aust.* Joker. *Ich weiß ganz genau, wieviel es bei dem Schmähtandler geschlagen hat.* "I know exactly what's what with that joker."

SCHMARR(E)N, *m., S.* Nonsense; trash (lit. pancake). *Das ist ein Schmarrn!* "That's a lot of rot." ***Jmdm. einen Schmarren angehen.*** To be no one's damned business (impolite, but not vulgar as: ***das geht dich einen Dreck/Scheißdreck an***). *Das geht dich einen Schmarren an!* "That's no concern of yours."

SCHMECKEN. 1. To taste; taste good. *„Lasst es euch schmecken!" sagte immer Mutter. Allein es schmeckte uns meistens nicht, denn sie war keine begabte Köchin.* " 'Enjoy the meal/dig in,' mother always said. But we didn't usually enjoy the food, since she wasn't a very good cook." ***Schmecken nach mehr.*** To taste terrific. *Deine Ochsenschwanzsuppe schmeckt nach mehr.* "Your oxtail soup tastes great." ***Schmecken wie eingeschlafene***

Füße/wie Hund. To taste terrible (lit. like feet that have fallen asleep/like a dog). *Der Salat schmeckt wie eingeschlafene Füße.* "The salad tastes yucky." **2.** To find/like. *Wie schmeckt dir der neue Job?* "How do you find/like the new job?"

SCHMEIßEN. 1. To throw. *Eine Lage/Runde schmeißen.* To buy a round of drinks. *Wenn ich die Mäuse hätte, würde ich noch 'ne Lage schmeißen.* "If I had the dough, I'd buy another round of drinks." *Den Laden/eine Sache schmeißen.* To run a business/do s.t. competently. *Ich muss den Laden allein schmeißen.* "I've got to run the whole show m.s." **2.** To give up, chuck. See HINSCHMEIßEN **1.**

SCHMIERE, *f.* **1.** Poor-quality theater (lit. grease; paint). *Die Filmdiva hat in dieser Schmiere angefangen.* "The movie queen started out in this humble theater." **2.** Lookout, in *Schmiere stehen* (from Hebr. for "sentinel" via ROTWELSCH; not rel. to *SCHMIEREN*). *Beim Banküberfall sollte ich Schmiere stehen.* "I was supposed to be the lookout during the bank robbery."

SCHMIEREN. 1. To smear, grease. *Jmdm. Brei/Honig um den Mund/Bart schmieren/Jmdm. Rotz auf die Backe schmieren.* To brownnose s.o. See ROTZ. **2.** To clout. *Pass auf, oder ich schmier dir eine.* "Watch out or I'll clobber you." **3.** To bribe. *Wenn wir nicht reichlich geschmiert hätten, hätten wir den Auftrag nicht bekommen.* "If we hadn't greased many palms, we wouldn't have had the contract." *Jmdm. die Hände schmieren.* See HAND.

SCHMIERENKOMÖDIANT/SCHMIERENSCHAUSPIELER, *m.* Ham (schmaltzy) actor. *Die Dorfpiefkes verstanden meine hohe Kunst nicht und schimpften mich einen Schmierenschauspieler.* "Those dumb rubes didn't understand my high art and called me a ham actor."

SCHMIERENTHEATER, *n.* Low-grade theater. *Ein Schmierentheater rauslassen.* (*Youth.*) To put/have s.o. on. *Willst du hier ein Schmierentheater rauslassen?* "Are you trying one of your stupid cons on us?" Cf. SCHMIERE **1.**

SCHMIERESTEHEN, *n.* Keeping a lookout. See SCHMIERE **2.**

SCHMONZES, *m.* Stupid chatter. *Solchen Schmonzes will ich mir nicht länger anhören.* "I don't want to listen to that drivel anymore."

SCHMONZETTE, *f.* Trashy movie/play. *Der Kritiker tat den Film als Schmonzette ab.* "The critic dismissed the film as trash."

SCHMU, *m.* Scam; finagling. ***Schmu machen.*** To cheat. *Bei der Abrechnung hat sie 'n bisschen Schmu gemacht.* "She finagled the figures a little when adding them up."

SCHMUS, *m.* Foolish talk; soft-soap, sweet nothings. *Red keinen Schmus!* "Don't give me that." ***Auf Schmusekurs gehen.*** To take a conciliatory tone. *Die Gewerkschafts-führung will keinen Streik und geht mit den Arbeitgebern auf Schmusekurs.* "The union leaders don't want a strike and are taking a friendly tack to management."

SCHMUTZ. See FEUCHT.

SCHNABEL, *m.* **1.** Mouth (lit. bird's beak/bill). *Halt den Schnabel!* "Shut your trap." **2.** Penis (*children*). *Er hat mir seinen Schnabel gezeigt und ich ihm meine Muschi.* "He showed me his willie, and I showed him my pussy."

SCHNÄBELN. To kiss. *Sie schnäbeln den ganzen Tag.* "They bill and coo all day long."

SCHNABULIEREN. To eat with gusto. *Das freut mich, euch beim Schnabulieren zu sehen.* "I love to see you all put it away."

SCHNACK = KLÖNSCHNACK.

SCHNACKELN, *S.* To go off well (lit. to click tongue/fingers). *'S hat alles geschnackelt!* "Everything clicked."

SCHNACKEN, *N.* To chat; talk. *Kannst Platt schnacken/snacken?* "Can you speak Low German?" Cf. AB-SCHNACKEN; KLÖNEN.

SCHNACKERL, *m., n., Aust.* Hiccups. *Pius XII hatte monate-lang 's Schnackerl.* "Pius XII had the hiccups for months."

SCHNALLE, *f.* Whore (lit. buckle). *Die Schnalle wird mit dir gleich ins Bett springen.* "That slut'll jump into bed with you right away."

SCHNALLEN. To understand (lit. to buckle). *Hast's jetzt endlich geschnallt?* "Have you finally caught on now?"

SCHNALLENTREIBER, *m.* Pimp. *Der Schnallentreiber kennt keine Gnade.* "That whoremaster shows no mercy." Cf. SCHNALLE.

SCHNAPPEN. To nab. *Einer der Ganoven wurde geschnappt.* "One of the crooks was nabbed."

SCHNAPSDROSSEL, *f.* Tippler (lit. booze thrush [bird]). *Onkel Otto ist 'ne drollige Schnapsdrossel.* "He's a comical lush."

SCHNAPSEN/SCHNÄPSELN. To drink hard liquor. *Das Bier schmeckt ihr noch, aber schnapsen kann sie nicht mehr.* "She still likes a glass of beer but she can't hit the hard stuff anymore."

SCHNAPSLEICHE, *f.* Drunkard (lit. booze corpse). *Es saßen lauter Schnapsleichen in der Kneipe.* "Just dead drunks sat in the bar."

SCHNATTERGANS/SCHNATTERLIESE, *f.* Talkative woman. *Von der Schnatterliese kommt man nicht so leicht los.* "It's not easy to get away from that chatterbox."

SCHNATTERMAUL, *n.* Talkative person. *Ihr Mann ist 'n richtiges Schnattermaul.* "Her husband's a real chatterbox."

SCHNATTERN. To chatter, natter. *Der schnattert einem ein Loch in den Bauch.* "He'll talk your head off."

SCHNAUFERL, *n., Aust.* Well-worn old car (lit. little wheezer). *Von seinem Schnauferl kann er sich nicht trennen.* "He can't part with his old car."

SCHNAUFPAUSE, *f., S.* Short pause (for stand. *Verschnaufpause*). *Ich brauch unbedingt eine Schnaufpause.* "I really need a breather."

SCHNAUZE, *f.* Mouth (lit. muzzle [animal]). *Halt die Schnauze!* "Shut your trap!" ***Die Schnauze (gestrichen)***

voll haben. To be (thoroughly) fed up. *Von deinen Versprechungen hab ich die Schnauze voll.* "I've had a snoot full of your promises." ***Jmdm. die Schnauze polieren/lackierern.*** To beat s.o. up (lit. to polish/varnish s.o.'s mouth). *Her mit der Kohle oder ich polier dir die Schnauze.* "Hand over the dough or I'll rearrange your face." See FREI.

SCHNECKE, *f., youth.* **1.** Slow car (lit. snail). *Ich brauch keinen Flitzer; meine alte Schnecke genügt mir schon.* "I don't need a fast car; my old buggy's good enough for me." **2.** Girl. *Wo hast du diese tolle Schnecke aufgegabelt?* "Where'd you pick up that nifty chick?"

SCHNEID, *m., S.* Courage. *Ich steh nur auf Autorennfahrer. Die haben Schneid!* "I just go for race car drivers. They've got guts!"

SCHNEIDEN/SICH IN DEN FINGER SCHNEIDEN. To be very much mistaken (lit. to cut o.s.). *Wenn du denkst, ich deck deine Schulden, dann hast du dich geschnitten.* "If you think I'm going to cover your debts, you're way off base."

SCHNEIEN. To snow. ***Jmdm. ins Haus schneien.*** To drop in on s.o. *Ich will nicht, dass deine Verwandten uns wieder so ins Haus schneien.* "I don't want your relatives dropping in on us again like that."

SCHNELLDURCHBLICKER = **DURCHBLICK-OLOGE; EXPRESSCHECKER.**

SCHNEPFE, *f.* Whore (lit. snipe [bird]). *Mit der Schnepfe hast du gepennt?* "You slept with that slut?"

SCHNICKSCHNACK, *m.* Junk; nonsense. *Wenn du diese Schnickschnackpartei wählst, wirfst du nur deine Stimme weg.* "If you vote for that Mickey Mouse party, you'll just be wasting your vote."

SCHNIEDELWUTZ, *m., hum.* Penis (from dial. ***Wutz,*** pig). *Lass mal sehen, wie dein Schniedelwutz aussieht!* "Let's have a gander at your porker!"

SCHNIEGELMANN. See MISTER SCHNIEGELMANN.

SCHNIEKE, *Berlin.* Chic; wonderful. *Sie ist immer schnieke gekleidet.* "She's always elegantly dressed."

SCHNIEKI, *m., youth, usually pej.* S.o. always smartly dressed; uptight bourgeois. *Diesen Schnieki kann ich nicht ab.* "I can't stand that fashion plate." Cf. KRAGEN; KRAWATTENDJANGO; MISTER SCHNIEGELMANN; SCHICKIMICKI.

SCHNIEPEL, *m., children.* Penis (var. of SCHNABEL 2). *Wir zeigten uns gegenseitig die Schniepel.* "We showed each other our willies."

SCHNIPPELN. To snip. *„Ich will meine Organe spenden, um das Leben zu umarmen, auch nach dem Tod." „Wenn's mit mir aus ist, lass ich mich nicht auseinander schnippeln."* " 'I want to be an organ donor, to embrace life, even after death.'—'Well, when it's over for me, I'm not having m.s. hacked away at.' "

SCHNODDERIG. Impudent. ***Ein schnodderiges Mundwerk haben.*** To be a loudmouth. *Mensch, hat der 'n schnodderiges Mundwerk!* "Man, has he got a mouth on him!"

SCHNORREN = SCHLAUCHEN 2.

SCHNÖSEL, *m.* Arrogant person. *Zuerst haben diese Schnösel auf der Uni meine große Erfindung ausgelacht.* "At first those snot-noses at the university laughed at my great invention." Cf. SCHICKISCHNÖSEL.

SCHNÖSELIG. Insolent. *Sie ist weniger schnöselig als ihr Bruder.* "She's not as sassy as her brother."

SCHNOTTERNASE = ROTZNASE.

SCHNUCKELCHEN, *n.* Sweetie pie. *Ich denk nur an dich, du mein kleines Schnuckelchen.* "All I think of is you, my little darling."

SCHNUCKELIG. Sweet; cute; snug. *Bist ja so schnuckelig.* "You're such a sweetie pie."

SCHNUCKI/SCHNUCKIPUTZI = SCHNUCKELCHEN.

SCHNUFFI, *m.* Inhaler of a narcotic substance (cocaine, etc.) *Der ist längst schon Schnuffi.* "He's been a sniffer for some time." Cf. KOKSER.

SCHNUPPE. *Jmdm. schnuppe sein.* To be indifferent to. *Uns ist das alles schnuppe!* "We couldn't care less about that."

SCHNUPPERSTUNDE/SCHNUPPERTOUR, *f.* Inspection (from **schnuppern,** to sniff; snoop). *Ich lud alle Eltern zu einer Schnupperstunde in meiner Tanzschule ein.* "I invited all the parents to check out my dancing studio."

SCHNURZ. *Jmdm. schnurz (und piepe) sein.* See SCHNUPPE.

SCHNUTE, *f.* Mouth. *Eine Schnute ziehen/machen.* To pout. *Zieh mir nur keine Schnute!* "Just don't pull a long face on me."

SCHOKORIEGEL, *m.* For *Schokoladenriegel,* chocolate bar. *Keiner mehr schenkt mir Schokoriegel und Seidenstrümpfe.* "Nobody's giving me chocolate bars and silk stockings anymore."

SCHOLLE, *f.* Flounder. *Jmdm. scholle sein.* Not to care. *Mir ist das ultrascholle.* "That gets no rise at all out of me." *Scholle sein.* **1.** To be without funds. *In Monte Carlo waren wir totalo scholle.* "We were flat broke in Monte Carlo." **2.** To be flabbergasted. See PLATT. **3.** Drunk. *Er ist schon voll scholle.* "He's already dead drunk."

SCHÖN. Beautiful, fine (often used ironically; sometimes intensified by *ganz*). *Die Hools haben ihn ganz schön verprügelt.* "The hooligans did some job beating him up." *Schöne Scheiße!* Some rotten mess!

SCHÖPPELN. To drink alcohol (cf. POKULIEREN; SCHOPPEN, *m.*). *In dieser Studentenkneipe hab ich oft einen geschöppelt.* "I enjoyed many a glass in that students' tavern."

SCHOPPEN, *m., S.* **1.** Glass of wine/beer. *Sich beim Schoppen treffen.* To meet over/for a drink. *Wir treffen uns beim Schoppen.* "We'll meet for a drink." **2.** Var. of SCHÖPPELN.

3. To shop (from Eng.). *Bis zur Erschöpfung will ich schoppen.* "I want to shop till I drop."

SCHOTTER, *m.* **1.** Money (lit. gravel; cf. KIES; STEINE). *Wenn ich den nötigen Schotter hätte, würde ich mich von der Welt abschotten.* "If I had the bread, I'd shut m.s. off from the world." **2.** Nonsense. *Die Alten haben mich wieder mit ihrem Schotter voll gesülzt.* "My parents bored me with their stupid drivel again."

SCHRAUBE, *f.* **1.** Screw. *Bei dem ist 'ne Schraube locker.* "He's got a screw loose." **2.** Unattractive woman. *Wer will so 'ne Schraube pflöckeln?* "Who wants to screw an old bag like that?"

SCHRECKSCHRAUBE = SCHRAUBE 2.

SCHREIBEN. To write. ***Sich etwas hinter die Löffel/ Ohren schreiben.*** To be sure to remember (lit. to write s.t. behind one's ears). *Von uns bekommst du keinen Pfennig mehr. Schreib dir das hinter die Löffel!* "You're not getting one cent more from us. Get that into your head!"

SCHRILL. Shrill; garish (youth sl. syn. for GRELL). ***Jmdm. schrill auf die Birne/Melone/Marille/Tomate schlagen.*** See ***Jmdm. auf den KEKS gehen.***

SCHRITT, *m.* Step. ***Auf Schritt und Tritt.*** Very closely. *Die Fotojäger verfolgten die Prinzessin auf Schritt und Tritt.* "The paparazzi dogged the princess's tracks."

SCHRÖPFEN. To fleece (lit. to bleed [as in former medical practice]). *Im Nepplokal wurde er total geschröpft.* "They really took him to the cleaners in that clipjoint."

SCHROTT, *m.* Nonsense (lit. scrap metal). *Was sülzt du da für hohlen Schrott zusammen?* "What's all that garbage you're going on about?"

SCHROTTHAUFEN/SCHROTTKISTE = BLECH-HAUFEN/BLECHKISTE.

SCHRULLE, *f.* **1.** Quirk; weird idea. *Was hast du wieder für Schrullen im Kopf?* "What crackpot ideas have you gotten into your head again?" **2.** Nasty old woman. *Tu sie nicht als alte Schrulle ab; von der Pflanzenheilkunde* *weiß sie viel.* "Don't dismiss her as an old crone; she knows a lot about herbal medicine."

SCHUBBEJACK/SCHUBIAK, *m.* Louse. *Diesen Schubiak soll mir nie wieder über die Schwelle kommen.* "I won't have that SOB in the house again."

SCHUBS, *m.* Nudge. *Ich gab ihm 'n Schubs, als er am Steuer einschlief.* "I nudged him when he fell asleep at the wheel."

SCHUFTEN/SICH SCHUFTEN. To slave away. *Ich schufte für zwei und du faulst nur.* "I'm knocking m.s. out doing the work of two, and you just lounge around."

SCHUFTI, *m., youth, pej.* Hard worker (rel. to SCHUFTEN [to work hard], not *Schuft* [scoundrel]). *Ja, wir lungern nur rum; mit Schuftis haben wir nichts am Hut.* "Yes, we just hang out; we have nothing to do with eager beavers."

SCHULSHERIF(F), *f., pej., youth.* Teacher; school principal. *Der Schulsheriff geht mir echt auf den Sack.* "That teach is a real ballbuster."

SCHUMMELN. To cheat. *Minnie schummelte beim Kartenspiel.* "Minnie cheated at cards."

SCHUMMELZETTEL, *m.* Crib sheet. Cf. SCHWARTE **3**; SPICKZETTEL. *Ohne Schummelzettel wär er in Mathe durchgefallen.* "Without a cheat sheet, he would have failed in math."

SCHUMMLER, *f.* Cheater. *Ihr Schummler, ihr habt alle Schummelzettel benutzt!* "You cheaters, you all used cheat sheets."

SCHUPPEN, *m.* Joint, dive; hovel (lit. shed; hangar). *Jetzt raus ausm Schuppen und in den Technoschuppen.* "Let's blow this hole and go to the disco." Cf. BUDE.

SCHUSS, *m.* **1.** Shot. *Ein Schuss in den Ofen/ins Knie.* A total waste of time. *Die ganze Debatte war nur ein Schuss in den Ofen.* "The whole debate was useless." *Einen Schuss setzen/drücken.* To shoot up dope. *Drück dir 'n Schuss, wenn du musst, aber nur mit Einwegspritzen.* "Give y.s. a fix if you have to, but only with disposable needles." ***Sich den goldenen Schuss drücken/setzen.*** To overdose on drugs. *Sie hat sich den goldenen Schuss gesetzt—vielleicht absichtlich.* "She OD'd, maybe deliberately." ***Einen Schuss haben.*** See SOCKENSCHUSS. **2.** Small quantity. *Mit Mozart und 'nem Schuss Humor geht alles besser.* "Everything goes better with Mozart and a touch/dash of humor."

SCHÜSSEL, *f.* Head (lit. bowl). ***Einen Sprung in der Schüssel haben.*** To be scatterbrained/foolish (lit. to have a crack in the bowl). *Der hat 'n Sprung in der Schüssel.* "He's a bit cracked." Cf. RISS; KNICK; PUPILLE.

SCHUTT = SCHROTT.

SCHÜTZE ARSCH, *m.* Common soldier. *Ich will gar nicht Offizier werden; bleib lieber Schütze Arsch.* "I don't want to be an officer; I'd rather stay a buck private." ***Schütze Arsch im dritten/letzten Glied.*** The lowest of the low. *Du bleibst lebenslänglich Schütze Arsch im letzten Glied.* "You'll always be at the bottom of the barrel."

SCHWABBELN. To talk nonsense (lit. to wobble). *Hast jetzt nicht genug geschwabbelt?* "Haven't you talked enough garbage now?" Cf. SABBELN; SCHWAFELN; WAFFELN.

SCHWÄCHELN. To be listless (*schwach* = weak). *Heute hat die Mannschaft echt geschwächelt.* "The team really had lead in their pants today."

SCHWACHFUG, *m., youth.* Nonsense (prob. a comb. of *Schwachkopf* [dimwit] and *Unfug* [mischief], thus s.t. a dunce would say/do). *Das ist jetzt genug Schwachfug!* "That's enough baloney now."

SCHWACHMANN = LAUMANN.

SCHWACHSTROMAKADEMIE, *f., youth, pej.* School for the mentally or physically retarded (lit. weak [electrical] current academy). *Sie ist 'n Genie, echt grell beleuchtet; warum hat man sie in die Schwachstromakademie geschickt?* "She's a genius, extremely bright; why'd they send her to a remedial school?"

SCHWAFELEI, *f.* Babble. *Bei den Sitzungen gibt's nur Schwafelei.* "Nothing but drivel at the meetings."

SCHWAFELN = **SABBELN.**

SCHWALLEN. To drone/babble on (from **Schwall,** flood [of words]). *Lass doch dein ewiges Schwallen!* "Quit going on and on."

SCHWANZ, *m.* Penis (lit. tail). *Wenn der Schwanz aufsteigt, fliegt der Verstand zum Fenster raus.* "When the cock rises up, reason flies out the window."

SCHWANZFUTTERAL, *n.* Condom (lit. penis case). *Es geht besser, wenn er ein Schwanzfutteral mit Gleitsubstanz benutzt.* "It's easier when he uses a lubricated condom."

SCHWARTE, *f.* **1.** Skin (lit. hide; rind). ***Bis/dass die Schwarte kracht/knackt.*** Till one drops. *Morgen müssen wir arbeiten, bis die Schwarte kracht.* "Tomorrow we'll have to work our fingers to the bone." See JUCKEN. **2.** Thick volume. *Hast du diese Schwarten alle gelesen?* "Have you read all these fat tomes?" **3.** Pony, crib sheet (cf. SCHUMMELZETTEL). *Die Lernfuzzis wissen, dass die meisten von uns Schwarten benutzen.* "The teachers know that most of us use trots."

SCHWATZ, *m.* Chat. *Die alte Schwatzbase war auf einen Schwatz gekommen.* "The old gossip came around for a chat."

SCHWATZBASE/SCHWÄTZBASE, *f.* Gossip. See previous entry.

SCHWEDE. See ALTER SCHWEDE.

SCHWEDISCHE GARDINEN, *pl.* Prison bars (lit. Swedish curtains, i.e. iron bars). *Der gehört hinter schwedische Gardinen.* "He belongs behind bars."

SCHWEIN, *n.* **1.** Pig. ***Den Schweinen wird alles Schwein.*** (*hum.*) If you're dirty minded, everything's dirty (lit. to pigs everything is piggish). *Ja, den Reinen ist alles rein, und den Schweinen wird alles Schwein.* "Yes, to the pure all things are pure, and nasty buggers reduce everything to their level." ***Mein Schwein pfeift!*** I can't believe it! That is incredible! (lit. my pig's whistling). Cf. STRULLEN; KLAVIER; ROTKEHLCHEN; ZWITSCHERN. **2.** Nobody at all. ***Kein Schwein.*** *Und wenn's nicht klappt, wird dir kein Schwein helfen.* "And if it doesn't work out, not a damned soul will help you." **3.** Luck. *Da haben wir aber Schwein gehabt!* "We really lucked out!"

SCHWEINCHEN SCHLAU, *n.* Smart person; smarty-pants. *Spiel nicht hier auf Schweinchen Schlau.* "Don't play the know-it-all here."

SCHWEINEGEIL. Intensifies GEIL.

SCHWEINEKERL = SAUKERL.

SCHWEINIGELN. 1. To talk dirty. *Viele Ärzte schweinigeln gern unter sich.* "Many doctors like to talk dirty when they get together." **2.** To make a mess. *Hört doch auf zu schweinigeln!* "Quit mucking things up!"

SCHWENGEL, *m.* Penis. *Schwingt sein Schwengel in mir, hör ich himmlisches Glockengeläute.* "He really rings my chimes when his tool's at work inside me."

SCHWIMMEN. To swim. ***Ins Schwimmen kommen.*** To get confused. *Mit dem Euro bin ich zuerst ins Schwimmen gekommen.* "At first I was all at sea dealing with the euro."

SCHWIPS, *m.* Alcohol-induced euphoria. ***Einen (kleinen) Schwips haben.*** To be (a bit) tipsy. *Ohne den kleinen Schwips hätte er nicht so gut getanzt.* "He wouldn't have danced so well if he hadn't been a bit lit up."

SCHWIRREN. See ABSCHWIRREN.

SCHWITZEN. To sweat. ***Jmdn. ins Schwitzen bringen.*** To make things rough for s.o. *Die neusten Enthüllungen haben den Präsidenten ins Schwitzen gebracht.* "The new revelations have made things rough for the president."

SCHWITZHÜTTE, *f.* Gym (lit. sweat hut). *In der Schwitzhütte spielt man jetzt schöne Mucke.* "They play nice music in the gym now."

SCHWOF, *m.* Dance. *Ich hab ihn beim Schwof kennen ge-*

lernt. "I met him at the dance."

SCHWOFEN. To dance. *Im Urlaub bin ich oft schwofen gegangen.* "When I was on vacation, I often went dancing."

SCHWUCHTEL, *f., pej.* Effeminate homosexual (prob. a comb. of WACHTEL and SCHWUL). *Er sagt, er sei nicht schwul, aber er verkehrt nur mit Schwuchteln.* "He says he isn't gay, but he hangs around only with swishy queens."

SCHWUL. Homosexual. *Ich glaub, er ist schwul.* "I think he's gay."

SCHWULENBAR, *f.*/**SCHWULENLOKAL,** *n.* Gay bar. *'S ist nur 'n Kaff, hat aber zwei Schwulenlokale.* "It's just a hick town, but it's got two gay bars."

SCHWULEREI, *f.* Homosexuality. *Manchmal glaubt er ein in die Schwulerei verirrter Normalo zu sein.* "Sometimes he thinks he's a straight who strayed into homosexuality."

SCHWULI, *m., youth.* Male homosexual. *Komm her, kleiner Schwuli!* "Come here, little fruit!"

SCHWULIBUS, *hum.* **In Schwulibus sein.** To be in a fix. *Ich bin wieder in Schwulibus, werde mich aber schon durchbeißen.* "I'm in trouble again, but I'll get through it OK."

SCHWULIGAN, *m.* Homosexual hooligan (play on SCHWUL and HOOLIGAN). *Er gehört einer Bande von Schwuligans an.* "He belongs to a gang of gay hooligans."

SCHWULITÄT, *f.* Trouble. *Er hat viel Schnaps und 'n Sechserpack getrunken und ist dann in Schwulitäten geraten.* "He drank lots of booze and a six-pack, and then got into hot water."

SCHWULSZENE. See SZENE.

SCHWUPP! Quick as a flash! *Schwupp war mein Kaninchen weg!* "My rabbit ran off just like that."

SECHS, *f.* Six (failing grade in school). ***Einer Sechs gleichzusetzen.*** A failure; dud. *,,In puncto Sex ist er 'ne Null." ,,Aber vielleicht war's nur das eine Mal, das er einer Sechs gleichzusetzen war."* " 'As far as sex is concerned, he's a zero.' 'But maybe it was just that one time that he failed to perform.' " ***Sechs Richtige im Lotto haben.*** To win the top prize in the Ger. lottery; to hit any jackpot. *Ein Bravo für den braven Wilhelm, der sechs Richtige im Lotto gehabt hat.* "Three cheers for good old Wilhelm, who won the lottery."

SECHSERPACK, *m.*/**SECHSERPACKUNG,** *f.* Six-pack (esp. of beer). *Von wegen Sechserpack! Heut gibt's Sekt! Im Lotto hat er 'nen Sechser gehabt.* "No way a six-pack! It's champagne today! He won the lottery."

SEELENKLEMPNER, *m.* Psychiatrist (lit. soul plumber). *Die Seelenklempner konnten ihm nicht helfen.* "The shrinks couldn't help him."

SEELENWÄRMER, *m.* Alcoholic pick-me-up. *Während der Predigt spürte er große Lust auf einen kleinen Seelenwärmer.* "During the sermon he really felt like having a little drink."

SEIBELN/SEIBERN = SABBELN; SABBERN.

SEICH, *m.* **1.** Urine. *Auch neben den Urinalen gab's überall Seich.* "There was piss all around the urinals too." **2.** Drivel = GESEICH.

SEICHEN. 1. To urinate. *Sauf weniger, wirst dann weniger seichen.* "Drink less and you'll piss less." **2.** To talk/write drivel. See SCHWAFELN.

SEITENSPRUNG, *m.* Extramarital affair (lit. jump to the side). *Ich hab dir schon zu viele Seitensprünge verziehen.* "I've already forgiven you for too many romantic escapades."

SEKT ODER SELTERS! Let's go for broke!/All or nothing!/Let's shoot the wad! (lit. champagne or soda water).

SELIG. Tipsy. *Sie sind schon alle selig.* "They're all a little plastered already." See ALKOHOLSELIG.

SEMESTER, *n*. Age group (lit. [school] semester). ***Älteres/höheres Semester.*** Older student/person. *In meiner Tanzbar kommen auch ältere Semester auf ihre Kosten.* "Even those who aren't spring chickens anymore will find what they want in my dance bar."

SEMMELN, *S.* To whack. *Dir möcht' ich eine auf die Nuss semmeln.* "I'd like to give you a shot in the head."

SENF, *m*. Mustard. ***Seinen Senf zu etwas geben.*** To put one's two cents in. *Natürlich musste der Sülzkopf seinen Senf dazu geben.* "Of course that idiot had to put in his two-cents worth." Cf. KREN.

SEXMUFFEL, *m*. Person wary of sex. *Die Angst vor AIDS hat viele zu Sexmuffeln gemacht.* "Fear of AIDS has scared many sexless."

SEXPROTZ, *m*. S.o. who pretends to sexual prowess. *Meistens sind Sexprotze enttäuschend.* "Sexual braggarts are usually disappointing."

SHIT, *m., from Eng. sl.* Heroin; dope. *Der Shit ist alle.* "No more dope left."

SICHERUNG, *f.* Fuse. *Ich sagte ihr die Wahrheit, und da ist ihr die Sicherung durchgebrannt.* "I told her the truth and she blew a fuse."

SIDDHARTIST, *m., youth.* Truth seeker (often interested in Buddhism and a variety of religions. From Siddhartha, the Indian prince who founded Buddhism). *Ich bin kein selbstgefälliger Spießer und versteh euch schon, ihr Siddhartisten.* "I'm no smug bourgeois, and I understand you young truth seekers." Cf. ZIPPIE.

SIFF, *m*. Dirt. *Dich kann keine Seife entsiffen, denn der Siff sitzt dir tief in den Knochen.* "You're beyond soap, because you're cruddy through and through."

SIFFKOPF/SIFFKOPP, *youth.* Stupid idiot. *Hau ab, Siffkopf!* "Beat it, dumb bastard."

SILBE, *f.* Syllable. ***Etwas mit keiner Silbe erwähnen/verraten.*** Not to say a word about s.t. *Mit keiner Silbe sollst du's verraten.* "Don't breathe a word to anyone about it."

SILBENSTECHER, *m., pej., youth.* Teacher (lit. syllable joker). *Der neue Silbenstecher kann mir gestohlen bleiben, und die andern auch.* "The new teacher can get lost, and the others too."

SKELETTI, *m., youth.* Old codger. *Dieser Skeletti ist ganz netti; er findet alles immer paletti.* "That old bag o' bones is real nice; he always finds everything cool."

SKIN/SKINNI(E), *m.* Skinhead (shortened from Eng.) *Der Skinnie ist Grufti geworden und trägt jetzt 'n Toupet.* "The skinhead's ancient now and wears a toupee."

SOCKE, *f.* Sock. **Die Socke machen.** (*Youth.*) **Sich auf die Socken machen.** To get going. *Macht euch jetzt endlich auf die Socken!* "Get going now, will you!" **Jmdm. auf die Socken gehen.** To get on s.o.'s nerves. *Dein Gesülze geht mir schrill auf die Socken.* "Your babbling's really getting on my case." **Von den Socken sein.** To be flabbergasted. *Ich hörte davon und war total von den Socken.* "I heard about it and was knocked for a loop." See AUSZIEHEN; NAHKAMPFSOCKE; QUALMEN.

SOCKENSCHUSS. **Einen Sockenschuss haben.** To be crazy. *Ich soll's bezahlen? Hast 'n Sockenschuss!* "I'm supposed to pay for it? You're nuts!"

SOFTI(E), *m.* Tender, caring male; wimp (as used by macho males). *Nach so vielen durchknallten Mackern, steh ich jetzt nur auf Softis.* "After so many freaked-out guys, I just go for softies now."

SOFTWAREFEHLER, *m.* = **SCHALTFEHLER.**

SOLO. Single (from It.). *Er war lange solo aber jetzt hat er 'ne neue Lebensgefährtin.* "He was unattached for some time, but now he's got a new significant other."

SOLOBERGER, *m., youth.* Loner. **Einen Soloberger hinlegen.** To go it alone. *Jetzt willst du deinen Soloberger hinlegen; später aber wirst du an mich denken.* "Now you want to go it alone; but you'll think of me later."

SONNE, *f., youth.* Beautiful girl (lit. sun). *Pass auf, das du dir an deiner Sonne nicht verbrennst; viele haben sich* *schon den Tripper bei ihr geholt.* "Watch out your sun doesn't scorch you; she's already clapped up lots o' guys."

SONNYBOY, *m., invented Eng.* Golden/fair-haired boy. *Alle finden ihn sympatisch, unwiderstehlich, dieser Sonnyboy.* "Everyone finds that charmer irresistible."

SOßE, *f.* Sperm, come (lit. sauce). *Im Zeitalter des Zapfenmantels vermissen viele die Soße.* "Many miss the spermal sauce in the age of the condom."

SOTT, *m., n., N.* Soot. **Sott haben.** To be lucky (from the folk belief that touching or even seeing a chimney sweep brings luck). *Mann, hast du Sott gehabt!* "You really lucked out, man!"

SPANNEN. To understand (lit. to tighten). *Nichts davon hat er gespannt.* "He didn't catch on to any of it."

SPANNER, *m.* Peeping Tom; lecher. *Mir macht's nichts aus, dass der alte Spanner von nebenan mich beim Ausziehen begafft.* "The old voyeur next door ogles me when I undress, but it doesn't bother me."

SPARFLAMME, *f.* Low flame; pilot light. **Auf Sparflamme kochen.** To soft-pedal. *Zuerst war der Chef ganz Feuer und Flamme für mein Projekt; jetzt wird aber auf Sparflamme gekocht.* "At first the boss was full of enthusiasm for my project, but now it's on the back burner."

SPARSCHWEIN, *n.* Piggy bank. **Sein Sparschwein schlachten.** To break into one's savings (lit. to slaughter one's piggy bank). *Ja, wir fahren in Urlaub; ich hab mein Sparschwein geschlachtet.* "Yes, we're going on vacation. I used my savings."

SPAßBREMSE, *f.*/**SPAßVERDERBER,** *m.* Killjoy. *Diese Spaßbremse hättest du zu Hause lassen können.* "You could have left that killjoy home."

SPAßVOGEL, *m.* Joker. *Ute ist echt 'n Spaßvogel; hat aber keineswegs einen Vogel oder ein Spatzengehirn.* "Ute's a real clown; but she's not crazy or birdbrained."

SPEICHER, *m.* Warehouse; computer memory (used by computer hackers for their emotional state). *Mein Spei-*

cher ist für heute ausgepowert. "I've reached a saturation point today."

SPEKULANTENHEINI, *m.* Speculator. *Hier kaufen jetzt die Spekulantenheinis alle Grundstücke auf.* "The speculators are buying up all the properties here."

SPEZI, *m., S.* Chum. *Wenn mei' Spezi und ich picheln gehen, trinken wir keine Spezis.* "When my buddy and I go drinking, we don't drink lemon Cokes."

SPEZI, *n.* Lemon-flavored cola. *Vielleicht aber doch ein kleines Spezi mit einem Schuss Rum.* "Well, maybe a lemon Coke with a shot of rum."

SPICKEN. 1. To lard. **2.** To bribe (cf. SCHMIEREN **3**). *Er hat 'ne gespickte Brieftasche und könnte den Senator spicken.* "He's got a fat (well-larded) wallet and could grease the senator's palm." **3.** To copy (*school sl.*). *Bei dem Dussel hast du gespickt?* "You copied from that idiot?" Cf. ABSCHMIEREN **1.**

SPICKZETTEL, *m.* Cheat sheet, trot; speaker's notes (Cf. SCHUMMELZETTEL). *Er hatte seinen Spickzettel verloren und kam bald ins Schwimmen.* "He'd lost his notes and soon was all at sea."

SPIEß, *m., mil.* Sarge (lit. spear; skewer). *Bei der Grundi hat uns der Spieß nicht geschont.* "The sarge didn't spare us during basic training."

SPINATWACHTEL, *f.* Cranky old woman (lit. spinach quail; cf. WACHTEL). *Du nennst sie 'ne Spinatwachtel, aber auch sie braucht Liebe und Streicheleinheiten.* "You call her a nasty old bag, but she too needs love and affection."

SPINNEN. To be a bit cracked/daft. *Du spinnst wohl!* "You must be nuts!"

SPINNERT, *S./***SPINNIG.** Slightly crazy. *Mit diesem spinnerten Hammel mag i' (ich) net (nicht) tanzen.* "I don't want to dance with that wacky oaf."

SPITZ. Horny (lit. pointed). ***Spitz wie Nachbars Lumpi sein.*** To be very horny (lit. as horny as the neighbor's dog). *Der/die ist immer spitz wie Nachbars Lumpi.* "He's always horny as an old goat/she's always as hot as a bitch in heat." *Auf jmdn. spitz sein.* To go for s.o. *Auf dich bin ich wirklich spitz.* "You really get me going." *Jmdn. spitz machen.* To turn s.o. on. *Ich versuchte, sie spitz zu machen, 's war aber verlorene Liebesmühe.* "I tried to come on to her, but it was wasted effort."

SPITZBEKOMMEN. See SPITZKRIEGEN.

SPITZE, *f.* **1.** Point/peak. *Spitze sein/Absolute/einsame Spitze sein.* To be (absolutely) first rate/tops. *Das Essen war Spitze!* "The food was terrific." **2.** Pointed remark. *Spitzen austeilen.* To make digs. *Für heute Abend hast du jetzt genug Spitzen ausgeteilt.* "You've been catty enough for one evening."

SPITZE. Classy/nifty. *Sie hat sich ein spitze Auto gekauft.* "She bought a swell car." Cf. KLASSE.

SPITZKRIEGEN. To get wise to. *Ich hab spitzgekriegt, dass da was nicht astrein ist.* "I've wised up to it that there's s.t. fishy there."

SPITZMAUS, *f.* Shrew. *Einst war ich seine süße liebe Maus; jetzt schimpft mich der Scheißkerl eine Spitzmaus.* "I was once his sweetie pie; now that bastard calls me a bitch."

SPLITTERNACKT/SPLITTERFASERNACKT. Stark naked. *Am FKK-Strand (Freikörperkulturstrand) laufen alle splitternackt herum.* "Everyone walks around butt naked on the nudist colony beach."

SPOMPANADE(L)N, *pl., Aust.* Foolishness; adventures. *Nach einem Leben voller Spompanadeln möcht ich mich jetzt an dich binden.* "After a lifetime of foolishness, I'd like to make a commitment to you now."

SPONTI, *m.* Uncommitted left-winger. *Wir versuchen jetzt die Spontis für uns zu gewinnen.* "We're trying to get the free-wheeling radicals on our side."

SPONTIGRUPPE, *f.* Left-wing group. *Unsere Sponti-gruppe ist mir zu doktrinär geworden.* "Our liberal organization has become too doctrinaire for me."

SPORTELN. To engage in sports. *In der Freizeit wird ge-sportelt.* "We play at sports in our leisure time."

SPORTFUZZI, *m., youth.* S.o. into sports; jock; sports-caster. *Mit Sportfuzzis hat sie nichts am Hut.* "She has nothing to do with sports freaks."

SPRACHFUZZI, *m., youth.* Linguist. *Er ist Sprachfuzzi, checkt aber kaum die Jugendsprache.* "He's a language dude, but he doesn't understand much young people's talk."

SPRUCHKASPER/SPRUCHVOGEL, *m., youth.* Fool full of wise sayings. *Der Spruchkasper geht mir echt auf den Keks.* "That pompous jerk gets on my nerves."

SPRUNG, *m.* Jump. ***Immer auf dem Sprung sein.*** To be always on the go/on the ball. *Du lungerst nur herum aber ich bin immer aufm Sprung.* "All you do is hang out, but I'm always on the go." ***Auf einen Sprung vorbeikommen.*** To come for a brief visit. *Kannst nicht auf 'n Sprung vorbeikommen?* "Can't you come for a little while?" ***Einen Sprung haben.*** To be cracked. See SCHÜSSEL; KNICK; PUPILLE.

SPUCKE, *f.* Spit. ***Jmdm. bleibt die Spucke weg.*** S.o. is floored. *Er ließ die Hose runter und mir blieb die Spucke weg.* "He dropped his pants, and I was breathless."

SPUCKEN. To spit. ***Es ist zum Spucken.*** Weaker equivalent of *es ist zum* KOTZEN. See also KOPF; WO MAN HIN-SPUCKT.

SPUCKTÜTE, *f.* Any reed instrument, esp. saxophone/clarinet (lit. spitbag). *Die Spucktüte und der Mundverkehr törnen Bill voll an.* "The saxophone and oral sex are big turn-ons for Bill."

STAMMFREIER, *m.* Steady boyfriend (lit. regular wooer). *Was ist aus ihrem Stammfreier geworden?* "What's happened to her boyfriend?"

STÄNDER, *m.* Erection. *Der Junge ist im Alter wo er fast ständig einen Ständer hat.* "The boy's at an age where he's got an almost perpetual erection." Cf. STEHEN; STEIFER.

STARK, *youth.* Wonderful (lit. strong). *Die Band spielt unheimlich stark.* "That band's playing is terrific." Cf. HART; SCHARF; STEINSTARK.

STAUB. See FEUCHT.

STAUCHEN, *youth.* To shoplift Cf. KLAUFEN. *Gehen wir zuerst 'n bisschen stauchen, dann saufen.* "Let's get in a little shoplifting before boozing it up."

STECHER, *m., youth, pej.* Guy/mack (lit. sticker). *Dieser Stecher kann mir gestohlen bleiben.* "That fucker can get lost." Cf. BIENENSTICH; SILBENSTECHER.

STECHSCHRITT, *m., youth.* Terrific dance/dancers (lit. goosestep). *Mann, war das ein turbotoller Stechschritt.* "Man, that was a really sizzling dance."

STECKEN, *pl., youth.* Money (lit. sticks). *Wo soll ich die Stecken herholen?* "Just where'm I supposed to get the bread?"

STEHEN. To stand. *Auf etwas/jmdn. stehen.* To be attracted to. *Die Chefin steht auf ihren jungen rothaarigen Sekretär.* "The boss really goes for her young, red-haired secretary." *Einen stehen haben.* To have an erection. *Ja, du hast einen stehen, aber 's ist mir schnuppe.* "Yes, you've got a hard-on, but I don't care."

STEHLEN. To steal. *Etwas/jmd. kann einem gestohlen bleiben.* S.t./s.o. might as well not exist as far as s.o. is concerned. *Der Sabbelheini kann uns gestohlen bleiben.* "That windbag can get lost."

STEIFER, *m.* Erection. *Er hatte einen strammen Steifen, kam aber zu schnell.* "He had a very firm erection, but came too fast."

STEIL. 1. Steep. *Eine steile Karriere machen.* To have a meteoric career. *Unser Lokalmatador macht jetzt in Amerika 'ne steile Karriere.* "Our local hero's now enjoying a sensational career in America." 2. Wonderful (used in youth sl. as a rhyming alternative to overused GEIL). *Das ist echt 'ne steile Band.* "That's one sensational band." See ZAHN.

STEINE/STEINCHEN, *pl.* Money. *Nur noch 'n paar Steinchen, dann ist's getan.* "Just a little more dough, and it'll be settled." Cf. KIES; KOHLE; SCHOTTER.

STEINSTARK, *youth, intensifies* STARK. Mind-blowing. *Ihr Sound ist steinstark.* "Their sound's the living end."

STENGEL, *m.* Stem, stalk. ***Vom Stengel fallen.*** To collapse; be floored. *Als ich davon hörte, fiel ich fast vom Stengel.* "When I heard about it, I was really staggered." See GLIMMSTENGEL.

STENZ, *m., pej.* **1.** Dandy. *Dieser Stenz gibt all sein Geld für Klamotten aus.* "That fop spends all his money on clothes." **2.** Pimp. *Für diesen Stenz will ich nicht mehr arbeiten.* "I don't want to work for that pimp anymore."

STEPPKE, *m., N., esp. Berlin.* Boy; kid. *Für die Steppkes im Kiez hat er 'n Sportverein gegründet.* "He founded a sports club for the neighborhood kids."

STERN, *m.* Star. ***Vom anderen Stern sein.*** See UFER.

STERNHAGELVOLL. Completely plastered (lit. full of stars and hail). Intensifies VOLL **2.**

STICH, *m.* **1.** Prick, sting. ***Einen Stich haben.*** **A.** To have turned sour/bad (food). *Warum hast du die Milch so lange draußen gelassen? Sie wird jetzt 'n Stich haben.* "Why'd you leave the milk out so long? It's probably gone sour." **B.** To be a little crazy. *Ich glaub, du hast 'n Stich.* "I think you're nuts." **2.** Trick (cards/sexual). ***Einen Stich machen.*** See NUMMER.

STIEFEL, *m.* **1.** Boot. ***Das sind zwei Paar Stiefel/zwei verschiedene Stiefel/zweierlei Stiefel.*** That's a horse of a different color/another breed of cat. ***Jmdn. aus den Stiefeln hauen.*** To flabbergast s.o. *Das haut dich aus den Stiefeln, wenn ich's dir sage.* "That'll knock your socks off when I tell you." ***Seinen (alten) Stiefel weitermachen.*** To persist in an old-hat routine. *Der Alte will nur seinen Stiefel weitermachen.* "The old man just wants to keep on with the same old stuff." ***Jmdm. in die Stiefel scheißen.*** To infuriate s.o. (lit. to shit in s.o.'s boots). *Willst du mir in die*

Stiefel scheißen? "Are you trying to piss me off?" See AUSZIEHEN. **2.** Beer stein/glass in the form of a boot. ***Einen (tüchtigen) Stiefel vertragen können.*** To hold one's liquor. *Bevor er picheln geht, isst er viel Käse damit er 'n tüchtigen Stiefel vertragen kann.* "Before going out drinking he eats lots of cheese, so that he can put away the booze."

STIEKUM, *N.* On the quiet/sly (from Hebr. for silence). *Er ist 'n verhinderter Spion und tut alles stiekum.* "He's a would-be spy and does everything on the sly." Cf. KLAMMHEIMLICH.

STIER, *S.* Without funds. *Sie sind fast stier.* "They're almost broke."

STIESEL, *m.* Oaf. *Was findest du an diesem Stiesel?* "What do you see in that lout?"

STIFTEN GEHEN. To scram. *Vor Ankunft der Bullen sind wir stiften gegangen.* "We cleared out before the cops arrived."

STIMMUNGSBOMBE/STIMMUNGSKANONE, *f.* Life of the party. *Ich weiß, er gilt als Stimmungskanone, aber ich finde seinen Humor aufgesetzt.* "I know he's considered the life of the party, but I find his humor forced."

STINK-. Intensifying prefix, as in STINKFAUL; STINKFEIN; etc.

STINKADORES, *f., hum.* Smelly cigar. *Mein Mann darf seine Stinkadores nur aufm Balkon rauchen.* "I allow my husband to smoke his stogies only on the balcony."

STINKEFINGER, *m.* Obscene gesture. *Der Fußballer gab dem Schiri 'n Stinkefinger und durfte nicht weiter spielen.* "The football player gave the referee the finger and wasn't allowed to continue playing."

STINKEN. To be fed up (lit. to stink). *Mir stinkt der Job.* "I've had it up to here with that job."

STINKFAUL. Extremely lazy. *Wenn du nur nicht so stinkfaul wärst!* "If only you weren't such a lazy bones!"

STINKFEIN. Terribly fancy. *Die Schickeria verkehrt in dem stinkfeinen Restaurant.* "The smart set hangs out in that swanky restaurant." ***Stinkfein tun.*** To give o.s. airs. *Tu nicht so stinkfein!* "Stop being so pretentious!"

STINKLANGWEILIG. Extremely boring. *Der Film war stinklangweilig.* "The movie was deadly dull."

STINKNORMAL. As normal as can be. *Alle hatten den Serientöter für 'n stinknormalen Macker gehalten.* "They all thought the serial killer was just an ordinary guy."

STINKREICH. Filthy rich. *Sie hatte den richtigen Riecher beim Aktienkauf und wurde stinkreich.* "She had the right instinct for buying stocks and got filthy rich."

STINKSAUER. Extremely annoyed. *Unsere Mannschaft verlor wieder, und die Zuschauer waren stinksauer.* "Our team lost again, and the crowd was really ticked off."

STINKSTIEFEL, *m.* Nasty person (lit. smelly boot). *Der Stinkstiefel ist echt 'n Spaßverderber.* "That louse is a real killjoy."

STINKVORNEHM = **STINKFEIN.**

STINKWUT, *f.* Rage. *Seine Stinkwut war nicht auszuhalten.* "His foul temper was unbearable."

STINT, *m., N.* Young boy (lit. smelt [fish]). *Der Stint wird sich drauf freuen.* "The lad will look forward to that."

STOCKBESOFFEN. Dead drunk. *Warst wieder stockbesoffen.* "You were smashed again."

STOCKSAUER = **STINKSAUER.**

STOFFEL, *m.* Lout. *Warum hast du mit dem Stoffel getanzt?* "Why'd you dance with that lout?"

STOFFLÖWE, *m.* Braggart; Milquetoast (lit. stuffed lion). *Wärst du nur nicht so 'n Stofflöwe!* "If only you weren't such a wimp!" Cf. LÖWE **2.**

STOSSTRUPP, *m., youth.* Police (lit. shock troops). *Der Stoßtrupp kam rasanto angepest.* "The fuzz drove up fast."

STOTTERN. To stutter; splutter. ***Auf Stottern kaufen.*** To buy on the installment plan. *Den Wagen haben wir auf*

Stottern gekauft; hoffentlich stottert der Motor nicht wieder. "We bought the car on the installment plan and hope the engine doesn't start spluttering again." Cf. AB-STOTTERN.

STRAHLEMANN, *m.* Golden boy. *Ganz aufn Hund gekommen ist er noch nicht, aber der Strahlemann von damals ist er längst nicht mehr.* "He hasn't totally gone to the dogs yet, but he's far from the golden boy he once was."

STRAMM. Tight; firm. *Stramm arbeiten.* To work hard. *Sie haben alle stramm und brav gearbeitet.* "They all did honest, hard work." *Die Hose/den Hosenboden stramm ziehen.* To spank (lit. to tighten s.o.'s pants/seat of pants). *Dir werd ich ganz schön den Hosenboden stramm ziehen.* "I'm going to give you a good hiding."

STRANG, *m.* Cord; rope. *Am gleichen Strang ziehen.* To pull together. *Wir müssen jetzt alle am gleichen Strang ziehen.* "We all have to pull together now." *Über die Stränge hauen/schlagen.* To run riot; get carried away. *Wir haben die Sau rausgelassen, richtig über die Stränge geschlagen.* "We had a wild time, really cut loose." *Wenn alle Stränge reißen.* See REIßEN.

STRAßENDIRNE. See DIRNE; STRICHMÄDCHEN.

STRAßENFEGERIN, *f.* Streetwalker (lit. street sweeper). *Politisch korrekt soll's jetzt „Sex-Versorgungs-Beschafferin" heißen; ich bin aber nur 'ne herkömmliche Hure, 'ne Straßenfegerin.* "The politically correct term now is 'Sex Care Provider;' but I'm just an old-fashioned whore, a streetwalker."

STRAßENKREUZER/STRAßENSEGLER, *m.* Big car (lit. street cruiser/sailer). *Mit dem Straßenkreuzer kommen Sie nicht durch die Altstadt.* "You won't get through the old part of town in that limousine." Cf. SCHLACHTSCHIFF 2.

STREEKDEERN, *N.* = **STRAßENDIRNE; STRAßENFEGERIN.**

STREICHELEINHEITEN, *pl.* Tender loving care. *Dem neuen Kätzchen müsst ihr oft Streicheleinheiten geben.* "You must often show affection to the new kitten."

STREIFEN. To touch against; scrape. ***Mich streift 'n Bus/ 'n Dampfer/'n Schiff/'ne Scholle/'ne Seilbahn.*** That's incredible!/Well blow me down! (lit. A bus/steamer/ship/ flounder/cable car's scraping me).

STREßBUDE, *f., youth.* Stressful workplace; school (lit. stress hut/dump). *Jetzt soll ich noch am Wochenende in der Stressbude malochen.* "Now I'm supposed to work in the salt mines even on the weekend."

STREUSAND = KIES; STEINE/STEINCHEN.

STRICH, *m.* **1.** Line; dash; stroke (pen). ***Dünn wie ein Strich/Nur ein Strich in der Landschaft.*** Thin as a rail (lit. thin as a dash/just a brush stroke in the landscape). *Wenn du bei deiner makrobiotischen Kost bleibst, wirst du nur ein Strich in der Landschaft sein.* "If you stick with you macrobiotic fare, you'll just be a stalk in the breeze." ***Unter dem Strich sein.*** To not be up to par. *Heute bin ich etwas unterm Strich.* "I'm feeling a bit down/under the weather today." ***Unterm Strich.*** In the last analysis. *Unterm Strich war das Ergebnis positiv.* "All things considered, the result was positive." **2.** Pile (rug); nap (fabric); direction of hair growth. ***Gegen den Strich.*** Against one's grain. *Selbst wenn's dir gegen den Strich geht, tu's doch mir zuliebe.* "Even if it goes against your grain, do it for me." ***Nach Strich und Faden.*** Right and proper. *Ich hab ihn nach Strich und Faden versohlt.* "I gave him a thorough hiding." **3.** Prostitution; streetwalking; red-light district. ***Auf den Strich gehen.*** To solicit for prostitution. *Mit 16 ist sie schon auf den Strich gegangen.* "She started hooking when she was 16."

STRICHER, *m.* Boy prostitute. *Als Stricher hat er ganz gut verdient.* "He made good money when he was on the streets."

STRICHJUNGE = STRICHER.

STRICHMÄDCHEN, *n.* Streetwalker. *Wenn ihr Vater, der so strenge Richter, je wüßte, dass sie Strichmädchen ist!* "If only her father, that stern judge, knew that she's a streetwalker!"

STRICK, *m.* Cord; rope. ***Jmdm. einen Strick drehen.*** To use s.t. against s.o. (lit. to wind a noose for s.o.). *Du hättest ihm nichts davon verraten sollen; jetzt dreht er dir 'n Strick.* "You shouldn't have told him anything about the matter; now he's going to use it against you." ***Sich einen Strick kaufen/nehmen.*** To commit suicide. *Da kann ich mir 'n Strick kaufen!* "I might as well end it all now." ***Wenn alle Stricke reißen.*** See REIßEN.

STRIPPE, *f.* Telephone (lit. string). *Ich hab sie jetzt an der Strippe.* "I've got her on the line now." ***An der Strippe hängen.*** To be on the phone/hog the phone. *Hängt er noch an der Strippe?* "Is he still on the telephone?"

STRIZZI, *m., S., esp. Aust.* **1.** Pimp. *I hob (ich habe) Streit mit mei' Strizzi koppt (gehabt).* "I had an argument with my pimp." **2.** No-good, rascal. *Mein Strizzi hat mich wieder geschlagen aber ich lieb ihn doch.* "That no-good of mine beat me again, but I love him anyway." **3.** Chum (ironic for **2**). *Willst mit, alter Strizzi?* "Do you want to come along, old buddy?"

STRULLEN, *N.* To urinate. ***Mein Haifisch strullt!*** Well, blow me down!/Well, I'll be damned! (lit. my shark's pissing).

STRULLERMANN, *N.* Penis. *Ich weiß nicht, warum er so stolz auf seinen winzigen Strullermann ist.* "I don't know why he's so proud of his piddling little pecker."

STUBE, *f.* Room. ***Die gute Stube.*** Parlor. *Der Weihnachtsbaum stand in der guten Stube.* "The Christmas tree was in the parlor." See KINDERSTUBE.

STUBENHOCKER, *m.* House mouse; stick-in-the-mud (lit. room squatter). *Ich geh gern schwofen, aber der alte Knacker ist Stubenhocker.* "I like to go dancing, but that old fogey's a couch potato."

STUSS, *m.* Nonsense. *Die Politpopper labern nur Stuss.* "The politicos just talk drivel."

SUBITO. Right away (taken unchanged from It.) *Aber subito soll's gemacht werden.* "I want it done immediately."

SUFF, *m.* Alcoholism. *Im Suff.* Under the influence (of alcohol). *Im Suff sagte er, er sei in mich verknallt.* "When he was under the influence, he said he was nuts about me."

SÜFFEL, *m.* Tippler. *Der Süffel ist immer voll.* "That tippler's always soused."

SÜFFELN. To tipple. *Dieser Sufi süffelt gern und bestreitet, dass der Wein im Koran wirklich verboten sei.* "That Sufi (Muslim mystic/dervish) likes to imbibe and denies that wine is really prohibited in the Koran."

SÜFFIG. Pleasant to drink. *Dies ist aber 'n süffiger Wein!* "This wine goes down real smooth!"

SUFFKOPF = **SÜFFEL.**

SULTAN = **SCHEICH 3.**

SÜLZEN. To babble; talk nonsense (lit. to pickle in aspic). *Wenn er nur zu sülzen aufhören würde!* "If he'd only stop droning on." See ANSÜLZEN; (SICH) AUSSÜLZEN; DUMM-SÜLZEN; RUMSÜLZEN.

SÜLZER/SÜLZKOPF, *m.* Dummy; babbler. *Diesen Sülzkopf hast du gewählt?* "You voted for that windbag?"

SUMPFEN. To live it up. *Gestern haben wir die ganze Nacht auf der Piste gesumpft.* "We had a blast barhopping last night."

SUMPFHUHN, *n.* **1.,** *youth.* Ugly girl (lit. moorhen). See SUMPFRALLE. **2.** Unreliable person. *Diesem Sumpfhuhn hast du getraut?* "You trusted that cowboy?"

SUMPFRALLE, *f., youth, pej.* Ugly girl; bitch (lit. swamp rail [bird]). *Die Sumpfralle macht ihm die Hölle heiß.* "That bitch is making life hell for him." Cf. BACHSTELZE; EULE; GEIERWALLY; NEBELKRÄHE; PUTE; SCHNEPFE; SUMPFHUHN; WACHTEL.

SYSTEMABSTURZ. See ABSTURZ.

SZENE, *f.* **1.** Scene. *Wie steht's mir der Diskoszene, der Kneipenszene in diesem Kaff?* "What's the nightlife like in this burg?" **2.** Milieu; subculture. *Er ist schwul, liebt aber die Bars in der Szene nicht.* "He's gay but doesn't like gay bars." See DROGENSZENE; SADO-MASO.

TACH!/TACHCHEN!, *N.* Good day! *Tach! Wie geht's?* "Hello! How are you?"

TALER, *m.*/**TALERCHEN,** *n.* Money. (Silver from St. Joachimstal in Bohemia was used to mint early "thalers;" Eng. "dollar" is rel.) *Hast noch 'n paar Talerchen für mich?* "Got a few more bucks/marks/euros for me?"

TAMTAM, *m.* Fuss; ballyhoo (lit. tom-tom [gong; drum]). *Warum macht man 'n solchen Tamtam drum?* "Why'd they make such a fuss about that?"

TANGIEREN. 1. To skirt (lit. to be tangent to). *Alles, was du sagst, tangiert nur das Problem.* "Everything you say is only incidental to the problem." **2.** To concern. *Deine Meinung tangiert mich nicht.* "I don't care about your opinion."

TANGOBRÜDER, *pl., youth.* Police (lit. tango brothers). *Die Tangobrüder waren hinter uns her.* "The cops were after us."

TANKEN, *youth.* 1 To take on alcohol (lit. to get gasoline). See ALKEN. **2.** To have sex. *Lola ließ alle tanken.* "Lola let everybody in."

TANKSTELLE, *f., youth.* Bar; disco; street with many bars/discos (lit. gas station). *Wir treffen uns auf der Tankstelle.* "We'll meet on the strip."

TANTE, *f., youth.* **1.** Woman over 30 (lit. aunt). *Mann, hat* *die Tante Holz vor der Hütte!* "Man, that broad's stacked!" **2.** Male homosexual. See TANTE HONEY; TUNTE.

TANTE HONEY, *m., youth.* Male homosexual (lit. aunt honey). *Wenn's mit den Törtchen nicht geht, wartet immer 'ne Tante Honey auf mich.* "When I don't make it with a tomato, some fruit's always waiting for me."

TANTE SCHLOTTERBECK, *f., youth.* Timid person (*schlottern* = to shake; tremble). *Und du hast keinen Finger gerührt mir zu helfen, du Tante Schlotterbeck.* "And you didn't lift a finger to help me, you chicken liver."

TANZBÄRENSCHRITT, *m., youth.* Slow, dragging dance rhythm (lit. dancing bear step). *Was ist denn in die Gruftis gefahren? So 'n toller Stechschritt, nicht ihr gewöhnlicher Tanzbärenschritt.* "What's gotten into those oldies? They're dancing up a storm, instead of doing their usual shuffle."

TAPERGREIS = **TATTERGREIS.**

TAPS = **HANS TAPS.**

TASSE, *f.* Cup. ***Nicht alle Tassen im Schrank haben.*** Not to have all one's marbles (lit. not to have all the cups in the cupboard). *Der Typ hat nicht alle Tassen im Schrank.* "That guy's not playing with a full deck." See HOCH DIE TASSEN!; TRÜB.

TASTENHENGST, *m.* Pianist (lit. keyboard stallion). *Stell den Flimmerkasten ab und lass Kai an den Tastenkasten ran; 'n turbogeiler Tastenhengst ist er.* "Shut the boob tube off and let Kai tickle the ivories; he's a terrific pianist."

TATTERERANSTALT, *f., youth.* Old-age home (lit. institution for the doddering). See TROTTELMUSEUM.

TATTERGREIS, *m., pej.* Doddering old man. *Der Tattergreis wollte mir sein Leben erzählen; vielleicht hätte ich ihm zuhören sollen.* "That old geezer wanted to tell me his life story; maybe I should have listened."

TATTERICH, *m.* The shakes. *Er ist Alker und hat mit zwanzig Jahren schon den Tatterich.* "He's an alcoholic and already has the shakes at 20."

TECHNO, *n., m., youth.* Electronic hard-driving disco dance music (hip-hop, acid jazz/rock, reggae, and such). *Techno törnt uns tierisch an.* "Techno's a tremendous turn on for us."

TECHNO-FREAKS/TECHNO-KIDS, *pl.* Techno music enthusiasts. *Beim Dancefloor hotteten sich die Techno-Kids.* "The techno kids worked up a steam when dancing." Cf. RAVER.

TECHNONOMADE, *m.* S.o. who conducts most of her/his business on the road using technology such as laptops, cell phones, etc. *Ich bin Technonomadin und könnt' es im Büro nie mehr aushalten.* "I work with mobile technology, and I'd never be able to stand working in an office again."

TECHNORAVE = RAVE.

TECHNORAVER = RAVER.

TECHNOSCHUPPEN, *m., youth.* Discotheque that features techno music. *Claro komm ich mit in den Technoschuppen.* "Of course I'll come along to the techno disco."

TECHNOTREFF, *m.* Party; dance with techno music. *Der Technotreff war elefantös.* "The techno party was fantabulous."

TEIL, *n., youth.* **1.** Penis (lit. part). *„Ich für mein Teil bin dagegen." „Mit deinem Miniteil solltest du lieber schweigen."* " 'For my part, I'm against it.' 'With a tiny dick like yours, you should shut up.' " **2.** Object of any kind (TV, clothing, vehicle, etc.). *Nicht schlecht das Teil.* "Not bad, that thing."

TELEFONITIS, *f.* Telephone mania. *Meine Töchter leiden an Telefonitis.* "My daughters are telephone addicts."

TELEFONANIERER. S.o. who talks endlessly on the phone (play on *telefonieren* and *onanieren* [to masturbate]). *Telefonanierer wie du gehen mir aufn Keks.* "Telephone babblers like you get on my nerves." Cf. VERBALO-NANIERER.

TELLERRAND, *m.* Narrow horizon (lit. edge of [one's] plate). *Der Chef ist unfähig, übern Tellerrand hinauszublicken.* "The boss can't see any further than the end of his nose."

TEMPO! Put some speed on!

TEMPOSÜNDER, *m.* Person caught speeding; speed demon. *Temposündern wird der Führerschein entzogen.* "Speed demons get their licenses taken away."

TERROR, *m.* Terror. *Terror machen.* (*Youth.*) To make a fuss/din/trouble. *Meine Hausdrachen wissen, dass ich kiffe und machen mir den vollen Terror.* "My parents know I'm a pothead and never stop giving me grief."

TICKEN. 1. To tick. *Nicht richtig ticken.* To be crazy. *Bei dem tickt's nicht richtig.* "He's off his rocker." **2.** To understand. See DURCHTICKEN.

TICKER, *m.* Telex machine. *Wir haben keinen Ticker.* "We have no telex."

TICKERN. To telex. *Sie hätten's faxen, nicht tickern sollen.* "You should have faxed it instead of telexing it."

TIERISCH, *youth.* Extremely; really (lit. bestial, savage). *Das hast du tierisch gut gemacht.* "You really did an A-1 job on that."

TIFFIG, *E., youth.* Nifty, neat. *War das 'n tiffiges Konzert!* "That was a real nifty concert!"

TIGERN, *youth.* To stalk; lurk; stride/drive pridefully; go out to pick up girls (all meanings are perceived as tigerlike). *Jede Nacht tigerte ich mit den Kumpels durch die Gegend; das waren Zeiten!* "Every night I used to go out prowling/cruising/wolfing with my buddies; those were the days!"

TILTEN. To be crazy (from Eng. to tilt). *Du spinnst, tiltst ja.* "You're off the beam, off your rocker."

TINNEF, *m.* **1.** Junk (from Hebr. for dirt). *Du verlangst zu viel für den Tinnef.* "You're asking too much for this junk." **2.** Nonsense. *Dein Tinnef interessiert mich nicht.*

"I'm not interested in your nonsense."

TITTE, *f.* Tit. *Er träumt von den Titten der Diana von Ephesos.* "He dreams of Diana of Ephesus' tits." See ARSCH . . . PRESSE; LINKE TITTE.

TITTENSCHWUNGPALAST, *m., youth, N.* Dance hall (lit. "tit swing palace"). *Im Tittenschwungpalast geht's voll geil zu.* "The disco's ecstasy land."

TO, *n.* From *die Toilette* (toilet) with infl. of *das Klo. Sie muss aufs To.* "She's got to go to the can."

TOBAK, *m.* Variant of *Tabak* (tobacco). ***Harter/starker Tobak.*** A bit much/thick. *Das ist starker Tobak, was du da vom Inzest in der Familie erzählst.* "That's strong stuff, what you say about incest in the family." See ANNO.

TOCHTER, *f., youth.* Young girl (lit. daughter). *Er tanzte mit 'ner klasse Tochter.* "He danced with a nifty chick."

TÖFFEL, *m.* Clumsy fool. *Geh doch weg, du Töffel!* "Go away, oaf!"

TOFFEL, *m.* Henpecked husband. *Der einstige tolle Hecht ist 'n totaler Toffel geworden.* "That former live wire's become a domesticated klutz." See PANTOFFEL.

TÖLE, *f.* **1.** Mutt. *Die Gören haben mir 'ne Töle ins Haus gebracht.* "The kids brought home a mutt." **2.** Bitch. *Die Töle geht mir aufn Wecker.* "That bitch gets on my nerves." Cf. ZIPPE.

TOLL. Wonderful (lit. insane). *Tolle Tussis gab's in der Disko.* "There were terrific chicks in the disco."

TOLLO, *youth sl. var. of* TOLL.

TOLLPATSCH, *m.* Clumsy person. *Mit diesem Tollpatsch will ich nicht tanzen.* "I don't want to dance with that clumsy guy."

TOMATE, *f., youth.* Head (lit. tomato). *Du hast wohl 'n Loch in der Tomate!* "You must have a hole in your head!" Cf. BIRNE; KÜRBIS; MELONE; PFIRSICH; RÜBE **2.**

TOP. Tops. *Die Band ist echt top.* "That band's tops."

TOPFIT. In great shape. *Wir glaubten den Wagen wieder*

topfit. "We thought the car was in perfect order again."

TORFKOPF, *m., N.* Idiot (lit. peat head). *Jetzt reicht's aber, Torfkopf!* "That's enough of that, meathead!"

TÖRNEN. See ANTÖRNEN.

TÖRTCHEN, *n.* Sweetie pie (lit. little tart [pastry]). *So ein tolles Törtchen wünschte ich mir.* "Boy, I'd love to have a creamy, dreamy piece like her."

TORTE, *f.* **1.** Pudgy girl (who may have overindulged in Torten [pastry tarts]). *Die Mageren mag ich nicht; ich steh eher auf Torten.* "I don't like the skinny ones; the plump ones are more my style." **2.** Sweetie pie. See TÖRTCHEN.

TOTAL. Thoroughly; wonderfully; extremely. *Dein Kleid ist total geil.* "Your dress is absolutely out of this world!"

TOTALINSKI/TOTALO, *youth sl. var.* of prev. entry. *Du törnst mich irgendwie echt an, aber totalinski!* "You really turn me on, like completely, you know!"

TOTE HOSE. Deadly dull (lit. dead pants). *Bevor Lola kam, war alles im Dorf echt tote Hose.* "Before Lola came, the village was absolute Dullsville." Cf. KALTE ASCHE.

TOTUS TUUS, *youth.* Lat. for *ganz dein* (entirely yours). *„Du weißt ja, ich bin totus tuus," schrieb sie mir.* " 'You know I'm entirely yours,' she wrote me." Cf. TUTTI/TUTTO.

TOUR, *f.* See HOCHTOUR; KRUMME TOUR.

TOURI, *pl.* From *Tourist* (tourist). *Die ganze Gegend ist jetzt von Touris überlaufen.* "The whole area's crawling with tourists now."

TOWARITSCH, *m., E.* **1.** Buddy, friend (from Russ. *tovarishch* [comrade]). **Den Towaritsch machen.** To have sex. *Im Trabbi haben wir den Towaritsch gemacht.* "We got it on in the Trabant." Cf. RASPUTIN. **2.** Mack, bud (hostile version of **1**). *Soll ich dir's Fell bügeln, Towaritsch?* "You lookin' for a fat lip, buddy?"

TRABBI, *m., Trabant* (satellite); car made in the former

GDR—the butt of many jokes). *Trabbifans gibt's jetzt auch im Westen.* "Now there are 'Trabbi' fans in the West too."

TRABBIFURZ, *m.* Crummy *Trabbi* (lit. *Trabbi* fart). *Mit seinem Trabbifurz wollte er meinen Mercedes überholen.* "He wanted to pass my Mercedes in his crummy Trabbi." Cf. PLASTIKBOMBER.

TRACHTENGRUPPE, *f., youth.* Traffic cops (lit. group dressed in traditional costume). Cf. GARTENZWERGE; TANGOBRÜDER. *Die Trachtengruppe holte die Kumpels auf den Mofas ein, uns nicht.* "The fuzz caught up with our buddies on the small mopeds, but not with us."

TRAMPEL, *m., n.* Oaf. *Dieser Trampel vom Land hat noch viel zu lernen.* "That country bumpkin still has much to learn."

TRAMPELTIER, *n.* Bactrian camel. In. sl. use = TRAMPEL.

TRAMPEN. To hitchhike. *Wir waren pleite und mussten trampen.* "We were broke and had to hitch." Cf. PER DAUMEN FAHREN.

TRAN, *m.* Fish oil. *Im Tran sein.* **1.** To be in a daze; be distracted. *Hast noch 'n Regenschirm verloren? Warst wohl wieder im Tran.* "You've lost another umbrella? You were probably daydreaming again." **2.** To be spaced out on drugs. *Er ist Fixer und immer im Tran.* "He's a junkie and always spaced out."

TRANE = **TRANFUNZEL 2.**

TRANFUNZEL, *f.* **1.** Lamp (orig. an oil lamp) that gives poor/gloomy light. *Bei dieser Tranfunzel kann ich nicht lesen.* "I can't read in this light." **2.** Slowpoke; dimwit. *Wenn du nur nicht so 'ne Tranfunzel wärst, könntest du's schon schaffen.* "If you weren't dopey and slow as molasses, you'd be able to swing it."

TRANFUNZLIG. Slow; dull. *Mensch, war der Film tranfunzlig!* "Man, what a drag that movie was!"

TRANSI, *m., f.* Transsexual; transvestite. *Seit ich Transi bin, fühl ich mich echt transzendental.* "Ever since I became a transi, I feel truly transcendental."

TRANSUSE/TRANTÜTE = **TRANFUNZEL 2.**

TRARA. See RIESENTRARA.

TRATSCHE, *f.* Gossip. *Diese Tratsche hat schon zu viel Unheil angerichtet.* "That scandalmonger's already done too much harm."

TRATSCHMAUL, *n.***/TRATSCHTANTE/TRATSCH-TASCHE,** *f.* = **TRATSCHE.**

TREBE, *f.* *Auf Trebe gehen.* To run away. *Ich halt's nicht mehr aus, ich geh auf Trebe.* "I can't take it anymore; I'm going to run away." *Auf Trebe sein.* To be a runaway. *Seit zwei Jahren bin ich auf Trebe.* "I've been a runaway for two years."

TREBEGÄNGER, *m.* Runaway. *Viele Trebegänger werden Stricher.* "Many runaways become prostitutes."

TRETEN. To walk, tread. *Jmdn./jmdm. in den Arsch/Hintern treten.* To give s.o. a kick in the ass/behind. *Wenn du diesen Tranfunzeln nicht in den Hintern trittst, kommt die Arbeit nicht voran.* "If you don't give those slowpokes a kick in the pants, the work won't get done."

TRIBAL RAVE, *m., n., youth.* Rave (big dance gathering) with a preponderance of African rhythms. *Beim Tribal Rave sind wir voll ausgeflippt.* "We totally freaked out at the tribal rave."

TRICK 17. Clever ploy; brilliant idea. *„Wie hast du's geschafft?" „Trick 17!"* " 'How'd you swing that?' 'Smarts!' "

TRICK 18, 18A. Youth sl. intensifications of TRICK 17.

TRIEZEN, *N.* To tease; annoy. *Hör doch auf, mich zu triezen!* "Quit bugging me!"

TRIP, *m.* Trip; drug trip. *Wir haben 'n geilen Trip nach den Südseeinseln gemacht.* "We took a terrific trip to the South Sea Isles."

TRIPPER, *m.* Gonorrhea (from *N.* Ger. *drippen,* to drip). *Aber leider haben wir uns da auch den Tripper geholt.*

"But unfortunately, we also got the clap there."

TRITTBRETTFAHRER, *m.* S.o. who profits from another's work (lit. running board rider). *Von wegen Trittbrettfahrer! Sie hat Wesentliches dazu beigetragen.* "What do you mean, free rider? She made significant contributions to it."

TRIVIALO, *m., youth.* Insignificant person. *Aus Neid nennst du sie Trivialos, aber du bist echt der Hohlste von allen.* "You enviously call them trivial, but you're the shallowest one around."

TROPFENFÄNGER, *m.* Condom (lit. drop catcher). *Der Tropfenfänger muss undicht gewesen sein; ich bin wieder schwanger.* "The bag must have leaked; I'm pregnant again."

TROTT, *m.* Routine (lit. trot). ***In den alten Trott verfallen/aus dem alten Trott herauskommen.*** To slip back into the same old rut/To get out of one's daily grind. *Der Zigeuner mit seiner Geige hat mir geholfen, aus dem alten Trott herauszukommen.* "The gypsy with his violin has helped me to get out of the rut I was in." Cf. ALLTAGSTROTT; EHETROTT.

TROTTEL, *m.* Imbecile. *Blöder Trottel, kannst nicht zählen?* "Dumb jerk, can't you count?"

TROTTELMUSEUM, *n., pej., youth.* Home for the aged (museum with jerks as exhibits). *Meine Fossilien gehören ins Trottelmuseum.* "My prehistoric parents should be exhibited in a (paleontology) museum."

TRÜB. Dreary; cloudy. ***Eine trübe Tasse sein.*** To be a wet blanket/drip. *Ach, versuch's doch mal, du trübe Tasse!* "Aw, come on 'n try it, you Gloomy Gus!"

TRUDELN. To play dice (lit. to go into a spin). *Beim Trudeln gewinnt er selten.* "He rarely wins when he rolls the dice."

TSCHABO = **DJANGO.**

TSCHAPPERL, *n., Aust.* Clumsy person. *Dem Tschapperl muss ich noch vieles beibringen.* "I've got lots to teach that oaf."

TSCHAU! Bye now! See you! (translit. of It. *ciao*). *Tschau, Bella* "Bye-bye, gorgeous!"

TSCHECHERL, *n., Aust.* Unpretentious little tavern/café. *Nach der Arbeit geht er ins Tschecherl.* "After work he goes to the little tavern."

TSCHECHERN, *Aust.* To drink alcohol. *Heut abend soll nicht getschechert werden!* "Don't do any tippling tonight!"

TSCHICK, *m., Aust.* Cigarette (from It. *cìcca*). *Nimm doch den Tschik aus dem Mund!* "Take that cigarette out of your mouth!"

TSCHÖ, *N.* Youth sl. var. of TSCHÜS.

TSCHUGGI, *youth.* Wonderful. *'S war alles tschuggi.* "Everything was terrific."

TSCHÜS/TSCHÜSCHEN! Bye!/Bye now./So long./See you.

TSCHÜSS/TSCHÜSSCHEN/TSCHÜSSI. Variants of the preceding entry, but pronounced with a short *ü*.

TSCHÜSSIKOWSKI. *E.* var. of TSCHÜSSI.

TUBE, *f.* Tube. ***Auf die Tube drücken.*** To step on it. *Wenn wir nicht auf die Tube drücken, kommen wir zu spät.* "If we don't step on it, we'll be late."

TUCH, *n.* Cloth. ***In trockne Tücher bringen.*** To straighten out. *Deine Probleme sind hausgemacht; du musst sie in trockne Tücher bringen.* "Your problems are of your own making; you've got to clean up your act."

TÜDDELN, *N.* To say/do foolish things. *Was tüddelst du da*? "What are you babbling about?"

TUNTE, *f., pej.* **1.** Effeminate homosexual (var. of *Tante* [auntie]). *Warum hast du zuerst mit der Tunte getanzt statt mit mir?* "Why'd you dance with that nelly-fag first instead of with me?" **2.** Girl who hangs out with a rock musician/band (cf. BRAUT **2**). *Willst diese Punkrocker-tunte heiraten? Das gibt's nicht!* "You want to marry that punk rocker groupie? You've gotta be kidding!"

TUNTENHAFT/TUNTIG. Fussy; effeminate. *Tu nicht so tuntenhaft!* "Stop being so prissy."

TÜR, *f.* Door. **Mach die Tür von außen zu.** Be on your way now and don't hurry back (lit. close the door from outside).

TURBO, *youth.* Fast. *Mach 'n bisschen turbo jetzt.* "Put a little snap into it now."

TURBO, *m., youth.* Speed. **Den Turbo reinhauen.** To step on it. *Haut doch mal den Turbo rein, ihr Kamele!* "Give it the gun, will you, you idiots!"

TURBO-. 1. Turbo- (in scientific compounds such as Turbodiesel). **2.** Extremely (*youth*), in compounds such as *turbogeil, turbohart, turbomäßig; turbostark. Das Konzert war turbotoll.* "The concert was totally terrific."

TURKEY, *youth.* Drug withdrawal (from Eng. "cold turkey"). *Total auf Turkey hab ich's nicht geschafft.* "I couldn't swing it, going cold turkey."

TÜRMEN. To clear out. *Ich wollte ihn packen, aber er ist getürmt.* "I wanted to grab him, but he beat it fast."

TUSCHER = HUSCHER 1.

TUSCHKASTEN, *m.* Box of watercolor paints. *Heute bist du 'n richtiger Tuschkasten.* "You've got all your war paint on today."

TUSSI, *f., youth.* Girl; broad; dame; tart. *Die Tussi macht mich total an!* "That chick really gets me going."

TÜTE, *f.* **1.** **Das kommt nicht in die Tüte!** That's out of the question!/No way! (lit. that won't go into the bag). **2. Tüten kleben.** To be in jail (lit. to paste bags together). *Er hatte große Pläne aber jetzt klebt er Tüten.* "He had great plans, but now he's making license plates." See PLASTIKTÜTE.

TUTTI/TUTTO, *youth.* Completely (from It. for "all;" an alternative to overused TOTAL and VOLL **2**). *Setzt du dich für mich ein, aber tutti?* "Will you go to bat for me, but I mean 100%?"

TUTTI PALETTI = ALLES PALETTI.

TWENS, *m.* Persons in their 20s. *Das ist 'ne Illustrierte für Teens und Twens.* "That's a mag for teens and people in their 20s."

TYP, *m.* Guy. *Was findest du an dem abgefuckten Typ?* "What do you see in that deadbeat guy?"

TYPE, *f.* Character, oddball. *Was weißt du von der Type nebenan?* "What do you know about that weirdo next door?"

ÜBERBELICHTET. Hypertense. *Du hast aber 'ne über-belichtete Birne heute.* "Man, you're really hyper today."

ÜBERDREHT. Hypertense/wired (lit. too tightly wound). *Dieser überdrehte Typ geht mir aufn Keks.* "That weirdo gets on my nerves."

ÜBERMACKERN, *youth.* To make too masculine. *Wir wollen die Fete nicht übermackern; lad mehr Mädchen ein.* "We don't want the boys to dominate the party; invite more girls."

ÜBERMACKERT. 1. Excessively macho, vain. *Bleib mir vom Leibe mit deinem Nietzsche und dem Übermen-schen; die waren wohl übermackert wie du.* "Don't talk to me about Nietzsche and the superman; they were proba-bly super machos like you." **2.** Past part. of ÜBERMACK-ERN. *Australien soll ein übermackertes Land sein.* "They say Australia's got an oversupply of guys."

ÜBERREIßEN. To understand. *Wer überreißt schon das Steuerrecht?* "Is there really anyone who understands the tax laws?"

ÜBERZIEHER, *m.* Condom (lit. overcoat). *So riesengroß ist sein Wunderhorn, dass er Überzieher in Übergröße benutzen muss.* "His dick's so huge that he has to use extra large condoms."

ÜBERZUG, *m.* Cover = **ÜBERZIEHER.**

U-BOOT, *m., for Unterseeboot.* Submarine. ***U-Boot Christ.*** Occasional Christian who "surfaces" only at Christmas or Easter. *Der ist nicht mal U-Boot Christ; er geht nie in die Kirche und würde am liebsten die Religion torpedieren.* "He isn't even an occasional Christian; he never goes to church and would like to sink the religion."

UFER, *m.* Shore. ***Vom anderen Ufer sein.*** To be a homosexual. *,,Ich dachte, er war vom andern Ufer." ,,Ja, aber er schwimmt oft vom einen zum anderen Ufer rüber."* " 'But I thought he was one of them.' 'Yes, but he often swings both ways.' "

ULK, *m.* Joke; practical joke. *Treib keinen Ulk mit mir.* "Don't try any of your tricks on me!"

ULKNUDEL, *f.* Joker; prankster. *Du bist 'ne richtige Ulknudel; solltest Berufskomiker werden.* "You're a real clown; you should be a professional comic."

ULTRAKRASS. See KRASS.

UMDOCKEN, *youth.* To bump off (lit. to change docks). *Die Gangster werden dich umdocken.* "The gangsters are going to put you in a cement suit and send you to the bottom of the river."

UMGEKEHRT. Opposite; inverse. ***Umgekehrt wird ein Schuh draus.*** The opposite is the case (lit. turning it the other way makes it a shoe). *Ich soll den Streit angefangen haben? Umgekehrt wird ein Schuh draus!* "I'm supposed to have started the quarrel? It's the other way around!"

UMHAUEN. To bowl over. *Die neue Band hat uns voll hingehauen.* "The new band really blew us away."

UMLEGEN. 1. To kill (lit. to put around; to knock down). *Der Profikiller hat den Falschen umgelegt.* "The contract killer bumped off the wrong guy." **2.** To lay, fuck. *Die hab ich längst schon umgelegt.* "I had her some time ago."

UMNIETEN, *youth.* To kill. *Zackig war er in seiner Niethose; schade dass man ihn umnieten musste.* "He looked real sharp in his studded jeans; too bad they had to rub him out."

UNGEIL, *youth.* Uninteresting. *Ihr neuer Macker ist total ungeil.* "Her new boyfriend's totally uncool."

UNHEIMLICH. Enormous; incredible (lit. eerie, uncanny). *Es hat unheimlich viel gekostet, aber wir haben uns unheimlich gefreut.* "It was incredibly expensive but we enjoyed o.s. enormously."

UNKE, *f.* **1.** Toad. See UNKENRUF. **2.** Woman with a negative/pessimistic outlook. *Jedes Mal, das ich mit der Unke spreche, hab ich Lust, mich abzuknallen.* "Every time I talk to that prophetess of doom, I feel like putting a bullet in my head." **3.** Pimply girl. *Die Unke hab ich gepflökelt, aber nicht geküsst.* "I screwed Miss Pimples but I didn't kiss her."

UNKEN. To foretell doom and gloom. *Er hat wieder was von Weltuntergang geunkt.* "He prophesied s.t. about the end of the world again."

UNKENRUF, *m.* Cry of doom/pessimism (lit. toad's cry). *Allen Unkenrufen zum Trotz hat sich die Chefin durchgesetzt.* "Despite all the cries of doom, the boss prevailed."

UNTERBELICHTET. Dim-witted (lit. underexposed [photography]). *Unterbelichtet ist sie nicht—nur 'n bisschen schüchtern.* "It's not that she's not very bright, she's just a bit shy."

UNTERBUTTERN. To push aside; suppress. *Wir Mädchen werden zu oft von den Jungen in der Klasse untergebuttert.* "We girls are often disadvantaged/dominated by the boys in the class."

UNTERHOSE, *f.* Underpants. ***Das zieht dir doch die Unterhose aus!*** (*Youth.*) That'll make you drop your drawers/knock your socks off.

UNTERJUBELN. ***Jmdm. etwas unterjubeln.*** To palm s.t. off on s.o.; to pin s.t. on s.o. *Das ist kein lupenreiner Diamant; man hat dir 'n fehlerhaften untergejubelt.* "It's not a flawless diamond. They palmed off a defective one on you."

UNTERKÜHLT. Dry, low-key (lit. hypothermic). *Nach den vielen giga-, galaktisch, Mammut-, hyper-, ober-, super-,* *ultra- usw. Übertreibungen, findet sie ihren unterkühlten untertreibenden Brilli megagalaktisch entzückend!* "After all that giga, galactic, mammoth, hyper, etc. exaggeration, she finds her cool, low-key, glasses-wearing Milquetoast supergalactically delightful!"

URALBÄR. See GEHEN.

URIG. Down to earth, natural; informal; ethnic. *Oma ist urig und besucht oft urige Kneipen.* "Granny's an original and often goes to ethnic/exuberant taverns."

URIN, *m.* Urine. ***Etwas im Urin haben/spüren.*** To have a gut feeling about s.t. (lit. to feel in the urine). *Im Urin spürte ich, dass ihm nicht zu trauen war.* "I knew in my gut you couldn't trust him."

URISCH, *youth.* Extremely; enormously. *Die Band ist urisch geil.* "That band's mind-blowing."

URLAUBSMUFFEL, *m.* Antivacation person. *Die Ferien verbringen wir wieder auf Balkonien statt nach Bali, Mali oder einem Balkanland zu fahren; mein Mann ist Urlaubsmuffel.* "We're spending the holidays on the balcony/porch again, instead of going to Bali, Mali, or the Balkans; my husband doesn't like vacationing."

URST, *youth.* Wild and wonderful; mind-blowing. *Mann, war das 'n urster Sound!* "Man, that sound was out of this world!"

URSTIG = URISCH.

URWÜCHSIG = URIG.

VEILCHEN, *n.* **1.** Violet. ***Blau wie ein Veilchen.*** Roaring drunk (intensifies BLAU **2**). *Man sah's gleich; er war blau wie 'n Veilchen.* "You could tell right away he was drunk as a skunk." **2.** Black eye. *Wo hast du dir das blühende Veilchen geholt?* "Where'd you get that prize shiner?"

VEILCHENBLAU. Dead drunk. *Er ist schon veilchenblau.* "He's already soused."

VERÄPPELN, *N.* Nonvulgar form of VERARSCHEN.

VERARSCHEN. To put s.o. on/make an asshole of s.o. *Willst du mich etwa verarschen?* "Are you putting me on?" Cf. VERSCHEIßERN.

VERBALONANIERER/VERBALONANIST, *m., youth.* Windbag (lit. verbal masturbator). *Die Lernfuzzis sind alle nur Verbalonanierer!* "The teachers have all got diarrhea of the mouth."

VERBEULEN. See GIEßKANNE.

VERBIEGEN. See GIEßKANNE; ROHR **3**.

VERBIESTERT. Grouchy; nasty. *Wenn meine Alten nur weniger verbiestert wären!* "If only my parents weren't such grouches."

VERBLEUEN. To beat up. *Die Hools verbleuten ihn ganz schön.* "The hooligans beat him black and blue."

VERBOTEN. Prohibited, forbidden. ***Verboten aussehen.*** To look grotesque. *Diese gepiercten Punks sehen viel-*

leicht verboten aus. "Those punks with lots of body piercing look really weird."

VERBRENNEN. To burn. *Sich das Maul/den Mund/den Schnabel/die Zunge verbrennen.* To say too much (lit. to burn one's mouth/beak/tongue). *Pass auf, dass du dir nicht wieder den Schnabel verbrennst!* "Be careful not to talk your way into trouble again."

VERBUDDELN. To dig. *Wo Wasserleitungen verbuddelt werden, können auch Kabelrohre verlegt werden.* "Wherever they install water pipes they can also lay cables."

VERBUMFIEDELN. To squander. *Was? Die Penunzen hast du alle verbumfiedelt?* "What! You fiddled away all that money?" Cf. GEBUM(S)FIEDELT.

VERBUTTERN. To spend (lit. to turn into butter). *Die Kohle haben wir gleich verbuttert.* "We spent the bread right away."

VERDAMMT! Damn it!

VERDAMMT NOCH EINS!/VERDAMMT NOCH MAL!/VERDAMMT UND ZUGENÄHT! Damn and blast!/Damn it to hell!/Goddamn it!

VERDAMMTE SCHEIßE! Holy fuckin' shit!

VERDAMPFEN = (SICH) VERDÜNNISIEREN.

VERDODELT/VERDÖDELT, *S.* Stupid. *Wenn du nur nit so verdodelt wärst!* "If only you weren't such a dodo/dumb yoyo!"

VERDREHT. Crazy. *Er findet die Welt überdreht, verdreht und hat sich in den Wald zurückgezogen.* "He finds the world tense, twisted and has retired to the woods."

VERDRÖSELN. To hang out/around; be lazy. *Ihr verdröselt nur die Zeit.* "You just waste your time."

VERDRÜCKEN. To eat a lot (lit. to crumple clothes). *Mensch, kann der was verdrücken!* "Man, that guy can really put it away."

(SICH) VERDRÜCKEN/VERDUFTEN = (SICH) VERDÜNNISIEREN.

(SICH) VERDÜNNISIEREN. To scram. *Wenn dieser Dreckskerl kommt, verdünnisier ich mich.* "If that SOB comes, I'm going to make m.s. scarce."

VERDUNSTEN = (SICH) VERDÜNNISIEREN.

VEREINSHUBER, *S./***VEREINSMEIER,** *m., pej.* Club enthusiast; joiner. *Der ist 'n richtiger Vereinsmeier.* "He's a real club nut."

VERFERKELN. To soil. *Du warst voll und hast das Bett verferkelt.* "You were soused and soiled the bed."

VERFLIXT! Darn it!

VERFLIXT NOCH MAL!/VERFLIXT UND ZUGENÄHT! Damn it to hell!/Damn and blast!

VERFLUCHT! = VERDAMMT!

(SICH) VERFRANZEN. To fly off course; to lose one's way. *Der Flieger Corrigan machte sich dadurch berühmt, dass er sich verfranzt hatte.* "The aviator Corrigan assured his fame by flying the wrong way."

(SICH) VERFRATZEN. To scram. *Verfratzt euch, meine Dinos kommen!* "Clear out, my parents are coming!"

VERFRESSEN. 1. Greedy; gluttonous. *Verfressen wie ich bin, hab ich mir den Bauch am Büfett voll geschlagen.* "Glutton that I am, I pigged out at the buffet." **2.** To blow one's money on food. *Er hatte 'n Bärenhunger und verfrass sein ganzes Geld.* "He was ravenous and blew all his money on food."

VERGACKEIERN. To pull s.o.'s leg. *Du versuchst, uns wieder zu vergackeiern.* "You're trying to put us on again."

(SICH) VERGAFFEN. To fall in love. *Ich hab mich in alle drei vergafft.* "I fell for all three of them."

(SICH) VERGALOPPIEREN. To be on the wrong track. *Du hast dich wieder vergaloppiert.* "You're way off the beam again."

VERGAMMELN. 1. To spoil. *Alles im Kühlschrank ist vergammelt.* "Everything in the fridge is spoiled." **2.** To waste time. *Das ganze Wochenende hab ich vergammelt.* "I didn't do a damn thing all weekend."

VERGAMMELT. Scruffy; decrepit (lit. spoiled). *In deiner vergammelten Schese fahr ich nicht.* "I don't want to ride in your broken-down jalopy."

VERGEIGEN. To make a mess of; lose. *Die Mannschaft hat das Spiel vergeigt.* "The team lost the game."

VERGRAULEN. To alienate. *Die träge Spielart des Stürmers vergraulte viele Zuschauer.* "The forward's (soccer player) listless playing put off many spectators."

(SICH) VERHAUEN. To slip up (lit. to beat o.s.). *Die Meinungsforscher haben sich bei der letzten Wahl schwer verhauen.* "The poll takers slipped up badly during the last election."

VERHEULT. Puffy faced and red eyed from crying. *„Siehst so verheult aus." „Ja, beim schmalzigen Film brauchte ich Unmengen von Taschentüchern zum Verheulen."* " 'You look as if you've been crying.' 'Yes, during the shmaltzy film I needed lots of tissues for bawling.' "

VERHINDERT. Would-be; frustrated. *Meine Frau ist 'ne verhinderte Schauspielerin, ich 'n verhinderter Politiker.* "My wife's a would-be actress, I'm a frustrated politician."

VERHOHNEPIPELN = VERÄPPELN.

VERHÜTERLI, *n., Swiss.* Condom (lit. protector). *Kauf welche Verhüterli im Automaten aufm Männerklo.* "Buy a little latex protection in the vending machine in the men's room."

VERJUBELN. To squander on pleasure. *Sein ganzes Vermögen hat er verjubelt.* "He lived it up and went through his entire fortune."

VERKATERT. Suffering from a hangover. *Mensch, ich bin total verkatert.* "Man, I've got one hell of a hangover."

VERKEILEN. To beat up (lit. to wedge). *Sein eigener Bruder hat ihn verkeilt.* "His own brother beat him up."

VERKLARTÜTTELN, *N.* = **VERKLICKERN.**

VERKLEMMT. Inhibited (lit. stuck/wedged). *Total verklemmt war er; aber ich hab ihn aufgeklärt und jetzt ist er geil.* "He was really uptight; but I put him wise, and now he's raunchy." Cf. KLEMMI.

VERKLICKERN. To clarify; elucidate (*klickern* = to play marbles). *Nixon verstrickte sich, indem er wiederholt versuchte, dem Volk sein Verhalten zu verklickern.* "Nixon got tangled up by repeatedly trying to make his behavior perfectly clear to the people."

VERKNACKEN/VERKNACKSEN. To send to prison; slap a fine on (from Hebr. for "to punish"). *Er wurde zu drei Jahren verknackt.* "He got sent up for 3 years."

(SICH) VERKNACKSEN. To sprain/twist. *Beim Schilaufen hab ich mir den Fuß verknackst.* "I sprained an ankle skiing."

(SICH) VERKNALLEN. To fall madly in love with. *Die Blöde hat sich in meinen Mann verknallt.* "That dumb broad's fallen madly in love with my husband."

VERKNALLEN. To explode. *Zu Sylvester hat er jede Menge Böller verknallt, und natürlich viel Kohle dabei verknallt.* "He set off lots of firecrackers for New Year's Eve, and of course squandered lots of money on them."

VERKNASSEN = **VERKNACKEN/VERKNACKSEN.**

VERKOKELN. To burn down. *Tim versuchte, das Elternhaus zu verkokeln.* "Tim tried to torch the family home." Cf. ABFACKELN.

VERKORKST. Ruined. *All ihre Kinder sind verkorkst.* "All their kids are screwed up."

(SICH) VERKRÜMELN = **(SICH) VERDÜNNISIEREN.**

VERLADEN. To deceive (lit. to load). *Dich hat man richtig verladen.* "They really took you for a ride."

VERLÖTEN. To solder. ***Einen/ein paar verlöten.*** To have a quick snort of alcohol/to knock back a few. *Verlöten wir 'n paar vorm Essen.* "Let's have a few before dinner."

VERMASSELN. To mess up. *Du hast mir meine Beförderung vermasselt.* "You screwed up my promotion."

VERMIESEN. To spoil. *Mit deiner Sauferei hast du mir den ganzen Abend vermiest.* "You and your boozing ruined the whole evening for me."

VERMÖBELN. To beat up. *Sie haben ihn richtig vermöbelt.* "They really beat him up."

(SICH) VERNARREN. To fall for; go for. *Ich hab mich in dich vernarrt.* "I'm nuts about you."

VERNASCHEN. 1. To make it with (lit. to eat up sweets; spend on sweets). *Die Ute hab ich mir am Strande von Sylt vernascht.* "I had Ute on the beach at Sylt." **2.** To defeat resoundingly. *Die Konkurrenz haben wir vernascht.* "We had the competition for lunch."

VERPÄPPELN. To pamper. *In der Penne wurden wir alles andere als verpäppelt.* "We were anything but coddled in that school."

VERPASCHEN, *Aust.* To sell off (at a loss). *Meine Briefmarkensammlung will ich verkaufen aber nicht verpaschen.* "I want to sell my stamp collection, but not at a loss."

VERPASSEN. 1. To miss. *Verpass den Bus nicht!* "Don't miss the bus." **2.** To give. ***Jmdm. eine/eins verpassen/ Jmdm. eine Ohrfeige/eine Tracht Prügel verpassen.*** To clout/whack s.o. *Hör auf, oder ich verpass dir eins!* "Cut it out or I'll give you a shot in the head!" ***Jmdm. einen Denkzettel verpassen.*** To give s.o. a warning; to teach s.o. a lesson. *Diesmal hab ich dir nur 'n kleinen Denkzettel verpasst.* "This time I just gave you a little warning." ***Jmdm. eine Zigarre verpassen.*** See ZIGARRE.

VERPATZEN. To spoil. *Er hat mir alles verpatzt.* "He ruined everything for me."

VERPENNEN. To oversleep; sleep through. *Die Vorlesung hab ich wieder verpennt.* "I slept through his lecture again."

VERPENNT. Half-asleep; dim-witted. *Wie gewöhnlich warst du verpennt.* "As usual, you were half-asleep."

311

VERPETZEN, *school sl.* To snitch on. *Wenn du uns verpetzt, reißen wir dir den Arsch auf.* "If you rat on us, we'll beat the shit out of you."

(SICH) VERPFEIFEN = **(SICH) VERPISSEN,** but not vulgar.

VERPFEIFEN. To inform on (*pfeifen* = to whistle). *Du hast den Bullen mein Versteck verpfiffen.* "You squealed to the cops about my hideout."

(SICH) VERPISSEN, *youth.* To scram. *Verpiss dich, Arschloch, oder du kriegst eine vor die Fresse.* "Piss off, asshole, or I'll knock your block off."

(SICH) VERPLAPPERN. To blab. *Der Präsident hat sich verplappert; man wird die Steuern erhöhen.* "The president let the cat out of the bag; taxes will be raised."

VERPLEMPERN. To squander. *Du verplemperst dich.* "You fritter your time away."

VERPRASSEN = **VERPULVERN.**

VERPUFFEN. To fail; fall flat. *Unsere Bemühungen sind alle verpufft.* "Our efforts were all for nothing."

VERPULVERN. To fritter away. *Er hat das ganze Vermögen schnell verpulvert.* "He quickly squandered the entire fortune."

VERPUTZEN = **WEGPUTZEN.**

VERQUAST. Mixed up; garbled. *Für so verquaste Ideen bin ich nicht zu haben.* "I'm not open to half-baked ideas like that."

VERRECKEN. To die a rotten death. *Verrecken sollen sie alle!* "Let them all croak!" ***Zum Verrecken sein.*** To be horrible/revolting. *Es ist zum Verrecken, wie er seine Eltern behandelt!* "It's just horrible the way he treats his parents." ***Nicht ums Verrecken/ums Verrecken nicht.*** Not for the life of me. *Das Geheimnis verrat ich keinem, nicht ums Verrecken.* "I won't betray the secret to anyone, no way!"

VERRÜCKT. Crazy. ***Verrückt und fünf ist neune!*** Insanity knows no bounds! *Unser alter Pfarrer will Transi* *werden; verrückt und fünf ist neune!* "Our old pastor wants to become a transsexual. Madness reigns supreme!" ***Verrückt spielen.*** To act/go crazy. *Weltweit scheint das Wetter verrückt zu spielen.* "The weather seems to be going crazy all over the world."

VERSAUBEUTELN. 1. To lose/misplace. *Meine Schlüssel hab ich wieder versaubeutelt.* "I've gone and lost my keys again." **2.** To make a mess. *Er wird's wieder versaubeuteln.* "He'll screw up again."

VERSAUEN. To screw up. *Du versaust alles.* "You make a rotten mess of everything."

VERSAUERN. To stagnate; turn sour. *Er ist arbeitslos und versauert.* "He's unemployed and embittered."

VERSCHÄRFT. See ECHT VERSCHÄRFT.

VERSCHAUKELN. To dupe. *Die Politiker haben uns verschaukelt.* "The politicians took us in."

VERSCHEIßEN. See VERSCHISSEN.

VERSCHEIßERN. To put s.o. on. *Hör doch auf, mich zu verscheißern!* "Quit shittin' me, will ya!" Cf. VERARSCHEN.

VERSCHERBELN. To sell (often at a loss). *Die Gräfin musste ihre Gemäldesammlung verscherbeln.* "The countess had to sell her collection of paintings."

VERSCHEUERN = VERSCHERBELN.

VERSCHIEßEN. To fire/use up ammunition. *Der Boxer wusste, dass er seine Kraft nicht zu früh verschießen sollte.* "The boxer knew he should pace h.s."

(SICH) VERSCHIEßEN. To fall madly in love with. *Sie waren alle in mich verschossen, aber dafür konnte ich nichts.* "They were all madly in love with me, but I couldn't help it." Cf. (SICH) VERKNALLEN.

VERSCHISS, *m.* Bad reputation. *Wegen seiner Sauferei kam er bei den Filmproduzenten in Verschiss.* "Because of his boozing, he became poison to the movie producers."

VERSCHISSEN. Shitty. *Er trägt seidene Unterhosen, die*

aber meistens verschissen sind. "He wears silk underpants, but they're usually shitty." ***Bei jmdm. verschissen sein.*** To be on s.o.'s shit list. *Er weiß, dass er bei ihnen verschissen ist.* "He knows he's on their shit list."

VERSCHLUCKEN. To swallow. ***Einen Besenstiel/Ladestock/Stock/eine Elle/ein Lineal verschluckt haben.*** To have a stiff/ungainly posture (lit. to have swallowed a broomstick/ramrod/stick/ruler). See BESENSTIEL.

VERSCHLUDERN. To mislay; mess up. *Hast wieder alles verschludert!* "You screwed up everything again."

VERSCHÜTTEN. To spill; bury; submerge. ***Es bei jmdm. verschüttet haben.*** To be on the outs with s.o. *Seit sie unser Geheimnis verraten hat, hat sie's mit der ganzen Familie verschüttet.* "Ever since she betrayed our secret, the whole family's been hostile to her."

VERSCHÜTT GEHEN. 1. To do a disappearing act. *Die Polente kam angepest und wir gingen verschütt.* "The police drove up and we beat it." **2.** To die. *Im Krieg ist mancher Kamerad verschütt gegangen.* "Many an old friend bought it (died) in the war."

VERSCHWITZEN. To forget (lit. to make sweaty). *Hast es wieder verschwitzt!* "You forgot again!"

VERSICHERUNGSHEINI, *m.* Insurance company employee. *Das hat mir der Verischerungsheini nicht gesagt, als er mir die Police verkaufte.* "The guy who sold me the insurance policy didn't tell me that when I bought it."

VERSIFFT, *youth.* Cruddy; disgusting (lit. "syphed up," from Syphilis). *Ich wollte mit ihm poofen, aber seine versiffte Bude törnte mich total ab.* "I wanted to sleep with him, but his filthy room turned me off totally." Cf. SIFFKOPF; ENTSIFFEN.

VERSILBERN. To sell (lit. to paint/plate with silver). *Er musste fast die ganze Sammlung versilbern.* "He had to sell most of the collection." ***Jmdm. die Hände versilbern.*** See HAND.

VERSOHLEN. To whip with a belt/strap. *Dir gehört richtig* *der Arsch versohlt.* "S.o. should take a strap to your ass."

VERSPIELEN. To gamble away. ***Es bei jmdm. verspielt haben.*** To have lost out with s.o. *Seit du mich betrogen hast, hast du bei mir verspielt.* "You betrayed me and I don't want anything more to do with you."

(SICH) VERSPIEßERN, *pej.* To become a typical petit bourgeois. *Der ehemalige Revoluzzer hat sich verspießert.* "The former revolutionary's become very square."

VERSTAND, *m.* Reason. ***Jmdm. den Verstand geklaut haben.*** To be crazy (lit. to have stolen s.o.'s reason). *Du hast ihm wieder verziehen? Dir hat man wohl den Verstand geklaut!* "You forgave him again? Have you lost your mind?"

VERSTEHEN. To understand. ***Nur Bahnhof/Wurstsalat verstehen.*** Not to understand anything. *Er hat uns voll gesülzt, aber ich verstand nur Wurstsalat.* "He babbled on and on, but I didn't understand a damned thing."

VERTICKEN, *youth.* **1.** To sell. *Das kauf ich dir nicht ab; vertick's jemand anders.* "I won't buy (believe) that; try to sell it to s.o. else." **2.** To explain. See VERKLICKEN.

VERTOBACKEN. To beat up. *Nach der Penne haben sie ihn vertobackt.* "They beat him up after school."

VERTRIMMEN. To beat up. *Den Kotzbrocken will ich vertrimmen.* "I'm gonna wallop that scuzzball."

VERTRÖDELN = VERGAMMELN 2.

VERTROTTELN. To go senile. *Nach dem Tod seiner Frau ist er vertrottelt.* "He's been gaga since his wife's death."

VERTROTTELT. Run down; decrepit. *Stell dich nicht so vertrottelt!* "Don't slump/slouch/drag about like that."

(SICH) VERTÜDERN, *N.* To get tangled up. *Er hätte lieber schweigen sollen, statt sich so zu vertüdern.* "He should have kept quiet, rather than tripping up like that."

VERULKEN. To make fun of; put on. *In ihrem neuen Song verulkt sie die Schlager der Fünfziger.* "She makes fun of 50s pop hits in her new song."

VERURSCHEN, *E.* To squander. *All die Mäuse hat er verurscht.* "He blew/went through all the dough."

VERUZEN = VERULKEN.

(SICH) VERZIEHEN. To scram. *Verzieh dich, aber dalli!* "Beat it, and make it fast!"

(SICH) VERZUPFEN, *S.* = **(SICH) VERZIEHEN.**

VIELLEICHT. 1. Really; intensely; extremely (all intensifiers; lit. maybe). *Das ist vielleicht 'n Wagen!* "That's some car!" *Bist du vielleicht 'n Dusseltier!* "You really are a stupid idiot." **2.** Not really (in questions). *Ist das vielleicht eine Antwort/Lösung/Aussage?* "What kind of an answer/solution/statement is that?" *Ist das vielleicht dein Ernst?* "You can't be serious/you don't really mean that, do you?"

VIERECKPALAST, *m., youth, ironic.* Small room (lit. "four-corner palace"). *Wie wär's mit 'ner Fete auf deinem Viereckpalast?* "How about a party at your pad?"

VIERECKRAKETE, *f., youth.* Car (lit. rectangular rocket). *Tim hat 'ne tolle Viereckrakete.* "Tim's got a fantastic set of wheels."

VIERRADJET, *m.* = **VIERECKRAKETE.**

VISAGE, *f.* See POLIEREN.

VITAMIN, *n.* **Vitamin B.** Connections ("B" for BEZIEHUNGEN). *Ohne Vitamin B hätt er den Posten nie bekommen.* "He never would have got the job without pull."

VOGEL, *m.* Bird. **Den Vogel abschießen.** To take the cake. *Das schießt den Vogel ab!* "That's the living end!" **Einen Vogel haben.** To be crazy. *Lucia di Lammermoor sang wie ein Vogel, vielleicht weil sie auch einen Vogel hatte.* "Lucia di Lammermoor sang like a bird, maybe because she had bats/birds in the belfry." **Jmdm. den/einen Vogel zeigen.** To tap one's head to indicate that one thinks s.o. is crazy. *Beim Autofahren zeigen mir viele den Vogel, aber ich kümmre mich nicht darum.* "When I drive, many give me the finger, but I don't let it get to me." **Einen toten Vogel in der Hose haben.** To fart. *Wer hat hier 'n toten*

Vogel in der Hose? "Who's been farting here?"

VÖGELEI, *f.* Screwing. *Seit die Schnepfe hier wohnt, gibt's nichts wie Vögelei im Haus.* "Since that bitch arrived, there's been nothing but fucking here."

VÖGELN. To copulate. *Damals waren wir richtige Turteltäubchen und vögelten Tag und Nacht.* "We were real lovebirds then and fucked night and day."

VOLL NULL. Intensifies NULL 2.

VOLL OPERN. See OPERN.

VOLL. 1. Full. See GEKNÜPPELT VOLL; GERAMMELT/GERAP-PELT VOLL. 2. Drunk. Cf. GRANATENVOLL; STERN-HAGELVOLL. *Der ist wieder voll.* "He's soused again." 3. Totally (youth sl. intensifier, in place of stand. *völlig,* as in *voll geil, voll ödig,* etc.). *Mann, ich war voll ausge-powert.* "Man, I was totally burned out." Cf. TOTAL.

VOLLE KANNE/VOLLE SOßE/VOLL GAS/VOLL SCHNUR/VOLL STOFF = VOLLE PULLE.

VOLLE PULLE. All out; at top speed. *Er war voll und fuhr volle Pulle.* "He was soused and drove at top speed."

VOLLNIETE, *f.* Deadbeat, dud (lit. complete blank). *In allem, was er unterfing, war er nur 'ne Vollniete.* "He was a dead loss at everything he attempted."

VOLLTREFFER, *m.* Direct/smash hit. *Ihre letzte Rille war ein Volltreffer in den Charts.* "Her last record was a smash in the charts."

VON WEGEN!/VON WEGEN OTTO! That's not true at all!/Not on your life, Otto (Charlie, Louie, etc.)! *Meinst du, sie hätten mir dabei geholfen? Von wegen Otto! Sie haben keinen Finger gerührt.* "You think they helped me with it? No way! They didn't lift a finger."

VORBAU, *m.* Breasts (lit. porch; balcony). ***Einen großen/schönen/üppigen Vorbau haben.*** To have big breasts. *Sie und ihre beiden Schwestern haben alle drei einen schönen Vorbau.* "She and her two sisters are really stacked, all three of them." Cf. HOLZ; VORSTEVEN.

(SICH AN ETWAS) VORBEIMOGELN. To be evasively dishonest about s.t. *Wie gewöhnlich hat sich der Senator an den Streitfragen vorbeigemogelt.* "As usual, the senator wormed his way around the issues."

VORBEREITEN. To prepare. *Etwas von langer Hand vorbereiten.* To prepare s.t. (usually hostile) well in advance. *Der Angriff wurde von langer Hand vorbereitet.* "The attack was planned well in advance."

VORGRUFTI, *m., youth.* S.o. 20–30 years old. *Nach unserer Verjüngungskur kommen wir uns fast so jung wie Vorgruftis vor.* "After our rejuvenation cure, we feel almost as young as the old wrecks in their 20s."

VORHALTEN. To hold in front of. *Mit vorgehaltener Pistole/Schusswaffe.* At gunpoint. *Mit vorgehaltener Pistole hat er uns bedroht.* "He threatened us at gunpoint." See HINTER . . . HAND.

VORHANG, *m.* Penis (lit. curtain, or what "hangs in front"). *Ich bin sehr erwartungsvoll, wenn der Vorhang aufgeht.* "I have great expectations when the dick goes up (lit. when the curtain rises)."

VORHAUT, *f.* Foreskin. *Sich etwas hinter die Vorhaut klemmen.* To take s.t. and shove it (lit. to wedge s.t. under one's foreskin). *Noch 'n wertlosen Schuldschein von dir? Den kannst du dir unter die Vorhaut klemmen!* "Another worthless IOU from you? You can stick that in your penis pipe and suck on it."

VORSTEVEN, *m.* Prow, bow (ship). *Einen großen/schönen Vorsteven haben.* See VORBAU.

VOTZE = FOTZE.

WA? Wa?; Eh?; No? (short for *was?* and *wahr* in *nicht wahr?*). *Dir müsste man echt die Fresse lackieren, wa?* "You really need your face bashed in, don't you?"

WABERN. To undulate; billow; flicker. See (SICH) DURCH-WABERN; RUMWABERN; (SICH) WEGWABERN.

WACHSEN. To grow. *Jmdm. wächst der Kopf durch die Haare.* To be growing bald. *Ihm wächst schon der Kopf durch die Haare.* "He's already losing his hair." Cf. RÜBERWACHSEN.

WACHTEL, *f.* Foolish female (lit. "quail"). Cf. ALTE SCHACHTEL; SPINATWACHTEL. *Alle hielten sie für 'ne alte Wachtel, aber alle hat sie ausgetrickst.* "They all thought she was a silly old goose, but she outsmarted them all."

WACKEL, *n.* *Auf den Wackel gehen.* To be a streetwalker; solicit for prostitution; cf. STRICH. *Mit so 'nem Knackarsch solltest du aufn Wackel gehen.* "With a sexy ass like yours, you ought to shake it and sell it."

WACKELN. To shake. *Dass die Wände wackeln.* See WAND.

WAFFEL, *f.* Head (lit. waffle). *Einen an der Waffel haben/Eine verbrannte Waffel haben.* To be crazy. *Wenn die Alte nur nicht 'ne verbrannte Waffel hätte!* "If only the old lady weren't bananas!"

WAFFELN. To babble, prate. *Du wirst nie müde, mich voll*

zu waffeln. "You never tire of babbling on endlessly." Cf.
NIEDERWAFFELN; SABBELN; SCHWAFELN.

WAFFENFUZZIS, *pl., youth.* Police. *Die Waffenfuzzis
waren hinter uns her.* "The cops chased us."

WAHLSCHLAPPE. See SCHLAPPE.

WAHNSINN, *m.* Madness. ***Des Wahnsinns fette/kesse
Beute sein/Vom Wahnsinn umzingelt sein.*** To be completely crazy (lit. to be lunacy's fat/sassy booty/to be sur-
rounded by madness). *Ich soll's bezahlen? Du bist wohl
des Wahnsinns fette Beute!* "I should pay for it? You're off
your blooming rocker."

WAHNSINNIG. Extremely (lit. crazy). *'S war wahnsinnig
heiß; wir haben uns aber wahnsinnig abgehottet!* "It was
extremely hot, but we had a terrific time."

WAHNSINNSFLITZER, *m., youth.* Wonderful, fast car. *In
seinem Wahnsinnsflitzer sind wir durch die Savanne
gedüst.* "We sped through the countryside in his out-of-
this-world car."

WALACHEI, *f.* The boonies. (Walachia, a province of Ro-
mania, is sl. for any remote place.) Cf. PAMPA; SAVANNE.
Ab in die Walachei mit diesem Hammel! "Put that jackass
out to pasture!"

WAND, *f.* Wall. ***Dass die Wände wackeln.*** Like all get out.
Wir wollen feiern, dass die Wände wackeln. "We want to
have a blast." Cf. BALKEN; FETZEN.

WANST, *m.* Paunch. ***Sich den Wanst voll schlagen.*** To stuff
o.s. *Wir haben uns den Wanst voll geschlagen.* "We
pigged out." Cf. FETTWANST.

WAPPLER, *m., Aust.* Jerk. *Was will schon wieder der Wappler?* "What's that idiot want now?"

WARMER/WARMER BRÜDER/WÄRMLING, *m., pej.*
Male homosexual. *Im Internat waren wir warme Brüder;
ich glaub irgendwie, er ist's noch, trotz der Frau und vier
Gören.* "We were both gay in boarding school; I sort of
think he still is, despite his wife and four kids."

WARMWASSERGEIGE, *f, youth.* Souped-up motorcycle (lit. warm-water violin). *Er nahm mich mit auf seine Warmwassergeige und ich kam ganz auf Touren.* "He took me with him on his bike, and my motor really got turned on."

WÄSCHE, *f.* Laundry; washing; underwear. ***Jmdm. an die Wäsche gehen.*** To make overt sexual advances to s.o. *Der wollte mir gleich an die Wäsche.* "He tried to get into my pants right away." ***Dumm aus der Wäsche gucken.*** See GUCKEN; cf. REIZWÄSCHE.

WASCHLAPPEN, *m.* Coward/weakling (lit. washcloth). *Ihr Mann ist 'n richtiger Waschlappen.* "Her husband's a real wimp."

WASERL, *n., Aust.* Helpless creature. *Mir tat's arme Waserl leid.* "I felt sorry for the poor thing."

WASSERN. 1. To splash down. *Man weiß nicht, wo das Raumschiff gewassert hat.* "They don't know where the spaceship splashed down." **2.** To swim. (*Youth.*) *Willst heute wassern?* "Want to go swimming today?" **3.** To urinate. (*Youth.*) *Die Frischlinge wassern alle im Schwimmbad.* "The little kids all piss in the pool."

WATSCHE(N), *f., S.* Slap. *Vom Vater hat's oft Watschen gegeben.* "My father often clouted me."

WATSCHEN, *S.* To whack. *Jetzt watsch ich dir eine, du Lausbub.* "I'm going to sock you now, you no-good brat."

WATSCHENMANN, *m.* Target of criticism (from an amusement park figure in Vienna's *Prater*). *Mutig, freimütig war ich; jetzt bin ich zum Watschenmann geworden.* "I was courageous, outspoken; now I'm the butt of all that hostile criticism."

WATTE, *f.* Cotton padding. ***Jmdn. in Watte packen.*** To look after s.o. with exaggerated concern. *Mutti hat uns in Watte gepackt.* "Mom brooded over us like a mother hen." Cf. PACKEN **1.**

WECKER, *m.* Alarm clock. ***Jmdm. auf den Wecker fallen/gehen.*** To get on s.o.'s nerves. *Kai fällt mir echt* *auf den Wecker.* "Kai really bugs me." Cf. GEIST; KEKS; ZEIGER.

WEDELN. See RUMWEDELN.

WEBFEHLER, *m.* Flaw in the weave. ***Einen Webfehler haben.*** To be crazy. *Die hat seit langem 'n Webfehler.* "She hasn't been right in the head for some time."

WEDER GICKS NOCH GACKS SAGEN/VERSTE-HEN/WISSEN. Not to say/understand/know anything at all. *Weißt weder gicks noch gacks davon, aber hörst nicht auf zu gackern.* "You don't know a damn thing about it, but you keep running your mouth."

WEGBALLERN. To kill. *Die Gangster haben sie alle weggeballert.* "The gangsters mowed them all down." Cf. ABKNALLEN.

WEGBÜRSTEN, *youth.* Var. of BÜRSTEN, to beat up. See NIEDERBÜRSTEN.

WEGBUNKERN. To stash away. *Die Ganoven hatten das ganze Moos weggebunkert.* "The crooks had stashed away all the dough."

WEGDACKELN = **ABDACKELN.**

WEGFLUPPEN = **LOSFLUPPEN.**

WEGGESCHLAFFT. All done in (*schlaff* = slack; list-less). *Siehst total weggeschlafft aus.* "You really look wasted."

WEGGETRETEN = **WEGGESCHLAFFT.**

WEGHABEN. See EINEN WEGHABEN; RUHE.

(SICH) WEGKLEMMEN, *youth.* To scram (lit. to wedge o.s. out). *Da klemmte ich mich rapido weg.* "I got m.s. out of there fast."

(SICH) WEGKLINKEN = **(SICH) AUSKLINKEN.**

WEGKLUNKERN, *youth.* To squander money. *Der ganze Kies ist schon weggeklunkert.* "All the dough's blown."

WEGMACHEN. To get rid of. *Sie wollte das Kind nicht wegmachen lassen.* "She didn't want to get an abortion."

WEGPUSTEN. To blow away. *Sie hat alle Konkurrenz weggepustet.* "She blew away the competition."

WEGPUTZEN. To polish off food (lit. to polish [dirt/a stain] off an object). *Im Nu hatte er den ganzen Kuchen weggeputzt.* "He polished off the whole cake in no time flat."

(SICH) WEGROBBEN. To slink away (from *robben,* to crawl like a seal). *Von seiner eigenen Entscheidung will sich der Schuft jetzt wegrobben.* "That bum now wants to back off from his own decision."

(SICH) WEGSCHALTEN, *youth.* To scram (*schalten* = to switch; change gear). *Schalt dich endlich weg!* "Get moving, will ya!"

WEGSCHIFFEN/WEGSCHIPPERN. To get going. *'S ist Zeit, wegzuschiffen.* "It's time to go."

(SICH) WEGWABERN, *youth.* To sneak off. *Warum hast du dich gleich weggewabert?* "Why'd you slink off right away?"

WEGZISCHEN = ABZISCHEN.

WEICH. See BIRNE; KEKS.

WEICHEI, *n.* Wimp (lit. soft-boiled egg. *Oft tu ich, was meine Frau mir rät; bin aber kein Weichei.* "I often do what my wife advises, but I'm not a Milquetoast."

WEICHKLOPFEN. 1. To soften up. *Er versuchte mich weichzuklopfen, aber ich blieb hart.* "He tried to soften me up, but I remained firm." **2.** To beat up. (*Youth.*) *Der Knuffi hat ihn weichgeklopft.* "The big bruiser beat him to a pulp."

WEICHKRIEGEN = WEICHKLOPFEN 1.

WEICHSPÜLER, *m.* Ineffectual person (lit. fabric softener). *Warum hat man diesen Weichspüler zum Parteichef gewählt?* "Why did they elect that wimp party chief?"

WEICHTEILE, *m., pl.* Private parts (lit. soft parts). *Sie interessiert sich besonders für die Weichteile harter Männer.* "She's particularly interested in tough guys' privates."

WEIDMANNSHEIL! Good hunting!

WEISHEIT, *f.* Wisdom. *Die Weisheit mit Löffeln gefressen haben.* To know all the answers. *Sie glaubt, die Weisheit mit Löffeln gefressen zu haben.* "She thinks she's got the inside track on everything."

WEISMACHEN. To hand a line to/take in. *Der Schwindler wollte uns weismachen, wir sollten das Grundstück im Sumpf kaufen.* "The swindler tried to get us to believe that we should buy that property in the swamp." *Das kannst du (einem) anderen weismachen!* Go tell it to the marines! *Der Sumpf soll zu einer blühenden Landschaft werden? Das kannst du andern weismachen!* "The swamp's gonna turn into a blooming landscape? Tell it to the marines!"

WEIß DER GEIER/KUCKUCK! Who knows! See GEIER.

WERT. Worth. *Keinen Pappenstiel/Pfifferling wert sein.* Worthless. *Diese Münzen sind keinen Pfifferling wert.* "Those coins aren't worth peanuts."

WESSI. See BESSERWESSI.

WESSILAND, *n.* Former W. Ger. *Diese windigen Glücksritter hätten lieber in Wessiland bleiben sollen.* "Those crooked money hunters should have stayed in the West." Cf. OSSILAND.

WICHSEN. 1. To whack (lit. to polish, wax). *Ich wichs dir eine.* "I'm gonna clobber you." **2.** To masturbate. *Meine Alte hat mich beim Wichsen erwischt.* "My old lady caught me whacking off."

WICHSER, *m.* Joker; guy one dislikes (lit. masturbator). *Was wollen diese Wichser hier?* "What do those fuckers want here?"

WIDERLING, *m.* Repulsive person. *Er ist herzensgut; nur in seinen Filmen spielt er immer den großen Widerling.* "He's really kindhearted; it's only in the movies that he always play the archvillain."

WIEHERN. 1. To laugh uproariously (lit. to neigh; whinny). *Zum Wiehern sein.* To be a scream. *Zum*

Wiehern war's, als der dicke Diktator vom Pferd runter-fiel. "What a howler, when the fat dictator fell off his horse." **2.** To complain. *Hör doch endlich auf zu wiehern!* "Quit grousing!"

WIENERN. To polish, clean. *Das Café wurde gewienert und hat jetzt seinen alten Scharm wieder.* "The café was polished up and has regained its old charm."

WIESE, *f.* Meadow; lawn. ***Auf der grünen Wiese.*** Out in the country. *Wir wären gern länger auf der grünen Wiese geblieben.* "We would have liked to stay longer in the country."

WILDFANG, *m.* Little devil. *Unsere jüngste Tochter ist 'n ziemlicher Wildfang.* "Our youngest daughter's s.t. of a tomboy."

WIND, *m.* Wind. ***In den Wind schreiben.*** To write off. *Unsere großen Hoffnungen können wir jetzt in den Wind schreiben.* "Now we can kiss our high hopes goodbye." ***Wind um etwas machen.*** To make a big fuss about. *Ach, mach doch nicht so 'n Wind darum!* "Oh, don't make such a big thing about it."

WINDBEUTEL, *m.* Frivolous, irresponsible person (lit. cream puff). *Diesem Windbeutel wird 'ne solche Arbeit nie gelingen.* "That lightweight will never manage a job like that."

WINDEI = WEICHEI.

WINDELWEICH. Very soft (lit. soft as diapers). *Sie braucht ihm nur schöne Augen zu machen, und er wird windelweich.* "All she has to do is make love eyes at him, and he becomes her pushover." ***Jmdn. windelweich hauen/schlagen.*** To beat s.o. to a pulp. *Sie haben ihn windelweich geschlagen.* "They beat the living daylights out of him."

WINSELTASCHE = BLASSACK; SPUCKTÜTE.

WINSELTÜTE, *f., youth.* **1.** Crybaby (lit. whimper bag). *Sei doch nicht so 'ne Winseltüte!* "Don't be such a cry-baby." Cf. HEULPETER; HEULSUSE. **2.** Loudspeaker; mega-

325

phone. *Die Winseltüte ist kapores.* "The loudspeaker's busted."

WIRRKOPF, *m.* Crackpot. *Diesem Wirrkopf sind sie alle aufn Leim gegangen.* "They all got taken in by that crackpot."

WOHNKLO, *n., youth.* Small room with a toilet (*Wohnung* = apartment; *Klo* = toilet). *In seinem Wohnklo mieft's immer.* "His pad always smells bad."

WO MAN HINSPUCKT. Wherever you look (lit. spit). *Wo man hinspuckt entstehen Hochhäuser.* "Wherever you look, high-rises are going up."

WONNEPROPPEN. Plump, little, darling child. *Du bist mein Wonneproppen, mein Eins und Alles.* "You're my little love dumpling, my everything."

WÖRKEN, *youth.* To work. Cf. ASTEN **2;** HINKELN; KEULEN; MALOCHEN; SCHUFTEN. *Wörken, Wörken, ewiges Wörken; 's erwürgt mich, wirklich!* "Slaving away and away; it's stifling me, really!"

WUCHTBRUMME, *f.* Powerfully built female. *Mit der Wuchtbrumme ist nicht gut Kirschen essen.* "Better not mess with that tough broad."

WÜHLEN. To work very hard (lit. to dig; rummage). *Genug gewühlt für heute!* "That's enough drudgery for today."

WUNDERHORN, *n.* Penis (lit. magic horn). *Mir ist sein Wunderhorn der Inbegriff aller Mythen, Musik und Literatur.* "For me, his dick is the essence of all myth, music, and literature."

WUPP!/WUPPDICH!/WUPPS! Whoops! *Mit einem Wuppdich.* In a flash. *Mit einem Wuppdich waren sie fort.* "They cleared out fast."

WUPPER, *f.* Wupper (a tributary of the Rhine). *Über die Wupper sein.* To be down the drain. *Er wusste nicht richtig damit umzugehen, und jetzt ist der Computer über die Wupper.* "He didn't know how to use it, and now the computer's had it."

WURSCHT/WURSCHTEGAL. Southern pron. of WURST/WURSTEGAL, but widely used in the North for emphasis.

WURSCHTL, *n., S.* Fool (lit. little sausage). ***Jmds. Wurschtl sein.*** To be s.o.'s patsy. *Ich bin doch nit dei' Wurschtl.* "I'm not your dummy/slave."

WURST, *f.* **1.** Sausage. ***Um die Wurst gehen.*** To be down to the nitty-gritty. *Es geht um die Wurst.* "The crunch has come." ***Wurst sein.*** To be of no concern. *Was du davon hältst, das ist mir Wurst.* "I don't care what you think about it." Cf. LEBERWURST. **2.** Turd. ***Eine Wurst machen.*** (*Children.*) To do #2. *Musst du 'ne Wurst machen?* "Do you need to do #2?"

WURST WIDER WURST. Tit for tat. *Du hast mich nicht unterstützt, jetzt pfeif ich auf dich. Wurst wider Wurst.* "You didn't support me, now I say to hell with you! Like for like."

WÜRSTCHEN, *n.* **1.** Turd (lit. small sausage). ***(Ein) Würstchen machen.*** See WURST **2.** **2.** Insignificant/pitiable person. *Ihr tat das arme Würstchen leid und sie tanzte mit ihm.* "She felt sorry for the poor thing and danced with him."

WURSTEGAL SEIN. To be indifferent to. *Geh oder bleib, mir ist's wurstegal.* "Go or stay, I couldn't care less."

WURSTELEI, *f., pej.* Muddling. *Trotz der Wurstelei bei uns im Büro wird manchmal gut gearbeitet.* "Despite all the farting around in the office, some work does get done occasionally."

WURSTELN. To muddle. *Wir haben lange genug gewurstelt, jetzt wollen wir klotzen.* "We've been putzing around long enough, now we're going all out."

WURSTIG. Totally indifferent. *Er ist weniger wurstig, seit er den Buddhismus und das Mitgefühl entdeckt hat.* "He has less of a what's-it-to-me attitude since discovering Buddhism and compassion."

WURSTIGKEIT, *f.* What-do-I-care attitude. *Seine Wurstig-*

keit nervte mich. "His no-skin-off-my-nose attitude used to get on my nerves."

WURSTKESSEL, *f.* Sausage vat. ***Noch in Abrahams Wurstkessel sein.*** Not born yet. *Du weißt ja nichts davon; da warst du noch in Abrahams Wurstkessel.* "You don't know anything about that; you were still a gleam in your father's eye."

WURSTSALAT, *m.* Cold meat salad. ***Wurstsalat verstehen.*** See VERSTEHEN.

WURZEN, *S.* To exploit s.o. *Schon vor der Scheidung hat sie ihn richtig gewurzt, und es geschah ihm recht.* "She got all she could out of him even before the divorce, and it served him right."

WURZEREI, *f., S.* Exploitation. *Ich wollte dir helfen, mich aber nicht der Wurzerei aussetzen.* "I wanted to help you, but I didn't plan to get fleeced."

WUSCHELKOPF, *m.* S.o. with curly/disheveled hair. *Kämm dich doch, du Wuschelkopf!* "Take a comb to that mop, will you!"

WUTSCH! Whoosh! *Wutsch war er weg!* "He ran off in a flash."

WUTZ, *f., S.* Pig. *Der Bauer Futz liebte seine Wutz.* "Farmer Futz loved his porker." ***Die Wutz rauslassen.*** See SAU.

WUZERLDICK, *S.* Fat. *Ein wuzerldicker Mönch begrüßte uns in der Klosterbrauerei.* "A tubby monk welcomed us to the monastery brewery."

X

XANTHIPPE, *f.* Shrew (name of Socrates' wife. Semantically but not linguistically rel. HIPPE and ZIPPE). *Mit seiner Xanthippe, dieser Zippe, geht er philosophisch um.* "He deals philosophically with his bitchy wife."

X-MAL = ZIGMAL.

YIF/YIFFI(E), *m., f.* From Eng. "young individual freedom freak." (As distinct from yuppies [young urban professionals], yiffies are less career oriented and not trendy or consumerist.) *Yiffis sehe ich gern um mich, aber nicht zu viele Yuppies.* "I like to have yiffies around, but not too many yuppies." See FRUPPIE; ZIPPIE.

ZACK, *m.* ***Auf Zack bringen.*** To get into shape. *Die neue Chefin griff hart durch and brachte alles schnellstens auf Zack.* "The new boss took decisive action and quickly got everything shipshape." ***Auf Zack sein.*** To be on the ball. *Sie ist dauernd auf Zack.* "She's always on the ball."

ZACK! On the double!. ***Zack machen.*** To make it snappy. *Hör auf rumzufummeln und mach mal 'n bißchen zack!* "Quit fumbling around and jump to it!"

ZACK/ZACK, ZACK. Just like that. *Und zack, zack war's fertig.* "And in a flash it was done." Cf. RUCK, ZUCK.

ZACKEN, *m.* **1.** Prong; tooth (comb); serrated edge. ***Einen (kleinen/ziemlichen) Zacken (in der Krone) haben/weghaben.*** To be (a bit) drunk/crazy. *Beim zweiten Bier hatte er schon 'n ziemlichen Zacken weg.* "Two beers and he was already plastered." ***Einen Zacken drauf haben.*** To speed. *Der Porsche hatte 'n gewaltigen Zacken drauf.* "The Porsche was speeding like all get out." See KRONE; ZULEGEN. **2.** Big nose. *Sie will sich 'ner Nasenkorrektur unterziehen; kein Wunder mit 'nem solchen Zacken.* "She wants to get a nose job; no wonder, with a beak like that."

ZACKIG. Dashing; snappy. *In seiner Uniform sieht er zackig aus.* "He looks snazzy in his uniform."

ZACKO, *youth sl. var. of* ZACK.

ZAHN, *m.* Tooth. ***Steiler Zahn*** *(50s–60s youth sl.).* Classy chick (lit. steep [wonderful] tooth). *Ist Nina vielleicht 'n steiler Zahn!* "Nina's a real knockout!" See ZULEGEN.

ZAPFEN. 1. To tap. *Es geht nichts über ein frisch gezapftes Pils.* "Nothing beats a freshly tapped Pilsener." **2.** *m.* Penis (lit. pine cone; icicle). *Deinem Zapfen bleib ich ewig grün.* "I'll always have a thing for that thing of yours."

ZAPFENMANTEL, *m.* Condom (lit. penis coat, cf. ÜBERZIEHER.) *Ohne Zapfenmantel gibt's bei mir keinen Zapfenstreich.* "No getting it on with me, unless you put a rubber on."

ZAPFENSTREICH, *m.* **1.** Time to return to barracks; last call for drinks. **2.** Sexual intercourse. *Lili Marleen wartete auf den großen Zapfenstreich.* "Lili Marleen waited for a super screwing."

ZAPPELPHILIPP, *m.* Fidgety child/person. *Warum kannst du keine fünf Minuten ruhig sitzen, du Zappelphilipp du?* "Why can't you sit still for 5 minutes, you wiggly Willy?"

ZAPPENDUSTER. Pitch black; gloomy. *Mit dem Projekt sieht's zappenduster aus.* "Things look bleak for the project."

ZASTER, *m.* Money. *Mit schmierigen Geschäften hat er viel Zaster gemacht.* "He made plenty of dough on his dirty deals."

ZAUPE, *f., rural.* Bitch (canine and human). *Du hältst mich für 'ne Zaupe, aber ich mein's gut mit dir.* "You think I'm a bitch, but I want to help you." Cf. ZIPPE.

ZAUSEL, *m.* Codger. *Einige sagen, der alte Zausel sei ein Schamane.* "Some say the old geezer's a shaman."

ZECHGELAGE = SAUFGELAGE.

ZECHGENOSSE/ZECHKUMPEL/ZECHKUMPAN = SAUFBRUDER.

ZECHPRELLER, *m.* S.o. who leaves without paying the bill for food or drink. *Uli ist 'n gewiefter Zechpreller.* "Uli's a sly bill dodger."

ZECHTOUR = **PICHELTOUR; SAUFTOUR.**

ZEIGER, *m.* Pointer; watch hand. ***Jmdm. auf den Zeiger gehen.*** To get on s.o.'s nerves. *Du gehst mir aber gewaltig auf den Zeiger.* "You really push all my buttons."

ZETT, *n.* Prison. *Er wurde zu 20 Jahren Zett verurteilt.* "They put him away for 20 years."

ZIBBE = **ZIPPE.**

ZICKE = **ZIEGE.**

ZICKEN, *pl.* Foolish things. ***Zicken machen.*** To do dumb things; cause difficulties. *Mach mir bloß keine Zicken!* "Just don't give me a hard time!"

ZICKIG. Foolish; prudish. *Tu nicht so zickig!* "Stop being such an uptight idiot."

ZIEGE, *f.* Nasty woman (lit. nanny goat; cf. ZIMTZIEGE). *Diese blöde eingebildete Ziege soll mir nur nicht vor die Flinte kommen!* "I better not get my hands on that stupid, stuck-up bitch."

ZIEGENBOCK. See STINKEN.

ZIEHEN. To pull. ***Jmdm. eine ziehen.*** See ZWITSCHERN.

ZIELWASSER, *m., hum.* Alcohol (lit. goal water; orig. alcohol drunk by hunters or those engaged in target practice). *Du schießt immer daneben; vielleicht hilft dir 'n bisschen Zielwasser aus meinem Flachmann.* "You always miss the mark; maybe a shot from my hip flask will help you."

ZIERFISCH, *m.* **1.** Dainty, attractive teenage girl (lit. ornamental fish). *Die Ute ist vielleicht 'n flotter Zierfisch.* "Ute's a real nifty number." **2.** Affected, talkative girl; (*Ziererei* = affectation, coyness). *Er wollte 'ne Nutte, keinen Zierfisch.* "He wanted a whore, not a prissy, prattling girlie."

ZIFFERBLATT, *n.* Face. *Vom Zifferblatt der Moslime waren nur die Gucker zu sehen.* "All you could see of the Moslem woman's face were her peepers."

ZIGARRE, *f.* **1.** Rebuke (lit. cigar). ***Jmdm. eine Zigarre***

verpassen. To tell s.o. off; scold. *Mutti wird dir 'ne Zigarre verpassen.* "You're going to catch hell from Mom." **2.** Zeppelin. *Die neuen Zigarren benutzen Helium statt Wasserstoff.* "The new zeps use helium instead of hydrogen."

ZIGMAL. Umpteen times. *Ich hab's dir schon zigmal gesagt.* "I've already told you umpteen times."

ZIGEUNERN. To wander around. *Du denkst nur ans Zigeunern; aber der Ernst des Lebens beginnt bald auch für dich.* "All you think about is roaming, but you'll soon find out about the serious side of life."

ZIMPERLIESE, *f.* Sissy (lit. prissy Lizzie). *Du hättest es schon machen können, wenn du nicht so 'ne Zimperliese wärst.* "You could have done it, if you weren't such a sissy."

ZIMT, *m.* **1.** Cinnamon (from Malayan for sweet wood). **2.** Junk; nonsense (from Hebr. for zero). *Du weißt, was du mit dem Zimt machen kannst.* "You know what you can do with that junk."

ZIMTZICKE/ZIMTZIEGE, *f., pej.* Dumb broad. *Die Zimtzicke kann mich mal.* "That stupid cow can kiss my ass."

ZINKEN, *m.* **1.** To mark cards. ***Mit gezinkten Karten spielen.*** To play with marked cards; use unfair tactics. *Der Ganove hat mit gezinkten Karten gespielt.* "That crook played with marked cards." **2.** Thieves' secret mark. *Der Gauner litt an der Alzheimer-Krankheit und erkannte die Zinken nicht mehr.* "The thief suffered from Alzheimer's disease and didn't recognize the marks anymore." **3.** Big nose. *Cyrano und Jimmy Durante waren stolz auf ihre Zinken.* "Cyrano and Jimmy Durante were proud of their schnozzes."

ZINNOBER, *m.* Junk; nonsense; fuss (lit. cinnabar; vermillion). *Ach, was musst ihr immer so 'n Zinnober machen.* "Oh, why do you always have to make such a fuss?"

ZIPFEL, *m.* Penis (lit. tip). See ZAPFEN.

ZIPFELMÜTZE, *f.* Condom with a pointed tip (lit. pointed cap). *Außer der Zipfelmütze trug er nichts.* "All he was wearing was a condom."

ZIPPE, *f., pej.* Ugly female; bitch. *So 'ne Zippe hat er sich verdient.* "He deserves that ugly bitch." Cf. TÖLE.

ZIPPELGUSSE, *f., youth.* Bitch; ugly girl (pun on *Zipfelgosse* [barroom urinal]). *Die Zippelgusse ist gerade die Richtige für dich.* "That dog-faced bitch is exactly right for you."

ZIPPIE, *m., f.* Eng. for "Zen-inspired professional pagan." Cf. SIDDHARTIST. *Viele Zippies glauben an ein globales Gehirn und an globale Zusammenarbeit.* "Many zippies believe in a global brain and working together globally."

ZISCHEN, *youth.* **1.** To tell (lit. to hiss). *Bin mal reich, mal arm gewesen; reich war besser, kann ich dir zischen.* "I've been rich, I've been poor; rich was better, I can tell you." Cf. FLÜSTERN. **2.** To fizz. *Ein Bier/einen zischen.* To have a beer/drink. *Gehen wir schnell einen zischen.* "Let's go have a quick beer." **3.** To clout. *Du bekommst gleich eine gezischt!* "I'm gonna clobber you now."

ZITTERKNOCHEN/ZITTERRÜSSEL, *m.* Timid person (lit. "tremble-bones/nose"). *Du hast mir nicht geholfen, du Zitterknochen.* "You didn't help me, you chicken liver."

ZOFF, *m.* Trouble; aggravation (from a Hebr. phrase for bad end). *Mit meinen Hausdrachen hab ich immer nur Zoff.* "All I have is bad news with my parents."

ZOHE = ZIPPE.

ZOMBIE, *m., youth.* Old fossil (lit. zombie). *Was wollen diese Zombies hier in der Disko?* "What are the living dead doing here in the disco?"

ZOMBIG. Brilliant, "wicked." *Sie hat wieder zombig Tennis gespielt.* "She played a mean game of tennis again."

ZONI, *m., pej., youth.* Inhabitant of the former GDR (the Soviet occupied zone of Ger. was often referred to as *die Zone*). *Die Wessis nennen uns Zonis; aber einst waren auch sie „die Eingeborenen von Trizonesien."* "West Germans call us Zonies, but they too were once 'natives of Trizonia.' " Cf. AMIZONE; NORDI; OSSI; WESSI.

ZOOKRÄHE = NEBELKRÄHE.

ZOTTE, *f.* Shaggy tuft of hair; pony. *Kalte Zotten kriegen,* youth sl. var. of *kalte Füße kriegen.* To get cold feet. *Hast gleich kalten Zotten gekriegt.* "You got scared right away." *Mit den Zotten auf Grundeis sein.* To be at the end of one's rope (lit. to be on thin ice with one's shaggy hair). *Damals war ich mit den Zotten auf Grundeis.* "I didn't know what to do next."

ZOTTEL, *m.* Ponytail. *Einen Zottel im Kapee haben.* To be crazy. *Der hat 'n Zottel im Kapee.* "He's off his rocker."

ZOTTELHAAR, *n.*/**ZOTTELKOPF,** *m.* Person with hair tied in a tail in back. *Siehst den Zottelkopf da?* "You see that rat tailer over there?"

ZUBÜRSTEN = ZUSAMMENBÜRSTEN.

ZUCKERJUNGE = PUPPENJUNGE.

ZUCKERPUPPE, *f.* Sweetie pie. *Sie heißt Elfriede und ist aus Wuppertal, ist aber keine Zuckerpuppe.* "Her name's Elfriede and she's from Wuppertal, but she's no baby doll."

ZUKNEIFEN/ZUSAMMENKNEIFEN. To press shut. *Den Arsch zukneifen/zusammenkneifen.* To die (lit. to shut one's ass). *Ich hätte ihm vergeben sollen, bevor er den Arsch zukniff.* "I should have forgiven him before he croaked."

ZUKNÜPPELN. Intensifies KNÜPPELN **1.**

ZULEGEN. To increase; add. *Einen Gang/Schritt/ Zacken/Zahn zulegen.* To step on it; speed up. *Wenn wir einen Zahn zulegen, kommen wir noch rechtzeitig an.* "If we put on some speed, we'll arrive on time."

ZUNDER, *m.* **1.** Tinder. *Jmdm. Zunder geben.* To give s.o. a severe reprimand/beating. *Dir müsste man dreimal am Tag Zunder geben.* "You're in need of a beating three times a day." **2.** Money. See ZASTER.

ZUNSEL, *f.* Bitch; battle-ax. *Die Zunsel geht mir auf den Keks.* "That bitch gets on my nerves."

ZUOPERN. See OPERN.

ZURÜCKPFEIFEN. To bring back into line (lit. to whistle back). *Die Präsidentin musste den General zurückpfeifen.* "The president had to put the general in his place."

ZUSAMMENBÜRSTEN, *youth.* Var. of *bürsten* in the sense "to beat up." See NIEDERBÜRSTEN.

ZUSAMMENFALTEN, *youth.* **1.** To reprimand (lit. to fold up). *Mutti hat ihn richtig zusammengefaltet.* "Mom really laid down the law to him." **2.** To beat up (for stand. *zusammenschlagen*). *Die Bande hat ihn voll zusammengefaltet.* "The gang really beat him up."

ZUSAMMENKLAPPEN, *youth.* **1.** To collapse (lit. to fold up). *Dieser Drogi ist dem Zusammenklappen nahe.* "That junkie's about to collapse." **2.** To beat up. See ZUSAMMENFALTEN **2.**

ZUSAMMENKNEIFEN = **ZUKNEIFEN.**

ZUSAMMENKRATZEN. To scrape together. *So viel Geld können wir nicht zusammenkratzen.* "We can't come up with that much money."

ZUSAMMENOPERN. See OPERN.

ZUSCHEIßEN. See LASS DICH ZUSCHEIßEN!

ZUSPITZEN. To put on; to importune. *Ich glaub, du versuchst mich zuzuspitzen.* "I think you're putting me on."

ZUSTEUERN. To steer/head for. *Ohne auf eine Platzzuweisung zu warten, steuerten sie auf einen Tisch am Fenster zu.* "Without waiting for s.o. to seat them, they headed for a table by the window."

ZUWAFFELN = **WAFFELN.**

ZWEIGLEISIG. Double-tracked. *Ein Zweigleisiger/eine Zweigleisige.* Married man/woman with a lover. *Ich bin eine anständige Ehefrau, keine Zweigleisige.* "I'm a respectable married woman and I don't want anything on the side."

ZWEITE HAUT, *m.* Condom (lit. second skin). *Als Lesbe, will ich von der Schlange Schwanz nichts wissen, mit* *oder ohne zweite Haut.* "As a lesbian, I want nothing to do with the snakelike dick, in or out of a bag."

ZWERCHFELL, *n.* Diaphragm. ***Jmdm. das Zwerchfell massieren.*** To tickle s.o.'s funny bone. *Die Komikerin hat uns das Zwerchfell massiert.* "The comedian really tickled our funny bone."

ZWIRN, *m., youth.* Clothes (lit. yarn; thread). *Warum trägst heute 'n so feinen Zwirn?* "Why are you all dressed up today?"

ZWISCHENBUNKERN, *youth.* To reside for a while. *Die Bullen suchen mich; könntest du mich nur für heut Nacht zwischenbunkern?* "The cops are looking for me; could you put me up, just for tonight?"

ZWITSCHERN. To chirp. ***Bei jmdm. zwitschert's.*** S.o.'s crazy. *Bei dir zwitschert's wohl!* "You must have bats in your belfry!" Cf. VOGEL; PIEP. ***Mein Goldfisch/ Krokodil/Nashorn zwitschert.*** "Well, I'll be a monkey's uncle!" (lit. my goldfish/crocodile/rhinoceros is chirping). Cf. KLAVIER; KNUTSCHEN; SCHWEIN **1;** STRULLEN. ***Jmdm. eine zwitschern.*** To slap s.o. *Nimm die Hand weg oder ich zwitscher dir eine!* "Take your hand away or I'll slap you!" ***Einen zwitschern.*** To have a drink. *Zwitschern wir uns einen jetzt!* "Let's have a drink now."